y of Congress Cataloging-in-Publication Data

Allen D.
cy research : concepts, methods, and applications / Allen D. Putt,
Springer.
        cm.
iography: p.
udes index.
N 0-13-684051-5
olicy sciences.   I. Springer, J. Frederick.   II. Title.
87   1989   88–29396
1--dc19   CIP

ial/production supervision: Roseann McGrath Brooks
 design: Lundgren Graphics, Ltd.
facturing buyer: Peter Havens

ed in the United States of America
 8 7 6 5 4 3   2   1

N 0-13-684051-5

ice-Hall International (UK) Limited, *London*
ice-Hall of Australia Pty. Limited, *Sydney*
ice-Hall Canada Inc., *Toronto*
ice-Hall Hispanoamericana, S.A., *Mexico*
ice-Hall of India Private Limited, *New Delhi*
ice-Hall of Japan, Inc., *Tokyo*
n & Schuster Asia Pte. Ltd., *Singapore*
ra Prentice-Hall do Brasil, Ltda., *Rio de Janeiro*

wledgment is gratefully made for permission to use material from the following sources:

*t D. Behn and James W. Vaupel, Quick Analysis for Busy Decision Makers. Copy-
© 1982 by Basic Books, Inc. Reprinted by permission of Basic Books, Inc.,
shers.*

*rd S. Bloom, "Lessons from the Delaware Dislocated Worker Pilot Program,"
ation Review, Vol. 11, No. 2, April 1987, pp. 157–177. Copyright © 1987 by
Publications, Inc. Reprinted by permission of Sage Publications, Inc.*

*acknowledgments are continued on page 384, which constitutes an extension of the copy
age.*

Policy Research
Concepts, Methods, and App

Allen D. Putt

California State University–Sacramento

J. Fred Springer

University of Missouri–St. Louis

PRENTICE HALL
Englewood Cliffs, New Jersey 07632

*This Book is Dedicated
to Our Families:
Anne and Holly
Sandy and Liam*

Contents

12 Analysis of Costs in Policy Research   309

13 Quick Analysis: Policy Research Under Pressure   339

VI PROJECT MANAGEMENT SKILLS

14 Planning and Managing Policy Research   357

Preface

The ideas reflected in this text emerged from lengthy discussions concerning discrepancies between ways in which research is typically taught in the classroom and ways in which research is actually produced and consumed in organizations. As teachers of methods courses in public administration and public policy programs and as practitioners of policy research, the authors remained frustrated in their search for course material that accurately portrayed the unique combinations of skills necessary to produce relevant information for policymakers. Frequently, texts in the field do not convey the interest and challenges analysts experience within the policy process. This text is designed to fill these gaps.

The objective of this book is to produce a basic text in policy research—the application of systematic information collection and analysis to organizational decision making. The text is appropriate to courses that share an emphasis on policy research, though they have varying titles (e.g., Quantitative Methods, Research Methodology, Administrative Decision Making, Methods for Policy Analysis, Scope and Methods of Public Administration, Program Evaluation, and Decision Methods). These courses are typically required in public affairs and administration programs and in other policy-related programs such as political science, applied sociology, criminal justice, counseling and social work, health and safety studies, urban planning, education, and park and recreation administration.

Policy Research is distinguished from other texts in the field by several characteristics. First, it is organized around five fundamental skills necessary in accomplishing effective policy research. Three of the skills—information structuring, information collection, and information analysis—encompass basic steps involved in conducting and interpreting research. Two of the skills—policy skills and project management—mediate between the producers of information and policy decisions. The former set of skills is critical to the relevance and value of policy research as a decision resource; the latter is critical to planning and managing policy research.

The five skills provide a simple organizing framework for presenting complex processes of generating and applying decision-oriented information. Students are introduced to the diversity of skills and to the linkages among these skills. Specific techniques such as cost-benefit analysis, *Delphi* techniques, and PERT are mentioned and sometimes presented as examples, but the emphasis is on giving students a solid grasp of the logic, approaches, and applications underlying these specialized tools. Many texts mistakenly emphasize specialized techniques, assuming students have an operational background in fundamental skills.

Second, the text emphasizes the intertwining of research activities and decision making in the policy process. Policy research is not conceived here as a compromised version of pure science applied in an alien environment. Rather, the systematic production of information is viewed as an ongoing process lodged in decision makers' need to know. Understanding *what* decision makers need to know, and *why*, is a fundamental part of policy research.

Third, a style of presentation designed to be readable and engaging has been consciously adopted. Key components of this style include extensive use of illustrations and case studies. The writing style is straightforward, employs technical language only as necessary, and reflects a conversational tone.

Teaching research is one of the most challenging tasks to be faced in the college classroom. The subject is vast, proper sequencing of topics is problematic, and student interest is difficult to stimulate and maintain. Problems are often compounded when instructors do not have professional experience in policy research. These kinds of difficulties in teaching courses involving policy research were prominent considerations in designing this text. In particular, the text addresses two major concerns in effective teaching in methods courses: the content concern and the anxiety concern.

The Content Concern

An issue in teaching courses related to policy research is determining which topics should be included. The diversity of course titles in the area is matched by a lack of faculty consensus on specific course content. Market surveys confirm that there is little agreement on course content or methods that should be covered in these courses.

This lack of agreement is related to the search for a limited set of specific techniques or methods perceived as most useful in policy analysis. The question of course content then becomes: Should the course cover program evaluation? PERT? decision trees? survey research? queing theory? optimum mix analysis? dynamic equilibrium analysis? and on and on. At this level of content specificity, the question is irresolvable with respect to basic policy research courses. By and large, these research technologies are closely linked to specific kinds of information needs. It is important to present a variety of such research technologies to demonstrate applications of research procedure to particular decision-making situations, but their use in foundation courses should be as examples, not as primary course components. Practicing producers and users of policy research must first possess the fundamental skills that allow them to understand specific techniques and assess their appropriateness for the particular decision situations they face.

Accordingly, the primary thrust of *Policy Research: Concepts, Methods, and Applications* is on the basic logic and skills that undergird the diversity of techniques for systematic production and use of information for policy decisions. The core of the text presents the fundamental skills of planning and managing research, conceptualizing problems, collecting information, interpreting results, and producing useful information for decision making. Some of these topics are included in other basic texts on policy research, but their treatment here has unique emphasis.

First, there is an emphasis on the fitting of research approaches to information needs relevant to a particular policy context. For example, information relevant to the initial evaluation of innovative peer counseling programs for the severely disabled may require open-ended, exploratory data collection techniques, a qualitative approach. Research on the impact of standardized campaign finance regulations on congressional races, on the other hand, may require structured collection of standardized information from a large number of campaigns, a quantitative approach. In this text, data collection techniques are compared not only for their methodological qualities (e.g., validity, reliability, obtrusiveness, generalizability), but also for their relative fit to different types of policy problems, decision settings, and resource levels. Thus, unnecessary debates such as the superiority of qualitative versus quantitative techniques are avoided.

Another theme is the use of "triangulation" to strengthen the quality and relevance of policy research. Because each data collection or data analysis technique carries its own assumptions and limitations, the principle of methods triangulation, for instance, posits that consistency of findings across different techniques provides a useful test of accuracy, adding to the dependability and usability of findings, conclusions, and recommendations. Similarly, since different data sources (e.g., agency records of a program plus legislative, judicial, and other records) provide differing perspectives on a research problem, consistencies and discrepancies between different sources are important considerations in interpreting and applying findings. The authors' experience in policy research confirms that effective use of triangulation strategies is an important component in policy analysts' arsenal of research strategies. Conflicting perspectives of policymakers, weaknesses of much available data, obvious limitations of single data sources in addressing complex policy questions, and restricted resources for conducting highly rigorous studies all contribute to the value of triangulation for producing accurate and useful information for policy decisions.

Discussions of data collection techniques are oriented toward the types of research tasks commonly faced by practicing policy analysts. For example, the chapter on sampling does not focus on the most sophisticated sampling problems (such as a national household sample) to demonstrate stratification, clustering, and other sampling tools. Rather, examples based on sampling documents, client groups, employees, citizens, and other more frequent applications are used. The discussion of sampling also addresses issues such as identifying the appropriate sampling unit (e.g., documents or respondents capable of providing the information relevant to the policy question at hand) and triangulation in sampling—issues critical to policy research but not discussed in most research texts.

The Anxiety Concern

A second concern in effective teaching and learning of research is the anxiety many students feel with respect to courses in research and analysis. This anxiety has multiple sources. Many students who pursue careers in areas involving policy research have avoided mathematics, statistics, and similar quantitative courses. Every teacher of research methods has experienced the frustration of attempting to overcome the barriers many students feel with respect to their performance in these areas. Another contributor to student anxiety is students' perception that the topic is not concretely related to the kinds of things they will be doing on the job. They do not have a clear sense of what producers and consumers of policy research actually do. In the authors' experience, many in-career students who actually produce and use systematic information in their jobs do not recognize these activities as research. *Policy Research* is designed to assist instructors reduce student anxiety regarding courses on research and analysis in several ways.

First, the presentation of materials is designed to stimulate student interest about a topic they expect to be dry and to put them at ease with the subject matter. From the beginning paragraphs, the text is strongly oriented toward conveying concrete impressions of the kinds of research activities analysts undertake. Initially this is accomplished through a vignette that follows a number of policy analysts through daily activities. The vignette conveys the interpersonal interactions and organizational dynamics typical to policy research tasks. It portrays policy research as an activity requiring the creative blending of a variety of skills, only some of which are technical in nature. The text is written to help the reader relate the general methods and approaches of research to concrete job-related activities.

Second, the extensive use of concrete examples and case studies is a central part of the strategy to reduce student anxiety. Examples are frequently used to introduce concepts and discussions of research procedure. Typically, abstract ideas are developed out of concrete examples, giving students constant indications of the relevance of research concepts to personally recognizable "real world" activities. Many of the examples and cases are drawn from the authors' own consulting and public sector research experiences. Firsthand knowledge of the cases allows a discussion of the subtleties that convey the challenge of public policy analysis.

Substantively, cases and examples are drawn from a wide variety of policy areas—vocational rehabilitation, health, criminal justice, human services, transportation, employment and job training, business regulation, campaign finance regulation, and education. They address a wide range of applications from needs assessments to the evaluation of program processes and impacts. Within this diversity, however, several major studies are cited repeatedly throughout the text. This continuity in examples allows readers to gain familiarity with these studies and allows parsimony in the presentation of examples.

Third, the sequencing of the discussion of five skills areas stems partly from the assumption that students will be less anxious about learning the abstract concepts of research methodology if they are familiar with the concrete situations in which policy research is used. Accordingly, Chapters 2 and 3 address policy skills—knowledge about policy problems, decision making, and research utilization that contributes to effective policy research. Attempts are made to treat these topics in ways that emphasize their relation to research procedures and that help ease students into thinking about researchable concepts and appropriate data. For example, the discussion of policy phases emphasizes the uniqueness of information needs at each step. The student is sensitized to the variety of research contributions to policy decisions and to the many constraints on the use of research-generated information to guide decisions. Policy research is not irrelevant in any of these decision settings; it simply takes differing forms in terms of fulfilling the information needs of policy participants.

Acknowledgments

This text reflects the contributions of a large number of people. The many examples of policy research used throughout are often drawn from actual projects conducted by practicing policy analysts. The authors thank Joël L. Phillips, president of EMT Associates, Inc., of Sacramento, California, for his contributions. He has been a strong supporter throughout this project and a principal in many studies cited here. The authors also wish to thank Peter A. Lauwerys, president of Northern California Research Associates, Inc., of Sacramento, California, for his contributions. Professor Guenther Kress, California State University at San Bernardino, has also been involved in many of the studies discussed and has contributed to the ideas presented here.

The authors acknowledge and appreciate the helpful comments of reviewers at various points in the development of the manuscript. These reviewers include Donald F. Kettl, University of Virginia; Stephen L. Percy, University of Virginia; T. McN. Simpson III, University of Tennessee–Knoxville. The California State University–Sacramento and the University of Missouri–St. Louis have supported the research behind this effort in numerous ways, including research grants and released time. The authors are particularly grateful to colleagues at these institutions who have listened, read, and improved the ideas presented in this text.

A number of people in the Department of Political Science and the Center for Metropolitan Studies at the University of Missouri–St. Louis skillfully produced the manuscript. Particular thanks go to Sandy Overton-Springer, Jan Frantzen, Lana Sink, and Pam Vierdag. Finally, our families merit special thanks for their support and understanding throughout the highs and lows that produced *Policy Research*.

1

Practicing Policy Research

Policy research takes place in and around the offices of decision makers. One way of introducing policy research is to examine what goes on in those offices as public officials make choices affecting citizens and consumers of governmental programs. The beginning pages of this chapter introduce policy research by "dropping in" on people who produce and use it. Generally, these persons are involved in the process of gathering and interpreting information which helps officials decide about the actions they should or should not take. The people observed possess a variety of work skills and have many different job titles, but are referred to generically as "policy analysts."

The remainder of the chapter provides an overview of those concrete activities that constitute policy research. Specifically, the chapter provides a brief history of the development of policy analysis as an integral contributor to policy and management decisions. It also provides an extended definition of what policy research is and how it fits into the administration of complex organizations and policies. Finally, the chapter outlines the organization of the text.

POLICY RESEARCH: A BEGINNING VIGNETTE

The California Health and Welfare Agency is located in sprawling, air-conditioned offices scattered through numerous buildings in downtown Sacramento—the state capital. Composed of nine separate departments, this agency is the largest public bureaucracy in the nation's most populous state. One component of the agency is the Department of Rehabilitation (DR), which administers governmental efforts to aid physically impaired persons. The DR is in turn divided into a diversity of programs aimed at specific problems of the disabled. One of these programs provides financial support for locally organized, not-for-profit organizations called Independent Living Centers (ILCs). These organizations deliver a variety of counseling, information, and support services for people with severe physical impairments. By dropping into Department of Rehabilitation offices, an observer would find a large number of policy analysts concerned with the state's policies toward these centers. These analysts are spread through several of the department's many subunits. The location of these units is depicted in the abbreviated organization chart presented in Figure 1.1.

The first opportunity to eavesdrop on policy analysts talking about Independent Living Centers is in the Management Analysis Section, a kind of watchdog over the operations of local Department of Rehabilitation offices scattered around the state. Management Analysis monitors local activi-

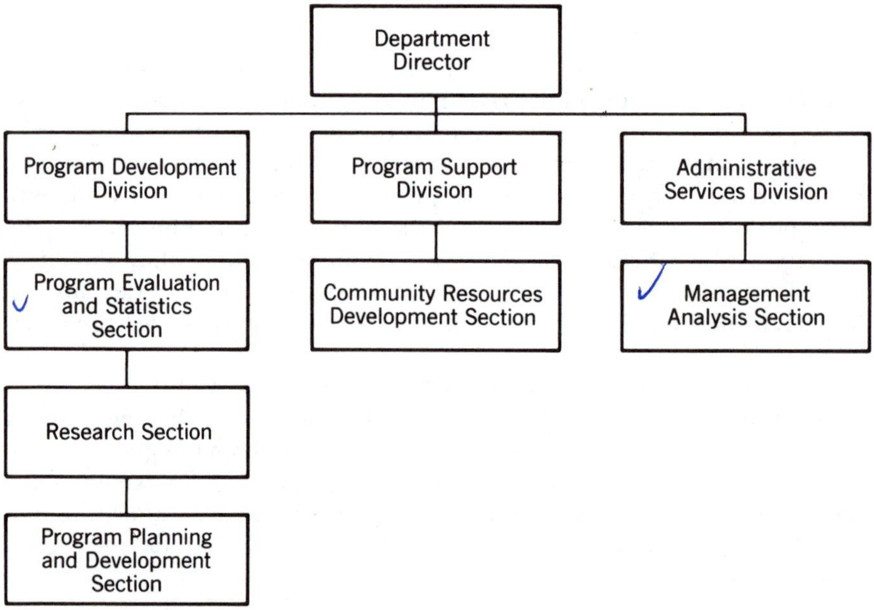

FIGURE 1.1 Partial Organization Chart: Department of Rehabilitation

ties to identify what local staff is accomplishing, and audits local offices to ensure that money is spent according to purposes prescribed under the law. Monitoring and auditing require a substantial amount of information—records of client contacts, records of eligibility for services, records of services provided, and accounting records, for example. Periodically, teams of management auditors are sent to the field to check on the accuracy and completeness of the records received from the office. Members of these teams are one sort of policy analyst.

In their first years of operation, Independent Living Center staff experienced many problems with these auditing teams. ILC staff were often inexperienced and professionally oriented toward protecting the individuality and independence of their clients—not toward program management. As a result, administrative failings in many ILCs threatened their eligibility for federal funds which the state depends on to support ILC activities.

Management auditing teams returning from the ILCs that summer, however, found program management much improved. One team leader, who clearly had a strong sympathy for the efforts of the ILCs, was encouraged about the turnaround that had been achieved. He told fellow department officials about the role his auditors had played in the improvement. High-ranking executive appointees in the Department of Rehabilitation had been urging the team leader's office to use compliance audits to evaluate the Independent Living Centers for some time. In response, last year's teams had carefully explained management problems to ILC staff, noted deficiencies, provided guidance toward solutions, and told them a record of deficiencies would be kept so that action could be taken if the problems were not corrected in the following audit session. It worked. Compliance monitoring had become management education, and the threat of a federal cutoff had been averted.

The Management Analysis Section and other administrative sections of California's Department of Rehabilitation are located in stately, restored brownstones along Sacramento's downtown Mall. Across the Mall, in stark modern office buildings, an observer will find the Program Evaluation and Statistics Section.

This section is responsible for conducting studies which measure the degree to which programs accomplish their intended objectives. These effectiveness evaluations serve a variety of purposes: they meet requirements for evaluation established through federal and state policies; they illuminate problem areas in a program and monitor program performance over periods of time; and they identify and justify budget requests by program managers. Ultimately, information gained through evaluations gives decision makers one perspective on whether programs should be continued or modified. In Program Evaluation and Statistics one can observe more policy analysts at work.

One morning in early June, a newly assigned program analyst was sipping coffee with one of several computer programmers who work in the section. She had just been put in charge of developing performance measures to evaluate Independent Living Centers. It was difficult, she explained. One responsibility of her section is to develop measures of efficiency and effectiveness for the department's programs. In standard programs designed to provide vocational training, for example, the section traditionally measured performance by examining the number of unemployed disabled clients who are able to reenter the labor force after receiving program services. To evaluate the economic benefits of the Vocational Rehabilitation programs, they also compared the income of clients when they entered the program to their income after they left.

The ILCs' programs stress peer counseling. A basic objective of peer counseling is to strengthen the self-reliance and confidence of the disabled client; it is thought that identification and discussion with a counselor who is also disabled is an important approach in achieving this objective. Unlike training to achieve employment, however, it is difficult to develop specific measures of performance in achieving peer counseling objectives. Still, if the ILCs are to ensure their continued funding by the state, concrete bases for demonstrating performance had to be developed. The task would require work, but the program analyst was convinced appropriate criteria could be developed to assess the effectiveness of the peer counseling program.

Across the hall in the Research Section a graduate intern from the local state university was perusing a volume of statistical tables and charts. She was orienting herself to her internship assignments, feeling fortunate to have been assigned to the Independent Living Research Project which was being funded through a grant from the Department of Health and Human Services. The project was a two-year effort to develop a client gains scale which would assess the degree to which services provided by the Department of Rehabilitation contributed to improved ability to care for one's personal household needs, to achieve mobility and involvement in the larger community, and to achieve a sense of self-reliance. The project was exciting to her because it was on the cutting edge of policy regarding services to the disabled. The gains scale was a pioneering attempt to define and measure clearly the benefits of recent rehabilitation programs. Beyond that, the process of developing an accurate and relevant set of questions to demonstrate client achievements promised to be stimulating.

Two floors above, in the other offices of the Program Planning and Development Section, a policy analyst holding the title of comprehensive services specialist was reading a thirty-page report titled "The Feasibility of Requiring a Non-State Match from Independent Living Centers Receiving State Support." In a time of decreasing government revenues, the Joint Legislative Budget Committee had asked the Department of Rehabilitation to take a hard look at the possibility of requiring the local centers to raise a specified percentage of their operating budgets from non-state sources, such as community organizations or fees for services. The specialist was nearing completion of the demanding task of compiling the report in time for the committee's hearings. The task had required telephoning around the state and analyzing fiscal records. She had developed a forecast of probable fiscal consequences which demonstrated that many of the smaller centers could not survive any match requirement in their first three years. Even after this initial period, her results demonstrated that a uniform matching requirement would jeopardize centers in cities with less adequate sources of local assistance.

The analyst felt a justifiable pride in her careful work and explicit recommendations, but it appeared the legislature would not benefit from the information in the near future. A friend from the legislative staff of the Joint Committee had just called and informed her that the committee would not be considering the issue, at least not now. Several members had received pressure from their districts and considered the issue too politically sensitive to take up. On the one hand, members did not want to turn down a potential revenue-saving measure; on the other, they did not want to vote against the severely physically impaired. Under the circumstances they felt it was best to do nothing at all.

Finally, moving past the brightly colored partitions which surround the offices of Program Planning and Development reveals the location of the Community Resources Development Section. At the center stands the section manager's cluttered desk. For the upcoming summer, the big issue in Community Resources would be Assembly Bill 2687, just passed by the legislature. On this morning, a task force of policy analysts (with various titles) was gathered around the section manager's desk to discuss the new bill. The legislation had important implications for the future of Independent Living Centers and offered the possibility of a new base for continued state funding. AB 2687 required the department to plan and implement five pilot projects which would provide funds for selected ILCs to operate as comprehensive service centers for the severely impaired.

The idea had a history. Regional comprehensive service centers had been used for years to provide a central point where parents of developmentally disabled children (e.g., mentally retarded) could gain information and referral to the variety of specific educational, medical, counseling, and support services they might require. However, the idea had not been tried in the area of physical and sensory disabilities in adults; nor had it been administered through independent, peer-oriented centers like the ILCs. Under the circumstances, the legislature decided that carefully evaluated, demonstration programs were necessary before making a full-scale public commitment of funds to this untried application of the comprehensive service center concept.

The department director had administratively delegated implementation of AB 2687 to Community Resources Development with the clear indication the project had a high priority. In the climate of fiscal constraint, the director knew that positive evaluation results were required to ensure continuation of the comprehensive service centers program. He hoped evaluation findings would demonstrate that pilot programs improved performance by severely disabled clients. The major focus of the task force discussion this morning was the detailed requirements for evaluation which had been established by the legislature. These requirements are contained within the following excerpts from AB 2687.

Excerpts from AB 2687

The people of the State of California do enact as follows:

SECTION 1.   Section 19801 of the Welfare and Institutions Code is amended to read:

19801. An independent living center shall:

(a) Be a private, nonprofit organization controlled by a board of directors. A majority of the board shall be comprised of disabled individuals;

(b) Be staffed by persons trained to assist disabled persons in achieving social and economic independence. The staff shall include as large a proportion as is practicable of disabled individuals;

(c) Provide, but not be limited to, the following services to disabled individuals:

(1) Peer counseling,

(2) Advocacy,

(3) Attendant referral,

(4) Housing assistance and

(5) Information and referral.

(d) Provide other services and referrals as may be deemed necessary, such as transportation, job development, equipment maintenance and evaluation, training in independent living skills, mobility assistance, and communication assistance.

Chapter 8.5.   Pilot Comprehensive Services Center for the Disabled

19810.   The purpose of this chapter is to study the feasibility and to plan for the establishment of pilot projects which would alter the delivery of services to the severely disabled through a system of comprehensive service centers.

The provisions of this chapter shall be administered by the Department of Rehabilitation.

19813. The department shall, through consultation with community based independent living centers, develop administrative and program standards and regulations for the development and provision of services. The department shall also formulate criteria for pilot comprehensive service centers for the disabled. The criteria shall include . . .

(g) Specifications for the evaluation of the proposals submitted for the pilot projects and for the evaluation of the pilot projects. Specifically the evaluation shall include, but not be limited to:

(1) The number and description of disabled individuals by disability, who receive services from the pilot project centers;

(2) The range of problems presented by the individuals serviced, and the services provided in response to those problems;

(3) The number of individuals who moved from an institutional setting to a more independent setting by type of setting;

(4) The number of individuals who entered vocational rehabilitation or employment;

(5) The impact of the services on medical and supportive service costs;

(6) The impact or benefits of the services on the disabled individuals' participation in family and community activities;

(7) The cost and savings to the General Fund and other public funds of providing the services;

(8) The cost effectiveness of the services provided;

(9) The effectiveness of data collection and output for program evaluation purposes;

(10) Other sources of funding independent living centers; and

(11) Other information specified by the department.

The department may enter into interagency agreements with other state agencies, independent living centers and such other consultants as deemed appropriate by the Health and Welfare Agency for purposes of planning, evaluation, site selection and such other factors to assure fiscal and management accountability of the projects.

Planning for the evaluation was a challenge, and the section manager wanted to anticipate any problems which might arise, even though the study itself was two years off. Accordingly, the task force was brainstorming the process to identify problem areas and to devise strategies for ensuring an accurate and useful evaluation of pilot project results.

An early decision had been reached regarding who would conduct the study. To maximize objectivity in designing and carrying out the research, and particularly to remove any reservations that the legislature might have regarding a study carried out by the department itself, it was decided that private research consultants or university-based researchers should conduct the study. This meant that department staff would prepare a request for (study) proposals (RFP) which detailed the information objectives of the evaluation study, and would circulate it among qualified research analysts outside the department. Determination of who would eventually conduct the research would be based on the department's evaluation of the study proposals submitted in response to the request.

Beyond this basic decision to have the evaluation conducted by outside consultants rather than internal staff, the task force had identified a number of potential difficulties in administering the experimental pilot program. When section decision makers reviewed applications from ILCs to serve as pilot sites, for instance, they would have to consider the degree to which successful applicants were representative of the thirty-some other ILCs in the state. If the pilot projects were not representative of most other ILCs, it would be difficult to convince the legislature that similar achievements could be accomplished elsewhere.

After lengthy discussions, members of the task force lapsed into a more relaxed conversation about the delicate task of negotiating participation in the study with the fiercely independent ILCs. The accuracy and usability of the research findings required cooperation and effort, and sometimes ILC management and staff could not see why all this data collection, interview time, and disruption of clients was necessary. Task force members agreed it was a situation requiring tact and skill on the part of analysts studying the program. Later, members headed for their individual offices, agreeing to meet a week later to further detail criteria for selecting pilot sites for the study.

Some Common Ground

The activities discussed in this beginning vignette are complex and fluid, depicting policy research as a widespread and diverse function defying easy and precise definition. For now, a few observations are ventured on the underlying characteristics of the activities witnessed in the department offices.

First, the Independent Living Centers vignette demonstrates that persons engaged in policy analysis hold a variety of job titles—both technical and managerial—and are scattered through a variety of organizational units. Indeed, the evaluators of the AB 2687 pilot program—external consultants—would not be employees of the Department of Rehabilitation at all. Most likely, they would be analysts in a private research organization or college teachers who contract to do policy research for the department. Some participants in the policy research process, such as the section manager for Program Planning and Development, do not actually conduct the research themselves. Rather, they consume the resulting information in helping to make decisions for which they are responsible. Thus, the policy research process includes both producers (those who actually collect and analyze information) and consumers (those who use that information in policy deliberations).

Second, the persons in the vignette were using a variety of technical skills in the course of their work. The auditors were trained in analyzing fiscal and management records. The director of the Independent Living Research Project was skilled in the construction of questionnaires designed to measure complex attitudes and perceptions, and in the techniques for statistical analyses of these questionnaires. The outside analysts who would eventually evaluate the pilot programs would have to demonstrate their skills in a variety of research techniques from the rigorous design of experimental studies to less-controlled methods of investigation such as personal interviews. Indeed, policy research draws on a broad spectrum of techniques for information collection and analysis, including adaptations of the scientific model of experimentation, applications of economic analysis to program costs and benefits, surveys of individuals, statistical analysis of large data sets, personal observation, and more. The list of particular data collection and analysis options available to policy analysts is constantly expanding as the technology develops, and an important part of any policy analyst's training is the acquisition of expertise in these techniques.

Third, analysts in the opening vignette were applying their technical skills to a series of specific information needs which had arisen in the processes of making decisions regarding the ILCs. Some of these decisions were necessary for planning future activities intended to accomplish public objectives. The proposal to create Comprehensive Service Centers in ILCs, for example, involved planning decisions. Other decisions related to the accomplishments of past government activities and their possible improvement. The evaluation of the ILC pilot projects would provide information for assessing whether the new service centers did accomplish what was intended.

Still other decisions focused on the actions of people within programs rather than on the performance of programs as a whole. Monitoring the activities of individual counselors, for example, may provide information for keeping them accountable to program intentions or for improving the efficiency of their work. Decisions of each type—planning, evaluation, and internal management—interrelate to influence the success or failure of public policy. Policy research provides information to meet the range of these decision needs.

Fourth, though they possessed technical skills, these policy analysts were not rote technicians performing standardized work to carry out the bidding of their administrative or political superiors. In many instances the analysts exercised significant discretion in determining what information was relevant to the problem they were working on and in deciding what questions should be asked to address aspects of the problem. For example, analysts developing the client gains scale for the Independent Living Research Project had discretion in formulating the questionnaire items which provided concrete definition to the "gains," or outcomes, which ILCs are attempting to achieve. The information analysts develop is not programmed or routine; it is developed with a view to its relevance for the issue at hand.

Fifth, it follows that effective policy research requires sensitivity and responsiveness to its users and to others affected by its use—policymakers, employees, clients, and citizens. If information generated through policy research is not considered in decision-making situations by these groups, it fails its intended purpose. Awareness of the many factors at work in the decision-making process is just as important as the use of technical skills. Such factors include the social, psychological, and political contexts in which decisions are made (Putt and Rehfuss, 1981:185).

Factors such as decision maker beliefs and values also influence outcomes of decisions. Differing views among contending groups shape the number and kinds of acceptable alternatives in policy-making situations. The legal environment of public policy establishes constraints on decision making. An appreciation of these factors at work in decision making is essential for understanding the potential of policy research to yield useful information.

Policy research, then, takes place alongside a diversity of organizations and stakeholders which cumulatively constitute public policy. The function of policy research is to facilitate public policy processes through providing accurate and useful decision-related information. The skills required to produce information that is technically sound and useful lie at the heart of the policy research process, regardless of the specific methodology employed. These basic skills of policy research are increasingly in demand within public (and private) organizations. This trend will not diminish; the use of policy research is part of a chain of interconnected social changes characterizing the information age of the 1990s and beyond. Following is an overview of major factors which launched and continue to propel the development of policy research.

THE DEVELOPMENT OF POLICY RESEARCH: A BRIEF HISTORY

Through the history of American public policy, influencing public decisions required skills in the traditional languages of politics. Successful political actors were able to combine the art of rhetorical communication with the public, and the art of wheeling and dealing with other political actors in more private settings of smoke-filled rooms. In the last two decades, however, successful maneuvering in the halls of government has increasingly required the ability to converse in a third language—the language of policy analysis. Discussion of statistical indicators, budgetary forecasts, social impacts, and environmental impacts has not replaced appealing public rhetoric or skillful negotiating, but it has become an essential component of public dialogue.

The development of research as an integral part of policy-making has not happened overnight, nor is the development of the research role complete. As with any complex technology which generates information for applied purposes, the development of policy research has necessitated the integration of new equipment, new techniques (ways of doing things), and new roles for people (Dutton and Danziger, 1982:4).

Along with developing an applied technology of policy research, scholars with an interest in policy analysis have worked toward defining a distinctive intellectual enterprise referred to as the policy sciences. The intellectual history of the policy sciences can be traced to American pragmatism in the early part of this century, as reflected in the writings of John

Dewey and others. Numerous scholars and practitioners in a variety of fields made major contributions to theory and technique of the policy sciences during this century. Throughout its history, policy science has focused on "problem-oriented, multimethod, and human-centered inquiry leading to purposeful action" (Brewer and deLeon, 1983:7).

A complete history of the intellectual and applied development of policy research is not a purpose here; however, the development of the interacting components of the endeavor can be portrayed in three major historical periods: experiments in policy research (1930–1960), the search for policy solutions (1960–1980), and facilitating the policy process (1980–?).

Experiments in Policy Research: 1930-1960

Seeking advice before making decisions is not new. Politicians have always had counselors bringing them information and participating in their decisions; but historically, the legitimizing base for this advice was often kinship, personal ties, and political agreement. The counsel of experts who base their authority on skills in systematic analysis evolved more slowly.

During the 1920s and 1930s, Charles Merriam at the University of Chicago made important contributions to the theory and technique of a science "devoted to the recognition of human problems and their alleviation" (Brewer and deLeon, 1983:8). The massive economic problems of the 1930s provided an impetus to applications of policy research to governmental decision making. President Hoover, facing the massive uncertainty of the Great Depression, commissioned prominent sociologist William F. Ogburn to produce the extensive volume *Recent Social Trends* (1933). This work foreshadowed the current development of statistical record banks which provide a continuous profiling of the social and economic state of the nation. As the depression ground on and the administration of Franklin D. Roosevelt sought innovative government action to revive the ailing economy, economists were brought into the government to provide "scientific" expertise. Social scientists achieved official status as expert advisers within the offices of government.

During World War II another sociologist, Samuel Stouffer, undertook a pioneering analysis of military morale problems when serving as research director of the Information and Education Branch of the United States Army. The resulting study was a landmark because it provided an explicit research foundation for policy decisions by the U.S. army (Finsterbusch and Motz, 1980:3), and demonstrated the utility of sociological and psychological research for improving organizational performance. The tragedy of a second world war prompted the development of other systematic approaches to informing policy decisions. Systems analysis, for example, was advanced through numerous applications by the military.

Through the late 1940s and 1950s, the increasing legitimacy of social science advice to government was reaffirmed through a series of seemingly unconnected steps. The Employment Act of 1946 established the Council of Economic Advisers (CEA) within the Executive Office of the President and charged them with preparing an annual report on the state of the economy. For the first time, the role of independent scientific analysis was institutionalized at the highest levels of the federal policy process.

The landmark *Brown v. Board of Education of Topeka* decision was a major breakthrough for the use of social research in judicial decision making. In resolving this case, the Supreme Court relied on psychological research that demonstrated impaired self-concepts among minority children in segregated schools. This testimony provided one foundation for the finding that racial segregation in the public schools was inherently unequal.

Many of these early uses of expert analysis to improve policy decisions were halting—brought about by crisis or by the idiosyncratic initiatives of individual policymakers. In a real sense, these initial efforts were experiments in the application of research to public problems. They demonstrated the possibilities of gathering systematic information bearing on questions of policy, and they provided examples of cases in which social analysis had significant input in policy-making situations. Several factors, however, slowed the development of policy research and its application in government.

First, development of the equipment necessary to large-scale information processing was in its infancy. Prior to the first-generation computers of the 1950s, information storage and retrieval was cumbersome, typically involving large physical file storage areas and numerous file clerks who accessed the information by hand. Early computers of the 1950s began to alter the capability to handle straightforward data files, but their dissemination through government was limited by cost, size, and limits in flexibility in handling multiple operations. Not until the 1960s did computerization take hold in government offices across the nation.

The period of experimentation was also characterized by rudimentary development in the techniques of policy research. Stouffer's study, for instance, produced new techniques for analyzing causal relations in survey data; the techniques simply had not existed prior to his effort. Similarly, techniques for measuring social phenomena which were the objects of policy had to be created. The development of economic indicators spurred by the 1946 Employment Act led the way. The full potential of policy research had to await the creation of more refined and standardized techniques in information collection and analysis.

In the scholarly literature, Lerner and Lasswell's edited volume *The Policy Sciences* (1950) summarized some of the policy research contributions made during the depression and World War II, but the academic community was slow to build upon the pioneering work of those early years. The policy sciences approach, as advocated by Lasswell, explicitly recognized that science was not the necessary "handmaiden of inevitable human progress" (Dunn, 1981:19). Policy research and analysis had to address the importance of specifying the human values that define human progress and dignity.

Lasswell continued to lead the way in articulating the need for a unique intellectual approach to the study and resolution of policy problems. Indeed, in 1956, Lasswell used his address as newly elected president of the American Political Science Association to outline the future policy challenges of nuclear weapons, energy use, expanded communications, and the prolonging of life through medical advances (Lasswell, 1956). Despite his challenge, the scientific community did not take it up until later.

Finally, the early stages of policy research were constrained by the lack of people trained in policy research skills—both as producers and consumers of information. Most of the early studies were conducted by professors who struggled to develop ways of adapting their training in scientific research to the subtle and changing world of public policy. Similarly, public officials who encouraged early policy research and who considered it seriously in their deliberations were the exception. This state of affairs was to change in the years ahead.

The Search for Policy Solutions: 1960-1980

A second phase in the emergence of contemporary policy research can be traced to the early 1960s—more specifically to the inauguration of John F. Kennedy. The Kennedy administration brought with it a renewed faith in the capability and responsibility of government to improve society. This belief in proactive government action was translated throughout the sixties into a steady march of significant social legislation. The Civil Rights Act of 1964, the Elementary and Secondary Education Act of 1965, the Economic Opportunity Act of 1967, the Omnibus Crime Control and Safe Streets Act of 1968, and many more pieces of federal legislation carried public policy into new areas of social concern.

Public officials increasingly turned to policy experts for information and analysis which would provide the solutions to society's ills. Many analysts were eager to respond and touted the potential of scientific analysis in meeting the challenge. If the commitment was made and the analysis performed, it was assumed that the problem could be solved.

A related characteristic of the sixties was the belief that the federal government could fashion, implement, and control far-flung programs which would efficiently and effectively implement solutions to social problems. Again, the systematic collection and analysis of information was expected to play a central role in controlling programs, keeping them accountable, and determining whether they were meeting their objectives (Mowitz, 1980:19). The proliferation of program monitoring, program evaluation, rational budgeting systems, and a variety of other management information tools demonstrated the increased reliance on policy research as a means of controlling public programs. Thus, the application of policy research to large-scale problems in the 1960s was characterized by an optimistic belief in the efficacy of policy research in solving social problems on a national basis.

As the assault on large-scale social issues increased the demand for policy research, technological advances improved the capacity of analysts to respond. The 1960s were a decade of rapid advance in the design and manufacture of large mainframe computers; computing facilities proliferated. The advent of flexible third generation computers in the seventies dramatically increased capabilities for storing, retrieving, and manipulating large data sets. Improvements in research technology were no less dramatic. Easy-to-use computer programs made complex statistical analysis of large data sets readily available to a wide variety of users. Opinion polling and the collection of statistics on crime, health, economic conditions, the environment, and a variety of other social conditions became routine.

The second period of development for policy research brought rapid growth in the number of trained specialists available to conduct policy research. "Policy research, analysis, and training were professional fads, and everybody wanted to get with it" (Brewer and deLeon, 1983:8). Courses and whole programs of study in the methods of policy research were introduced into a growing number of universities and colleges. In addition, as the academic marketplace dried up in the late 1960s, many holders of advanced degrees in the social sciences entered government as an appealing opportunity to apply their skills and knowledge. The employment of trained analysts in government increased rapidly, and cadres of experts found their niches at all levels of the public service.

The combined effects of public policy oriented to large-scale social problems and improvements in the technology of policy research contributed to a brief honeymoon for advocates of centralized, large-scale uses of policy research. Comments from a 1964 press conference by the late Senator Hubert H. Humphrey demonstrate the increased acceptance and even solicitation of policy research by public officials.

> We have vast needs in education, in transportation, in communications, in weather control, air and water pollution, in medical facilities and technology, housing, and many, many more areas.... These problems are admirably suited to the ... "analysis" approach.... (quoted in Quade, 1975:6)

Possibly the zenith of high-placed optimism regarding the potential of policy research for solving public problems came in 1965 when President Lyndon Johnson ordered the expansion of systematic budgeting in the federal bureaucracy. The president proclaimed the introduction of

> a very new and very revolutionary system of planning and programming and budgeting throughout the vast Federal government, so that through the tools

of modern management the full promise of the finer life can be brought to every American at the lowest possible cost. (quoted in Mowitz, 1980:9)

The Program Planning and Budgeting system (PPB) was a massive and ambitious undertaking. The system required the categorization of budget expenditures into programs with specifiable objectives. Analysis of the costs and benefits of achieving these objectives was to be used to allocate public monies in the most beneficial and efficient manner. Systematic collection and analysis of information was the technique of PPB, but the intent was no less than to "recast federal budgeting from a repetitive process for financing permanent bureaucracies into an instrument for deciding the purposes and programs of government . . ." (Schick, 1966:55). PPB epitomized the second period in the evolution of policy research because of its optimistic assumption that policy research technology would lead directly to improved policy decisions.

In its inflated belief in the powers of policy analysis to provide policy solutions, the second historical phase of policy research carried the seeds of its own destruction. Brewer and deLeon (1983:8) observed that for policy analysis, "the decade of the 1970's was, with minor exceptions, a time of exuberant oversell, burgeoning activity, and limited performance." PPB and other applications of comprehensive, systematic analysis were criticized on a number of grounds. A major criticism attacked the basic assumption that analysis could solve social problems. In the words of Victor Thompson (1975:57),

> I must be blunt: science cannot solve social problems. . . . The solution of a social problem is properly described with such words as "compromise," "consensus," "majority," "negotiation," "bargaining," "coercion," etc. If the "solution" cannot be described in such terms, then it is not the solution of a social problem.

The presumption that scientific analysis alone could dictate optimum policy conjured visions of an Orwellian society in which technocrats operating under the cloak of science invade individual privacy and manipulate society for their purposes.

Other critics observed that analysis could clarify and inform but could not eliminate or resolve value differences. Insistence on the objectivity of policy research information masks this limitation and threatens to "make each and every technocrat the overt or covert agent or fomentor of his or her own private ideology. In such circumstances . . . the policy analysts . . . are no more than accidental political agents . . ." (Benveniste, 1977:29).

Additional criticisms focused on the technical inadequacies of policy research itself. Donald Schon (1971), a noted futurist, argued that the quality of information about social problems, the bewildering array of potentially relevant variables, and the limited ability to analyze this complexity

renders the search for technically valid solutions futile. Schon (1971:227) argued that "conclusions will not hold steady over time." In a world of rapid change, the time required to plan, test, and verify centralized policy solutions will very possibly extend beyond the duration of the concern itself.

The most telling criticisms of policy research in this period came from advocates of policy science itself. Much of the work done in the name of policy research did not reflect the basic characteristics of the approach. Critics argued that most of the studies of the period were dominated by technical or bureaucratic definitions of problems, rather than being truly responsive to social problems. The "failure was most apparent in [the] neglect of the humanistic aspects" (Brewer and deLeon, 1983:8) of policy science.

The failure of policy research to meet its optimistic promises led some critics to proclaim its death in government. Others disagreed. "Whether judged by the number of planning and evaluation units, program analysts, or actual analysis done . . ." (Rose, 1977:68), there was a substantial increase in policy research activity even after the demise of PPB. It was not the commitment to analysis that was waning, but the notion that analysis alone was sufficient basis for dictating solutions and controlling programs. A revised and competing view of the role of policy research in decision making was and currently is emerging.

Facilitating the Policy Process: 1980-?

Putting a precise starting date on the third stage in the changing roles of policy research is elusive: the characteristics of this stage are emerging. However, by the mid-1970s the reactions against second-stage thinking were consolidating. Most notably, there has been a reawakening of the importance of recognizing the limitations of analysts' ability to provide technical solutions to human problems. Policy analysis in the third stage is perceived as facilitating policy decisions, not displacing them.

Third-stage analysts decreasingly serve as producers of solutions guiding decision makers to the one best way of resolving complex policy concerns. Policy research in the third phase is not expected to produce solutions, but to provide information and analysis at multiple points in a complex web of interconnected decisions which shape public policy. Policy research does not operate separated and aloof from decision makers; it permeates the policy process itself. Lynn (1980:1) explains:

> To aid them in thinking and deciding . . . , public officials have been depending to an increasing extent on knowledge derived from research, policy analysis, program evaluation and statistics to inform or buttress their views. Elected and appointed officials in the various branches and levels of government, from federal judges to town selectmen, are citing studies, official data, and

expert opinion in at least partial justification for their actions more often than in the past.

Two implications follow. Where policy research in the second stage was focused in the administrative branch and focused on budgeting and control functions, third-stage policy information is tailored to and accessed by multiple stakeholders. Legislatures; federal, state, and local agencies; contracted service providers; advocacy groups; political parties; courts—all are involved in producing and consuming policy research.

Policy information facilitates the decisions of these disparate stakeholders in a variety of ways. Policy research helps administrators clarify the nature of issues facing them; it aids planners by scanning social indicators for emerging policy problems; it assists program managers in identifying points of organizational breakdown; it provides information on the desires of citizen groups, and on and on. Policy research increasingly provides a broad range of information needs called for in public sector policy making.

Policy research in the third stage is characterized by a restrained view of the contribution it can make to policy deliberations. Many decisions involve delicate balancing acts between competing views. Programs to prevent child abuse, for example, must balance prevention of abuse with protection of privacy in the family and home. Policy research can help document the extent and nature of child abuse, and can evaluate the efficacy of programs in preventing abuse, but it cannot provide definitive answers in resolving the proper balance between the issues of child abuse and governmental intervention in family and home affairs. Janet Weiss (1980:1227) concludes:

> Research has ... a useful contribution to make, but it is necessarily a partial contribution. . . . Even in those situations where all actors agree on desired policy outcomes and are merely searching for optimal means, [analysts] must be content with being useful only when complemented by other sources of feedback to the policy process. In a case such as child abuse, where the nature of the problem is itself highly controversial, we have much more reason to be modest.

The transformation of policy research into a mechanism for facilitating decisions throughout the policy process has been propelled by ever-more dramatic changes in technology. The most far-reaching of these is the distributed data processing revolution of the 1980s. The development and marketing of small, remarkably powerful computers allows decentralized storage, access, and use of a diversity of information sources. No longer does the centralized mainframe computing facility with its high priesthood of computer specialists dominate information technologies. Flexibility and adaptation to varying needs is replacing centralized and standardized sources of policy information characteristic of the mainframe era.

A similar tendency toward flexibility and diversity has characterized advances in techniques of analysis. The second-stage emphasis on large data sets, economic analysis, quantitative statistical analysis, and hypothesis-testing research designs is being augmented by the continuous evolution of a diversity of flexible approaches to information collection and interpretation. Improved methods of exploratory data analysis allowing the analyst to describe large data sets without preconceptions (i.e., hypotheses) are one illustration. Underlying the surge in available techniques for analysis is the recognition that these methods must fit the nature of the particular situation being researched. The application of policy research to a broad range of concerns necessitates an increasing array of research techniques tailored to specific situations.

The third stage of policy research is also being influenced by fundamental changes in the roles of policy analysts. Guy Benveniste (1977) observed that the United States has a tradition of standards and procedures for politics and a separate tradition of standards and procedures for science, but it does not have standards for the appropriate application of science within politics. The result, he argues, is that the roles of analyst and politician have been viewed as contradictory. A challenge now and in the future is to make politics and systematic analysis more complementary without jeopardizing their distinctive contributions.

First steps in the creation of this modified relationship have already taken place. It is increasingly recognized that information produced by policy research is not neutral and apolitical but is itself based on assumptions and preferences. It does not and should not replace politics. The emerging role for policy analysts "is one . . . actively engaged in an intellectual partnership with the decision maker throughout the policy process" (Mayer and Greenwood, 1980:16). Indeed, as with the section chief in the beginning vignette, the roles of analyst and decision maker often converge in the same individual.

While PPB-type budgeting systems epitomized the aspirations of the second stage of policy research, the third stage is characterized by a network of decentralized uses of information. The evolving California Fiscal Information System, or CFIS, represents one variant of third-stage technology. This ambitious system provides detailed data on the operation of California's major state agencies (Cowden, 1981). The information is diverse, including budget information, cost accounting data, a variety of performance measures (e.g., workload, program outputs), nature and movement of legislation affecting programs, and more.

When fully operational, the data base will be accessible to analysts, administrators, legislative staff, and others needing the information. Access is thus decentralized, and the data can be utilized for a variety of purposes including day-to-day program management, legislative oversight, budget forecasting, and legislative bill tracking. CFIS will provide an unprecedented flow of information between programs and between the executive and legislative branches of government.

Understandably, the advent of CFIS raises serious questions about its impact on the policy process. Even though access is hypothetically widespread, will CFIS data actually be used by a large number of decision makers, or will a small coterie of knowledgeable staff dominate its uses? What will be the quality of CFIS information? Some public officials believe that information systems such as CFIS will increase political tensions and conflicts. Detailed information previously controlled by separate organizations is becoming widely available, facilitating advocacy of some programs and attacks on others.

In the third stage of policy research, information is increasingly used to strengthen or undermine policy orientations held by contending factions. "Increasingly, officials from the President on down lose influence in policy debates when they cannot get their numbers right or when their ideas are successfully challenged by opposing experts" (Lynn, 1980:2).

Finally, policy research in the third stage is characterized by the complexity and intractability of many of the problems facing policymakers. What should be done about the health threat posed by toxic wastes in the environment? Indeed, just what is the nature and degree of that threat? How should government respond to escalating health costs? What can be done about the downward spiral of inadequate education, inadequate services, and persistent crime in America's inner cities? These questions and new ones arising place increasing demands on policymakers. In the foreseeable future, policymakers will continue to turn to policy analysts for help in addressing these complex issues.

POLICY RESEARCH IS . . .

By now a series of impressions about policy research has been formed. Policy research is a differentiated set of activities that touch public policy at numerous points. Yet policy research activities do share characteristics discussed below.

Human Centered

The fundamental characteristic of policy research is that it addresses human problems emerging from an evolving community. The function of policy research is to help create a future contributing to human dignity and to human development, and to analyze problems with the goal of benefiting the human condition. Human needs, interests, and values are core concerns of policy research. Policy research is based upon the belief that "there is no reason for study beyond the contribution that can be made to the human future" (Meehan, 1981:4). The human-centered feature of policy research will be evident throughout the text.

Pluralistic

As a human-centered enterprise, policy research cannot be separated from the conflict of values and interests which characterizes political and social processes. Policy research can clarify ideas and provide empirical evidence, but it cannot erase value differences or make them irrelevant. The beginning vignette demonstrated the potential—indeed the inevitability—of conflict and opposition in policy deliberations. Turning over more resources to Independent Living Centers threatens traditional vocational rehabilitation counselors in the department who fear a decrease of resources in their own programs. The development of productivity measures concerns interest groups for the severely disabled, who fear a decrease in services and programs provided for them. It is inevitable that research information will be used to advocate particular policies and decisions.

An example illustrates the impact of differing points of view on the use of policy research information. The situation concerned questions regarding the appropriate support level for recipients of county General Assistance welfare grants. In most states, General Assistance is the last source of public economic assistance for persons who are financially indigent, but do not qualify for any other form of public assistance (such as unemployment insurance or aid to the disabled). The support level for this form of welfare has traditionally been modest ($100 to $150 per month was not uncommon in the state where this research was accomplished).

Recently, an interest group representing the poor in several western states undertook a campaign to raise grant levels to an "adequate" level for subsistence. The interest group selected policy analysts to conduct a series of studies which would (1) identify standards for an adequate level of subsistence, and (2) survey selected counties to determine the actual minimum cost of attaining that adequate level of subsistence. The studies yielded a recommended level of support 50 to 100 percent higher than existing welfare grants.

This information was used by the interest group to advocate for increased levels of support. Although none in the sponsoring interest group knew what an appropriate level of support would be, they were certain that existing levels were too low. The study provided a concrete, systematically supported recommendation for an appropriate level.

These recommendations did not go unopposed. Opponents objected to the recommended increases despite the evidence, citing a lack of funds. Others attacked the recommendations for a food budget which would allow nutritionally sound diets, arguing that this diet would not be purchased by welfare recipients. They attacked the requirement that grant amounts should allow the rental of housing meeting federal standards of adequacy, arguing that many working people live in substandard housing. They argued that these standards reflected value choices—and of course they were right. Still, it was clear that the studies improved the bargaining position of the interest group, and, in county after county, boards of supervisors compromised, raising grant levels to a point between what they were and what was recommended in the studies. Information generated by policy research provides a resource for strengthening the influence of stakeholders in the political process.

Multi-Perspective

The pluralistic nature of public policy requires a pluralistic research approach. Policy research must accommodate multiple perspectives on issues, and this has implications for the organization and conduct of policy research.

A major implication is that policy research is interdisciplinary.

> None of the policy-relevant disciplines—including philosophy, history, economics, political science, law, sociology, psychology, and the biological and physical sciences—has precisely [the policy research] frame of reference, although each has something positive to contribute. (Brewer and deLeon, 1983:9)

Policy analysts are open to and conversant with the differing ways in which policy problems can be defined and the differing perspectives that can be brought to their solution. Only then can the range of human values be reflected in public policy, and only then can research information be useful to stakeholders.

The complexity of public issues also means policy analysts incorporate multiple research methods and multiple data sources into their studies. Policy problems and the information relevant to their resolution cannot be simply portrayed, and the research procedures used by policy analysts reflect this complexity. Subsequent chapters discuss this need for multiple research perspectives in terms of research "triangulation," which refers to an emerging measurement strategy in policy research.

Systematic

Policy research frequently uses the fundamental logic and procedures of science as a way of gaining information about policy issues. Science as a way of creating knowledge involves two basic steps. First, science requires the systematic clarification of ideas, or concepts, so that they have a clear relationship to the real, or empirical, world—a world that corresponds to shared understandings and experiences. Scientific statements are established through the ability to observe persons, objects, and events in the world.

The second basic step in scientific research is to collect and interpret information through standardized procedures. A basic characteristic of standardized procedures is that the activities through which observations are made and interpreted are explicit, well-defined, and replicable by other analysts. Other characteristics of scientific inquiry follow naturally from the application of standardized procedures. For example, scientific research is systematic in that consistent criteria are provided for selecting what to observe and for placing observations into categories of information. In the Independent Living Research Project, the process of constructing the gains scale would allow the categorization of individual questionnaire responses according to a systematic set of criteria for determining independent living skills. The same conceptual definition of independent living would be used to classify responses of all questionnaire respondents.

Science does not rely on personal intuition or individual authority to determine what is real. Rather, it depends on empirical evidence, on systematic and concrete observation of events. The processes used in producing this information are made explicit. Because of its explicit character, the procedures used in any scientific study are subject to scrutiny and criticism. Further, study procedures can be replicated to see if comparable findings result, serving to confirm or disconfirm original findings.

Decision-Relevant

Third-stage policy analysts do not assume policy decisions can be reduced to neat, determinate calculation of the best solution. They do assume that decisions can be improved through carefully produced information, and that stakeholders will not dismiss such information out of hand. Future chapters show that the relevance of information for policy-making depends on numerous factors: the nature of the policy concern, the constellation of interests surrounding the problem, the degree of power to make policy decisions, and the type of organization in which the decision will be made (e.g., administrative agency or legislature). A few basic observations about producing information that is decision relevant are appropriate here.

First, producing decision-relevant information depends upon the definition of policy decisions themselves. Scholars have established a tradition of attempting to define policy decisions as distinct from other kinds of decisions. Bauer (1968:2), for instance, has proposed that the term *policy* be reserved for decisions "which have the widest ramifications, the longest time perspective, and generally require the most information and contemplation." Yet research (Weiss and Bucuvalas, 1980:38) has revealed that even the highest-ranking governmental officials express "a fairly general reluctance to admit making decisions of any substance," i.e., the type of decision that would define policy as viewed by Bauer. Even top decision makers see their latitude restricted by past events, legal and economic constraints, the definition of the problems which they are expected to address, and the actions of other individuals and organizations which will affect policy once their decision is made. The diffused nature of much decision making makes it hard to delineate specific points when decisions are made.

It follows from this conceptualization of policy decisions that policy research is not limited to top policy decisions: it has relevance at multiple points in the policy process. Relevant policy research does not require addressing centralized, comprehensive policy questions. Rather, it involves a broad range of information needs ranging from matters such as the addition of a reporting item to be included in quarterly evaluation reports to more major information needs regarding whether the funding of ILCs as comprehensive service centers will produce intended policy effects.

Creative

Policy research requires creativity and imagination. In the fluid world of public policy, experienced policy analysts are astute observers of the situations in which particular issues arise. They are able to select that combination of research techniques adapted to a specific policy issue. Further, they are capable of translating the results of their research into a form usable by decision makers, each of whom may have differing preconceptions and policy preferences.

The requirement to tailor policy research to particular situations, to particular information needs, and to particular groups of stakeholders puts a premium on the ability of analysts to adapt to new situations. Futurist Donald Schon has stressed the importance of a situational approach to the practice of policy research (1971:231):

> No theory taken from past experience may be taken as literally applicable to this situation, nor will a theory based on the experience of this situation prove literally applicable to the next situation. . . . It will need to be tested against the experience of the next situation, and the next situation will turn out to be different.

Policy analysts cannot rest on routinized approaches to policy problems; they respond creatively to the uniqueness of each problem situation.

Policy research is a challenging endeavor which provides an opportunity for creativity and initiative. Policy research is a highly social activity, involving the exchange of ideas and information with others. Policy analysts have an opportunity to develop an insider's knowledge about the workings of society and the organizations which compose it. Indeed, they are charged

with creating a significant part of society's knowledge about its own collective workings. One of its most enticing features is the opportunity to be on
the cutting edge of transformations contributing to public policy. This reason alone keeps policy analysts motivated despite the disappointments and
frustrations inherent in a diffused, changeable, and value-laden work environment.

CONCLUDING COMMENTS

The growth of policy research as a decision resource has created a demand
for skills in both producing and consuming relevant technical information.
Producers need effective training in the skills of policy research to maximize the accuracy and usefulness of the information they produce. Consumers need the skills to understand and assess accuracy and relevance in
the information presented to them.

The skills required may be placed in two major categories. The first
category consists of scientific skills, including the clarification of ideas and
the development of standardized procedures for collecting and analyzing
data. These skills are used in carrying out competent and creative research
and in assessing the quality of research done by others. Systematic scientific
skills lie at the core of policy research as a technical endeavor.

The second broad area consists of facilitative skills. These skills apply
the fundamentals of policy analysis to the often chaotic world of policy-
making. Scientific skills are necessary to make policy research technically
sound; facilitative skills are necessary to make it relevant to the policy
process.

In subsequent chapters, scientific skills are presented in three categories. Information-structuring skills sharpen the analyst's ability to clarify
policy-related ideas and to examine their correspondence to real world
events. Information-collection skills provide the analyst with approaches
and tools for making accurate observations of persons, objects, or events.
Information-analysis skills guide the analyst in drawing conclusions from
empirical evidence. These skills do not stand independently, but build on
each other in the research process. Though these scientific skills are discussed sequentially, the practice of policy research requires the simultaneous consideration of all three skills areas.

Mediating between the core scientific skills and the policy-making environment are two facilitative skills. Relevant policy research requires an
understanding of the policy-making process—differing ways in which policy
decisions are made, types of policy and their major objectives, organizational and interpersonal influences on policy decisions, and the factors
which may affect the use of information. This knowledge of the policy process is referred to as policy skills. Policy research also involves the efficient

and effective use of organizational resources to accomplish research tasks. Planning and management skills are as important in policy research projects as they are in other organizational endeavors. Research management skills are critical to successful project outcomes.

The remainder of the text is organized around the five skills which cumulatively contribute to effective policy research. The next section of the text (Part II) emphasizes policy skills. These skills are discussed first because they provide an essential foundation for conceptualizing policy problems, considering the various data-collection sources relevant to policy issues, and understanding the application of systematic procedures to policy decisions generally.

Following the introduction to the research implications of the policy process is a discussion of each of the three scientific skills. Part III addresses information structuring; Part IV information collection; and Part V information analysis. Research management skills are discussed in Part VI; they are taken up after the scientific skills because problems of planning, coordinating, and communicating policy research will be more understandable once a working familiarity with the activities making up policy research tasks are known.

REFERENCES

Bauer, Raymond A. 1968. "The Study of Policy Formation: An Introduction," in R. A. Bauer and K. J. Gergen, eds., *The Study of Policy Formation.* New York: Free Press.

Benveniste, Guy. 1977. *The Politics of Expertise.* 2d ed. San Francisco: Boyd Fraser.

Bingham, Richard D., and Marcus E. Ethridge. 1982. *Reaching Decisions in Public Administration: Methods and Applications.* New York: Longman.

Brewer, Garry D., and Peter deLeon. 1983. *The Foundations of Policy Analysis.* Homewood, IL: Dorsey Press.

Cowden, Anne C. 1981. "California's New Fiscal Information System: Increasing Oversight or Redressing an Imbalance of Power." Paper presented to the American Society for Public Administration, Detroit, MI.

Dunn, William N. 1981. *Pubic Policy Analysis: An Introduction.* Englewood Cliffs, NJ: Prentice-Hall.

Dutton, William H., and James N. Danziger. 1982. "Computers and Politics," pp. 1–21, in James N. Danziger, William H. Dutton, Rob King, and Kenneth L. Kraemer, *Computers and Politics: High Technology in American Local Governments.* New York: Columbia University Press.

Finsterbusch, Kurt, and Annabelle B. Motz. 1980. *Social Research for Policy Decisions.* Belmont, CA: Wadsworth.

Langbein, Laura Irwin. 1980. *Discovering Whether Programs Work: A Guide to Statistical Methods for Program Evaluation.* Santa Monica, CA: Goodyear Publishing.

Lasswell, Harold D. 1956. "The Political Science of Science," *American Political Science Review* (December 1956):961–79.

Lerner, Daniel, and Harold D. Lasswell, eds. 1950. *The Policy Sciences.* Stanford, CA: Stanford University Press.

Lynn, Laurence E., Jr. 1980. *Designing Public Policy: A Casebook on the Role of Policy Analysis*. Santa Monica, CA: Goodyear Publishing.

MacRae, Duncan, Jr., and James E. Wilde. 1979. *Policy Analysis for Public Decisions*. Belmont, CA: Duxbury Press.

Mayer, Robert R., and Ernest Greenwood. 1980. *The Design of Social Policy Research*. Englewood Cliffs, NJ: Prentice-Hall.

Meehan, Eugene J. 1981. *Reasoned Argument in Social Science: Linking Research to Policy*. Westport, CT: Greenwood Press.

Mowitz, Robert J. 1981. *The Design of Public Decision Systems*. Baltimore: University Park Press.

Ogburn, William F., ed. 1933. *Recent Social Trends*. Washington, DC: U.S. Government Printing Office.

Putt, Allen D., and John Rehfuss. 1981. "Decision-Making," in Thomas P. Murphy, ed., *Contemporary Public Administration*. New York: Peacock.

Quade, Edward S. 1975. *Analysis for Public Decisions*. New York: Elsevier Science.

Rose, Richard. 1977. "Implementation and Evaporation: The Record of MBO," *Public Administration Review* (January/February).

Schick, Allen. 1966. "The Road to PPB: The Stages of Budget Reform," *Public Administration Review* (December).

Schon, Donald A. 1971. *Beyond the Stable State*. New York: W. W. Norton.

Thompson, Victor A. 1975. Without Sympathy or Enthusiasm: The Problem of Administrative Compassion. Huntsville, AL: University of Alabama Press.

Weiss, Carol H., and Michael J. Bucuvalas. 1980. *Social Science Research and Decision Making*. New York: Columbia University Press.

Weiss, Janet A. 1980. "Dilemmas of Evaluating a Balancing Act: Policies for Prevention of Child Abuse," *Policy Studies Journal* 8,7:1222–28.

2

Orienting Research Efforts
Mapping the Policy Terrain

The preceding chapter portrayed the task of policy analysts as complex and multifaceted. Far from being narrow technocrats, policy analysts are persons who understand and appreciate the subtle factors entering into the ways that stakeholders perceive and grapple with policy questions. When confronting a policy problem, the initial thoughts of skilled analysts emphasize questions such as, "What is the problem as the decisionmaker is likely to view it? What is the decisionmaker's reality that I must address? How is the decision likely to be reached? What are the 'Particulars?'" (Lynn, 1980:6).

An orientation to the rich complexity and detail of the public policy terrain is necessary to accurate and useful policy research. Part II identifies policy skills crucial to laying the groundwork for policy analysis. This chapter identifies phases in the process of making and carrying out policy decisions and discusses how policy research contributes to the phases. Chapter 3 discusses principles and activities making policy research information more useful to its consumers.

THE LAY OF THE LAND

In his first term, President Ronald Reagan unveiled his administration's criminal justice policies in a speech before the International Association of

27

Chiefs of Police. Following a recitation of threatening crime statistics, the president dramatically established a focus for his remarks. "From these statistics a portrait emerges. The portrait is that of a stark, staring face, a face that belongs to a frightening reality of our time—the face of a human predator, . . . the habitual criminal" (Weekly Compilation of Presidential Documents, 1981:1040). The president went on to affirm his administration's support of a policy theme that had been evolving for more than a decade. The thrust of this theme (referred to here as "career criminal policy") was to use federal influence and resources to focus criminal justice efforts (particularly prosecution) on habitual criminals thought to account for a large volume of street crime.

The history of career criminal policy provides a case study for an introduction to the processes of public policy-making and the ways in which analysts contribute to these processes. The purpose is to provide an orientation to the ways in which public policies are developed, enacted, and modified (or even terminated). The intent is not to provide a comprehensive analysis of policy processes, but to clarify how policy analysts contribute to policy at each phase in its life cycle. To organize the discussion, an intellectual map of the policy-making terrain is used.

Like any map, the framework presented here is not a detailed and accurate picture of any particular policy process on any particular day. Road maps do not forewarn drivers of slow-moving farm equipment, deep patches of fog, or detours due to local flooding and road repairs. They do provide information on the general character of the terrain that may be relevant at specific points en route. The skillful cross-country driver will be alert for merging traffic and backed-up autos when traveling major metropolitan freeways, but will scan the roadway for trucks, tractors, and unfenced animals when negotiating rural lanes. Similarly, a map of the policy terrain provides analysts clues to the obstacles and opportunities that typify certain cycles in the policy process, and to what types of information are likely to be most pertinent at these times.

Before beginning a discussion of the major phases through which policies typically pass, some prominent features of the policy terrain require clarification. A basic feature of policy processes is that specific policies rarely follow identical routes. A useful map of the policy terrain incorporates the likelihood of detours, interruptions, and even permanent barriers in attempts to complete an intended journey. Alternative policy routes may be necessary as unforeseen events block the way.

In the mid-1970s, for example, career criminal policy at the national level was being implemented through federal grants-in-aid to local prosecutors. Despite the program's great popularity and apparent successes in dealing with habitual offenders, federal grants were terminated because Congress eliminated the larger agency administering the career criminal program. The reasons for terminating the larger agency had little to do with career criminal policy, but the action effectively blocked one popular route to confronting habitual felons. Policymakers pursuing career criminal objectives had to reorient their efforts and search for alternative routes. The information needs of decision makers changed as they searched for new policy approaches.

Another characteristic of the policy process provides further explanation for the circuitous routes traveled by most public policies. The assumption that policies follow direct and orderly routes to their eventual outcomes presumes a single driver will be charting the course, or all drivers involved agree on the same course. In policy-making, this assumption cannot be made. "It has become apparent that the steering wheel is often but loosely connected to the rudder. The impact of policies depends in good part on the performance or reaction of people not under the direct control of the policy maker" (Nelson, 1977:34).

Policies are shaped through the actions of many drivers, or policy participants. For example, decisions necessary to formulate and implement public policies are made by groups or individuals in many different organizations. Frequently these organizations operate independently, with little or no coordination or communication among their members. The federal impetus for career criminal policy was primarily the initiative of a few individuals in the federal bureaucracy, but it was put into action in prosecutors' offices in widely dispersed communities around the country. Furthermore, the effectiveness of prosecution programs in implementing career criminal policies depends in part on the actions of other agencies in the local criminal justice system—law enforcement, courts, and corrections.

Not only are there multiple drivers within organizations that formulate and carry out public policy; there are numerous external interest groups and individuals influencing public policy. These individuals and groups often have different conceptions of the need for and the purposes of public policy. They carry different priorities for what constitutes appropriate public policy, different moral and ethical commitments, and different conceptions of what causes social problems and how to resolve them. In an open and competitive political system, all have a legitimate voice in shaping public policy. In the area of career criminal policy, for example, these divergent outlooks led local prosecutors to define the problem of career criminality differently and thus stress different solutions.

In understanding the policy terrain, analysts consider the information needs that follow from different value premises. Methods of incorporating the values and perspectives of various stakeholders into policy research are detailed in subsequent chapters.

Finally, the mapping of public policy requires a recognition of the varying levels of specificity at which policymakers operate. A road map of the United States is of little use in planning a Sunday drive through the byways of New England; nor is a map of Louisiana of use in locating the

French Quarter in New Orleans. Similarly, the career criminal policy guidelines developed at the federal level could not provide local prosecutors with specific guidance in implementing their habitual offender programs within the context of their local criminal justice system. Although policy guidelines may be set at higher levels, the specific steps in the policy process must be specified and respecified within differing contexts.

In sum, mapping the policy terrain orients analysts to the environment in which they will work. However, specific policies move through the policy process in subtle and convoluted ways. The reality of policy-making is characterized by unrelated and unexpected changes in the environment, multiple decision makers in a fragmented system of governance, the pulls and tugs of varying value perspectives, and the necessity of adapting policy to different contexts.

The Policy Process

To orient policy analysts, a process framework composed of identifiable stages or phases in the history of a policy has particular advantages. "A problem initially conceived is not equivalent to one of long standing, where experience and efforts to contend with it have amassed" (Brewer and deLeon, 1983:10). As a policy matures from an initial idea to institutionalized programs impacting the lives of citizens, the kinds of decisions facing policymakers change. Needs for information change correspondingly. Conceiving of the policy process as a series of interrelated phases allows policy to be tied to evolving information needs and to different applications of policy research.

Dividing policy-making into a series of stages represents an attempt to separate a continuous and interactive set of activities into an orderly sequence of phases. Partly because of the difficulty of this task, different authors have identified different numbers of phases. Nakamura and Smallwood (1980) identify three phases—formulation, implementation, and evaluation; Alexander (1985) proposes four phases—stimulation, policy, program, and implementation; Brewer and deLeon (1983) offer six—initiation, estimation, selection, implementation, evaluation, and termination. The exact specification of stages varies with the purposes of the authors.

For the present purpose of orienting producers and users of policy research to the policy process, the map here is visualized in five stages of activity:

Stimulation: recognizing and defining issues

Clarification: specifying needs and solutions

Initiation: deciding to go forward

Implementation: putting programs into practice

Evaluation: assessing results

Each stage is discussed in the following sections. The focus is on the concerns that characterize each stage and on the ways in which policy analysis contributes to a resolution of the concerns.

POLICY STIMULATION

Fifteen years ago, career criminal policy—the treatment of habitual offenders—was not an issue on the nation's criminal justice agenda. Individual prosecutors may have prosecuted repeat offenders vigorously, but such actions were situational judgments about what a particular defendant deserved. These judgments did not constitute systematic public policy. Within a decade, however, $30 million in federal money and many more millions in state and local funds had been invested in programs for the prosecution of career criminals (Springer, Phillips, and Cannady, 1985). How did this national policy effort get started? Through what processes were the individual concerns of countless prosecutors (e.g., repeat offenders constitute a particularly serious threat to society) translated into a systematic governmental effort?

The first stage in the processes shaping public policy is a period of policy stimulation. A number of activities characterize this stage: relevant groups and individuals sense potential problems or opportunities that may require public action; different means to approach the problem or opportunity may be tentatively sketched; and groups and individuals with interests in the issue express support or opposition to potential governmental actions. The duration of the stimulation phase is variable. Issues may rise quickly in the policy agenda, or issues may languish in this phase awaiting the right combination of need and opportunity to vault them into the public focus.

Since the period of policy stimulation involves the initial process of sensing and assessing a need or opportunity and of developing ideas, it is an intuitive and interpretative process. It is also a difficult stage to outline or map because different policies are stimulated by unique combinations of events. Further, conditions sending a policy initiative past the stimulation phase during one time period may compel no further governmental attention at another point in time. Social policies spawned by the resource-rich environment of the 1960s would have been considered unthinkable in the cutback eras of the following decades.

The nature of activities characterizing the stimulation phase is further explored by examining how emerging policies are sensed and defined, the role of policy communities in stimulating policy efforts, and the role of policy analysts in this initial stage of policy development.

Recognizing and Defining Issues

C. Wright Mills (1976:8) distinguishes between "troubles," which are personal matters, and "issues," which are public matters.

> In these matters, consider unemployment. When, in a city of 100,000, only one man is unemployed, that is his personal trouble, and for its relief we properly look to the character of the man, his skills, and his immediate opportunities. But when in a nation of 50 million employees, 15 million men are unemployed, that is an issue, and we may not hope to find its solution within the range of opportunities open to any one individual. The very structure of opportunities has collapsed. Both the correct statements of the problem and the range of possible solutions require us to consider the economic and political institutions of the society, and not merely the personal situation and character of the scatter of individuals.

Beginning activities in policy stimulation include distinguishing issues, which require public responses, from troubles, which lie in the realm of individual responsibility.

Issues are rarely self-evident. The world does not often present policy-makers with clearly defined problems for which solutions are readily apparent. Consequently, the early stages of policy stimulation include diagnosing whether a problem even exists. "It is not clear problems, but diffuse worries, that appear. . . . There are signals . . . of a problem, but no one knows yet what the problem is" (Rein and White, 1977:262). Early signs of an emerging issue may be disturbing trends in social indicators (e.g., increased teenage pregnancies), new stories about local problems (e.g., massive fish kills in remote northern lakes), increased activity by political interest groups (e.g., MADD—Mothers Against Drunk Driving), or other indications that certain troubles are becoming widely recognized.

At this stage in the policy process, problems (or opportunities) are just beginning to be sensed, recognized, and defined. Since the extent of a problem, its causes, and its potential solutions are not immediately evident, the values, beliefs, and philosophical orientations of individuals involved in the issue come to the fore. Issues gain their attributes through a continuous definition process shaped by the values, goals, assumptions, and understandings of its participants.

Vocational rehabilitation, one of the oldest social programs in the federal government, provides an example of the ongoing nature of problem definition in policy processes. State departments of rehabilitation around the country address a similar issue. Large numbers of persons in society sustain physical impairments (including sensory loss, paralysis, loss of limbs, disabilities from birth, severe disease, and more) that limit their entry into productive employment. Results are severe personal difficulties and the loss of fully productive members of society.

Traditionally, rehabilitation policy has been based on an individual adjustment model in which the disabled person was aided in making necessary psychological accommodations and in gaining relevant training for appropriate employment. Placement in a sheltered workshop where, for instance, the blind might make brooms, would represent an extreme of this model in which the individual was expected to accommodate to the restrictions of the environment.

The 1960s brought a major redefinition of the problem of disability. Medical advances increased survival and longevity after disabling trauma or disease; Vietnam returned thousands of young disabled veterans; and, as a consequence, a new generation of leadership grew up within organizations for the impaired. By the early 1970s rehabilitation policy was incorporating a new view of the problem of disability. In this view, social barriers, not individual inability, were responsible for many of the vocational limitations of disabled persons. Workplaces and transportation were inaccessible to wheelchairs; employers and coworkers discriminated (knowingly or unknowingly) against the disabled; and disabled children were denied equal educational opportunities.

A redefinition of the problem related to disability demonstrates how policy is shaped in early stages of policy stimulation. As Dery (1984:5) puts it, "Problem definition . . . is a framework for doers." The way a policy problem is interpreted, clarified, and designed implies the range of solutions that may be applied to its resolution, providing a guide for future policy action. Thus, the revised view of disability does not call for programs of counseling to help disabled individuals to adjust to their limitations. Rather it calls for programs to make workplaces and public places barrier-free; it calls for mainstreaming of disabled children in regular school classrooms; it calls for affirmative action policies to combat discrimination in employment. Where counseling is appropriate, it stresses assertiveness, self-confidence, and independent living—not acceptance and accommodation.

The example underscores a fundamental point. The initial definition of a problem during the policy stimulation phase reflects the outlooks, purposes, and understandings of those participating in creating the policy agenda. The makeup of the group of participants involved in early policy definition is a crucial factor in shaping policy outcomes. These policy communities vary according to policy area, as illustrated in the following discussion.

Policy Communities and Policy Stimulation

The initial creation of the National Career Criminals Program provides an example of the makeup and importance of a policy community in stimulating and defining policy efforts. The 1968 Crime Control and Safe Streets Act created a significant institutional participant in the stimulation of the career criminal grants program. The act created the National Institute of Law Enforcement and Criminal Justice, a governmental research institute charged with soliciting and funding basic and applied research regarding crime and criminal justice policy.

The institute (now the National Institute of Justice) provided a national focus for guiding research and the dissemination of knowledge concerning criminal justice issues. Two areas of institute-sponsored research were particularly important for the stimulation of the career criminal program. First, the institute began sponsoring research projects and conferences to produce and disseminate basic research findings on criminal careers—the development of patterns of criminal behavior in individuals. Early studies on the topic had produced an intriguing core finding—a small portion of individuals committing crimes account for a very large proportion of total street crime (Wolfgang, Figlio, and Sellin, 1972).

A second set of projects also stimulated interest in developing policy related to habitual offenders. The federal government funded the development of a computerized management information system for prosecutors known as PROMIS. This system was marketed to local prosecutors to improve statistical reporting of office performance. Data produced by the PROMIS system demonstrated how frequently a small number of offenders came before the courts, reinforcing the idea that a small number of individuals commit a great amount of crime. The PROMIS studies suggested that more careful case preparation, fewer charge dismissals, and less plea bargaining for these repeat offenders would help incarcerate them more frequently, reducing their repeated contacts with the law.

In addition to encouraging research and disseminating knowledge on career criminals, the newly created federal agencies played a role in strengthening the network of local prosecutors who were possibly interested in implementing career criminal programs. The institute worked with the National District Attorneys Association to sponsor national seminars for the discussion of possible solutions to the emerging career criminal problem. These seminars sparked interest in doing something about more effectively prosecuting career criminals and highlighted several existing legal approaches for accomplishing this.

By the mid-1970s the policy community that would dominate the definition of the career criminal problem was visible. The network consisted of elected officials (particularly in Congress) who were champions of stronger law enforcement, a small number of federal employees in the newly created offices of the Law Enforcement Assistance Administration, researchers in several universities and private research organizations, the National District Attorneys Association, and interested local prosecutors. This core of key stakeholders could also point to the presumed support of a large segment of the public who supported law-and-order candidates in the late 1960s and early 1970s. The "career criminal" policy community highlights several general points.

Governmental agencies are central components of most policy communities. They provide a locus for specialized information and problem definition. In the career criminal case, a national response to the career criminal problem might not have emerged if the way had not been paved through the creation of a new federal agency directly involved in improving state and local law enforcement.

Interest groups are also key figures in policy communities. The fact that the national prosecutors association showed an early interest in the career criminal problem strengthened the likelihood that the policy solution would focus on prosecution efforts.

Another major component in policy communities is the knowledge industry—university and private researchers interested in the policy area. Indeed, a major study of federal policy-making concluded that "after interest groups, the collection of academics, researchers, and consultants is the next most important set of nongovernmental actors" (Kingdon, 1984:57) in setting the policy agenda.

The example also demonstrates the effects of the policy community on early problem definition and on guiding the development of public policy. Early studies on career criminality yielded information beyond the disproportional incidence of crime among a minority of offenders. It documented, for instance, the early onset of the career pattern, the high incidence of drug involvement in this group, and the relation of the career pattern to poor family conditions. If these findings were generated within a policy community focused on drug abuse or on family problems, early problem definition would likely have focused on these findings and led toward programs dealing with these contributing factors. However, the policy community that did emerge was dominated by criminal justice organizations. Accordingly, problem definition and subsequent policy actions moved toward law enforcement solutions.

Policy Research and Policy Stimulation

Policy research contributes to policy-making in the stimulation phase in several ways. First, policy research provides basic descriptive empirical information concerning the existence and extent of emerging troubles. An example is the various economic and employment indicators regularly gathered by the Departments of Commerce and Labor. When the unemployment rate rises beyond a generally accepted level or when an upward trend is evident, it triggers pressure to take policy actions designed to stimulate the economy.

In other instances, the identification of issues is more ad hoc. Policy studies of a diagnostic, exploratory nature increase the awareness and understanding of a problem by analyzing its prevalence and severity. Documentation of the prevalence and spread of AIDS (acquired immune deficiency syndrome) in a locality is an example.

A second function of policy research in the stimulation phase is to encourage creativity in problem definition. The fact that most problem definition occurs in established policy communities means that prevailing problem understandings and preferred solutions can be self-sustaining; the ways of the past weigh heavily in future responses. At a broad level, research into social problems encourages new perspectives. Early research on career criminals introduced innovations in the way some decision makers perceive the use of incarceration. Former perspectives on incarceration emphasized either rehabilitation of inmates or the deterrence of crime through swift and sure punishment. The career criminal research suggested that incarceration might be most efficient and effective if extended prison terms were reserved for the minority of chronic offenders.

In a more specific sense, policy research increases the likelihood of innovation in problem definitions by seeking out and presenting contrasting points of view. Policy participants on varying sides of an issue are queried and their views incorporated in study design and result. A significant part of the analyst's contribution at this point may be to broaden existing understandings about problems and to help decision makers unlearn dated and unworkable problem understandings and solutions.

Policy analysts play a particularly important role in the identification of alternative means of addressing problems. In discussing the development of policies for controlling the escalating problem of health care costs, Kingdon (1984:59) noted, "While academics were not responsible for the prominence of that problem on the agenda, they were prominent among the people to whom politicians turned for ideas on how to cope with it." In a variety of ways, policy analysts and their information play an influential role in the stimulation of policy problems and responses.

POLICY CLARIFICATION

In policy stimulation, original perceptions concerning a problem (or opportunity) are generated. Policy clarification activities involve the refinement of the problem, developing alternative policy solutions, evaluating the feasibility of alternative solutions, and estimating what stakeholders can expect to happen once proposed solutions are implemented. The following subsections identify tasks that policy analysts undertake to aid decision makers in the policy clarification stage.

Refining Need Estimates

Early research on career criminals had only been suggestive in documenting the severity and magnitude of the habitual offender problem, and in recommending possible policy solutions. The empirical research demonstrating that relatively few career criminals commit a great majority of street crime was limited. The most important studies examined the number of police contacts by a sample of juveniles over a ten-year period (Wolfgang, Figlio, and Sellin, 1972), and the number of times the same offenders appeared in prosecutors' caseloads (Williams, 1979). The emerging awareness that these same individuals commit a disproportionate number of street crimes was an extrapolation from this record of criminal justice contacts.

While this information base was sufficient to stimulate the career criminal policy concept, clarification of the concept required more detailed knowledge related to career criminals. As part of their continuing research program in the area, the federal government funded a series of studies by the Rand Corporation (a large private research corporation) to improve knowledge about the nature and quantity of crime committed by career criminals.

One of these studies (Petersilia, Greenwood, and Lavin, 1977) was based on personal interviews with more than four thousand state prison inmates in five states. Inmates in the study sample were questioned extensively about their personal background and, in particular, their past criminal behavior. The truthfulness of their responses was checked by comparing their responses to official criminal records. These data quality checks indicated that the inmates were often willing to report accurately their past criminal behavior. The findings of the study helped clarify knowledge about the extent of street crime committed by high-rate offenders. In their study, the analysts classified approximately one-fifth of the burglars and robbers in prison as high-rate offenders, and found that these offenders had committed an average of over 150 serious street crimes a year. The Rand study, and other less ambitious research efforts, began to clarify the potential public benefit that could be achieved through effectively controlling the career criminal.

Developing Alternative Solutions

More refined understanding of the need represented in a policy problem paves the way for developing appropriate and feasible policy response(s). This search for solutions begins with a thorough inventory of current policy efforts in the area and an assessment of their performance and effectiveness. Growing knowledge about the behavior of career criminals clarified the need for action in the area, but did not confirm that pursuing prosecution programs was an adequate policy approach.

Based on growing knowledge of the career criminal problem, a number of policy analysts began to argue that the appropriate policy response was "selective incapacitation." The premise of this policy is simple. Since a minority of criminals commit the majority of crimes, and since this minority are persistent in their criminal behavior, society can be most effectively and efficiently protected by imprisoning these career criminals through extended sentences. How to carry out this policy approach, however, is not clear.

The fate of criminal defendants is a product of the relatively independent actions of police, prosecutors, judges, and corrections agencies. Furthermore, the ability of these stakeholders to influence sentencing of a targeted group of offenders, individually or collectively, depends on the sentencing provisions of state criminal codes. Clarification of the policy approach would require (a) identifying the role of these various stakeholders in affecting sentencing, and (b) identifying the potential for improvement over current levels of performance.

Comparing the potential effectiveness of different points of leverage is important to identifying alternative policy approaches or to identifying promising combinations of actions that may improve an approach. However, the momentum of policy approaches initially envisioned in the stimulation stage can restrict or circumvent consideration of alternative or expanded policies. In the early development of career criminal policy, attention focused on deficiencies in prosecution that were presumed to reduce the potential incapacitation of career criminals. Thus, the initial policy thrust was restricted to funding prosecution programs. It was not until several years later that career criminal policy was expanded to include coordinated police-prosecution programs to identify, apprehend, and prosecute career criminals.

Evaluating Policy Feasibility

The consideration of alternate policy approaches involves the feasibility of achieving certain actions as well as the potential efficiency, effectiveness, and fairness of the actions. Assessments of feasibility include several considerations. First, the fiscal and human resource requirements of potential actions impact the probability of adoption. Recommended alternatives are more likely to be implemented if they do not require major infusions of new resources or a major reorientation of available resources.

Second, the feasibility of specific approaches depends upon the complexity of the decision processes that are necessary to initiate them. The simplicity of initiating career criminal units within local prosecutors' offices added to the program's appeal for federal decision makers. Coordinated approaches to career criminal policy that encouraged police, prosecutors, and courts to integrate their efforts may have offered advantages in potential effectiveness; but they would have been unwieldy, and consensus would be difficult to achieve. Changes in state sentencing laws might provide important new tools to combat career criminals, but they would require action by state legislatures. The uncertainty of legislative approval made sentencing law an unlikely focus for a federal initiative.

The feasibility of a given action is further influenced by the magnitude of change that will be required of established organizations and their members. Policies that ask people to abandon familiar patterns require strong commitments of resources and efforts to achieve acceptance. One observer has largely attributed the popularity of career criminal policy among prosecutors to the minimal demands for change in their behavior. "The program in effect provided prosecutors with the opportunity to improve their operations in a way they defined for themselves, an understandably appealing prospect" (Chelimsky and Dahmann, 1980:135).

Feasibility should not be the sole consideration in specifying the policy approach. Indeed, the most feasible policy is often to maintain the status quo, whether or not it adequately meets current and future needs. As is so often the case in policy decisions, the ultimate weight given to considerations of feasibility involves balancing what is desired against what can be achieved. Policy analysts help weigh these factors.

Estimating Policy Impacts

The policy clarification stage also involves estimating future impacts of a particular policy alternative. How effective will a policy be in meeting current and future needs? For policymakers, the value of accurate prediction of future policy consequences cannot be denied. Perfect foresight would not eliminate disagreement about policy objectives, but it would eliminate the uncertainty and risks surrounding policy outcomes. The ability to develop precise quantitative estimates of policy impacts, however, is dependent on a number of factors, including the clarity of the problems and the availability of relevant information.

If the selective incapacitation objective is adopted, for example, analysts would like to estimate the numbers and types of crimes that could be prevented through a policy that incapacitated the most active 10 percent of the habitual felons that enter the prosecutor's caseload. What would analysts have to know to make reasonably accurate estimates of the consequences of this policy objective? The key data element in this analysis would be an estimate of the rate at which the targeted offenders would commit crimes if they were on the street (Petersilia, Greenwood, and Lavin, 1977). Of course, the estimate of this rate must be indirect since it concerns future behavior, but this is only the beginning. Rates of crime differ greatly between types of crime: shoplifters and check forgers commit many more crimes than burglars, who commit more than robbers, who commit more than rapists—on the average.

And, assuming analysts come up with appropriate estimates adjusted by crime type, there is the additional concern of adjusting for changes in crime rate through offenders' life cycles. Criminologists have documented that individual crime rates typically peak in the late teens and early twenties and fall by age thirty. Thus, estimates of the number of prevented crimes will depend upon the age at which individuals are incarcerated, as well as the length of sentence. Very long sentences for older inmates may prevent little crime through incapacitation.

The point of this discussion is not to deny the importance of estimating policy impacts but to clarify limits on the ability to forecast events. In the career criminal instance, and with respect to many social issues, the ability to produce accurate predictions of policy impacts is limited. It is not surprising or irrational that federal decision makers decided to pursue career criminal policies despite the lack of precise estimates of effects. Need, feasibility, apparent public support, and the reasonable expectation that the program would have a positive effect were sufficient to continue support of the policy.

Where problems are better understood and information is of better quality, precise estimates of policy impacts are significant aspects of policy clarification. Attempts at precise estimation are particularly important when the problem has widespread aggregate effects. Economic, environmental, energy, and defense problems, for example, are frequently the topics of studies concerning widespread consequences of policy actions.

When precise empirical estimates are infeasible, policy analysts use "intuitive" (Dunn, 1981) methods for focusing attention on plausible future effects. The use of expert opinion in assessing a proposed solution, for instance, alerts stakeholders to potential consequences of implementing a policy option. Focusing attention on plausible future impacts also has the important effect of alerting decision makers to possible unintended negative consequences of a policy.

Policy Research and Policy Clarification

Once an issue has been identified as a candidate for public action, the policy process enters a phase rich with challenges and opportunities for policy analysts. Recommendations for improving policy decisions have frequently focused on the need for more adequate "planning"—the process of setting goals, forecasting the future, and developing alternatives so that policy choices are more informed.

Despite its importance, policymakers and policy analysts recognize that thorough planning is an ideal only roughly approximated. Pressure of limited time and limited resources, disagreements about specific objectives, varying value priorities, and limited ability to collect relevant information place limits on the degree to which policy decisions are based on thorough planning.

Nevertheless, the refinement and clarification of information needs and alternative solutions are important contributions to informed decisions. Policy analysts are central in providing these decision resources.

POLICY INITIATION

At some point, policymakers decide whether or not to put policy alternatives into practice. This decision depends partly on decisions made in earlier stages. Policy is molded throughout the policy process, but different
stages tend to emphasize different kinds of decisions. A variation on the
travel analogy introducing this chapter clarifies the point.

The decision stream that accompanies policy developments begins at
the stimulation phase. A problem is discerned (boredom—We need a vacation) and increasingly defined (I'm tired of this cold weather). Problem definition is followed by a period of clarification and data gathering (Is it
warmer in Florida or New Orleans? Which is less expensive?).

The initial problem definition has narrowed the options that are acceptable (we will not go North), and the effort spent gathering travel brochures has assisted in developing and assessing proposed solutions; but
none of the decisions has yet committed participants to any specific action.
We know we want to be warm and stimulated, but still may decide that a
trip South is not the best way to achieve those goals.

At some point, dictated by time constraints and the level of satisfaction with a knowledge of the options (The French Quarter looks so intriguing in these brochures) and other factors (I can get off next week, but after
then not for a couple of months), the period of clarifying ends and decisions
are made. The specific location is decided, reservations are booked, bags
are packed, and we walk out the door. This decision to spend money, to
purchase a ticket to a particular destination, and to go is of a different order
from those that went before. Further decisions remain to make the trip a
success (Where shall we eat? Shall we go shopping or ride the riverboat?),
but the decision to initiate the vacation has been taken.

The policy initiation stage is where policymakers decide to commit
resources and to carry out programs, that is, courses of action toward particular goals. An example of initiation in public policy is the passage of legislation enabling new programs, but policy is also initiated by decision makers
in the executive and judicial branches of government. Again, career criminal policy provides an example.

As noted above, career criminal policy at the federal level was formulated within the Law Enforcement Assistance Administration, a new federal
agency created by the Crime Control and Safe Streets Act of 1968. This
legislation was a policy initiation decision; it committed hundreds of millions of dollars to new federal action to improve state and local criminal
justice systems. However, the law is more appropriately seen as a related
collection of policies; it mandated several simultaneous courses of action
toward broad goals for improving the administration of justice.

These separate policies were represented by various titles of the act.

Some, such as the program for dispersing educational grants and loans to upgrade skills among the nation's enforcement officers, were detailed and specific, leaving little room for administrative discretion in program activities. Others, such as the research program earlier described, were less specific about the exact ways in which funds were to be used. Indeed, a portion of LEAA's budget was reserved for "discretionary grant programs." Referring to this discretionary budget, a Twentieth Century Fund report (1976:49) on LEAA concluded the agency "cannot help but make policy through the way in which it invests these funds." In the discretionary grant program, the legislature had delegated broad policy-making authority to the executive branch. The resulting policy was largely fashioned by a small group of individuals within the agency.

Brewer and deLeon (1983:18) observe that the selection of proposed policies "is the most political of the . . . steps" in the policy process. Their reference to politics refers to the environment of "multiple, changing and sometimes conflicting goals held by those interested in the problem and its resolution." As a result, the decision to initiate policy requires bargaining, compromise, building coalitions of like interests and objectives, and the exercise of power and influence.

Policy Research and Policy Initiation

Policy research makes substantial contributions to initiation activities. Policy analysts are asked to make recommendations among policy alternatives and to provide information on the nature and extent of support for particular policy actions.

Policy research cannot dictate whether the intended objectives of a policy are right or wrong, given the diversity of values and priorities among stakeholders, but it can assess the degree to which policies meet specified decision criteria. Adapting Dunn (1981:232), there are several decision criteria that stakeholders and policy analysts use to make recommendations: effectiveness, efficiency, equality, and responsiveness.

- Effectiveness refers to the magnitude of a valued outcome (objective) that a policy will provide. Effectiveness is typically measured in some unit of outcome (years of incarceration is an effectiveness measure for career criminal policy).
- Efficiency is the magnitude of a valued outcome that a policy will provide for a given level of effort. Efficiency is usually measured in terms of the ratio of outcome units to dollars expended (years of incarceration produced for each dollar spent on career criminal prosecution).
- Equality refers to the distribution of the costs and benefits of a policy throughout society's members. Career criminal policy could be potentially effective and efficient, but be judged inequitable because those

mistakenly identified as future high-rate offenders are concentrated among the socially disadvantaged.

- Responsiveness refers to the degree to which a policy will meet the preferences of particular groups or interests. A strong impetus to career criminal policies was provided by the high degree of responsiveness to the preferences of local prosecutors and criminal justice practitioners.

The above categories of criteria are not exhaustive; particular policy analyses may employ other criteria to recommend policy choices. However, the more standardized and widely applied techniques for policy recommendations draw on these criteria, particularly efficiency and effectiveness. Chapter 5 provides a more detailed discussion of "choice" decisions and chapter 12 introduces cost-effectiveness and cost-benefit analysis as techniques used to compare the efficiency and effectiveness of alternative policies. The application of these decision criteria to policy alternatives in a variety of policy areas represents a significant contribution of policy analysts to the initiation stage.

Policy research findings concerning probable program impacts are just one consideration for policymakers faced with policy initiation decisions. Regardless of the certainty of information produced in the policy clarification stage, policymakers will continue to disagree in their underlying values, assumptions, understandings, and preferences for policy outcomes. Policy analysis may demonstrate that a construction moratorium in a coastal zone is necessary to preserve an endangered species of waterfowl, and that the moratorium would cost several hundred jobs in the local economy. The position stakeholders take on this issue is going to depend as much on personal values concerning job loss and economic growth and environmental preservation as it will on policy research findings.

Policy analysts improve the relevance and credibility of their analyses through a careful awareness of the value context in which findings are used. Short-term economic costs that concern policymakers (e.g., the impact of passive restraint requirements on new car costs), for instance, can be placed in the context of larger economic savings (e.g., savings in medical costs and lost human resources).

Policy analysts also help decision makers interpret the ideological implications of their perspectives by making their value-laden assumptions clear. The concept of selective incapacitation, for example, implies certain value assumptions concerning effective and equitable criminal justice policy. It takes the utilitarian perspective that good policy is that which most effectively and efficiently protects society from crime. Value perspectives that stress the use of criminal sanctions as retribution for a particular act are more likely to stress uniform and equitable, as opposed to selective, sentencing.

Because policymakers and other stakeholders do not necessarily agree on values and objectives, bargaining and consensus building are necessary to initiate policy. Compromises are shaped, in part, by coalitions of political support that reflect varying levels of power and influence and interest in the issue. Policy research also helps policymakers understand the constellation of support and opposition surrounding policy alternatives, and to incorporate this knowledge into their approaches of formulating and initiating policy. Though policy initiation is perhaps the most political stage of the policy process, policy research makes important contributions through recommending solutions and assessing levels of support among stakeholders.

POLICY IMPLEMENTATION

The National Career Criminals Program was introduced amidst much fanfare in Washington, D.C. It was presented as the centerpiece of the federal government's new efforts to "bring [the career criminal] to a speedy trial, and to make sure that, if found guilty, he is sent back to prison" (Gerald R. Ford Presidential Documents, 1975:1188). The program was to be administered through a federal grants program that would fund local jurisdictions to operate career criminal prosecution units. Successful applicants for project funding would write proposals demonstrating the need for a career criminal program in their jurisdictions. The proposal had to contain a statement of program objectives, a budget, a staffing plan, and procedural policies to be used in prosecuting career criminals.

Vague and general goals are a well-recognized characteristic of policy processes. In order to achieve agreement among legislative factions, for instance, enabling statutes are often little more than authorization to take action to solve a vaguely stated problem. Even in a relatively focused policy such as the career criminal program, policy initiation leaves program specifics largely up to lower-level administrators who implement the policy.

The federal definition of the program was simple. Local prosecutors were encouraged to

- establish small prosecution units staffed by senior, experienced attorneys;
- develop selection criteria that clearly identify the defendants to be prosecuted as career criminals in the jurisdiction;
- reduce the active caseload for the unit to facilitate more concentrated effort in prosecuting career criminals; and
- develop management policies to limit plea bargaining, ensure continuous attention to cases, and ensure a firm stance on sentencing.

How these guidelines were to be implemented was up to local policymakers. Clearly, the success and substance of career criminal prosecution policy would be significantly determined by the quality of its implementation in local jurisdictions, and by the quality of ongoing monitoring and management of the program.

Policy implementation is the series of activities and decisions that transform policy statements into practice. Stimulation, clarification, and initiation produce statements of intent; implementation produces results.

> Public policies are rarely self-executing. The Supreme Court may hand down a decision to desegregate schools, Congress may pass legislation to restrict immigration, or the President may order troops to rescue U.S. hostages in Tehran—but little progress toward accomplishing these goals may occur. Without effective implementation the decisions of policy makers will not be carried out successfully. (Edwards, 1980:1)

Implementation requires innumerable decisions and actions, e.g., issuing and enforcing directives and regulations, disbursing or withholding funds, recruiting and assigning personnel, awarding grants or contracts, creating new organizational units, supervising staff, making budget requests, creating forms, writing reports.

The sheer range and detail of implementation decisions tend to mask their importance. Yet implementation failures have been noted across a broad range of program areas. Many failures of policy are failures of implementation.

> [Policy] accomplishments are a pale reflection of their intentions. The big ideas that have shaped policy—maximum feasible participation, equality of opportunity, self-sufficiency, compensatory treatment, to name a few—seem to have become caricatures of themselves the moment they ceased to be ideas and began to be translated into action. Concern about the implementation of social programs stems from the recognition that policies cannot be understood in isolation from the means of their execution. (Elmore in Brewer and deLeon, 1983:250)

Improved implementation actions and decisions are critical to whether policy changes make a difference. As in prior stages, analysts make important contributions to successful implementation. Indeed, implementation-stage activities constitute a great volume of day-to-day policy research.

Specifying Needs and Objectives

Policy goals may remain vague at the initiation stage, frequently reflecting highly generalized statements of need. A major implementation task is to specify objectives more precisely in concrete, specific empirical terms. In the case of career criminal programs, the requirements for proposals included a needs assessment for the local jurisdiction. In many of these jurisdictions, prosecuting attorneys found themselves fulfilling policy analyst roles in undertaking these tasks. Skills in identifying and interpreting crime statistics, trends, and current levels of performance were central to their efforts to document the need for career criminal programs in their jurisdictions.

Wholey (1983) stresses the importance of carefully establishing program objectives. If objectives are to be useful, they must be more than a symbolic statement of some intent or preference. They must be specific, attainable, and concrete. For instance, a major intent of career criminal policy was crime reduction, but what that meant in actuality was too vague to be useful for local managers. The intent to reduce crime gave program managers no clear indication of workable program policies and procedures useful in achieving this goal.

In one state, analysts helped decision makers develop several program objectives that provided more specific guidance. To accomplish this, group interviews were arranged with representatives of the major agencies and others that would be affected by the program—local prosecutors, judges, public defenders, the State Department of Corrections, law enforcement, and the State Office of Criminal Justice Planning (OCJP). Analysts aided the administering agency (OCJP) to identify specific objectives that reflected the priorities of these groups. For example, one objective was to increase the percentage of convictions that are convicted to top charge (the most serious charge filed by a prosecutor in the case). This specific objective allowed program managers to devise specific policies to accomplish it, e.g., severely limiting the conditions under which a guilty plea would be accepted in exchange for a reduction in charge. Specific objectives of this type also provide a basis for subsequent evaluation of performance, discussed in the following section of the chapter.

Decision Criteria

Implementing policy means developing specific empirical criteria for making decisions that meet the policy's intent. In the career criminal example, local prosecutors had to develop specific criteria for selecting appropriate defendants for the program, i.e., on what basis will offenders be prosecuted as career criminals? The identification of individual persons, organizations, or events that are the intended targets of policy action is a fundamental part of public policy analysis.

The criteria for defining career criminals lies at the center of career criminal policy. The career criminal concept was pursued through the stimulation, clarification, and initiation stages largely because of its potential utility in reducing the risk to society posed by repeat offenders. To accomplish this, the decision criteria used for selection had to meet two major standards.

First, the criteria had to be reasonably accurate empirically. If they did not identify the true high-rate offender population, the very purpose of the program was threatened. Policy analysts consequently turned their attention to defining and identifying the career criminal. Greenwood and Abrahamse (1982), for example, attempted to develop a methodology for predicting which defendants are most likely to be high-rate offenders. The career criminal can be identified through adult criminal records, but other characteristics improve the prediction of potential repeat offenders. Juvenile offenses, particularly juvenile drug use, were particularly important in Greenwood's findings.

Considerations of empirical accuracy must be balanced with a second consideration—pragmatic usefulness. If prosecutors are routinely to use criteria to select career criminal defendants, necessary information must be available and accepted as appropriate for that use. Predictive criteria based on juvenile records are problematic on both counts; such records are often sealed and unavailable in the juvenile courts, and many people would oppose the use of juvenile records to augment negative sanctions as an adult. As a result, selection criteria for most programs rely almost entirely on adult criminal records. In Chicago, for instance, defendants accused of a violent felony (assault, rape, or robbery) who have been convicted of two prior felonies as adults will be prosecuted in select Repeat Offender Trial Courts.

Developing accurate and useful criteria and procedures for identifying the targets of policy lies at the core of program implementation. Policy research is an important contributor to developing accurate and useful decision criteria.

Resource Decisions and Levels of Effort

Policy implementation requires decisions about budget and productivity. Federal guidelines for career criminal programs encouraged local units to adopt a lower caseload for career criminal prosecutions than would occur in regular felony cases, making the assumption that case preparation and trial readiness would improve with more time.

Decisions concerning tradeoffs in quality and quantity are ubiquitous in program implementation. Organizational incentive systems too heavily weighted toward quantity (e.g., the number of cases "closed into employment" for a vocational rehabilitation counselor), can encourage decision makers to focus only on the easiest cases (i.e., the least impaired clients who are more readily employable). On the other hand, an inordinate application of program resources to the few most difficult cases may deny adequate services to the broad range of a program's clients.

Policy research includes a variety of techniques for aiding in decisions about appropriate levels of effort. Measures can be developed to monitor both quantity and quality of effort, providing managers with continuous feedback on program performance. In vocational rehabilitation, for example, studies have been conducted to estimate the counseling time required to place clients with differing degrees of disability. These have provided a foundation for developing productivity measures that do not penalize counselors for accepting and seriously serving difficult cases.

Policy Research and Policy Implementation

The above examples do not exhaust the contributions that policy research makes during implementation activities. Analysts aid in developing adequate descriptions of job duties and responsibilities, in developing improved incentive systems, in improving communication between managers and employees. "Organization Development," for example, is a branch of applied social science that uses a variety of research and feedback techniques to address problems impairing effective and efficient organizational performance. These types of focused analysis improve policy performance by facilitating program implementation and goal achievement. The need for relevant policy research information is ongoing during implementation activities.

POLICY EVALUATION

Evaluation is a principal feedback stage of the policy process. Policy analysts provide several types of information in this phase. Policy evaluation provides information which lets stakeholders know what happened following the initiation of a policy; it provides a description of implementation activities. At a greater level of complexity, evaluation is intended to identify the degree to which a policy has succeeded in achieving its intended objectives. Finally, evaluation can provide insight into reasons policies have succeeded or failed and can suggest courses of action for improving the attainment of policy objectives.

The underlying purpose of the evaluation stage is to learn from past experience. Without examining the implementation and outcomes of policy efforts, there is little possibility of programmatic improvement. The potential for improvement takes a variety of forms because specific evaluations of policy serve various purposes (Glaser, Abelson, and Garrison, 1983:222–24), such as

- determining the overall worth and value of the policy in achieving intended purposes;
- identifying the most and least successful components of the policy;
- ascertaining the programmatic strategies that best contribute to the successful implementation of the policy; or

- assessing unexpected side effects or the unintended consequences of policy efforts.

The results of evaluations are used to contribute to decisions about program continuation and modification.

The prominence of evaluation in policy research has been fueled by concerns of taxpayers, politicians, and administrators. Frequently, their enthusiasm for evaluation research is based on the anticipation of subsequent policy improvement. After a congressional mandated review of LEAA programs, for instance, the General Accounting Office concluded that "there has not been sufficient systematic evaluation to advance the Nation's knowledge as to how to effectively fight crime" (U.S. House of Representatives, Committee on the Judiciary, 1976:21). In a congressional review of the career criminal program, legislators deferred judgment on its effectiveness pending the completion of ongoing evaluations.

Evaluation is not simply an abstract learning mechanism. It represents an attempt to control and guide policy efforts. Rein and White (1977:225) point out that "because of recent pressures for accountability... research now serves as a management device to ensure that agencies do what is expected of them."

The hopes for enhanced accountability by managers, politicians, and the public have contributed to the widespread institutionalization of evaluation of public policies. Increasingly, federal and state legislation requires evaluation of programs as a prerequisite for continued support. Control agencies, such as the General Accounting Office or state departments of finance, have extensive evaluation staffs; private consultants and university researchers offer evaluation services; larger public agencies may have internal evaluation staffs. Major activities of evaluators can be summarized in three major areas—monitoring program performance, conducting impact evaluations, and conducting process evaluations—each of which is discussed in subsequent sections.

Program Monitoring

Program monitoring involves the ongoing systematic collection of data on program activities. The information is primarily of two types.

- *Inputs* are resources consumed by carrying out program activities. Budget dollars and person-hours are basic inputs, serving as efficiency measures.
- *Outcomes* are the products of program activities. Number of cases processed, number of convictions, number of state prison sentences, and so forth, are examples of outcome measures serving as effectiveness indicators.

Program monitoring includes the development of standardized performance indicators and reporting systems. All grant recipients for the career criminal program, for instance, were required to submit quarterly reports that detailed inputs in terms of dollar expenditures and staff hours. A variety of output measures were required, including number of cases accepted, number of prosecutions, number of prosecutions to top charge, and number of prison sentences. These reports were then aggregated into national program statistics by the Bureau of Criminal Justice Statistics. Regular monitoring of performance provides public officials with information on the status of major services and highlights strengths, deficiencies, and problem areas. When collected over time, monitoring information indicates trends, supplying warning signs for areas needing corrective attention.

Impact Evaluation

Impact evaluations are conducted to determine the degree to which a policy achieves its intended objectives. Impact evaluations are more elaborate than program monitoring since impact evaluations focus changes in social and physical conditions. For example, in programs for teaching English as a second language, monitoring may document the numbers of hours students spend in instruction. Impact evaluations focus on the results of that instruction—such as the percentage of students reaching a given level of reading proficiency after a period of instruction. Analysts performing impact evaluations develop measures that focus on short-term and long-term intended and unintended program results, and not simply the work performed.

Impact evaluations ideally provide more than a description of the changes in measures of program objectives that follow program implementation. Analysts attempt to design studies that allow them to determine how much of this change is attributable to the policy that is undergoing evaluation. For example, immigrant children would be expected to gain some proficiency in the English language simply through being immersed in an English-speaking classroom. An evaluator of a program for teaching English as a second language would want to know how much the program increased proficiency over what might be expected through simple immersion in a classroom.

Impact evaluations provide conceptual and technical challenges for policy analysts. An evaluation of career criminal policy provides a case in point. A few years after LEAA began funding local career criminal prosecution programs, they commissioned a national impact evaluation of the program. The study was conducted by the MITRE Corporation, a private research firm, and demonstrates some of the difficulties in determining whether a policy is effective.

First, the lack of explicitly stated goals in the national program made it difficult for policy evaluators to establish clearly the criteria by which the program was to be assessed, a common problem in impact evaluation. Initial agreements with LEAA indicated that the research firm would evaluate the impact of the program on crime levels in each of four jurisdictions. By the time the study was complete, the research firm was forced to abandon that research approach. It proved too difficult to construct a research design that would isolate changes in the crime rate that could be clearly attributed to career criminal programs rather than to other events occurring in the jurisdiction. For example, a general "get tough" attitude in the community could produce lower crime rates. The final study examined program impacts on more proximate indicators—conviction rate, top charge conviction rate, incarceration rate, and sentence length.

Second, the results of the national evaluation were not clear-cut, another common outcome in evaluation studies. Programs showed mixed results in achieving their objectives. In some instances, improvements in performance were documented but were not of sufficient magnitude to suggest adequacy in meaningfully addressing the crime problems of a jurisdiction. In other instances, there were meaningful improvements in some performance measures and negligible change in others. Despite the considerable effort devoted to evaluating career criminal program impacts, the studies did not produce clear and definitive answers concerning the extent to which the policy actions achieved intended objectives. Indeed, the record of the MITRE study and other local evaluations of career criminal prosecution suggests that some local programs are much more successful than others. The importance of local implementation looms large.

Impact evaluations are primarily concerned with determining whether a program works—whether it produces the improvements in social conditions that were intended. The fact that impact evaluations examine the success or failure of program activities makes them of particular interest to higher level decision makers and agencies with the responsibility for supervising and controlling programs. Thus, legislators who make decisions concerning funding of one program over another often value information that provides an indication of how well different programs are achieving their objectives. Accounting authorities in the Office of Management and Budget use impact evaluations in setting budget request priorities. Project managers for federal programs use impact evaluation results to help determine whether project funding should be continued.

Despite their potential use in making high-level decisions about policy directions, impact evaluations are less useful to program managers themselves. Knowing that their programs are not performing up to expectations does not provide operational guidance for how to improve them. Process evaluations, in contrast to impact evaluations, are better oriented to the needs of program-level managers.

Process Evaluation

Process evaluations determine why a program is performing at current levels, and what can be done to improve that performance. Accordingly, process evaluations are concerned with identifying specific links between policy implementation activities and program performance. Study findings are not intended to determine whether a program is meeting specified goals, as in impact evaluations, but to develop recommendations for improving program implementation procedures. In the words of one program-level administrator, "we are interested not so much in whether X causes Y as in the question if Y is not happening, what is wrong with X" (Sylvia, Meier, and Gunn, 1985:135).

As experience with career criminal programs accumulated and jurisdictions commissioned impact evaluations to meet grant requirements, some policy analysts began to criticize the research findings. In particular, analysts noted the lack of attention to process considerations. One critic of career criminal program evaluations argued that

> the design of the evaluation research is incomplete and should be enhanced to answer the next logical questions: why does the program fail or succeed and what can be done about it? Until this enhancement occurs, these studies cannot avoid generating frustrations among practitioners and policymakers alike. (Bartolemeo, 1980:117)

The "second generation" of evaluation research on career criminal programs emphasized process questions. The National Institute of Justice, for example, contracted with EMT Associates, a private research firm, to evaluate programs in seven jurisdictions nationwide. Their process evaluation differed significantly from earlier studies of career criminal programs. Rather than simply focusing on measures of program success, the analysts oriented their research to identifying the problems prosecutors experienced in implementing their programs, and in identifying ways in which implementation efforts could be improved.

To accomplish this research objective, analysts followed a three-phase process. First, they interviewed prosecutors, judges, defense attorneys, law enforcement officials, and other knowledgeable persons to determine the most significant problems in implementing career criminal programs and to identify current approaches to solving these problems. Second, they gathered information (from prosecutors' files and intensive interviews) to help assess the adequacy of current implementation procedures and to help identify opportunities for improvement. Third, they worked with an advisory committee made up of representatives of the criminal justice policy community to develop guidelines for improved implementation of career criminal programs.

The study identified a number of important problem areas in the organization and management of career criminal programs (Springer, Phil-lips, and Cannady, 1985). This discussion typifies the primary intent of pro-cess evaluations. Process evaluations focus on concrete concerns of program implementation with the goal of helping program managers over-come barriers to achieving intended specific objectives.

Policy Research and Policy Evaluation

In the past two decades policy evaluation has become a major channel for policy research contributions to the policy process. Evaluation involves policy analysts in a variety of activities ranging from the design of informa-tion systems for monitoring programs, through the conduct of complex studies to test the results of policy, to making recommendations for the improvement of program implementation activities. While evaluation stud-ies encompass a broad scope of research endeavors, they share the goal of assessing the past performance of policies to provide guidance for future continuance and modification (including termination) of programmatic ef-forts.

The fact that evaluation involves the assessment of past performance makes it a particularly delicate and sensitive phase in the policy process. Prosecutors who have publicized their career criminal program as evidence of anticrime efforts may be hesitant about allowing analysts to evaluate the program. What if the evaluation finds the program makes little difference in the fate of repeat offenders? Such a finding provides information to be used against an elected prosecutor in the next election. Evaluations man-dated by federal agencies carry the threat of funding reduction or termina-tion if program performance is inadequate. Similarly, legislatures may use evaluations as part of "sun-setting" measures which require periodic reau-thorization of policies and programs implementing that policy. Evaluation often poses a potential threat to the interests of politicians, administrators, interest groups, program recipients, and other stakeholders.

The spread of evaluation as a policy-making and management tool has highlighted the importance of nontechnical skills in policy analysis. Ana-lysts work with users of evaluation studies to develop clear understandings of evaluation objectives and to create realistic expectations of what findings a study can produce. They work with program managers and employees to collect accurate and complete information about program performance. They communicate results in ways maximizing the chances that information will contribute to policy decisions.

Evaluation is an activity requiring constant interaction with policy-makers, managers, and others—many of whom feel threatened by the evalu-ation process itself. Policy analysis requires more than knowledge in the techniques of data collection and analysis; it also requires knowledge of the policy process in a particular context and requires skills in working with people who are part of it. People skills, as well as technical research skills, are emphasized in subsequent chapters of this text.

CONCLUDING COMMENTS

Mapping policy terrains to orient research efforts is a basic policy skill. This chapter presented a conceptual map of the process through which policies are made and implemented, and how policy research information contributes to these processes. While the routes of particular policies through this terrain are typically circuitous or incomplete, the map does provide a useful orientation to the distinctive types of decisions—and the accompanying information needs—that confront stakeholders at various stages in public policy life cycles.

Policy analysts—in universities, private research firms, governmental agencies, and other affiliations—are members of policy communities that often *stimulate* new or modified policy through identifying emerging problems. Policy analysts provide indicators of political, social, and economic conditions to help policymakers scan society for emerging policy problems. Policy analysis also helps provide a forum for developing contrasting and broadened interpretations of the causes and consequences of emerging problems. This forum can help stimulate policies that avoid recycling past understandings that are no longer accurate. Policy research contributes to the conceptual and empirical accuracy of initial problem definition, thereby strengthening the foundation for future action.

As problems enter the agenda of possible public action, the information needs of decision makers become more specific. The central contribution of policy research shifts from helping determine whether there is a problem and what the problem is to specifying the extent of the problem and alternative policy solutions. The dialogue has narrowed. Major analysis tasks in policy *clarification* include detailed descriptions of the magnitude and severity of a problem, developing policy alternatives, assessing the feasibility of implementing the alternatives, and assessing their potential to achieve the desired solutions. Analysis at the clarification stage focuses on information that elaborates the nature of a policy problem and alternative policy responses.

In the *initiation* stage, individuals with decision-making authority ultimately determine whether a given policy will be selected. Analysts contribute to these decisions in a number of ways. They help articulate value-laden assumptions behind policy alternatives, test policy alternatives against specified decision criteria, and identify patterns of support or opposition to policy options. In the initiation stage policy research information becomes one of numerous considerations that decision makers weigh in their deliberations.

Once a commitment to action has been made and programs are being *implemented,* the nature of information needs changes again. The needs of program managers are specific and detailed. "Much like driving cross country, policy analysis requires large quantities of very specific factual information ... Events are ... everchanging" (Brewer and deLeon (1983:10). The ongoing needs of program managers to adapt their programs to reality provide a great deal of grist for the practice of policy research.

Policy analysts also play a major role in helping policymakers and program managers learn from past experience. The *evaluation* of policy implementation and results has become a regular part of the policy process, providing information and feedback on programmatic activities.

While it is easiest to conceptualize the policy process in the context of large policy efforts, such as career criminal policy, it is important to reemphasize that the map presented here is more analytic than descriptive. Policy applies to decisions at all levels of government in varying degrees of complexity, not just major programs reflecting national initiatives. Even smaller policy efforts pass through a necessarily shortened process of stimulation, clarification, initiation, implementation, and evaluation.

REFERENCES

Alexander, Ernest E. 1985. "From Idea to Action: Notes for a Contingency Theory of the Policy Implementation Process," *Administration and Society,* 16, 4:403–26.

Bartolomeo, John S. 1980. "Practitioners' Attitudes Toward the Career Criminal Program," *Journal of Criminal Law and Criminology,* vol. 71.

Brewer, Gary D., and Peter deLeon. 1983. *The Foundations of Policy Analysis.* Homewood, IL: Dorsey Press.

Chelimsky, Eleanor, and Judith Dahmann. 1980. "The MITRE Corporation's National Evaluation of the Career Criminal Program: A Discussion of the Findings," *Journal of Criminal Law and Criminology,* vol. 71.

Dery, David. 1984. *Problem Definition in Policy Analysis.* Lawrence, KS: University Press of Kansas.

Dunn, William N. 1981. *Public Policy Analysis: An Introduction.* Englewood Cliffs, NJ: Prentice-Hall.

Edwards, George C., III. 1980. *Implementing Public Policy.* Washington, DC: Congressional Quarterly Press.

Ford, Gerald R. 1975. *Presidential Documents: Gerald R. Ford. 1974,* vol. 10. Washington, DC: U.S. Government Printing Office.

Glaser, Edward M., Harold H. Abelson, and Kathalee N. Garrison. 1983. *Putting Knowledge to Use: Facilitating the Diffusion of Knowledge and the Implementation of Planned Change.* San Francisco: Jossey-Bass Publishers.

Greenwood, Peter W., and Allan Abrahamse. 1982. *Selective Incapacitation.* Washington, DC: U.S. Department of Justice.

Kingdon, John W. 1984. *Agendas, Alternatives, and Public Policies.* Boston: Little, Brown and Company.

Lynn, Laurence E., Jr. 1980. *Designing Public Policy: A Casebook on the Role of Policy Analysis.* Santa Monica, CA: Goodyear Publishing.

Mills, C. Wright. 1962. *The Sociological Imagination.* Glencoe, IL: Free Press.

Nakamura, Robert T., and Frank Smallwood. 1980. *The Politics of Policy Implementation.* New York: St. Martin's Press.

Nelson, Richard R. 1977. *The Moon and the Ghetto: An Essay on Public Policy Analysis.* New York: W. W. Norton.

Petersilia, Joan, Peter W. Greenwood, and Marvin Lavin. 1977. *Criminal Careers of Habitual Felons.* Santa Monica, CA: Rand.

Rein, Martin, and Sheldon S. White. 1977. "Policy Research: Belief and Doubt," *Policy Analysis* 4:239–71.

Springer, J. Fred, Joel L. Phillips, and Lynne Cannady. 1985. *Selective Prosecution: Lessons from Career Criminal Programs.* Sacramento, CA: EMT Associates.

Sylvia, Ronald D., Kenneth J. Meier, and Elizabeth M. Gunn. 1985. *Program Planning and Evaluation for the Public Manager.* Monterey, CA: Brooks/Cole Publishing.

Twentieth Century Fund. 1976. *Law Enforcement: The Federal Role.* New York: McGraw-Hill.

U.S. House of Representatives, Committee on the Judiciary. 1976. *Law Enforcement Assistance Administration, Hearings,* 94th Congress, 2nd Session. Washington, DC: U.S. Government Printing Office.

Weekly Compilation of Presidential Documents, Week Ending Friday, October 2, 1981. Washington, DC: U.S. Government Printing Office.

Wholey, Joseph S. 1983. *Evaluation and Effective Public Management.* Boston: Little, Brown and Company.

Williams, Kristen M. 1979. *The Scope and Prediction of Recidivism.* Washington, DC: PROMIS Research Project Publication No. 10.

Wolfgang, Marion, R. Figlio, and T. Sellin. 1972. *Delinquency in a Birth Cohort.* Chicago: University of Chicago Press.

3

Producing Usable Information

Linking Research and Policy

> If ... knowledge is ... to enhance our existence individually and collectively, that knowledge must reach the people who need it in a form that they can put to use. Putting what is known (and validated) to use is, indeed, the problem of our age. (cited in Glaser, Abelson, and Garrison, 1983:3)

Chapter 2 described ongoing contributions of policy research, emphasizing its use in fulfilling different information needs of decision makers at different stages of the policy process. Investing resources in policy research to meet these differing information needs is justified by the belief that resulting findings will make a positive contribution to the quality of policy-making. In other words, the benefits of information generated by policy analysts cannot be realized unless that information is used by public managers, elected officials, and other stakeholders in formulating, implementing, and evaluating policies. Unless research information is used as policies are made, it fails in its major objective.

Too often analysts assume research results will be used based on the quality or worth of the research alone, an oversimplified and counterproductive assumption.

> The old-fashioned concept of knowledge transfer [and use] went something like this: "Build a better mousetrap and the world will beat a path to your door." In other words, the dissemination and use of research was supposed to depend primarily on the goodness or intrinsic worth of the research itself. Only gradually over the last generation have we begun to realize that such an attitude almost guarantees the nonutilization of most research. (Havelock, 1980:11)

The point is that the use of research findings and recommendations by decision makers cannot be assumed or taken for granted. Simply because information is accurate and relevant does not ensure its use in policy-making.

Using policy research information is a more complex and uncertain activity than the better-mousetrap approach suggests. Putting information to use involves political, organizational, social, and attitudinal factors in addition to the specific knowledge generated through policy research. This chapter explores factors influencing the use of policy research information, focusing on approaches analysts employ in enhancing research usage. The assumption underlying the discussion is that policy research can be useful to stakeholders if ongoing attention is given to research use by producers and by users of the information. Illustrations of effective and ineffective research use are compared in the following two case studies.

RESEARCH IN ORGANIZATIONS: CASE STUDIES IN UTILIZATION

Alpha Agency

Alpha Agency is part of a state department created in the mid-1970s. The department was established to consolidate the operation of a variety of programs committed to assisting citizens in obtaining safe, sanitary, and affordable housing in suitable living environments. The housing programs operate largely through technical assistance, research and development, information dissemination, and loans and grants to eligible recipients, e.g., local governments and not-for-profit organizations. Over time, loan and grant programs have become a significant vehicle in fulfilling the mission of the department.

A written report to the legislature by the state's Office of the Auditor General criticized the department's handling of loans and grants, documenting numerous management and procedural problems needing improvement in administering the programs. The legislature requested that the department make necessary improvements.

In response, the department issued a request for research services to aid in

- developing better management information capabilities in the programs (in monitoring and evaluating projects, in improving criteria for assessing program effectiveness, and so forth);
- clarifying, documenting, and standardizing administrative procedures in loan and grant programs (e.g., developing standardized procedure manuals); and
- improving program performance in designated areas (ensuring program compliance with relevant statutes and regulations, reducing delays in disbursing funds to loan or grant recipients, improving fiscal controls, and so forth).

The services requested by the department were fragmented and technical. While ostensibly asking for concrete improvements in operating the loan and grant programs, the request was primarily a response to the auditor general's criticism.

What appeared to be straightforward requests for technical improvements had problematic implications. Many of the department's requests for improvement focused on standardizing reporting requirements (progress reports and financial reports) submitted by its loan and grant programs. The contents of the required reports and their frequency of submission varied among housing programs, thereby hampering the department's ability to meet its reporting requirements to legislative and executive officials. But past attempts to standardize the content and frequency of the reports had been resisted by individual housing program managers who strongly believed in the efficacy of their current reporting practices. Further, plans for an automated management information capability remained uncertain because the department was scheduled to become part of a new, statewide, integrated information system at some unspecified future date. Given these problems, the requested technical improvements would be of uncertain benefit or would meet with considerable resistance from housing program managers.

If technical recommendations generated through the research services were to be of any use, aggressive management would be needed to implement a series of procedural changes. It seemed unlikely this aggressive management style would materialize. Upper-level department managers were aware they would meet with resistance from program managers should they push the issue of standardization. Also, their attention was diverted by a series of resignations and transfers of senior organizational personnel associated with the research project. During the course of the study:

- The Division Chief, who had assumed formal responsibility for the research contract, resigned approximately six weeks after contract initiation, rescinded the resignation, and then resigned shortly before the end of the contract period. The Chief of a parallel division was appointed to fill the vacancy.
- The project officer, an Assistant Chief, transferred to a Section Chief position in the same division shortly before the end of the contract. (A Section Chief is one rank below an Assistant Chief.)
- The Chief of Administrative Affairs, a key person in a key unit involved in the project, resigned midway during the course of the project.

The discontinuities and uncertainties created through senior personnel changes produced adverse consequences for the success of the project. New managers needed to learn procedures, processes, and personalities. Little time was available to commit to a study designed to correct prior department problems. The arrival of new upper-level managers produced a "pulling back" from the research project among subordinate managers who were awaiting clear management signals from the changed leadership.

The organizational chaos brought about by the changes clearly undermined the project. New incumbents were reluctant to embrace a project midstream or to trust analysts unknown to them. When they did provide input to the study team, it frequently meant the introduction of new problems and information needs. Project objectives were expanded without the ability to make adjustments in timetable and funding.

As a consequence, relations with the department were sporadic. Initial attempts to build working relations with department and program managers were frustrated by their reluctance to put themselves at the center of the project. Instead, contact persons were scattered throughout the department with little representation from senior management among them.

In addition to a lack of focus and commitment to project objectives by senior personnel, essential resources to implement improvements were nonexistent. Fiscal commitments necessary to implement comprehensive management information systems were absent and uncertain in the foreseeable future. Program managers implementing many of the recommended improvements would resist changes, believing more in the systems and procedures they had developed. Regardless of whether they cared about the improvements or saw them as threats, the lack of resources to correct problems reduced program managers' commitment to the project.

The outcome of the project reflected its difficulties. A draft report was prepared providing technical remedies and recommended changes in resources and program coordination. Despite the documentation of immediate and concrete problems and the legislative mandate to correct them, little use was apparently made of findings and recommendations. The draft

report was submitted to the department: no reply or response was ever received.

Beta Agency

Beta Agency is a program in a state department of health services. The
program evolved when the department entered into a cooperative agreement with the Federal Centers for Disease Control to establish a diabetes
control program in the state. Diabetes is one of the leading causes of death
in the nation and is a major cause of blindness and other disabling conditions.

The program mission is to conduct collaborative activities aimed at
developing community-based programs designed to improve the quality, accessibility, and effectiveness of diabetes care throughout the state. The program focus is to reduce the complications, risk factors, and costs associated
with the disease.

The program mission included provisions for conducting a series of
public hearings in the state focusing on problems and solutions related
to diabetes. The diabetes control program staff, along with its advisory committee members, formed a diabetes coalition for formulating and conducting the hearings. Major purposes of the public hearings were to

- survey the magnitude of the problems posed by diabetes in the state;
- identify possible remedies to the cited problems;
- assist in developing an advocacy network among private and voluntary
  diabetes organizations; and
- heighten public awareness of diabetes as a major public health
  problem.

Hearings were typically chaired by state and local elected officials,
members of the advisory committee, and leaders in the local diabetes community. Most hearings included expert witnesses who testified on selected
aspects of diabetes. Witnesses were asked to identify diabetes-related problems and to suggest remedies designed to resolve them. Such persons included health care, education, and research professionals; patients and relatives of patients; members of voluntary health organizations; state and local
government officials; and representatives of concerned professional and
private organizations. To accommodate persons unable to attend the hearings, written testimony was accepted up to four weeks after completion of
the hearings. Policy analysts were asked to conduct an analysis of the written and oral testimony, and to prepare reports summarizing major findings
and recommendations. The final report would serve as a basis for possible
governmental action in combating diabetes in the state.

From a research-use perspective, outcomes were more positive with

Beta Agency than with Alpha Agency for a number of reasons. First, the information objectives of the research were generated internally, rather than being imposed from the "outside" (the Auditor General or the legislature). Information objectives of the analysis were clear and agreed upon, understood and accepted by diabetes program staff, concerned federal representatives, and representatives of the diabetes coalition.

Second, management and staff were actively involved in all phases of the research project, as was the advisory committee representing the major interests and perspectives of the program's policy community. A high level of commitment by program staff and the diabetes coalition was evident through the life of the project. The project was seen as important, receiving widespread support and sustained attention by potential users of the information. No significant changes in program leadership or in program direction occurred during the life of the research project. Unlike Alpha Agency, Beta Agency experienced little change in management while the project was in progress.

Third, effective communication linkages were established and maintained among program management, diabetes advisory group members, and policy analysts. Frequent meetings were held to elicit and to disseminate information relative to the project; much information was exchanged in more informal one-on-one settings. Program staff and coalition members were involved in all phases of the project, including the development of research tools and the review of preliminary findings and recommendations. Relations between producers and users remained cordial and professional throughout the project, with both attempting to be responsive and flexible in their work relations with the other.

Program stability, agreed-upon information needs, and effective linkages and collaboration between producers and consumers contributed significantly to the subsequent use of study results. Additionally, management's strong commitment and sustained attention to the study, along with that of the diabetes advisory group, produced a final report tailored to their concerns. The final report was presented in two volumes. The first briefly summarized the major findings of the hearings and emphasized the implications for legislative, agency, and public actions to control the hardships of diabetes. The second volume presented hearing results in detail.

Findings and recommendations emerging from the analysis of oral and written testimony were well received by Beta Agency and the diabetes coalition; some recommendations were incorporated into the state plan for diabetes control. The final two-volume report was published and disseminated to a variety of organizations and individuals interested in the control of this major health problem.

What Went Wrong? What Went Right?

The two case studies suggest that research results were used by Beta Agency but remained unused in Alpha Agency. The cases clearly differed in their dynamics, e.g., the interest and involvement of program staff and other interested parties, patterns of communication between producers and users, and the degree of stability in the agencies. The remainder of this chapter discusses major factors inhibiting and facilitating the use of policy research information in policy decisions.[1] An enhanced understanding of the dynamics of research utilization helps identify "what went wrong" in Alpha Agency and "what went right" in Beta Agency.

RESEARCH USE IN POLICY-MAKING

An initial concern in understanding research utilization is to define just what it means to "use" information produced by research. A straightforward interpretation is that use occurs only when there is an obvious, direct, and immediate application of findings and recommendations to specific decisions. Research usage, viewed through these lenses, is measured by determining whether findings are acted upon by policymakers in a clear, prompt, and rational fashion.

> The expectation is that specific findings point to a specific answer and that responsible policymakers proceed to implement that answer in policy or practice. Research makes a difference ... only if it changes a decision from what it would have been had there been no research to one fully in accord with what the research results imply should be done. (Weiss and Bucuvalas, 1980:10)

This view of utilization is too narrow for most policy research. It assumes decision points are clear, direct, and centralized. More frequently, policy is produced through a series of shifting decisions by changing sets of stakeholders whose influence changes over time. Decision making in public settings is typically fragmented, rarely the province of a single policymaker.

Further, the results of analyses are simply one of several sources of information policymakers consider in making decisions. Competing sources include personal views and experiences, legal rules and regulations, and the preferences of other stakeholders involved in policy outcomes. Decision makers have obligations to honor prior commitments, to balance opposing forces, to "respond to the political give and take that is part of the institutional 'cement' of our pluralist system" (Springer, 1985:490). The world of action, inhabited by persons and groups with competing values, is too varied and policy-making processes too diffused for such a limited conception of research use.

Additionally, this simple view of utilization ignores more subtle, indirect, less immediate uses of research in policy-making and administrative processes. Research results alter the ways in which stakeholders view issues without producing specific recommendations for a particular decision. Providing an understanding of issues and facilitating discussions without reference to concrete, immediate decisions is research usage. Policy research raises new concerns and possibilities, promotes administrative introspection of internal policies and procedures, corrects inaccurate assumptions and beliefs about the delivery of services, gains attention for an issue, and assesses the nature of support and opposition to proposed policy.

An expanded view of research utilization is necessary, one recognizing that policy analysis is but one source of information to decision makers and that research has multiple uses, entering choices in direct and indirect ways over immediate and long-term time periods. This view of utilization makes the concept less obvious and more difficult to measure, but better reflects the context and complexity of policy research.

In application, the broadened definition of research utilization implies that assessing the use of policy analysis is complex rather than simple. Policy research is consumed in a variety of ways, and criteria and bases for evaluating the user relevance of research results are themselves a proper topic for negotiation and agreement between information producers and users. Since the uses of research results vary with situations, policy research must be utilization focused, application oriented. Planning for improved utilization should be continuous, integrated into research activities from their inception to completion. Subsequent sections elaborate on this expanded view of utilization, discussing approaches employed in making research results more useful. The discussion begins with a clarification of major factors influencing the use of policy research information.

Determinants of Research Use

If analysts are to take steps to improve the usefulness of their research information to policymakers, they first make themselves aware of factors impeding research use. A number of the most important constraining factors can be categorized under (a) personal attitudes and characteristics of analysts and policymakers; (b) communication of project objectives, progress, and results; and (c) characteristics of the policy terrain.

THE PERSONAL FACTOR

The role of personal and interpersonal factors in impeding research use has been emphasized in many utilization studies (Springer, 1985:482). Working from interviews with decision makers, policy analysts, and project officers, Patton and others (1977:155) documented repeated mention of the importance of personal attributes such as interest, enthusiasm, and commitment to the project when the effects of research efforts were being explained. Respondents pointed to these factors "as the single most important element in the utilizing process" (Patton et al., 1977:155). This "personal factor" manifested itself in a number of ways, such as resistance to change, limited commitment to project objectives, and divergent orientations of decision makers and analysts.

Resistance to change among stakeholders is a commonly cited personal barrier to utilization. What Rothman (1980:99) calls the "force of custom" reflects a generalized resistance to change on the part of those affected. In the case of employees, for example, the expectations of requirements to shed current and familiar work roles and to learn new ones may produce uncertainty and insecurity. Glaser, Abelson, and Garrison (1983:81–84) suggest several specific sources of resistance, including:

- *Fear of loss of status or prestige or power.* Those benefiting the most from an existing situation are least likely to embrace major changes recommended by analysts.
- *Threatened job security.* Recommendations for change may require knowledge and skills different from those presently required.
- *Threatened work philosophy and practice.* Learning new methods of work and new orientations may be resisted when viewed as threatening to one's established point of view and work routines.
- *Fear of loss of self-esteem.* The exposure of individual weak points identified in research findings creates resistance since it affects one's sense of competency and self-worth. This source of resistance is particularly evident in evaluation studies, introduced in the preceding chapter.
- *Fear of the unknown.* People resist change when they do not understand it. Resistance may stem from a lack of understanding of a policy recommendation's effects and implications or from an incomplete understanding of the change itself.
- *Forced change.* Resistance emerges when change is demanded of—forced upon—those affected.

Recognizing and coping with personal sources of resistance is crucial to the successful application of research results. Conditions generating personal resistance to change were evident throughout the Alpha Agency study, particularly in relation to program managers. Existing work practices were threatened, and the status and effectiveness of program staff were put in question.

Lack of interest and commitment to project objectives is another major factor impeding research use. Policymakers and program staff have numerous competing demands on their time and attention (March and Olsen, 1979). Analysts compete with other issues requiring the attention of high-level decision makers, and compete for attention with the daily responsibilities of program staff.

Fragmented attention to project objectives can also be attributed to personnel turnover and changing priorities (Kress and Springer, 1988). As evidenced in the housing study, transitions in leadership during the course of the research reduced management support of and attention to the project. New incumbents were unable or unwilling to commit themselves to a study not of their own making. More pressing priorities demanded their attention. In the diabetes study, by way of contrast, the continuity of program staff facilitated effective working relations between information producers and users, contributing to the use of research results.

The *divergent roles and orientations* of policy analysts and decision makers are further obstacles to utilization. The belief that analysts and decision makers occupy two separate "communities" having different purposes, approaches, perspectives, interests, loyalties, and values has become a widely cited explanation for inadequate research use (Patton et al., 1977).

Chelimsky (1980:1177–84) comments on the reluctance of legislators to accept research findings sponsored by the executive branch because they doubt its objectivity, its credibility. Others such as Rothman (1980:101) observe that some decision makers adopt an "intuitive intellectual style" that places high value on personal judgment, past experience, and a feeling for the situation in making decisions—not on empirical research findings.

Attitudes and behaviors of analysts, the producers themselves, also influence research uses. A familiar observation is that "Researchers' formulations of problems for study often do not match decision makers' definitions of problems" (Weiss with Bucuvalas, 1980:17). Analysts may formulate problems in ways not adequately recognizing what is relevant and feasible for policymakers. They may oversimplify problems, ignoring factors relevant to decision makers' concerns. They may conceptualize problems to fit the methodologies in which they are particularly skilled, limiting the comprehensiveness and quality of resulting findings.

"Aloofness" on the part of analysts is a commonly cited personality characteristic influencing research usage. Rothman (1980:103–6) reports that aloofness generated a lack of trust among policymakers, negatively influencing the use of policy analysis. Aloofness can be personal and intellectual. A demeanor of arrogance and a tendency to avoid personal contact on the part of analysts inhibit trust and cooperation on the part of users. Analysts may be seen as too academic and theoretical, not anchored in reality. They may fail to address the real concerns of decision makers by becoming absorbed in minor technical concerns or overly abstract concerns rather than immediate, important, and real problems of the agency. Weiss (1972:99) adds to this analyst profile, observing that

the researcher is likely to be a detached individual, interested in ideas and abstractions. He thinks in terms of generalizations and analytical categories. His interest is in the long-term acquisition of knowledge, rather than the day-to-day issues of program operation. He seems cool, uncommitted to any program philosophy or position, without personal loyalties to the program or the organization.

Weiss adds that differences in work roles between producers and users may be more significant in assessing research usage than any underlying personality variable such as aloofness. Practitioners have to believe in what they are doing and how they are doing it; analysts have to question those programmatic beliefs and practices. This difference in orientations and behavior creates inevitable tension. Whatever their initial personal characteristics, once practitioners and analysts go about their divergent tasks they are likely to see things differently.

The health (Beta Agency) and housing (Alpha Agency) studies provide contrasts in relations between the two communities of analysts and decision makers. In the case of Beta Agency, a high level of commitment continued throughout the life of the diabetes-related project. The analysis was seen as relevant, receiving ongoing attention and support among potential user groups. Producers and consumers worked together in major phases of the project, e.g., designing the analysis plan and reviewing preliminary findings and recommendations. Relations between the two communities remained friendly, professional, and goal-directed throughout the project. In Beta Agency, personal and social factors promoted research usage, enhancing the worth and utility of the resulting information.

A contrary conclusion is drawn in Alpha Agency. In that housing case, there was little sustained interest in the project by upper-level decision makers and by program managers. Individuals responsible for implementing many of the recommended improvements resisted them for a variety of reasons, personal and otherwise. Collaboration was hindered due to a lack of commitment to the project and to the resignations and transfers of key agency personnel associated with the study. The inability to develop effective working relations contributed to the utilization outcomes experienced in Alpha Agency.

COMMUNICATION LINKAGES

Effective communication between information producers and users is a necessity in joining research and policy. Effective communication involves the technical accuracy and quality of research reports and presentations, and the quality of collaboration among key participants in the research project.

Certainly the technical quality of the research itself affects subsequent use. Technical quality includes how a study is designed and implemented. Research studies often signal increased funding, and a policymaker

> wants to be convinced that a designated need is real, that it has been demonstrated in a technically sound way sufficient to justify the allocation of scarce

funds being sought by parties with conflicting claims. Certain findings may require practitioners to change accustomed ways of work or to take additional responsibilities. They want to make sure that these extra demands on them are totally justified and that the service implications are safe for clients. (Rothman, 1980:139)

In addition to technical quality, research use is influenced through language and writing styles employed in reporting results. Understanding study results may be impeded due to excessive jargon and technical language unfamiliar to readers. Research reports may be too lengthy, unnecessarily detailed, requiring too much time to read and absorb. Their contents may overpower consumers through statistical overkill. Chapter 14 provides guidelines in producing well-written and relevant research reports.

Research information is likely to be devalued when there is a lack of ongoing collaborative relations between analysts and policymakers (Rothman, 1980:69–91). If users of research results have no say in decisions made during the course of the study, they will have less investment in study results. Working together in defining problems to be investigated, in carrying out research tasks, in making recommendations, and in disseminating results promotes an increased awareness of information needs and study limitations by producers and users alike.

Effective collaboration improves the mutual identification and definition of issues, enhancing the relevancy of research information. In the diabetes study, such interactions served to generate trust between analysts and users, resulting in a greater commitment to implementing research findings. Collaborative activities between producers and users relate closely to subsequent research uses.

While recognizing collaboration as an essential approach in improving research use, analysts avoid becoming entangled in program politics in such a way as to threaten the credibility and integrity of research findings. It is never appropriate to become so absorbed in program cultures that the accuracy and objectivity of research procedures and research results are compromised.

The dissemination of research results, another mechanism linking producers and users, may be haphazard, leaving out relevant policy participants. Berg (1978:43) correctly points out that the dissemination effort—distributing the results of research to stakeholders—all too often "tends to be nobody's job." Making sure the right decision makers get the right information implies that analysts assume an active role in ensuring that findings and recommendations are communicated "assertively and on a sustained basis within the organization" (Rothman, 1980:77). Well-designed dissemination strategies are central to research usage.

Shortcomings in communication linkages between analysts and decision makers—whether due to ineffective collaboration, inadequate dissemination, or inadequate research products—partly determine the subsequent worth and utility of study results.

SITUATIONAL FACTORS

Policy research is action oriented. It is designed to help decision makers respond to issues arising in changing environments. But research usage is not determined entirely by the people involved in producing and consuming it. Whatever their commitments and intentions, uses of information are affected by the context in which problems arise.

Resistance to change, for example, may have situational as well as personal bases. Resistance may be seen as a function of individual opposition, when its actual roots are constraints imposed by the situation. In other words, resistance may signal real impracticalities of proposed recommendations for changes, not personal insecurities. Situational barriers to research use may stem from the organization structure, competing political interests, and the availability of resources; each is briefly discussed.

The structure and design of organizations affect utilization outcomes. Some studies (Rothman, 1980:56) suggest that relatively flat organizations (those with few layers of management) facilitate circulation and communication of information among units. More open communications in these less-structured organizations encourage the dissemination of research information, leading to greater attention to findings and acting as an impetus to use.

In other cases, the political climate inhibits the application of research findings and recommendations. Policy issues shift rapidly. Concerns that fueled a policy analysis may have been resolved, forgotten, or significantly changed by the time of its completion, undermining its usefulness. When new programs and other major changes are recommended, the support of stakeholder groups, internal and external to the agency, is imperative in acquiring the legitimation and endorsements necessary to implement reforms.

Economic resources, in addition to political support and consensus, are often required to carry forward the implications of research. In Alpha Agency, for example, essential fiscal resources for implementing needed improvements such as automated management information systems were absent in the short term, uncertain in the foreseeable future. Recommendations not taking account of resource limitations stand little chance of being accepted and implemented. The accessibility of financial resources in implementing recommendations is a pervasive and frequently determining variable in the usefulness of research results.

In summary, determinants of research use can be identified at multiple points along the route from research production to policy action. The preceding discussion outlined only a sample of potential inhibitors stemming from contextual features, personal and social variables, and communication networks.[2] Research usage is ultimately shaped by a combination of such variables operating in unison. Given the thicket of potential obstacles to research use, the conclusion seems inescapable that

> getting appropriate research information to one individual and having that individual incorporate the information in her selection of decision options begins to seem no mean feat in itself, but producing information that will influence the actions of a bureaucratic organization is several orders of magnitude more complex. (Weiss with Bucuvalas, 1980:23)

Improving Utilization Potential in Policy Research

The preceding discussion suggests a variety of obstacles to the effective use of research information, to linking research and practice. Obstacles to research use inherent in the fluid and fragmented world of public policy are not underestimated by experienced analysts.

Analysts know they cannot expect a fortuitous string of events leading to the discovery and intended uses of their research information. Assuming research use occurs as a normal byproduct of a quality study, that no special efforts are necessary in enhancing utilization, is a guarantee of undervalued findings and recommendations. Instead, utilization occurs "as the result of ingenuity, resourcefulness and commitment" (Caplan, 1980:9).

Analysts do not wait until a final research report is presented before thinking about potential uses of research information. Producing usable information begins with initial meetings between analysts and users. These meetings provide the opportunity to alert consumers to utilization concerns, and to prompt them to consider these concerns on an ongoing basis.

Analysts should be alert to how usage can be enhanced throughout the course of the study. New aspects of the issue and new dissemination opportunities usually emerge as research progresses and as the project gets known among the policy community. Utilization plans, like the total research plan, should be flexible enough to admit new possibilities. The following sections offer guidelines in achieving utilization objectives. Sections are organized by major phases in policy research projects.

PLANNING RESEARCH

The participation of decision makers, implementers, and others in designing research projects is essential to subsequent use of research products. Producers and users should get together and decide the questions that need to be researched before conducting the study and attempting to apply the results. Utilization is enhanced when there is an early and explicit under-standing between analysts and decision makers regarding reciprocal re-sponsibilities and expectations arising from the research.

An early objective of collaboration is to discuss and specify purposes of the project. Analysts and users discuss and clarify information objec-tives—the specific research questions to be answered—and utilization ob-jectives, the planned applications of the research information. Effective col-laboration is a learning situation for producers and consumers.

Research planning is often improved by seeking the participation of a broad range of stakeholders. Different participants may have different expectations of questions that need to be asked, what the study should ac-complish, and how results might be used. Time and effort invested in the early planning stages produce important contributions toward research us-age. An evaluation of California's Political Reform Act (PRA), which will be referenced throughout the book, demonstrates the point.

The Political Reform Act evaluation was a broad-based study. Its objec-tives included assessing the effectiveness of legal provisions requiring de-tailed reporting of campaign finance information by candidates for state offices, assessing the effectiveness of provisions requesting the expenditures of lobbyists, and making specific recommendations for improving the administration of the PRA by the commission responsible for its implemen-tation—the Fair Political Practices Commission (FPPC).

Given the ambitious and far-reaching objectives of the evaluation, user involvement in planning the project was critical if study recommendations were to be used. A planning committee was formed consisting of analysts, top management from each of the agencies' three major offices, and the commission chairperson. All but one of the Fair Political Practices Commis-sion participants were attorneys with little or no experience in policy re-search.

Several weeks were spent in planning the four-month research study. The process included formal and informal meetings and written exchanges. By the end of the process, producers and consumers had agreement on the information objectives of the study and on the research tasks that would be used to produce it. There was also mutual awareness of the type and quality of information that could be produced and its potential uses and applica-tions. Not all research projects warrant such an involved planning process, but ongoing collaboration between producers and stakeholders during project planning is closely linked to the usefulness of research results. If a number of decision makers are required to support or approve research actions, linkage mechanisms such as advisory groups are created to provide research direction and to gain support for subsequent research applica-tions.

Dissemination approaches for communicating research results (who receives the information and in what form) are also developed in the plan-

ning phase. Additionally, analysts along with users examine the fiscal resources accessible for implementing study recommendations, evaluate the
technology available to do so, and assess the skills and professional capabilities of personnel responsible for applying results. Where legal questions
may be involved, recommendations are considered in the light of their compliance with legal mandates of the organization.

Developing effective working relations with users, then, is an important task for analysts in planning research. Its major objectives are to

- establish a sense of credibility and trust with stakeholders;
- identify user groups and their planned applications of research results;
- develop effective communication networks;
- clarify mutual understandings and expectations for the research; and
- develop dissemination plans for communicating results.

The extent to which these objectives are realized in the planning phases of
research bears a close relation to subsequent use of research information.

IMPLEMENTING RESEARCH PLANS

Although the involvement of decision makers in the planning phases
of policy analysis is important, the need to maintain collaborative relations
in carrying out research plans is equally important. Policymakers and others are kept informed and given opportunities to express ideas and concerns as the project evolves. Analysts ensure that data collection instruments and procedures are understandable and relevant; a way of doing so
is to include users in decisions regarding data sources, collection instruments, and research procedures.

Further, analysts remain accessible to policymakers and relevant others during the course of the study. Through such ongoing meetings, analysts
are able to learn of and share perspectives as data are analyzed and their
meanings interpreted. In large research projects, formal communications
networks between producers and consumers may be established. For instance, advisory committees are sometimes used as a linkage mechanism,
particularly in larger research projects.

Advisory committees are usually composed of members of the group of potential research users, other producers of research, and the source of funding.
The research producer can gain useful advice and knowledge of sources of
information and perspectives from a committee comprised of both experts
and interested parties. (Seidel, 1983:53)

Advisory committees should contain representatives of senior management, particularly managers possessing policy-making powers relevant to the research focus. Additionally, advisory group membership may include political officials and representatives of client groups, labor organizations, other agencies, and other levels of government.

In other instances, accessibility and communication are achieved in less formal ways. Informal meetings—coffee, lunch—as well as formal meetings may enhance utilization (Caplan, 1980:94–97). The point is that utilization of research information is improved when influential persons are involved in major research processes. "Those who have a significant part in planning and decision making are not only better informed but also more committed to making use of the findings" (Glaser, Abelson, and Garrison, 1983:374).

In carrying out these collaborative activities, analysts avoid an air of aloofness in attitude or behavior by adopting a responsive, respectful role toward users (Rothman, 1980:174). While maintaining a professional perspective, they involve themselves in the dynamics of organizational processes, for example, taking an interest in and becoming informed through attending agency meetings and events or engaging in conversations with program personnel. Such activities help analysts understand agency concerns and better focus their efforts on them.

During the course of the study, analysts strive to minimize their demands on the organization—to disrupt agency operations as little as possible. A characteristic of much policy analysis is that it takes place in an action setting. Something else besides research is going on; there are programs serving people and pressing daily responsibilities to be met. "The research is an appendage, an also-present, a matter of secondary priority" (Weiss, 1972:92). Analysts should adapt the study to program requirements, restricting their demands on personnel as much as possible.

Experienced analysts adapt themselves to the working environment they are researching. When collecting data from records, for instance, they minimize their intrusiveness by learning procedures for checking out records on their own, by being willing to work in out-of-the way areas that do not disrupt normal activities, and by strictly observing rules on confidentiality, returning records, and so forth. Interviews are arranged to suit the respondent, not the analyst.

Of course, data have to be collected and staff members and others queried and asked to complete forms. But Weiss observes that too often analysts request more information that they need or will use. They

> impose heavier demands than their needs warrant. They ask eighty questions instead of twenty; they administer twelve batteries of tests when four would suffice. The reason is usually that they are not clear about what they are looking for, and they take all possible precautions not to miss anything that may turn out to be important. Better focus of the study at the outset ... would lessen the zeal to cast a wide and undiscriminating net. (Weiss, 1972:106)

Unnecessary demands strain working relations, increase friction, and endanger use of subsequent research information.

COMMUNICATING RESULTS

Collaboration as an aid to utilization continues to be a dominant theme in communicating research information. To keep potential users informed, analysts transmit periodic progress reports through written and oral means. Insights and suggestions of policymakers and relevant others are sought as alternatives, conclusions, recommendations, and action plans are developed. Dissemination plans formulated in earlier research stages are reviewed and updated, the focus being to improve the diffusion of research information. Written drafts of final reports are reviewed with key persons and groups, and their comments considered in revising findings, conclusions, alternatives, and recommendations.

Research results are communicated in a number of ways. The written word is unsurpassed for many purposes. Easily transmitted and retrieved, it is absorbed at the user's pace and convenience. If it is concise, cogent, authoritative, and open—inviting readers to participate in the research experience—written communications are effective in achieving utilization objectives. Chapter 14 provides guidelines in producing useful and well-written research reports.

Involving decision makers and other stakeholders in reviewing drafts of final reports is necessary in identifying and correcting factual errors, omissions, misinterpretations, unworkable alternatives and recommendations, vague, unfair, or misleading statements, and so on. Having key persons review drafts "is especially important where the confidence and support of key individuals may be at stake; for where policymakers or administrators come to believe that the analysis is unfair or invalid, the proposed solution is not likely to be adopted or implemented" (Ruchelman, 1984:32). Officials, agency personnel, and other stakeholders involved in the adoption and implementation of recommendations should be included in the list of potential reviewers of research documents.

Methods of communicating research results are not limited to written reports. Research usage is frequently enhanced through personal communication networks linking producers and users. "The literature is replete with studies that demonstrate the efficacy of face-to-face contacts as an influencer on knowledge utilization and change" (Glaser, Abelson, and Garrison, 1983:298).

Personal communications may take the form of informal contacts or workshops and conferences where research findings and their action implications are presented and discussed with policymakers. Depending on the nature of research products, demonstrations, or site visits may be valuable in displaying the usefulness of systems and procedures developed through analysis. Whatever methods are used to communicate results, the value of interpersonal contacts, of personal communications as a mechanism for facilitating usage, is well established.

Of course, all forms of written and personal communications should be considered in conveying research information to user groups. In larger projects,

> the use of audiovisual briefs also holds great promise. Data available . . . reveal that eight-to-ten minute films . . . produced to illuminate findings on ten projects were shown 152 times to a total audience estimated at 6,700 professionals. Final reports seldom reach so large an audience. (Engstrom, 1975:361)

Similarly, telecommunications offer innovative opportunities for effective research dissemination in large organizations. Preliminary information shows such communication networks to be effective and beneficial in cost in terms of message conveyance to clients, administrators, and others (Engstrom, 1975:362).

UTILIZATION AS A SHARED RESPONSIBILITY

Improving research usage requires a series of ongoing tasks in planning and implementing research and in communicating results. In each phase, analysts can choose among multiple strategies to better link research and policy. The use of these approaches by analysts does much to assure utilization objectives and to narrow the gap between research and application.

But no guarantees come with these strategies. Situational variables reflecting features of user settings may constrain the application of results, evidenced in the case of Alpha Agency. There, rapid changes in management and leadership and inadequate fiscal resources combined with other factors to produce findings and recommendations of limited use.

Collaboration between analysts and decision makers, a core approach in utilization, may go awry, breeding antagonism instead of generating commitment among participants. Advisory committees, for instance, may not work out as intended.

> In some cases, the committee members considered themselves the true representatives of the interested parties and became adversaries of the researcher. The committee members may view themselves as the supervisor of the researcher and therefore may not adequately consider the suggestions of the researcher. (Seidel, 1983:53–54)

Collaboration also assumes an interactive, ongoing relationship with decision makers, consuming time and attention in the process. But there are other demands on participants' time, many of them obligatory. Collaborative efforts may suffer since these activities are vulnerable to shifts in attention on the part of decision makers.

Research use is consequently shaped by multiple forces, only some subject to control by analysts. Analysts have a responsibility in achieving utilization objectives, but that responsibility is shared with others such as decision makers and implementing officials. Eventual utilization outcomes are a function of producer-user efforts and contextual features making up the policy terrain.

In fulfilling their responsibilities in generating useful information, policy analysts assume an active role, alerting stakeholders to utilization issues at the onset and continuing that emphasis throughout the project life cycle. Analysts help consumers identify how research results may be used, develop explicit understandings of utilization objectives, and determine their role in helping to ensure the attainment of utilization objectives. The effectiveness of analysts in influencing policy and practice depends in large measure on how well these tasks are performed.

Utilization-focused policy analysis better ensures the use of research products. But this focus cannot blind analysts to the necessity of voluntarily disclosing research limitations due to time and funding, the scope of the study and the methods and procedures used, the generalizability of findings, the underlying assumptions, and so forth. It is a rare occurrence when a single piece of policy research can be considered "authoritative," without flaws, and it should not be presented as such to encourage utilization. Limitations should be clearly communicated to give users the opportunity to assess information quality.

CONCLUDING COMMENTS

Billions of dollars are spent by governments in supporting policy research in the United States. The assumption underlying the expenditures is that there will be a reasonable return on these investments—that research results will be used in improving public policies and in improving programs serving to enhance the quality of existence. This chapter explored how analysts increase the likelihood of research results' being applied in policy settings.

Research usage assumes multiple meanings and forms in policy research. In some studies, findings and recommendations may have clear, direct, and immediate impacts on policy, but if so, "usually on relatively low-level, narrow-gauge decisions" (Weiss, 1985:206). More frequently, policy research is but one part of a complex decision process incorporating experience and personal insight, political pressures, precedence, and judgment. This use of policy research information refers to building up a frame of reference based on data as well as providing a more informed basis for decision making.

Research then fulfills multiple uses in policy considerations. Its effects may be short term and long term, direct and indirect, intended and unintended. The implication of this expanded view of usage is that if study findings and recommendations are to make a difference, their potential applications should be agreed upon by producers and users in the planning stages of a study. Indeed, planning for utilization is best viewed as continuous, integrated in research activities from project inception to completion.

Even well-planned ongoing efforts intended to facilitate utilization encounter obstacles arising from multiple sources. Personal and social factors are a major determinant of research usage. Organizationally, requirements to shed current work roles and to learn new ones may produce uncertainty and insecurity in those potentially affected by research recommendations, creating resistance to utilization. The commitment and orientation of policymakers toward the underlying worth of a study serve as additional influences impeding or facilitating usage.

Communication linkages between analysts and decision makers represent a second set of determinants impeding or enhancing research applications. Research information is likely to be undervalued when there is a lack of collaboration and effective work relations between producers and users. The dissemination of findings and recommendations may be unplanned, haphazard, leaving out relevant policy participants. The technical quality of the research itself may be flawed, as may the language and writing style employed in communicating results.

Situational variables—those related to features of the action setting— symbolize a third set of determinants influencing research usage. As discussed in the housing study, resignations and transfers of key organization personnel associated with the research eroded management support, placing severe constraints on research usage. Political support of relevant groups internal and external to the agency may be lacking. Even if there is political consensus, economic resources required to carry forward the action implications of research may be absent or uncertain.

Given the hurdles to joining research and policy, analysts take an active role in increasing the potential use of study results. Assuming that research usage occurs as a normal by-product of a technically sound study, that no special efforts are necessary in enhancing research use, is a guarantee of undervalued research findings and recommendations.

Producing usable information begins with initial meetings between analysts and decision makers. These planning sessions provide the opportunity to alert one another to utilization concerns, and to develop utilization objectives jointly. Such discussions also promote research studies more accurately reflecting user interests and concerns. They help analysts determine how and in what ways information may be applied in user settings, and how to orient efforts to those potential applications.

In the planning stages of research, analysts establish formal and informal communication networks linking them with stakeholders. They assess contextual factors influencing research usage—policymakers' interests and constraints, how and by whom decisions are made, likely sources of resistance, organization structure, human and fiscal resources—in the attempt to tailor subsequent alternatives and recommendations to the distinct policy terrain. Developing dissemination plans for communicating research results is another task in the beginning stages of research.

Utilization continues to be a focus in implementing policy studies. Stakeholders are kept informed and provided opportunities to express ideas and concerns as research proceeds. Analysts avoid an air of aloofness by adopting a responsive, flexible role toward users. A mutual professional and problem-solving relationship is continued and promoted in carrying out research. During implementation of the research plan, analysts strive to minimize their demands on personnel—to disrupt agency operations as little as possible.

In communicating research information, analysts transmit periodic progress reports through oral and written means. Oral communications take the form of informal, interpersonal contacts and committees, workshops, and conferences where research findings and their implications are discussed with stakeholders. Written drafts of research reports are reviewed with users and their comments considered in revising alternatives, recommendations, and action plans. The contents of research reports are specifically oriented to agency problems and concerns, and are brief, clear, and presented in operational and cost-benefit terms when appropriate.

Using the preceding approaches in planning, implementing, and communicating research enhances usage, narrowing the gap between research and practice. But utilization outcomes are shaped by a variety of interacting forces, only some within the control of analysts. Eventual outcomes are a function of producer-user efforts and contextual features of the policy setting.

Of course, the nature of the eventual uses may be for purposes other than planned—as a post hoc justification for previously agreed-on decisions, to rally opposition or support for a policy or program, or "to neutralize opponents, convince waverers and bolster supporters" (Weiss, 1985:207). Policy research takes place in social, political, and organizational settings; its uses are shaped by its context and by its participants. Nevertheless, in meeting their responsibilities to improve research usage, analysts maintain a utilization focus through the life of the project.

NOTES

1. For a comprehensive treatment of variables related to research use, see Glaser, Abelson, and Garrison (1983); Rothman (1980); and Weiss with Bucuvalas (1980).
2. Rothman (1980) and Caplan (1980:91–97) provide detailed utilization enhancement checklists for use by producers and users of research information.

REFERENCES

Berg, Mark R. 1978. *The Use of Technology Assessment Studies in Policymaking.* Ann Arbor, MI: Center for Research on Utilization of Scientific Knowledge, Institute of Social Research, University of Michigan.

Caplan, Nathan. 1980. "Summary: Common Themes and a Checklist," pp. 91–97, in Larry A. Braskamp and Robert D. Brown, eds., *New Directions for Program Evaluation: Utilization of Evaluative Information.* San Francisco: Jossey-Bass Publishers.

———. "What Do We Know About Knowledge Utilization," pp. 1–10, in Larry A. Braskamp and Robert D. Brown, eds., *New Directions for Program Evaluation: Utilization of Evaluative Information.* San Francisco: Jossey-Bass Publishers.

Chelimsky, Eleanor. 1980. "Evaluation Research Credibility and the Congress," *Policy Studies Journal* 8, 7:1177–84.

Engstrom, George. 1975. "Research and Research Utilization—A Many Faceted Approach," *Rehabilitation Counseling Bulletin* 19:357–64.

Glaser, Edward M., Harold H. Abelson, and Kathalee N. Garrison. 1983. *Putting Knowledge to Use: Facilitating the Diffusion of Knowledge and the Implementation of Planned Change.* San Francisco: Jossey-Bass Publishers.

Havelock, Ronald G. 1980. Foreword, pp. 11–14, in Jack Rothman, *Using Research in Organizations: A Guide to Successful Application.* Beverly Hills, CA: Sage Publications.

Kress, Guenther, and J. Fred Springer. 1988. "Service Utilization in Public Sector Consulting," *American Review of Public Administration* 18, 2:327–42.

March, James G., and Johan P. Olsen. 1979. "Attention and the Ambiguity of Self-interest," in James G. March and Johan P. Olsen, eds., *Ambiguity and Choice in Organizations.* Bergen, Norway: Universites Lorlaget.

Patton, Michael Quinn, Patricia S. Grimes, Kathryn M. Guthrie, Nancy J. Brennan, Barbara D. French, and Dale A. Blyth. 1977. *In Search of Impact: An Analysis of Utilization of Federal Health Evaluation Research.* Minneapolis: University of Minnesota.

Rothman, Jack. 1980. *Using Research in Organizations: A Guide to Successful Application.* Beverly Hills, CA: Sage Publications.

Ruchelman, Leonard I. 1984. *The Formulation and Presentation of Alternatives for Public Programs.* Croton-on-Hudson, NY: Policy Studies Associates.

Seidel, Andrew D. 1983. "Producing Usable Research: A Selected Review," *Policy Studies Review* 3:52–56.

Springer, J. Fred. 1985. "Policy Analysis and Organizational Design," *Administration and Society* 16:475–508.

Weiss, Carol H. 1972. *Evaluation Research: Methods of Assessing Program Effectiveness.* Englewood Cliffs, NJ: Prentice-Hall.

———. 1985. "The Many Meanings of Research Utilization," pp. 203–12, in Eleanor Chelimsky, ed., *Program Evaluation: Patterns and Directions.* Washington, DC: American Society for Public Administration.

Weiss, Carol H., with Michael J. Bucuvalas. 1980. *Social Science Research and Decision Making.* New York: Columbia University Press.

4

Structuring Policy Research

Matching Information Needs and Research Activities

Policy research is one aspect of a complex process of policy making and implementation. As contributors to a process that involves multiple organizations and individuals, policy analysts do not exercise independent control over the problems they address. Analysts may establish specializations in a policy area (e.g., environment, housing, criminal justice, health) or in a research methodology (e.g., program evaluation, cost-benefit analysis, survey research), but the policy issues they address are determined in large part by specific needs for information by decision makers.

The ability to respond to information needs of others is a central skill in policy research. Effective response requires analysts to understand what decision makers need to know and to determine research tasks required to meet this need. The previous chapter emphasized ways in which policy analysts interact with stakeholders to improve the use of research products. The following two chapters discuss ways in which analysts structure research tasks to meet information needs. Chapter 4 identifies five types of information needs that require distinctive research approaches. Chapter 5 discusses concepts and techniques policy analysts employ to measure empirical events of interest to stakeholders. Together, these chapters address fundamental skills necessary to clarifying policy problems and to making them amenable to research activities.

Following sections of this chapter present five examples, each representing a distinctive type of information need policy analysts encounter. Subsequent sections examine each of these types of research need in detail. These sections identify (a) the characteristics of each type of information need, (b) research approaches appropriate to addressing each type of need, and (c) the contributions that research on each type of need can make to the policy process. Skills in recognizing and clarifying these distinctive types of needs help policy analysts apply their research skills in ways most responsive to policy concerns.

THE POLICYMAKER'S NEED TO KNOW

In policy research, ways in which data are collected and analyzed follow from information needs; an effective research response is problem focused. Developing an understanding of information needs involves three basic considerations. First, how much is currently known about the issue? Policy research addresses everything from little-understood concerns to detailed refinement of established programs. What information is needed depends on what is already known.

Second, information needs are shaped by the intended uses of the information. What types of problems is the research expected to address? A program evaluation, for example, can be intended for use in budget decisions (should funding for this program be increased or decreased?), for improvement of program practices (are clients satisfied or dissatisfied with current services?), and for numerous other purposes. What information is needed depends on what stakeholders want to do with it.

Third, information needs are shaped by the importance of the issue being addressed. Policy decisions are made in an environment of competing demands on resources. The level of effort allocated to a given research project and the type of information produced by it are tailored to the significance of the concern as perceived by stakeholders. The following discussion demonstrates how different combinations of existing knowledge, problem type, and problem salience produce distinctive information needs for policymakers.

TYPES OF INFORMATION NEED: FIVE EXAMPLES

To apply research skills effectively, policy analysts carefully analyze information needs. This is not a passive activity. Decision makers often understand that they need information more clearly than they understand just what specific information they need. The following examples illustrate five major types of research information commonly needed by stakeholders.

Rural Drug Abuse: An Exploration Problem

A small county in the hills of a coastal state provides an illustrative case of an issue requiring exploratory research information. In the 1940s and 1950s the county had been a ranching and summer resort community that depended on its clear lakes for economic livelihood. The next two decades brought significant changes. The lake country spawned a minor retirement community, and a free way connection in a metropolitan area brought an increase in the numbers of families migrating to the area from the city.

The county remained primarily rural, but county residents were increasingly concerned with social problems that were traditionally urban. For example, church and parent groups began pressuring the county government to respond to the county's drug problems. Fortunately, the state had recently made funds available to rural counties to help identify the scope and extent of drug abuse in their counties and to propose appropriate programs.

The responsibility for writing a proposal for state drug abuse funds fell to the director of the County Health Department, a longtime county employee whose experience was in traditional areas of health inspection and preventative public health. While local public opinion indicated a heightened concern about drugs, the Health Department had no experience in the area and had no documented evidence of just what the county's drug problem was—or even if a drug problem existed.

In order to prepare the proposal for state funds, the directed instructed a policy analyst to conduct a "needs assessment" of the county's drug problems. The charge was broad. The director wanted to know what types of drug problems existed in the county, how serious they were, and what the county might do about them.

The distinguishing characteristic of this policy problem is the lack of prior knowledge concerning drug abuse in the rural county. Local decision makers did not have experience in the area, and there was little local information on the topic. Information and experience were undoubtedly available in urban areas, but their applicability to the local situation was uncertain. As noted by Mayer and Greenwood (1980:51), "Under such circumstances, the only choice open to the investigator is to assume a probing or exploratory approach to the subject." Faced with an exploratory problem, policy analysts formulate research approaches that clarify the nature of the problem, estimate the scope and importance of the problem, and recommend appropriate policy responses.

Who Rides the Bus?: A Description Problem

Public transportation planners in the United States frequently face difficult decisions. Public transit systems, usually buses, play an important part in providing mobility for the elderly, the disabled, the poor, and other transit-dependent persons. However, to make public transit as economically self-sustaining as possible, service must be planned to appeal to a broad segment of the public. Efficient and effective planning of routes and schedules is particularly difficult in less densely populated areas where routes cover large areas and ridership is often low.

Facing large budget deficits, the managers of a regional transit system decided to revise routes and schedules extensively to increase ridership and to respond better to transit-dependent groups. Transit service had not been significantly changed in a decade, a period in which the area had experienced significant population growth in some suburban areas. As a base for planning, transit managers needed information on who currently did or did not ride the bus, and why. The information would provide input to decisions modifying the number, timing, and routing of bus lines.

The responsibilities of the analysts who did the study were straightforward. Transit planners had several specific information requirements. From the agency's records they knew the number of riders, popular routes, and peak hours. However, they did not have specific knowledge of the composition of their ridership: What is the age, gender, occupation, and income of bus riders? Where do they live, where do they board the bus, where do they go on the bus, and how often do they ride? Answers to these questions would provide the base of information that transit planners desired concerning current ridership.

This information requirement has characteristics distinguishing it from the exploratory problem outlined above. In the transit situation, decision makers had sufficient knowledge about the issue they were facing to specify what they needed to know. Analysts needed to collect and present an accurate description of the population served by the transit system. The focus was consequently on quantitative description—accurate numerical estimates of the numbers of riders or nonriders falling in the defined categories. Faced with a descriptive problem, policy analysts formulate a research approach that accurately fulfills specific information requirements about an existing concern such as public transit.

Did Operation Safe Street Reduce Crime?: A Causation Problem

Through the 1980s, St. Louis, Missouri, experienced rapid redevelopment of its riverfront downtown. But the development was uneven. Office and commercial development took the lead, while residential growth lagged. (The city lost more than half its population between 1940 and 1980.) Policy initiatives were consequently formulated to stimulate residential development and to improve the desirability of urban living.

Operation Safe Street was one of these initiatives. It was designed in the mayor's office as a program to strengthen urban neighborhoods and to involve citizens in preventing crime. First, the city offered to install dead-bolts, basement window bars, and other security devices at cost (free to senior citizens). Second, meetings were organized in the neighborhoods to initiate a neighborhood watch program. Third, citizens were encouraged to turn on their porch lights at night. Finally, barricades were erected on selected neighborhood streets to restrict access and cut down on through traffic. The major objective of the program was to reduce neighborhood crime—primarily residential burglary.

The mayor selected nine neighborhoods for a two-year test of Operation Safe Street. Toward the end of the test period and with an election approaching, the mayor asked his staff to gather evidence on the effectiveness of Operation Safe Street. To what extent, if any, did the program cause a reduction in crime in the nine neighborhoods?

Asking whether the program reduced crime requires determining whether the program was responsible for observed changes in crime, or whether other factors were responsible for observed changes. To answer this question, the mayor's staff gathered information on crime rates in the neighborhoods and compared the decreases in the neighborhoods to the continuing escalation of crime in the city as a whole. The fact that the Operation Safe Street neighborhoods experienced decreased crime and the rest of the city did not was cited as evidence that the program caused reductions in crime.

This question introduces the problem of causation, a more complex information need than description. The difficult problems of demonstrating causation are of particular importance to policy analysts involved in evaluating the effects of public policies and programs. Methods for developing evidence on causal questions are discussed later in this chapter and in Chapter 11.

How Many Classrooms?: An Estimation Problem

The number of students enrolled in the public schools of an older city peaked in 1939. As in many older cities, the end of the baby boom generation and changing residential patterns brought steady enrollment declines through the 1960s and 1970s. With the exception of slight increases in 1963 and 1976, total enrollment dropped from 8,510 in 1959 to 6,104 in 1980, a decline of 28 percent. After 1980, enrollment trends continued to decline but in a less consistent pattern.

Appropriate assignment of classrooms in each school, hiring and assignment of teachers, and long-range planning for closing or converting unused facilities depend on how many students will be enrolling at each grade level in future years. As trends in enrollment patterns began to change in the mid-1980s, the school district asked a policy analyst to estimate enrollment patterns through 1990.

The distinguishing characteristic of estimation problems is that they require analysts to use current knowledge to make estimates about future events. Estimation problems in policy analysis are of two major types. First, policymakers require information concerning future needs or opportunities—trends that may require future action. The estimation of future school enrollments is an example of this type of information need.

A second type of estimation problem involves the desired outcomes and effects of policy actions. The central question in this type of estimation is, Will the proposed policy work: will it meet its intended objectives? Policymakers who planned Operation Safe Street would have liked to know how much crime they could expect to deter through the program before going forward. Estimating program effectiveness would involve estimations of the relationship between crime and the neighborhood conditions affected by the program—home security, street lighting, organized neighborhood watch, and traffic patterns. Faced with estimation problems, policy analysts develop procedures to forecast future needs or to predict the effects of policy actions.

What to Do About Solid Waste?: A Choice Problem

A city has experienced difficulty in meeting air quality standards required by the Environmental Protection Agency (EPA). Periodically the EPA has issued requirements that steps be taken to remedy particular sources of serious emissions problems. In one of these actions, the EPA required that the city's two obsolete solid waste incinerators meet emissions standards by a specified date. Failure to meet the requirement could result in a $20,000 daily fine to the city.

The obsolete technology of the thirty-year-old incinerators made it economically infeasible to meet emissions standards at these facilities. Accordingly, the city waste management agency was under pressure to develop alternative methods for disposing of the 650 tons of residential solid waste collected in the city each day. Several months of work in searching for realistic alternatives to the incinerators had produced two feasible alternatives.

One option would simply increase the use of landfills currently used to dispose of incinerated residue or waste that exceeds the capacity of the incinerators. Most communities in the metropolitan region currently use landfills as the means of waste disposal. However, fees charged to use landfills escalated rapidly in recent years and would likely continue to rise. Diminished capacity, as current landfill sites reach capacity, and new requirements to protect the environment from toxic leaks would maintain upward pressure on landfill disposal costs.

The second alternative was a resource recovery system to be constructed and operated by the Bi-State Development Agency, a nonprofit organization that operates the metropolitan transit system. The proposed resource recovery system would incinerate solid waste and use the heat to create steam for the city's downtown steam loop. The steam loop sells steam for heating, cooling, and manufacturing to approximately 250 business and government locations in the downtown area. Currently, the system is fueled entirely by oil. The proposal would reduce the use of expensive oil through construction of new trash-fired boilers. The proposed system would have sufficient capacity to burn the entire amount of residential waste collected by the city.

A member of the planning staff in the city waste management agency was assigned responsibility for analyzing the alternatives and for making a recommendation to the city legislative body. The staff member was presented with a choice problem. Choice problems focus on decisions about whether to undertake specified courses of action or not. Faced with choice problems, policy analysts develop research approaches that (a) clarify the alternative courses of action, (b) identify criteria (standards) for deciding which alternative(s) to choose, (c) compare the alternatives according to the criteria, and (d) recommend a choice.

POLICY RESEARCH AND INFORMATION NEEDS

The situations described above exemplify five types of information need encountered by policy analysts: exploration, description, causation, estimation, and choice. The types are important because they provide research frameworks analysts apply to issues emerging from the policy process. The research frameworks help analysts make decisions about the design of research projects.

If, for example, the decision situation facing an analyst poses an exploratory information need, the appropriate research design is oriented to broad clarification of understanding about the problem. Research tasks emphasize gathering a variety of information reflecting different points of view. Information collection techniques are oriented toward gathering a broad range of information, rather than concentrating resources in data reflecting a focused point of view.

On the other hand, if an information need is primarily descriptive, information collection is more focused. Relevant techniques involve statistical sampling and analysis to produce precise, focused information. Each type of information need carries its own implications for data collection and analysis. Understanding the type(s) of information required by stakeholders helps analysts generate relevant and useful analysis. Following sections discuss the research implications of each type of problem.

EXPLORATORY RESEARCH PROBLEMS

When problems or opportunities first arise in the policy process, they are characterized by a lack of developed knowledge about the nature of the issue, its extent and seriousness, and its causes. This lack of prior knowledge means that initial inquiry is broad, casting a wide net to capture relevant information. The appropriate research approach is exploratory in fulfilling these information needs.

Objectives of Exploratory Research

Making policy is often a process of funneling from broad possibilities to specific options and recommendations. Focusing on details too quickly may misrepresent the nature, scope, and severity of the problem. Exploratory research differs from other types of research problems in eschewing detail for breadth and in the consideration of a broad range of ideas and observations. The operating principle for exploratory problems is to cast a wide net. As Mayer and Greenwood have observed (1980:51): "the objective of the study undertaken at this stage must be primarily that of formulating the basic concepts" relevant to the problem situation.

Consider the exploratory research problem that introduced this chapter. The health administrator was confronted with citizens' perceptions of a drug problem in the county. However, individual citizens in the county viewed this problem in different ways. Some perceived a crime problem related to the selling of drugs and the crime necessary to finance user drug dependency; others were concerned about the moral effects of drugs on youth; still others were concerned specifically about the pervasive use of alcohol in the county. A major initial task for analysts aiding the health administrator was to identify the various ways in which the problem was viewed—to decompose the complex term *drug problem* into its major dimensions.

Once the health administrator had a more refined idea of the various forms that drug abuse problems might take in the county, it would become clearer what information was appropriate to assess the actual degree of these various dimensions of the problem in his county. A second objective of exploratory research is to provide initial indications of the actual occurrence of various dimensions of policy issues. The next section introduces information collection and analysis methods often used in exploratory research. Most of these methods are discussed more fully in following chapters, particularly Chapters 6, 9, and 13.

Appropriate Methods: Cast a Wide Net

Exploratory research tasks are characterized by a relative lack of prior knowledge concerning a problem. In some instances, experiences of other jurisdictions that have confronted the issue provide guidance in formulating ideas. In other situations the lack of experience with the problem is more pervasive; a minimal amount of information is available. In any instance, analysts look for information that provides empirically based clarification of the policy issue.

Several principles are used in conducting exploratory research. Of course, the general principle remains to cast a wide net by gathering information from multiple data sources. A corollary of the need to gather a broad range of information reflecting multiple perspectives is an emphasis on sources that quickly yield relevant information, and on methods for generating a range of ideas on an issue. The following techniques are applied in exploratory research and reflect the requirements of this type of information need.

BRAINSTORMING

Brainstorming refers to open discussions among groups of interested and knowledgeable persons with the objective of identifying multiple perspectives on a policy issue. These discussion sessions for generating ideas vary in composition and in formality of organization. They may be ad hoc meetings of available staff, for example, or organized and scheduled sessions including staff, experts, and affected parties. Analysts for the county health administrator organized short sessions with the administrator, law enforcement representatives, and representatives of clergy and parent groups.

While brainstorming sessions are conducted at varying degrees of formality, an early advocate of the technique set forth basic guidelines for improving the generation of group ideas (Osborne, 1948). Brainstorming is freewheeling; innovative ideas may provide the stimulus for productive new points of view. Participants are encouraged to expand on the comments of others. A record is kept of the ideas generated in the session, and a follow-up session may serve to categorize, screen, and refine suggestions. Brainstorming is useful for expanding the boundaries of problem definition and for suggesting possible problem solutions.

SELECT INTERVIEWS

Interviews with selected individuals involved in an issue are a rich source of current and relevant information. Select interviews are commonly used in exploratory research tasks because they allow analysts to obtain information from strategically located individuals in a short period of time.

The selection of respondents is the key to the breadth and quality of information collected in exploratory research. The operative principle is to identify respondents who reflect a variety of perspectives on the issue. Initial interviews often include program managers, high-level staff, politicians, and experts (e.g., academics, consultants) who can provide a broad perspective on the issue. Contacts are frequently by telephone to save time and resources.

Analysts for the county health administrator conducted initial interviews with the administrator himself and with staff in the state Department of Drug and Alcohol Abuse. Follow-up interviews were conducted with selected physicians working in the community, the county sheriff and a local chief of police, school principals and counselors, major local employers, and local clergy. Techniques for conducting personal interviews are discussed in Chapter 6.

AVAILABLE STUDIES AND RECORDS

The majority of policy issues have been the subject of prior investigations. Analysts in the drug needs assessment carried out a library search to identify books, journal articles, and prior studies concerning drug abuse problems. These sources provided a number of prior conceptualizations of drug problems and provided data on their occurrence in other locations.

In order to maximize the scope of information collected within limited resources, analysts rely heavily on available records, documents, and reports. Government agencies are a rich source of statistical information and records relevant to local problems. Information on components of the rural county's drug problem was gathered from several sources.

Records of admissions to emergency rooms in the two local hospitals provided information on the number of drug-involved cases during the last two years. Relevant data included the seriousness of the crisis, the drugs involved, and the age of the patient. Police arrest records provided data on the number of arrests for sales or possession of drugs; court records indicated convictions. Records in the offices of school principals allowed analysts to determine the prevalence of drug-related incidents in the local schools.

Government agencies are involved in a wide variety of data collection efforts ranging from census data and the monitoring of social conditions to client records kept by specific agencies. These records are a valuable source of available data for exploratory research tasks.

Legal documents are another important source for clarifying the nature of policy issues. Policymakers in the United States system of constitutional government must operate within the areas of discretion allowed them through the rule of law. All government action is bounded by constitutional limits, and many policy decisions must conform with a variety of more specific state and local legal constraints.

A legal review may involve several areas of inquiry, depending on the policy issue. Analysts may need to understand the legislation that enables administrative programs in given policy areas. At more specific implementation levels, analysts may need to be familiar with administrative law regulations that govern decision procedure or substantive decision criteria in a given program. Chapter 9 provides an extended discussion of the analysis of available data.

The preceding discussion identified sources and methods of information collection that typify exploratory research. Next discussed are information products derived from exploratory research.

Exploratory Information Products

Analysts in the drug abuse study presented a written report to the County Board of Supervisors. The report described the ways in which the analysts had gathered information, and presented the findings of their study. The initial section of the report emphasized that drug abuse was a complex issue affecting the lives of county residents in various ways.

The analysts drew upon their review of the literature and the information they had collected in the county to clarify the nature of drug problems. Specifically, they presented a discussion that refined the vague term *drug problem* into three major dimensions: health problems, criminal justice problems, and social problems (Figure 4.1).

To focus discussion and research concerning the drug problem, the analysts identified further subdivisions within each dimension. Health problems were classified as chronic, referring to ongoing health problems attributable to continuous drug use, or as crisis problems, referring to life-threatening situations (e.g., overdose). Criminal justice problems were further designated as sales-related (the illegal trafficking of drugs) and use-related —theft, traffic, or other crime committed by drug users. Finally, social problems were divided into school-related problems and problems of job performance related to drug use.

This part of the report clarified the meaning of the drug problem

FIGURE 4.1 Making Drug Problems More Specific

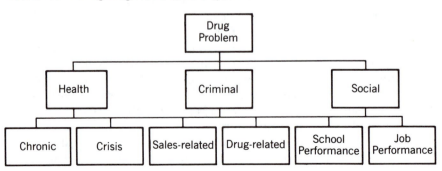

by defining it through more specific terms. While improving the ability to communicate about the problem, the improved specificity also guided analysts in identifying and communicating information pertinent to the problem.

The second major section of the report presented information on the empirical incidence of each problem dimension within the county. Emergency room data, for instance, were presented as an indicator of the extent and nature of life-threatening health crises related to drug use in the county. Interviews with major employers provided an indicator of job performance problems.

While empirical findings had to be presented within the clear constraints of available information and available resources, they did provide a preliminary profile of the drug problem in the county. In brief, the study findings yielded little indication of crime problems related to drug use—in either trafficking or the commission of crime by drug users. Similarly, evidence indicating the use of drugs among school-age children was limited mostly to marijuana use by high schoolers (though this appeared widespread). Employers reported extensive effects of alcohol use on job performance, but saw little explicit linkage to other drugs.

Evidence in the above areas ran counter to the darkest fears of many county citizens. Other findings revealed that physicians perceived problems involving alcohol-drug interaction among the county's citizens—particularly involving prescription drugs among the growing population of retirees. Emergency room data reinforced these interview findings; the majority of drug-related admissions involved alcohol interaction. This written product of the exploratory study provided decision makers with a clearer framework for thinking about programs to address the drug problem in the county and a preliminary empirical indication of the most important dimensions of the problem.

DESCRIPTIVE RESEARCH PROBLEMS

For other policy questions, information needs are specific enough to require precise descriptions of characteristics of large numbers of persons, organizations, or events. Descriptive research is appropriate for these policy questions.

Objectives of Descriptive Research

The objectives of analysts conducting descriptive research are different from those pursued in exploratory research. While exploration provides a basic understanding of issues, description is more focused and involves more precisely determining empirical characteristics of aggregate phenomena to develop a more detailed understanding of problems or solutions. Exploratory analysts select empirical observations for the primary purpose of developing a general understanding of an issue; descriptive analysts use this understanding to guide the collection of precise empirical information.

Descriptive research provides stakeholders with information about widespread phenomena they cannot possibly observe themselves. The characteristics of bus riders, the preferences of a city's residents, the number of unemployed persons in the nation, all require information about large populations that are beyond the ability of any individual or small group of individuals to observe directly. Providing information that accurately represents the true condition of these widespread phenomena is yet another distinction between exploration and description. Exploratory information is based on small numbers of observations from multiple sources; it rarely claims to represent accurately a larger population. Descriptive analysis, in the special meaning of description used here, provides quantitative statements about the condition of large populations. Statistical methods are used in descriptive analysis to specify the accuracy of those statements.

The information needs of transit planners trying to determine who rides the bus exemplify descriptive research tasks. Since they had prior knowledge of transit problems and of what they needed to know to make planning decisions, planners were able to ask analysts to provide specific and well-defined information. For instance, planners knew that demographic characteristics of riders were important for modifying routes to serve better the areas in which their clientele was concentrated. Therefore they specified that they wanted information on the age, gender, occupation, and income of riders.

In fulfilling descriptive research requirements, analysts rely on numbers. In the above example, the objective would be to tell transit planners how many (or what percentage) of their riders fall in each category of demographic description (e.g., specific age ranges), and how many do not. Similarly, analysts would provide counts of the numbers of riders who are males or females, and so on. It is in this sense of counting that the objectives of description are quantitative communications.

Descriptive information provides a basis for generalized descriptions of large numbers of observations. Analysts provide information about the typical characteristics of a large number of observations, e.g., what is the most common destination of bus riders? They may also provide information about the variety in characteristics, e.g., what proportions of bus riders most often go to several different categories of destination? Information on the size and distribution of characteristics in the population of interest (e.g., persons, events, organizations) is a basic objective of descriptive analysis.

Transit planners also requested information about relations or associations between variables. For example, planners asked the analysts to gather information about nonriders as well as riders. This information allowed answers to such questions as, Are area residents over sixty years of age more likely to ride the bus than residents under sixty? Descriptive information provides precise data on, for example, how much more frequently persons over sixty use public buses. Information concerning relations between variables is an important contribution of descriptive research.

Appropriate Methods: Accuracy and Precision

Where the methods of exploratory research are multiperspective, casting a wide net, those of descriptive research are focused and detailed. Methods used in descriptive analysis are oriented to accuracy and precision. (Accuracy and precision refer to the degree of error between findings and the actual empirical events being researched.)

Accuracy incorporates two dimensions—selection of observations and measurement of concepts. While exploratory analysis involves relatively few observations selected from multiple sources, descriptive research involves relatively large numbers of observations selected from carefully defined populations. The transportation analysts were expected to generate information about transit riders. Gathering information from all riders is not feasible—or necessary. Descriptive research is typically based upon a sample of observations (e.g., riders) that represent in important ways the full population. The accuracy with which the sample will represent the entire population depends on size and method of sample selection. Generally, accuracy is improved through larger sample sizes and selection methods that proportionally reflect all segments of the population. Selecting observations to maximize accuracy and precision of findings is discussed in Chapter 7.

Skills in statistics are central to descriptive analysis. The field of sampling statistics provides guidance in the selection of samples and allows analysts to specify the accuracy and precision of their sample findings. Descriptive statistics provide methods for analysts to summarize the characteristics of the members of a sample. These methods may describe the distribution of characteristics in a sample (such as the numbers and percentages of transit riders in differing age-groups), and describe typical characteristics of a sample (such as the average age of transit riders). Statistics also provide a basis for comparing subgroups (e.g., differing age-groups) within a sample, and provide techniques for identifying relationships among variables. Statistical methods are essential tools in descriptive research. (Chapter 10 discusses the uses of descriptive statistics.)

Descriptive Information Products

Descriptive research findings are quantitative and focused. From the transit survey, planners learned the numbers and percentages of riders within specified age ranges, the numbers and percentages who were students, the numbers and percentages who lived within each of the eight communities in their area, and so on. They also learned information based on the association between variables. For example, 80 percent of bus riders under sixty years of age use the bus primarily for commuting purposes (to school or work), while only 12 percent of the riders over sixty use the bus for these purposes. Such information helps planners anticipate changes in ridership as patterns of work, recreation, and residence change, enabling them to make changes responding to the needs of riders.

Many consumers of policy research information are not well versed in statistical methods used in descriptive research. Policy analysts are responsible for clearly communicating the meaning and limitations of the data they report; it is their professional and ethical responsibility to do so. In particular, reports of statistical information should indicate the degree of accuracy and precision of findings and other limitations influencing data quality.

Descriptive findings are also used as a basis for more complex research tasks. They provide information about the larger world that policy is meant to affect. As later sections of this chapter demonstrate, descriptive research often provides basic data necessary to causal, estimation, and choice problems. Providing accurate and precise information about large numbers of observations requires a specific research approach, but the resulting information frequently contributes to more complex research endeavors necessary for making policy decisions.

CAUSAL RESEARCH PROBLEMS

Exploration and description address basic building blocks of knowledge—ideas and observations. But information needs often go beyond basic understandings. Policy-making is designed to bring about change. Deciding what future actions might produce desired change or determining whether past actions have produced desired changes requires information concerning the links between policies designed to produce change and the conditions or events that created the policy issue. The appropriate research approach is causal in these situations.

Objectives of Causal Research

Causal, or explanatory, research involves questions of cause and effect. This type of policy research is important because it increases the possibility of controlling events in order to achieve policy objectives. Descriptive information concerning the growth of lung cancer as a cause of death in the United States provides an indication of the magnitude and urgency of this public health issue, but in itself provides no information concerning what to do about it. Description provides an indication of the need for policy action without indicating what might be done about the problem.

Knowledge of causes provides guidance for developing appropriate policy interventions, a major objective of causal research in policy analysis. The accumulation of research that demonstrates the role of tobacco in caus-ing lung cancer provides a basis for health policy—reducing smoking will reduce lung cancer (and other diseases). Further knowledge about why indi-viduals smoke or do not smoke may provide a basis for developing specific policy initiatives. In recent years, for example, smoking has increased dra-matically among females under twenty-five, while dropping throughout the rest of the population. To develop means of countering this trend, knowl-edge of the reasons for increased smoking among young women (distinct from other groups) may be important. Having information regarding the causes of policy problems is fundamental to successfully doing something about the problems.

A second major objective of causal research is to improve policy through learning from experience. Operation Safe Street was a policy initia-tive based upon certain expectations concerning conditions that contribute to street crime—dark streets, easy access, a lack of neighborhood awareness, and inadequate home security. Action was taken to ameliorate these condi-tions and thereby reduce crime. Once the program has been implemented, policy analysts use causal research to determine whether the actions taken caused a decrease (or increase or no change) in neighborhood crime, and use findings to recommend improved responses to the problem. Given the uncertainty of much knowledge about policy effects, evaluation of program impacts is an important part of the policy process.

Appropriate Methods: Controlled Comparisons

Operation Safe Street was based on the belief that easy access, poor lighting, nonsurveillance, and poor home security are causes of neighbor-hood crime. Improvement in these neighborhood conditions would be ex-pected to cause reductions in crime. An important objective of causal analy-sis is to help produce empirically substantiated information regarding the impact of policy initiatives.

A challenge confronting analysts conducting causal research is that policy problems tend to stem from multiple causes. Multiple causes compli-cate analysis because it is difficult to determine how much change in pro-gram recipients is caused by the specific actions taken in a program. If resi-dential burglaries decline in Operation Safe Street neighborhoods, the decline cannot automatically be attributed to the program. Faced with situa-tions of complex causation, analysts identify additional factors that may ac-count for changes in the conditions a policy is intended to affect. For Oper-ation Safe Street, possible alternative causes could include changes in law enforcement practices, changes in economic conditions, demographic changes in the neighborhood, and so forth.

Another challenge in establishing causes stems from the importance of the context in which particular causal links occur. An apple seed causes an apple tree to grow only under a limited range of conditions—soil, light, temperature, and moisture. Similarly, specific programs may be effective in some contexts but not in others. The stability of neighborhoods, for example, may be critical to determining whether Operation Safe Street produces its desired effects. The identification of the conditions under which causal links will hold is important if analysts are to determine the degree to which causal findings apply to similar problems in other jurisdictions.

The preceding discussion introduced conceptual and empirical challenges confronting analysts addressing causal questions. In policy research, the interest in policy evaluation has spurred advances devoted to analyzing empirical evidence of causal relations between programmatic initiatives and programmatic outcomes. A prominent strategy has been to adapt quantitative, experimental approaches in evaluating ongoing programs (Campbell and Stanley, 1966).

Three major types of experimental designs are true experiments, quasi-experiments and pre-experiments. True experiments are the most powerful of the three in evaluating program effects, and are characterized by the use of controlled comparisons to assess changes in experimental and control groups.

Designs often used in evaluating program effectiveness are quasi-experimental designs. These designs only approximate the ideal of controlled comparisons. Operation Safe Street provides an example of the principles and limitations of quasi-experimental approaches. Two years after the program was implemented, the program director released statistics that displayed the numbers of residential burglaries in the program neighborhoods. The statistics showed a downward trend in burglaries. This information was favorable to the Operation Safe Street program, but was inconclusive without also knowing the effects of nonprogram factors (such as a general decline in crime, increased law enforcement effort, and so forth) on this trend.

To address this possibility, the office released statistics demonstrating that city neighborhoods outside of the program did not experience a comparable decline in residential burglary. This data did increase confidence that the program was effective but still could not claim to be conclusive. The program analysts could not control which neighborhoods received the program and which did not. As a result, it was possible that the comparison neighborhoods were systematically different from the program neighborhoods. It was possible, for instance, that Operation Safe Street neighborhoods shared characteristics other than the program that led to the decrease in crime, and that these characteristics were not present in the comparison neighborhoods. Chapter 11 discusses experimental methods in detail; the following section discusses causal information products.

Causal Information Products

Information on causal relations makes essential contributions to decision making. Policy actions seek to produce changes in existing conditions, either to ameliorate problems or to take advantage of opportunities to improve. In either case, the ability to intervene successfully often depends upon knowing the conditions or events producing the problem and knowing in what ways public action can assist in resolving such problems.

In addition to being an important component of the process of developing future policy actions, causal research is a central component in learning about the successes and failures of prior policy initiatives. The impetus for formal evaluation studies began at the federal level (Patton, 1982:22), but has become a standard requirement at federal, state, and local levels. Indeed, evaluation studies that assess whether policy actions have caused their intended results have become an institutional part of organizational life.

Because of the implications of their findings, evaluation studies become controversial. Program staff and clientele worry that study findings will threaten continued support of programs they firmly believe in or which bring them benefits. The complexity of establishing causal findings also makes findings of causal analysis controversial. The tobacco industry has argued for decades that evidence linking smoking to widespread health problems is not scientifically certain. At the level of program evaluations, reviews of current practice often reveal examples in which study findings are challenged because critics argue that study design is inadequate (Springer and Phillips, 1988:105). In sum, the information products of causal research may be particular targets of controversy by competing stakeholders in the policy process.

ESTIMATION RESEARCH PROBLEMS

The only factual basis for knowledge is what has already happened, yet policy actions are designed to affect future events. Even when policy-making is reactive—responding to present problems—the intents of decision making are oriented to the future. While decision makers have clear uses for knowledge concerning future events, analysts have no direct evidence about them. Estimation problems involve the central task of determining the degree to which past knowledge provides an accurate and useful guide to future events.

Estimation Research Objectives

Policymakers have two kinds of questions about the future. The first concerns future needs for policy decisions: What will happen if no action is taken with respect to a particular policy issue? The second concerns future impacts of possible policy actions: What will be the effect of policy X on a particular policy issue? The similarity in these objectives is that they focus on events that have not yet occurred.

The need of a school district to project future student enrollment provides an example of both types of need. By district policy, principals are to ensure that certain standards—such as a maximum class size of thirty pupils in grades K–5—are followed in delivering this education. To anticipate future needs for teachers, numbers of classes, and other managerial decisions, the district wants estimates of future need, e.g., estimated numbers of students at each grade level.

Table 4.1 provides a sample projection of future needs for education services in a medium-sized city. The table displays enrollment for different grade categories from 1984 through 1988 and projects enrollment through 1994. These estimates provide a basis for calculating the results of a no-action alternative. For example, analysts can calculate average class size for each grade grouping, given current teacher strength with no attrition, hiring, or reallocation. The results of this calculation indicate areas in which action is necessary to maintain minimum standards, achieve equity in service delivery, or improve efficiency.

The student enrollment projections provide a straightforward basis for estimating the future effects of policy decisions. The district can, for example, estimate the effects of a no-hire policy (allowing a reduction in teachers through normal retirements and resignations) on the ratio of stu-

TABLE 4.1   Projected Enrollment, City School District

	K THROUGH 2	3 THROUGH 5	6 THROUGH 8	9 THROUGH 12
1984	6,104	2,820	1,465	1,819
1985	5,961	2,680	1,474	1,804
1986	5,627	2,412	1,482	1,733
1987	5,386	2,288	1,375	1,723
1988	5,250	2,252	1,294	1,704
PROJECTED				
1989	5,120	2,226	1,137	1,757
1990	4,970	2,207	1,067	1,696
1991	4,833	2,214	1,005	1,614
1992	4,671	2,224	972	1,475
1993	4,526	2,213	966	1,347
1994	4,439	2,211	973	1,255

dents to teachers. In many instances, however, estimating the future effects of policy actions is more difficult. Sometimes accurate historical information which provides a basis for making projections is not available. In other instances, complex policy objectives, such as intentions to improve behavior or social conditions, make the estimation of policy effects more difficult. If the school district wanted to estimate the effects of reduced class size on achievement test scores, for example, the estimation of effects would be more difficult and projections less certain.

Appropriate Methods: Stability and Change

Estimation involves the analysis of change over time. To estimate patterns of future change, analysts draw on the products and techniques of exploration, description, and causation as means of projecting past experience into future expectations. The precise method of estimation depends upon information objectives, existing knowledge and information concerning the issue, and available time and resources. Techniques of estimation can be grouped into three major areas: forecasting, modeling, and expert intuition.

FORECASTING

Forecasting techniques estimate future conditions based on information about past conditions and trends. Student enrollment projections provide an example; future enrollment in City School District was estimated by forecasting past patterns of enrollment into the future and adjusting forecasts in the higher grades to reflect past patterns of attrition or growth. Forecasts are descriptions of the past that are assumed to hold for the future. The accuracy of that assumption is the key to their usefulness as a decision resource.

A simple form of forecast is the "straight line" projection. Figure 4.2 displays a hypothetical projection of future population based upon past trends in Sun City. In this case, the consistency of the population rise since 1950 adds confidence to the utility of a straight-line projection.

The straight-line technique is straightforward and appealing, but its use is only justified if the past trend is essentially straight. In many instances, past trends may show cyclical fluctuations, significant increases or decreases in the rate of change. In these cases, straight-line projections may not produce accurate estimations of future conditions because the established pattern of change is not straight line.

As long as there is some regularity in the past pattern, however, other mathematical techniques are used to improve estimation. A historically regular cyclical pattern, for instance, is mathematically described and projected into the future. The less regular (i.e., the more random) the pattern

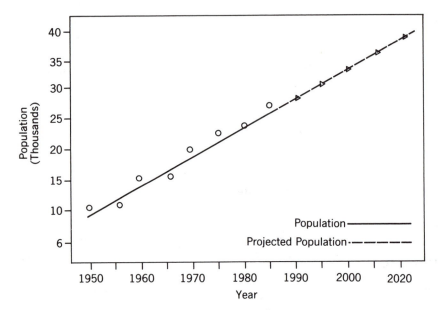

FIGURE 4.2 Projected Population Increase in Sun City: 1950–2020

of historical change, the less confidence one has in the accuracy of the estimate.

The ingenuity of analysts is instrumental in identifying techniques to
forecast for particular information needs. The value of any forecast, however, depends on adequate past description—accurate and precise data on
past trends in relevant indicators. In forecasts, the analyst is also sensitive
to changing events or new conditions that may interrupt the persistence of
trends, even if they have been stable in the past.

MODELING

Forecasts are well suited to providing information about future needs
that are a projection of existing trends—an extension of the past into the
future. However, decision makers are often interested in taking action that
will change future events—that will intervene in the simple extension of
the past into the future. To provide estimates of the future effects of policy
actions, policy analysts construct models allowing decision makers to anticipate the results of actions they may take.

Models are simplifications of reality that make relatively specific
(often mathematical) statements about the interrelationships between a limited set of elements of the real world. "A model is nothing more than in-

formed speculation about . . . behavior of some system whether human or nonhuman" (Patton and Sawicki, 1986:206). Of course, this speculation may be based on varying degrees of understanding and precision. Models are formulated in a great variety of ways, with varying degrees of rigor.

Study of career criminal programs has demonstrated that many of them are based on a behavioral model of offenders. This model might be verbally stated in the following way. "Offenders who have been convicted of serious crime in the past are more likely to commit new serious crimes than those who have no past convictions." The implication for action is to prosecute past offenders more vigorously, thereby preventing them from committing future crimes.

The model can be made more complex and precise in a variety of ways. Specific probabilities of committing new crimes may be specified, giving greater precision to the "more likely" relation stated in the verbal model. More predictive factors, e.g., age of the offender, may be added to improve the precision of the model. In any case, the value of the model as a predictive device for prosecution decisions will depend on the degree to which the model accurately represents real-world behavior.

Other more rigorous models are applied to policy problems. They come in a variety of forms.

- Statistical models provide mathematical statements of the probabilistic relations between factors included in the model.
- Simulations provide models of the interrelations among complex systems of variables. They allow estimation of the outcomes produced by changes in input variables to complex dynamic systems.
- Decision trees display the probability of different outcomes following a decision point. They are useful for estimating the probable outcomes of lengthy sequences of decisions.

Comprehensive discussions of the variety of approaches to modeling for purposes of estimation are available (Gass and Sisson, 1974; Crenson and Crissey, 1976). However, some generalizations can be made about estimation models.

Models are simplifications of reality; they are not reality itself. As in any simplification, models reflect one or a few perspectives on an issue. While they provide valuable information, experienced decision makers critically assess the assumptions and perspectives that underlie them. The fact that a model or any forecasting technique can produce a precise estimate of future conditions (e.g., a 4.8 percent rate of inflation in the next year) does not guarantee that the estimate will be accurate (the actual rate of inflation may be 7.2 percent).

EXPERT INTUITION

Inadequate historical data bases, a lack of understanding about future events, limited time, and limited resources combine to make intuitive forecasting techniques "the ones most often employed in policy analysis" (Patton and Sawicki, 1986:220). Intuitive techniques rely on the expertise and judgment of knowledgeable individuals to estimate future conditions. In its most basic application, intuitive forecasting involves interviews with persons knowledgeable about the issue. Analysts who must quickly develop an estimate of the impact of a new compensation policy on office productivity, for example, may conduct telephone inquiries to discover perceptions of personnel officers who have experience with the policy.

More rigorous (and resource-consuming) approaches to intuitive forecasting have been developed. One of the most widely used approaches is the *Delphi* technique developed at the Rand Corporation and named after the Greek oracle. In its most rigorous form, the technique uses questionnaires to survey the opinions of a panel of anonymous experts concerning future developments in their area of expertise. Through several rounds, survey responses are aggregated and returned to participants. After considering the aggregate opinions, participants are asked if they want to modify their own judgments. The objective of a Delphi study is to arrive at a consensual estimate within the anonymous panel. While the technique is applied in a variety of ways, the principles of expertise, anonymity, and several iterations of feedback provide useful guides in developing intuitive estimations (Dunn, 1981:196–202).

Scenario writing provides another intuitive approach to estimating future conditions. For example, knowledgeable persons may be asked to create freeform and innovative visions of possible conditions at some time in the future. The census departments has used scenarios of this type to generate creative and innovative ideas concerning future agency activities (Dunn, 1981:129). In other applications the exercise is more focused on desired future conditions. In this case, scenarios are oriented to identifying step-by-step sequences through which future conditions might be created from present realities. "The scenario especially lends itself to estimation requirements in that it usually relies on a verbal (and hence accessible), tentative (and hence alterable), and future-oriented (and hence policy-relevant) depiction of . . . both likely and desired future possibilities" (Brewer and de-Leon, 1983:153).

Estimation Information Products

Policy analysts produce a variety of responses to policymakers' need to know about future events. In some instances, estimation is an integral part of institutionalized data collection and analysis. Local planning agencies regularly provide forecasts of population growth, housing need, needs for public services, and so forth. Federal agencies produce forecasts of population shifts and use models to issue regular reports concerning the future of the nation's economy. Anticipating future needs is an institutionalized activity in established areas of government policy.

Government will occasionally seek creative estimation projects that anticipate emerging new areas of policy concern or generate creative new opportunities for public action. These types of activity rely less on precise historical data and analysis, and more on intuitive techniques.

The most common uses of estimation are those that accompany decisions policymakers encounter on a frequent basis. How many first grade teachers will be needed next year? What will be the effects of a 5 percent hike in the downtown sales tax? How much revenue will be generated by a new downtown parking lot? While the concerns that generate these questions do not necessarily generate fully researched estimation studies, they do benefit from the application of relevant estimation methods.

QUESTIONS OF CHOICE

The most precise and accurate understanding of the future consequences of policy actions cannot dictate whether the action should be taken or not. To act or not is a choice, and choices depend on intent—on what stakeholders are trying to achieve. Indeed, increased knowledge about the results of actions "actually forces man to become a moral agent by providing him with the capacity to produce change deliberately, thereby forcing him to choose, to select one of a number of possible and foreseeable options" (Meehan, 1981:20). Choices are not necessarily reasoned; students of organizational decisions have documented the ambiguous and fortuitous nature of many decisions (March and Olsen, 1979). But when choices are reasoned, they involve the systematic consideration of alternatives in the light of stated criteria.

Objectives of Choice Analysis

It is tempting to suggest that the major objectives of analysts facing a choice situation is to recommend the best or the most correct decision. This is an inappropriate objective because it presumes that the meaning of *best* or *correct* is shared and self-evident. Prior discussions of the policy process and the multiple stakeholders that influence it make it clear that no single conception of what is best exists.

Informed decisions require accurate and relevant information, and the discussion of prior types of information need emphasized the role of policy analysts in producing quality information relevant to each need.

Quality information for choice analysis means that "the decision maker will be able to weigh the consequences of changes in assumptions, values, and uncertainties and come to an independent decision" (Patton and Sawicki, 1986:13).

Analysts confronting choice problems initially identify criteria that express human intentions with respect to the policy question. The process involves identifying the values and objectives that stakeholders pursue in making the policy decision. It incorporates utilization skills identified in Chapter 3, and often involves articulating multiple values and objectives.

Decision criteria are often stated in abstract terms, applying to the broad range of policy actions. These criteria reflect values that largely transcend specific situations and are held by some as basic standards underlying choice. Efficiency, equality, effectiveness, and adequacy are examples discussed in Chapter 2.

Two tasks confront the analyst in articulating these criteria in specific decision situations. First, each criterion is specified within the context of a particular policy problem (e.g., what exact changes in the criterion will indicate effectiveness). Facilitating choice at this level often involves dialogue with stakeholders in specifying policy objectives.

Second, these criteria are often mutually contradictory in specific problem situations; maximizing one means settling for lower levels of another. Facilitating choice at this level often involves helping decision makers set priorities for competing criteria (what intentions take precedence over others). Additional tasks associated with researching choice questions involve selecting appropriate methods, discussed in the following section, for making comparisons among alternatives.

Appropriate Methods: Precision or Elaboration

Several techniques for making comparisons among decision alternatives have been developed and applied by policy analysts. These techniques reflect decisions about the kind of choice-related information wanted. First, decision makers would like precise empirical indicators concerning the criteria they consider relevant. Did the program work? Is the policy efficient? Second, decision makers often want to make decisions according to multiple concerns and objectives.

The desire for precise, concrete data and the desire for information on complex, multiple criteria are often not easy to resolve. This discussion focuses on approaches to facilitating choices that demonstrate the tension between these aspects of choice information, that is, precision or elaboration.

Cost-benefit analysis and its variants are examples of techniques designed to reduce comparisons of policy alternatives to a single criterion. The idea is appealing. All policies entail costs. These costs are undertaken because they are expected to accomplish the intents of decision makers—to provide benefits. If costs exceed benefits in a given policy proposal, the logic goes, implementing the policy will result in a net loss to the public.

With respect to policy alternatives, the logic of cost-benefit analysis yields an approach to developing a single precise criterion for deciding which alternative to choose. Policy analysts calculate the dollar value of the benefits of each policy alternative; then calculate the dollar costs of each alternative. That alternative with the greatest surplus of the value of benefits over costs is most cost effective.

Cost-benefit approaches offer a concrete response to the objectives of choice information—to specify criteria (net benefit), to relate information to criteria (dollar value), and to communicate findings in a manner clearly related to criteria (value of benefits minus value of costs). Nevertheless, cost-benefit approaches have been controversial.

> The appeal of cost-benefit analysis, and one of the major reasons for its unintentional as well as intentional misuse, lies in the simplicity of the concept of comparing gains and losses. . . . The difficulty comes in the application . . . to large-scale government projects whose costs and benefits are seldom clear to the evaluators or the interested public. (Sylvia, Meier, and Gunn, 1985:47)

The identification of specific costs and benefits is a highly subjective process, particularly in evaluating complex social policies. Should the analyst charged with comparing the solid waste disposal alternatives consider potential environmental damage as a cost? The answer depends on values—the orientations and perspectives of decision makers. Chapter 12 provides a detailed discussion of cost-benefit techniques.

Recognizing the limitations of reducing complex choice problems to a single criterion such as cost benefit, analysts have developed approaches to help decision makers compare alternatives using multiple criteria. Typically, these approaches incorporate matrix systems to display the assessment of each alternative according to each of the relevant criteria. The *Goeller Scorecard* (Patton and Sawichi, 1986:276) provides one means of summarizing alternatives according to selected criteria. It provides a summary of the evidence for comparison and a priority indication for alternatives on each criterion. Aggregating this information into a choice and weighing the importance of criteria are left to the decision maker.

Figure 4.3 provides a hypothetical application of the technique to several alternative policies for reducing prison populations. In this application, the choice made by policy makers depends on the relative value placed on different criteria. A decision maker concerned most about control of crime, for example, would select "intensive probation" even though it is relatively costly.

Other matrix methods have been developed to quantify the assess-

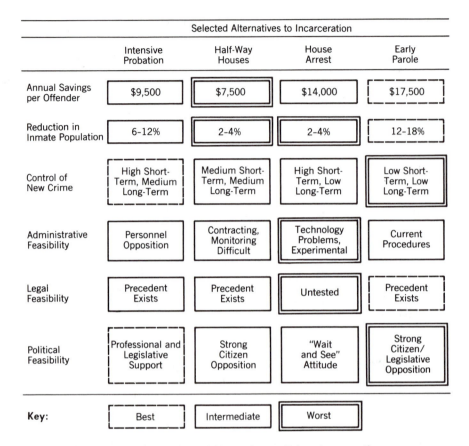

FIGURE 4.3 Scorecard Comparison of Alternatives to Prison Incarceration

ment of alternatives based on multiple criteria. The most rigorous employ weighting systems to quantify the relative importance of each criterion, thus allowing a single score to be calculated for each option. These approaches are useful if there is consensus on the relative importance of different criteria, if accurate data are available, and if resources are available for extensive research and analysis.

Choice Information Products

The products of choice analysis provide clarification of the values and intentions underlying a policy initiative and provide a method for comparing and choosing alternatives through the use of specified criteria. The ways in which these objectives are achieved vary in the degree of focus, quantification, and rigor.

The products of choice analysis are used as tools of communication, debate, and selection of alternatives in the policy-making community. Consequently, the products of choice analysis need to be clearly communicated and must include indications of their accuracy and usefulness.

> All analyses contain uncertainties and unintended side effects, and even broadly supported alternatives may not be implemented as expected. These possibilities must be explained to the client. No matter how careful and diligent the analyst is, errors in prediction will occur, new information will be discovered late in the analytical process, participants will change positions and so on. Analyses must therefore be recycled as new data become available. (Patton and Sawicki, 1986:295)

CONCLUDING COMMENTS

The five types of research problems introduced in this chapter suggest the variety of information needs arising in the policy process. The role of analysts is to respond to those needs with the purpose of improving the basis for informed decisions. Effective policy research requires the ability to categorize information needs so that appropriate research strategies are adopted. This chapter identified five distinctive types of information needs: exploration, description, causation, estimation, and choice. The five categories of information need provide a guide for breaking decision situations into research frameworks and research approaches.

Different information needs may predominate at each phase of the policy process identified in Chapter 2—stimulation, clarification, initiation, implementation, and evaluation. Indeed, Mayer and Greenwood (1980:57) observe that the nature of information needs

> characteristically varies with the stages of policymaking. Thus, in the early stages of the process, knowledge about the policy problem is invariably much less than it is in the later stages. As a consequence, there is a tendency for the [types of information need] to be associated with particular stages of policymaking.

However, no single type of research fully meets the information needs of a decision situation. Instead, information needs identified for each stage will typically involve multiple types of information.

Identifying the information needs most important to a given policy issue, and planning research and analysis activities most appropriate to meeting this combination of needs are fundamental skills of policy analysts. The combination of information needs identified in a decision situation provides a link between policy decisions and the data collection and interpretation techniques discussed in subsequent chapters.

REFERENCES

Brewer, Gary D., and Peter deLeon. 1983. *The Foundations of Policy Analysis.* Homewood, IL: Dorsey Press.

Campbell, Donald T., and Julian C. Stanley. 1966. *Experimental and Quasi-Experimental Designs for Research.* Chicago: Rand McNally.

Crenson, Matthew A., and Brian L. Crissey. 1976. *Models in the Policy Process.* New York: Russell Sage.

Dunn, William N. 1981. *Public Policy Analysis: An Introduction.* Englewood Cliffs, NJ: Prentice-Hall.

Gass, Saul I., and Roger L. Sisson, eds. 1974. *A Guide to Models in Governmental Planning and Operations.* Washington, DC: Office of Research and Development, Environmental Protection Agency.

March, James G., and Johan P. Olsen, with Soren Christensen, Michael D. Cohen, Harold Enderud, Kristian Kreiner, Pierre Romelaer, Kåre Rommetviet, Per Stava, and Stephen S. Weiner. 1979. *Ambiguity and Choice in Organizations.* Bergen, Norway: Universitiesforlaget.

Mayer, Robert R., and Ernest Greenwood. 1980. *The Design of Social Policy Research.* Englewood Cliffs, NJ: Prentice-Hall.

Meehan, Eugene J. 1981. *Reasoned Argument in Social Science: Linking Research to Policy.* Westport, CT: Greenwood Press.

Osborn, Alex F. 1948. *Your Creative Power.* New York: Charles Scribner.

Patton, Carl V., and David S. Sawicki. 1986. *Basic Methods of Policy Analysis and Planning.* Englewood Cliffs, NJ: Prentice-Hall.

Patton, Michael Quinn. 1982. *Practical Evaluation.* Beverly Hills, CA: Sage Publications.

Springer, J. Fred, and Joel L. Phillips. 1988. "Evaluating Drug Abuse Prevention: Current Directions," in A. M. Mecca, ed., *Prevention 2000: A Public/Private Partnership.* San Rafael, CA: California Health Research Foundation.

Sylvia, Ronald D., Kenneth J. Meier, and Elizabeth M. Gunn. 1985. *Program Planning and Evaluation for the Public Manager.* Monterey, CA: Brooks/Cole Publishing.

5

Measurement Strategies
Linking Concepts to Events

Newspaper stories regularly inform the American public of the health of national and regional economies. A standard piece of information conveyed in these stories—often in the headlines—is the unemployment rate. Recently a metropolitan newspaper reported unemployment in the metropolitan area at 6.2 percent, a rise of .3 percent from the prior month. The story expressed concern that the area's economy was not rebounding as quickly as other urban areas.

This commonplace story is one example of the need to measure concepts in public policy. The unemployment rate is a measure of the availability of jobs in an economy, one of many measures of economic health. The unemployment rate is a measure in the sense it provides a means of linking a concept—job availability—to real-world events.

While seemingly straightforward, the unemployment rate demonstrates the complexity of measuring concepts related to public policy. For example, the unemployment rate is criticized for the way in which it empirically defines the unemployed. Persons who have not worked in the week prior to being surveyed and who had not made specific efforts to find work during the preceding four-week period (e.g., registering at a private or public employment agency) are termed not in the labor force. These "discouraged workers" are not counted as unemployed. Critics argue that the result-ing unemployment rate underestimates true unemployment in the work force.

As with most measures of policy-related concepts, the unemployment rate has different meanings to different people. Some see the rate as an indicator of human tragedy—unpaid mortgages, broken homes, lowered self-esteem. Others see it as an inevitable consequence of a free-market economy—one that cannot be reduced too far without undesirable conse-quences such as increased inflation. Still others see the unemployment rate as an indication of the extent of their own job opportunities. The fact that concrete events such as the unemployment rate are interpreted differently according to individual values and interests is a fundamental concern of analysts defining policy concepts.

Developing adequate measures of policy-related concepts is conse-quently a challenging task. Accurate measures may have to be technically complicated; appropriate information sources may be unavailable. Policy participants with differing values and differing concerns will not agree on what a concept really means and how it is best measured.

Nevertheless, measurement is a critical part of policy research. For the policy analyst, developing measurement strategies is a continuation of the processes of refining research tasks and clarifying concepts. Specifying what concepts are to be measured—whether unemployment or drug abuse—comes before deciding how such concepts are to be measured. Measure-ment procedures guide analysts in the "how" of producing dependable and relevant information for decision making.

This chapter discusses measurement from a variety of perspectives. First, the links between concepts and measures are considered. Second, spe-cific types of measures are discussed. Finally, approaches to improving the accuracy and usefulness of measures in policy research are presented. The following case study demonstrates the role of measurement in one policy area.

DEFINING THE DEVELOPMENTALLY DISABLED: A CASE STUDY IN MEASUREMENT

Most citizens are familiar with one or more of the multiple social programs characterizing the growth of the American welfare state. This illustration relates federal attempts to develop acceptable measurement procedures for determining eligibility for public assistance to the developmentally dis-abled.

The 1963 Mental Retardation Facilities and Community Mental Health Centers Construction Act (P.L. 88-164) initiated federal action on the care and treatment of the developmentally disabled. Sponsors of the act recognized that given the broad range of disabling conditions affecting this population, services were required from a network of agencies and professionals. In ensuing years, amendments to the legislation sought to improve and refine service delivery to those who had been disabled through conditions preventing typical mental or physical maturation.

A key concern of the amending legislation has been to clarify the population of clients, that is, who should have the right to public assistance in obtaining services related to developmental disability? Through the sixties and seventies, Congress defined this population by specifying diagnosable medical conditions that inhibit development, e.g., cerebral palsy, epilepsy, autism, dyslexia, and neurological conditions related to mental retardation. This approach sought to define the concept the developmentally disabled by using medical measures.

With the growing political awareness of disabled persons and allied groups during the 1970s, the medical approach to defining the developmentally disabled came under criticism. Studies commissioned by the Department of Health, Education and Welfare (now Health and Human Services) demonstrated that such a narrow definition allowed significant numbers of persons needing services to be denied services because they did not manifest the recognized medical conditions. A victim of child abuse, for instance, may sustain trauma that interrupts mental or physical development, or both. This person may be in need of services available to the developmentally disabled yet be ineligible for federal assistance because medical criteria were not satisfied.

In essence, advocates of improved services to the developmentally disabled perceived a problem of measurement—what specific observable attributes should qualify a person as developmentally disabled? The medical approach, they believed, was narrow: it classified many persons in need of services as ineligible. In response to these criticisms, the 1978 amendments to the Developmentally Disabled Assistance and Bill of Rights Act modified the meaning and definition of the concept developmentally disabled. Congress discarded the traditional medical approach and substituted a functional definition. Eligibility for federal assistance was now based on a person's limitations in performing designated life activities, whether or not that person met diagnosed medical measures. The new federal definition of developmental disability follows:

1. It is attributable to mental or physical impairment or a combination of mental and physical impairments;
2. It is manifested before the person attains age 22;
3. It is likely to continue indefinitely;
4. It results in substantial functional limitations in three or more of the following areas of major life activity:
    a. Self-care,

    b. Receptive and expressive language,
    c. Learning,
    d. Mobility,
    e. Self-direction,
    f. Capacity for independent living,
    g. Economic self-sufficiency; and
5. It reflects the person's need for a combination and sequence of special, interdisciplinary, or generic care, or treatment of extended duration which are individually planned and coordinated.

The changed definition of the concept developmentally disabled had important consequences for disabled persons, implementing agencies, and taxpayers. Persons previously ineligible for federal assistance were now eligible under the new definition. How many were unknown, since Congress had mandated the new definition without estimates of the increased eligibility for services and without estimates of the increased costs to taxpayers.

Administratively, no specific measures for assessing the eligibility of potential recipients existed under the new definition. Current intake forms, service applications, and other procedures and policies applied by agency employees for measuring eligibility reflected the prior medically oriented definition; the new law made that definition obsolete. If state agencies wanted to continue to qualify for federal grants-in-aid for developmental disability programs, they had to create new procedures and forms to measure accurately which citizens were entitled to assistance, using the new functional definition as a guide.

From the viewpoint of agency officials, the change in eligibility measures was seen as an administrative and organizational issue; for the disabled as a moral and political issue; for the citizenry as a moral, social, and financial issue; but from the viewpoint of analysts, developing appropriate indicators of the concept developmentally disabled was a measurement issue. How can accurate and relevant measures of the term developmentally disabled be developed for specifying which citizens qualify within the modified definition passed by Congress?

This was not an easy question, but some things were clear. State agencies could no longer use medical measures then in place, e.g., a physician's diagnosis of cerebral palsy. These measurement criteria would systematically deny services to persons falling within the definition and intent of the new legislation, and would result in an irrelevant measure of eligibility under the new definition.

Equally clear, it would be unacceptable to allow individual case workers to exercise undue discretion concerning whether applicants qualify for services under the changed meaning of developmental disability. A person found eligible by one case worker might be denied services by another. In the absence of agreed-upon and uniformly applied indicators of who constitutes the developmentally disabled, inconsistent, inaccurate measures of who qualifies for service would result.

The case demonstrates that measuring concepts such as developmentally disabled in policy research is fluid, subject to change. A concept's substance is shaped and reshaped through the interplay of political, social, organizational, and individual influences. The new federal definition of developmental disability also represents a common measurement problem. The ideas expressed in the definition are not specific, well defined, concrete. Further, the ideas are subtle and multifaceted. They are not reducible to a single empirical indicator that would be fair and adequate to all concerned individuals and groups. The remainder of this chapter clarifies major tasks involved in defining and measuring complex concepts in policy research, and suggests strategies for improving measurement quality.

COMPONENTS OF THE MEASUREMENT PROCESS

Measurement in policy research provides procedures designed to match concepts such as developmentally disabled to their observable (empirical) roots. Empirical measurement represents the attempt to merge ideas with their real-world counterparts. Developing working definitions is an initial phase in the measurement process.

Working Definitions

The new federal definition of developmental disability represents a typical measurement concern in policy research. The ideas expressed in the definition are not precise. For example, key aspects of the concept developmentally disabled, such as "substantial functional limitations" are not further specified through real-world indicators of their existence. Yet developing working definitions requires the analyst to identify concrete, replicable, empirical references for what is meant by "substantial functional limitations." Only then can legislative intent be clearly related to the life circumstances of individuals. Working definitions tell analysts the empirical meanings of a concept, serving as a manual of instructions in collecting real-world observations.

The significance of working definitions cannot be overemphasized. Research, though often not viewed as such, is a process of communication. When concepts such as developmental disability and substantial functional limitations are subject to multiple interpretations, communication becomes clogged. Analysts strive to improve communication through a clarity of

TABLE 5.1   Concept: Police Effectiveness

DIMENSION	INDICATORS
Prevention of Crime	Reported crime rates, by type of crime
	Percentage of households and businesses victimized
	Number of physical casualties in crime-related police work
	Dollar property loss from crimes for households and businesses
Apprehension of Offenders	Percentage of reported crimes solved, by type of crime
	Percentage of arrests surviving preliminary court hearing and percentage dropped for police-related reasons, by type of crime
	Percentage of arrests resulting in conviction or treatment, by type of crime (effectiveness of arrest)
	Percentage of cases cleared in less than "x" time, by type of crime
	Percentage of stolen property recovered.

Source: Harry Hatry et al., *How Effective Are Your Community Services?* (Washington, DC: The Urban Institute, 1977), 86. © 1977 The Urban Institute. Reproduced by permission.

meaning exceeding that called for in everyday discourse, attempting to convey what is meant with sufficient precision so that users from diverse backgrounds and perspectives understand how key concepts are defined and viewed.

Working definitions are constructed on the basis of observable properties and characteristics of people or things. Assume, for purposes of illustration, analysts in a city police department have been asked to evaluate the effectiveness of a department's performance in two areas: the prevention of crime and the apprehension of criminals. An initial measurement task includes the development of indicators specifying the meaning of departmental effectiveness in these two areas or dimensions of the concept. Sources for creating these indicators include discussions with potential users of the resulting information and with experts in the field; reviews of related documents and research reports; and personal experience and observations. Table 5.1 displays sample indicators of policy performance in crime prevention and in apprehending offenders (Hatry et al., 1977:86).

Table 5.1 also illustrates that dimensions of concepts such as the prevention of crime are frequently measured through multiple and overlapping indicators. When combined for purposes of analysis, multiple indicators provide a more complete, accurate, and in-depth portrait of a complex dimension of a concept like crime prevention. Multiple indicators enable analysts to explore its varying aspects and in the process ensure increased coverage of important dimensions of a complex concept.

Working definitions are limited in scope, serving as only partial indicators of concepts. Kerlinger (1973:32) comments:

> Though indispensable, operational [working] definitions yield only limited meanings of constructs [concepts]. No operational definition can ever express all of a variable. No operational definition of intelligence can ever express the rich and diverse meaning of human intelligence. This means that the variables measured by scientists are always limited and specific in meaning. The "creativity" studied by psychologists is not the "creativity" referred to by artists, though there will of course be common elements.

In policy research, working definitions are often situation specific; they are used in a particular context for particular policy-related purposes.

The major obstacle in developing adequate working definitions in much policy research rests in the nature of the complexity of concepts under investigation. Concepts such as the developmentally disabled or deserving poor are subtle, multifaceted, changing, imbued with organization, economic, political, and social stakes.

The 1978 amendments in the case study on the developmentally disabled demonstrated the problem of constructing working definitions in a policy context. The political difficulty of precisely resolving sensitive issues that directly impact eligibility for benefits or impact the magnitude of benefits meant that legislative language remained vague, stressing general intent rather than specific criteria. Additionally, since legislators are not technical specialists, they may pass legislation which lacks detail.

> Skeletal legislation, as it is frequently called, is phrased in occasionally grand and, therefore, fuzzy terms. The implementing agency is told by the legislature to provide a safe environment for workers, to see that school children are served meals with adequate nutritional content, to assist the visually impaired, to maintain adequate income levels, and so on. (Lerner and Wanat, 1983:502)

The implementing agencies are then left with the task of meshing political mandates with administrative realities, of linking legislative intent with organizational practice.

> When bureaucrats are given . . . [such] legislation to implement, they are likely to find that the legislation as it stands provides too little guidance for crisp implementation. . . . Legislation saying that the poor shall be eligible for a service somehow becomes translated into an administrative regulation that single persons with net assets under $10,000 and an income under $5,000 per year may receive the services. (Lerner and Wanat, 1983:502)

The frequent vagueness that accompanies legislative policy statements requires the development of adequate working definitions if legislative intent is to be fulfilled.

Developing working definitions of concepts is an essential step in measurement. Policy research cannot proceed without working definitions because without them concepts cannot be photographed accurately through empirical lenses. Still, specifying empirical meanings of a concept is just the first step in the process of measuring policy concepts. For example, data sources must be identified that will provide information on empirical indicators underlying concepts.

Data Sources

Obtaining data on indicators is not only a primary tool of policy research; it is a method all use for gaining information about the world around them. Opening the blinds to see if the sun is shining is an indicator of current weather conditions. Listening to the morning news provides evidence of the immediate state of local, state, and national affairs. Looking before crossing a street is a measure of whether it is safe to proceed. Everyone is constantly engaged in obtaining cues about the environment through the use of empirical indicators. This information-seeking process becomes systematic research to the extent that it "serves specified research needs and is planned; that observations are recorded systematically; and that the resulting findings are analyzed as to their quality" (Selltiz et al., 1966:200).

Numerous techniques exist to gather evidence on empirical indicators and concepts. One way to classify these methods is whether *obtrusive* or *nonobtrusive* approaches are used in gathering information. Obtrusive approaches to data collection are those that intrude into the conscious awareness of those being observed. Unobtrusive methods are the opposite, made without the conscious awareness of research participants.

OBTRUSIVE DATA SOURCES

Generally, the most obtrusive data collection techniques are those that ask persons to self-report their behavior or opinions (e.g., in-person interviews, telephone surveys), those that make people aware their behavior is being studied. When individuals are aware of being observed, they feel self-conscious, aware they are the focus of attention, and respond and act in atypical ways, distorting the collection of dependable and accurate data.

The degree to which obtrusive data sources threaten data quality depends upon the objectives of the research. But policy analysts are particularly sensitive to biased self-reports. Respondents may perceive—often correctly—that their responses may influence policy decisions that will in turn affect their future interests, e.g., placing a trash-fill near their homes. In this situation, policy analysts guard against accepting self-reports as the sole indicator of the concept under investigation.

To illustrate, one objective of an evaluation of California's Political Reform Act was to assess the burden of reporting requirements on lobbyists required to submit monthly financial reports under the provisions of the act. As one means of accomplishing this objective, a mail questionnaire to a sample of registered lobbyists included the question outlined in Figure 5.1.

The potential bias in this obtrusive measure is clear. Lobbyists who object to being regulated under the act (and there are many) are more likely to express difficulty with the forms. Their response will measure their opposition to the requirement rather than measure a true assessment of the difficulty of reporting requirements.

In the social and political climate that surrounded the evaluation of this controversial act, it was important that the views and concerns of lobbyists be considered. However, analysts would seriously err if these perceptions were accepted as a sole genuine indicator of the burden of various reporting requirements. Methods of compensating for the obtrusiveness of such techniques are presented later in this chapter.

UNOBTRUSIVE DATA SOURCES

Unobtrusive approaches avoid direct interaction with research participants. Individuals are not directly questioned or aware they are being observed. Analysts need not be concerned with possible response biases of

FIGURE 5.1 Lobbyist disclosure forms under the Political Reform Act require information in a number of different reporting areas. Each of the topics listed below represents a major reporting area within the forms. Please indicate the degree of difficulty, if any, you find in keeping complete and accurate records of your activities in each area. (*Source:* J. F. Springer and A. D. Putt, "The Impact of the Political Reform Act of 1974 on California Politics." Sacramento, CA: Evaluation Research Consultants, p. 482.)

	NO PROBLEM	SLIGHTLY DIFFICULT	VERY DIFFICULT	NOT SURE
Lobbyist Activities (specific description of legislation or administrative action attempted to influence)	_____	_____	_____	_____
Payments Received	_____	_____	_____	_____
Deposits to the Account (sums received for the purpose of paying expenses)	_____	_____	_____	_____
Overhead	_____	_____	_____	_____
Petty Cash	_____	_____	_____	_____
Exchanges of money and other things of value with individuals	_____	_____	_____	_____
Exchanges of money and other things of value with businesses	_____	_____	_____	_____

respondents who are influenced by the presence of interviewers or by the knowledge that they are participants in a study.

Observation is unobtrusive when "the observer has no control over the behavior . . . in question, and plays an unobserved, passive, and nonintrusive role in the research situation" (Webb et al., 1966:112). Observers have been placed in courtrooms to record the nature of courtroom dialogue during plea negotiations. The effectiveness of antilitter or cleanup campaigns can be gauged through observation and rating the amount of litter and debris.

Documentary analysis (Chapter 9) serves as an example of a method that is frequently used to obtain information unobtrusively. Instead of asking respondents their ages, birth documents are consulted. Complaint files maintained by agencies are analyzed to provide an indication of service delivery satisfaction. Accident reports can be examined to evaluate the safety of bus service. Reports, records, and other recorded information maintained by organizations provide a ready source of unobtrusively obtained information for analysts.

All documents and records are not unobtrusive. The degree of obtrusiveness depends on how the original information was collected. Census data, for example, is based on interviews and questionnaires which may produce misreporting and distortion of data. Crime statistics based on "reported crime" will be biased by the unwillingness of certain individuals and groups to interact with law enforcement by reporting crimes they observe. In these instances, distorted data are possible since obtrusive approaches were used in collecting the original data.

This excursion into unobtrusive data collection approaches does not exhaust the multiple variations these methods assume in practice; the only limit is the reaches of the imagination. Yet they share the characteristic of not directly involving research participants. Analysts can consequently have increased confidence that the data gathered are not a reflection of the research methods selected in gaining information.

Sources of data, then, are distinguished on the basis of the degree of awareness of those being observed that they are part of a study. The higher the levels of awareness of research participants, the more likely the data collection technique itself produces changes in the behavior under study, adversely influencing the integrity of research findings. Any data collection strategy, e.g., interviews, mail surveys, experiments, or documentary analysis, can be assessed in terms of its obtrusiveness. When feasible, analysts incorporate multiple data collection methods, obtrusive and unobtrusive, in the analysis of a single policy problem. The use of multiple data collection approaches compensates for the biasing effects of any single approach.

Levels of Measurement

When working definitions and relevant indicators are specified and data sources and methods identified, analysts continue with detailed decisions regarding exactly how a concept will be measured. To implement the new definition of developmental disability, for example, eligibility forms had to be developed incorporating questions used to rate applicants according to their degree of functional limitation in the seven areas of life activity.

One element of this task was to determine the appropriate level of measurement at which to measure developmental disability. Higher levels of measurement produce more refined and specific information. Determining levels of measurement is a continuation of the analyst's attempt to be precise in the meaning of a concept. Three levels of measurement are commonly used in collecting data: nominal, ordinal, and interval. (A fourth level of measurement—the ratio level—is similar to the interval level except the ratio level of measurement has a true zero point as its origin.)

NOMINAL MEASUREMENT

Nominal measures yield basic information. These measures provide two or more distinct and nonoverlapping categories into which observations can be placed. For instance, a criterion for developmental disability benefits is that the disability "is manifested before the person attains age 22." Only nominal information is called for: either the applicant *did* develop the impairment before 22 or the applicant *did not* develop the impairment before 22. The categories are clear and mutually exclusive; deciding whether an individual is older than 22 or not is straightforward. Every observation can clearly be put into one or the other category without "gray areas" of interpretation. There are no shades of meaning, no in-between, no middle ground.

Nominal measurement is a labeling device that categorizes observations as different without implying degrees of difference. Gender, for example, divides persons into one of two categories. Indicators of ethnic background place people in one of several categories. A person's place of residence can be an important nominal measure for many policy purposes because it signifies differences in social and economic conditions.

The level of measurement used in categorizing data—whether nominal, ordinal, or interval—is a function of information needs, e.g., did or did not the person develop the impairment before age 22, and of the nature of the concept itself, e.g., gender is a nominal level concept.

ORDINAL MEASUREMENT

Ordinal-level information is typically more precise in comparison to nominal data. At this level of measurement, observations are ranked or ordered according to some criterion.

The name "ordinal measurement" derives from the ordinal numbers: first, second, third, etc. These allow the *ranking* of a set of objects (or events or phenomena) with respect to some characteristic, but they do not indicate the exact distances between the objects. For example, in an election the order of finish of the candidates does not say anything about the number of votes each one received. The order of finish indicates only that the winner received more votes than the runner-up, who in turn received more votes than the third-place finisher. (Meier and Brudney, 1981:102)

Ordinal measurements specify the relative position of people or things with respect to some criterion but with no implication as to the distance between positions. It is possible to say that something possesses more or less of a characteristic; it is not possible to say how much more or how much less.

Ordinal level information is frequently gathered for perceptual or atti-tudinal information. Assessing lobbyists' perceptions of difficulty in meet-ing reporting requirements (Figure 5.1) is a typical example in the applica-tion of ordinal measurement. In many perceptual applications, there is a presumed underlying dimension (e.g., difficulty) along which respondents can perceive greater or lesser magnitudes. However, there are no clear crite-ria for specifying the exact amount of difficulty. Categories for ordinal ranking provide a pragmatic resolution for measurement of these concepts.

INTERVAL MEASUREMENT

Interval measures produce the highest and most refined level of infor-mation. The reason: interval measures are based on constant intervals or units which are accepted as common standards. Age is measured in *years* and *months,* income in *dollars* and *cents,* weight in *pounds* and *ounces.* Refer-ring to the effectiveness indicators listed in Table 5.1, variables such as *per-centage* of households victimized, *number* of physical casualties in crime-related police work, and *dollar* property loss from crimes for households and businesses are all being measured at the interval level. Unlike ordinal measures, interval measurement allows analysts to report precisely how much more or less of a characteristic something possesses. Since the units of measurement are accepted as standard, analysts may state that 20 percent fewer households were victimized in comparison to last year; there were also 10 fewer physical casualties in crime-related police work; and the dollar property loss from crimes for households and businesses increased by 1.83 million dollars.

Interval measures are readily attainable when items or events can be counted. The effectiveness of a referral service for senior citizens might be partly gauged by the number of telephone calls received in a month. Success in vocational rehabilitation programs may be partially measured through the number (or percentage) of clients subsequently entering the work force.

Distinguishing between levels of measurement may seem a technical exercise, but the policy implications can be significant. An example from an administrative law hearing in a major United States city demonstrates the point.

DETERMINING LEVELS OF MEASUREMENT: A CASE STUDY

Under equal employment opportunity regulations, a group of black fire fighters brought legal action against a city fire department. The action alleged that a promotional exam identifying fire fighters eligible for promotion to lieutenant was discriminatory.

Expert witnesses for the city produced statistical tests that demonstrated no statistically significant difference in the test performance of blacks as compared to other fire fighters, i.e., the exam was not discriminatory. Expert witnesses for the black fire fighters produced statistical tests that did demonstrate statistically significant differences in test performance between blacks and other fire fighters, i.e., the exam was discriminatory.

A policy analyst was asked by the state Equal Employment Commission to provide an analysis of why the two expert witnesses supported directly contradictory conclusions. The answer hinged upon levels of measurement. Here is how.

The test scores for the promotional exam could be measured in any one of three ways.

1. Individual raw scores on the exam could be used. Raw scores ranged from a theoretical minimum of zero (no correct answers and no years of service) to a maximum of more than 1000 points. Individuals received scores based on correct answers to a variety of paper and pencil tests, performance on a decision simulator, and bonus points for years of service. Scores were calculated to two decimal points. The measurement level is *interval*.

2. Individual scores can be assigned according to the applicant's rank in comparison to the scores of other applicants. Since 577 applicants took the exam, the highest score would be assigned a rank of 1 and the lowest a rank of 577. This measurement system would identify the order of applicants from highest to lowest, but would erase the absolute magnitude of differences between their raw scores. The measurement level is *ordinal*.

3. Finally, individual scores could be assigned according to whether the applicant passed the exam (and was therefore eligible for promotion) or failed the exam (and was therefore ineligible for promotion). In this case the top 250 applicants or all of those who had raw scores at

or above 625.24 would qualify as passed, the remaining 327 failed. The measurement level is *nominal.*

The choice of level of measurement in gathering supporting statistics by expert witnesses explained differences in conclusions regarding the test performance of blacks and other applicants.

The expert witness for the fire fighters used raw test scores and individual ranks. Tests of statistical differences were based upon (a) comparison of average raw scores for blacks with other applicants, and (b) comparison of average test rank for blacks with average test rank for other applicants. These tests revealed very large differences in performance between blacks and other applicants—differences that would have occurred by chance less than 1 in 1000 times for raw scores and less than 1 in 100 times for ranks.

The city's expert witness used nominal categories of pass or fail to test differences between blacks and other applicants. While more blacks (66.7 percent) than others (40.7 percent) failed the exam, this difference could have occurred by chance more than 5 times in 100, a standard that the courts have recognized to indicate no adverse impact.

Thus, differences in expert conclusions about whether the fire fighter's promotional test demonstrated adverse impact on blacks were explained to the administrative law judge as a product of the level of measurement at which individual test results are scored.

The case demonstrates that measurement strategies—including appropriate levels of measurement—have policy implications. Resolution of whether the test demonstrated adverse impact on blacks would necessitate deciding whether the relevant outcome of the test was a raw score, a rank, or whether an applicant passed or failed.

The case also reinforces the difficulty of separating technical and political considerations in policy decisions. It was probably no accident that the experts measured test scores in ways that supported the preferred position of their respective clients. Furthermore, in this particular application, it was not clear that any particular level of measurement was the correct one to use.

The black fire fighters pointed out that only about 160 of the 250 eligible fire fighters would be promoted before the next test was given in two years. Promotions would be determined through a rule of one—the fire fighter with the highest score would be promoted first, the next highest score second, and so on down the list. Therefore, they argued, the most appropriate measure was the rank. The final decision would have to be made by the judge.

Finally, the case demonstrates the increased precision that comes with higher levels of measurement. Say the analyst is interested in the relative positions of persons who did not pass the test; how close were black applicants to passing as compared to others? With nominal measurement, no distinctions of this type could be made. Either an applicant passed or did not pass. At the ordinal level of the ranking, individuals below the passing level can be determined. Thus, the relative ranks of individual blacks not passing can be compared with others.

Similarly, the interval measurement of raw scores allows analysts to compare the average score of those black fire fighters who did not pass (330.87) with the average score of other ineligible applicants (540.98). While the nominal measure tells us only that individuals passed or failed, ordinal and interval measures provide increasingly precise measurement of how far different individuals or groups of individuals were from the passing score.

A benefit of the increased precision of higher levels of measurement is mathematical. Only interval-level measures can legitimately be added, subtracted, multiplied, or divided because only interval-level measures express quantities of some standard unit that can be counted. Precise measurement is a prerequisite for advanced forms of statistical analysis.[1]

MEASURING COMPLEX CONCEPTS

Policy analysts develop measures of concepts emerging from the policy process. These concepts are often complex. For purposes of developing adequate measurement strategies, several sources of this complexity have particular significance.

First, concepts are complex due to purposeful abstraction and vagueness. Vagueness is an essential element in policy-making because it allows compromise and accommodation among individuals and groups with differing values and perspectives.

Second, policy concepts are complex because they are multidimensional, possessing more than one aspect or component. Regional planners and economic development agencies, for example, have an ongoing interest in measuring the quality of life in their communities. High scores on this concept are useful in attracting economic activity. Quality of life, however, has many dimensions—aesthetics, health, culture, recreation, jobs, housing, and more. Quality of life is a composite of many dimensions, making it a complex concept.

Third, policy concepts are complex because their empirical indicators vary across time or location. Analysts may want to compare the cost of ambulance services in different localities or in different years. The task is complicated because the need for ambulance services and the difficulty of providing them (e.g., traffic conditions, distances) vary between communities and change over time.

Policy analysts apply several strategies for translating complex concepts into a single measure. The remainder of this section briefly describes commonly used strategies—scales, typologies, indexes, and ratios.

Scale Construction

Some concepts of interest to policy researchers are simple, concrete, direct, e.g., gender, age, annual salary, number of rides on the bus last week. Data concerning these simple concepts are usually captured through a single indicator—a single question in a survey, for example. Other concepts are more complex; no single indicator adequately reflects their richness and diversity.

Scales are multiple-item indicators used to measure unidimensional concepts. Figure 5.2 provides an example of a unidimensional scale intended to measure strength of self-concept among the physically disabled.

Respondents are asked to indicate the extent of their agreement with each of eleven statements. These statements (items) express a variety of assessments of the adequacy of one's own behavior. While each statement refers to a slightly different facet of behavior, they all emphasize a single dimension—the strength of one's self-concept.

> When we say that an attitude scale is unidimensional we mean that it measures a single attitude. A person's attitude score therefore reflects only his position on the underlying attitude continuum, and two or more persons who have the same attitude score will be at the same position on the latent continuum. If the attitude scale is not unidimensional, it means that more than one attitude (or other characteristic) is being measured by the scale. In this case, individuals having the same score may have widely different attitudes. (Shaw and Wright, 1967:20)

The particular items that compose a unidimensional scale meet both conceptual and empirical standards. Conceptually, they must be logically defensible indicators of the underlying concept. Empirically, each item must be correlated with the total score for the scale. In the process of constructing scales of this type, items are first selected for their conceptual content and administered to test samples of respondents. Items which do not correlate with the total score are not included in the final questions.

Other scaling procedures have been developed and applied in policy research.[2] Regardless of the exact format, scales provide measures of complex unidimensional concepts by combining multiple items that tap a variety of related empirical behaviors of a concept.

Typologies and Indexes

Scales measure complex unidimensional concepts through the use of multiple interrelated items. Ongoing attempts are made to ensure the unidimensionality of a scale, including the application of statistical tests to discard items not correlating with other items.

In the complex world of policymakers, concepts may not lend themselves to simple, unidimensional analysis and measurement. They may instead be subtle combinations of phenomena, multidimensional, incorporat-

Please indicate how much you agree or disagree with the following statements by checking the appropriate response.

	STRONGLY AGREE	AGREE	UNCERTAIN	DIS- AGREE	STRONGLY DISAGREE
I take good care of myself physically.	( )	( )	( )	( )	( )
I am satisfied to be just what I am.	( )	( )	( )	( )	( )
I solve my problems easily.	( )	( )	( )	( )	( )
I am as sociable as I want to be.	( )	( )	( )	( )	( )
I feel that people almost always treat me right.	( )	( )	( )	( )	( )
I find it easy to start a conversation with a stranger.	( )	( )	( )	( )	( )
I feel that I can accomplish the things I want to do.	( )	( )	( )	( )	( )
I like to take on new and important responsibilities.	( )	( )	( )	( )	( )
I start work on a new project with a great deal of enthusiasm.	( )	( )	( )	( )	( )
I am usually confident of my abilities.	( )	( )	( )	( )	( )
My friends seem to have a better time than I do.	( )	( )	( )	( )	( )

FIGURE 5.2 Scale for Measuring Self-Concept Among Physically Disabled Persons. (*Source:* Gene Hiehle, "Client Effectiveness in Independent Living Centers" (Sacramento, CA: California Department of Rehabilitation, 1981).)

ing a number of different major characteristics and properties. In these circumstances, a unidimensional scale consisting of several interrelated indicators is inadequate since only a single dimension of the variable is being measured. When multiple indicators measuring multiple dimensions of a concept are required, analysts use typologies or indexes.

Research on the prosecution of felony defendants provides a simple example of a typology. Research suggests that two dimensions are of central importance to the way defendants are viewed—the nature of their crime and the extent of their prior criminal involvement (Springer, Phillips, and Cannady, 1985). A typology based on these two dimensions might categorize defendants according to (a) whether they had been convicted of a felony crime before or not, and (b) whether the crime they were being held for was a violent, personal crime (e.g., robbery, assault, homicide, rape) or a property crime (e.g., burglary, theft, forgery).

Figure 5.3 presents a typology that identifies four separate types of defendant according to combinations of the two dimensions. The typology yields four nominal categories, or types, of offenders. If research expectations are correct, judicial decision makers should consider different options for case resolution to be appropriate for each type.

Constructing Indexes

Because policy-relevant concepts are frequently multidimensional, indexes are necessary to translate these concepts into single measures. The Consumer Price Index measures changes in retail prices. The index incorporates several dimensions, such as changes in price of health care, housing, food, and transportation. Each dimension in turn is based on individual indicators.

The Index of Leading Economic Indicators is another key measure compiled and published by the United States Department of Commerce. The index is the single most important predictor of the future course of America's economy. As such, it is "of overwhelming interest to business planners, stock and bond operators, consumers, workers and economists, not to mention politicians with eyes fixed on election day" (*New York Times,* September 28, 1984:29). The index has twelve dimensions, including average workweek, initial unemployment claims, vendor performance, stock prices, money supply, housing permits, new orders for consumer goods, sensitive materials prices, business equipment orders, business plant investment, business and consumer borrowing, and new business formations. Each dimension requires careful definition and relies on complex information collection procedures in itself.

Major economic and social indexes represent years of development

FIGURE 5.3 Types of Felony Defendants

		Type of Crime	
		Property Crime	Violent Crime
Prior Criminal Involvement	One or zero prior felony convictions	Property Offender	Violent Offender
	Two or more prior felony convictions	Career Criminal	Violent Predator

and massive systems of coordinated collection of information. In many instances, policy analysts want to make use of indexes for less sweeping purposes. A more limited example illustrates the process of developing an index.

Assume analysts are asked to evaluate the "effectiveness" of a community's recreation services. The initial task is to refine the concept effectiveness of recreation services. Included in this task is the specification of the dimensions to be measured. Analysts employ a multidimensional approach for this example, defining effectiveness as the degree to which recreation services "provide for all citizens a variety of enjoyable leisure opportunities that are accessible, safe, physically attractive, and uncrowded" (Hatry et al., 1977:42). In this definition, six overlapping dimensions of the concept can be identified:

A *variety* of interesting activities

The *enjoyableness* of recreation services

The *accessibility* of recreation programs

The *physical attractiveness* of recreation facilities

The *safety* of recreation programs

The avoidance of *crowdedness*

Once dimensions have been specified, indicators representing each dimension are created. Developing indicators can be straightforward, since each dimension may suggest concrete empirical measures of its existence. Indicators of the "enjoyableness of recreation services," for instance, may be measured through the degree of community satisfaction and user satisfaction, and rates of participation in recreation services. Indicators of the "safety of recreation services" may be assessed through the number of injuries to participants in recreation programs, the number of criminal incidents, user perceptions of the safety of recreation services, and nonuser satisfaction (percentage of nonuser households citing safety concerns as a reason for nonuse of recreation services).

After indicators have been developed for measuring various dimensions of a concept such as the effectiveness of recreation services, the final index is constructed. Index scores are derived by aggregating the values of individual dimensions. Each dimension may be assigned the same weight in computing the index number or may be weighted unevenly, depending on the way in which the composite concept is defined. For example, policymakers responsible for recreational facilities may consider safety to be of prime importance—more important than variety, for instance. In this case, the score for safety indicators might be counted as twice as important as the variety score in the final index.

Because indexes combine different dimensions into a single overall portrait of a complex concept, they present problems of interpretation. A given index score may be produced by very different patterns of values on individual dimensions. Accordingly, to assess fully the meaning of an index score, it is important to examine scores on individual dimensions. A low score on the "safety of recreation services" dimension may indicate an area which needs attention. It will not indicate whether the appropriate actions are to increase police surveillance or to make activities less physically dangerous.

Ratios

If, for example, an unemployment measure is to be useful as an indication of economic health at different times and at different places, it needs to be comparable in these different settings. The number of unemployed is not comparable because the labor force may grow or shrink over time, and different places (e.g., states or cities) have labor forces of different sizes.

Unemployment, therefore, is measured as a ratio (or percentage). Specifically, it is the number of unemployed as a percent of the civilian labor force. It is calculated through the following ratio.

$$\text{Unemployment Rate} = \frac{\text{number of unemployed}}{\text{number in civilian labor force}}$$

Measuring unemployment as a ratio has the major advantage of making the concept comparable across time, across regions, and across identifiable groups in the population. Thus, policymakers can assess whether persons seeking work in western states are relatively more or less successful than those in the east, or whether a greater percentage of women in the civilian labor force is unemployed than men.

Rates such as employment rates are particular, time-based ratios that express the number of events that occurred in a given time period as a percentage of the number of events that could have occurred in the time period. Thus, police clearance rates are the percentage of crimes reported in a given time period for which arrests are made. For prosecutors, conviction rates are the percentage of case dispositions in a given period (e.g., one month) that result in guilty pleas or guilty verdicts. Rates are commonly used to compare performance in different settings or across time. They are frequently used in policy research.

Ratios take other forms also. Percentages are used to compare groups in many ways other than the time-based use for rates. The city's expert witness in the fire fighters' promotion case compared the percentage of black fire fighters who passed the exam with the percentage of others passing. Ratios are used to indicate the rapidity of change, to measure efficiency, and to compare the relative value of different policies through cost-benefit ratios. These uses are explored in later chapters.

IMPROVING MEASUREMENT QUALITY

Scales, indexes, and other components of the measurement process serve as means of relating research concepts to their empirical counterparts. Effective measurement means that end results produce useful and accurate information, reflecting the assumption that the process through which the information was generated is free of error.

But error-free measurement is an ideal, not an operating reality. In policy research, measurement takes place in complex situations where numerous factors converge to influence what is measured and how it is measured. Given situational constraints, the challenge to analysts is to reduce sources of error to a minimum—no small challenge.

Sources of Measurement Error

Errors in measurement emerge in all stages of research, from conceptualization to data processing (Bailey, 1982:75–77). Vaguely defined concepts, for example, result in the use of incomplete measures or in measuring variables other than those intended. The credibility of the resulting information is predictably diminished. No matter how carefully subsequent phases of the research are conducted, the quality of findings is undermined due to errors in initially clarifying, defining, and specifying the empirical meanings of concepts.

Even when concepts are well specified, data collection approaches create their own sources of error. The use of obtrusive methods, e.g., in person surveys, may confound attempts to collect quality information since respondents are aware that the information they supply may affect decisions concerning them or because they want to answer in a socially acceptable manner. The misapplication of sampling techniques is a common source of error. Small sample sizes, a lack of randomization in selecting sample members, incomplete or outdated sampling frames, and nonresponse problems all present threats to the integrity of findings.

Errors occur after data have been collected. Coders incorrectly categorize responses in transferring data from questionnaires to the computer. Simple clerical errors or illegible responses are reasons for these mistakes. Scoring, tabulation, machine analysis all produce errors. The list of potential errors is endless.

Through applying quality control techniques at all stages of research, errors can be reduced but not eliminated. Those that remain are unequal in their consequences for data quality. Some errors will be *random*, fluctuating without any particular pattern. Coding errors, for instance, may occur on both the higher and lower ranges of the value of some variable. When errors are random, the assumption is that these errors are equally divided between positive and negative variations. To the extent the assumption is correct, errors should cancel out each other. Still, the resulting measure will lack precision because of the meaningless variation introduced by random errors. It will lack reliability. Random errors can be minimized but not totally controlled.

> The existence of random fluctuations is . . . a feature of the process of measurement. With greater care in the performance of the measurement the random variation may be expected to decrease, as shots carefully aimed at a bullseye are likely to be less widely dispersed than if they were just roughly directed to the target. But even Robin Hood cannot split arrows indefinitely—some random variation always remains. (Kaplan, 1964:200)

Other errors may be nonrandom, unequally divided between positive and negative variations from the actual value. These *systematic* errors fall into a pattern and do not cancel out each other. Instead of randomly fluctuating, coding errors, for example, may remain constant throughout the entire information processing phase. Perhaps the error is due to a coder who has consistently misinterpreted coding instructions or to a consistent tendency for respondents to say what they think the interviewer would like to hear. Whatever the reasons, variations are not random but lean to one side or the other of the actual value based on the particular distorting factors at work. Systematic errors result in invalid research information, in turn creating a misleading source of information for users.

IMPROVING MEASUREMENT QUALITY: RELIABILITY

Reliability refers to the precision and accuracy of measurement procedures used in generating data. A reliable measure has a small error component; scores do not significantly fluctuate from one moment to the next.

> By contrast, consider an unreliable instrument, an *elastic* ruler. If you tried to measure your height by standing on one end of the elastic ruler and holding the other to the top of your head, you would get a slightly different reading each time you measured because you would pull a little more or less on the ruler each time and it would stretch or shrink accordingly. An elastic ruler has a large error component, and that makes the observed scores unreliable. The larger the error component in relation to the true score, the less reliable the instrument. (Kidder, 1981:126)

Reliable measures provide accurate and precise information to the extent measurements are free from random fluctuation. High reliability alone is no guarantee of data quality (perhaps the wrong concept is being measured with great precision), but there can be no guarantee of data quality without reliable results. "In brief, reliability is a necessary but not sufficient condition of the value of research results and their interpretation" (Kerlinger, 1973:455). A number of general research strategies are used to improve the reliability of research information.

Standardize research procedures.   Clear and specific instructions for coders, interviewers, respondents, and so forth, reduce errors of measurement. Training and practice of coders and interviewers in the designated procedures minimize errors arising from misunderstandings of intent and process. Measuring instruments such as performance tests should be administered under standard conditions to compare results adequately. If measurement situations significantly differ, the results may reflect the differences through a large error component.

Use proven measures.   Ensuring the reliability of complex measures requires extensive testing and refinement. Before developing their own measures, analysts conduct a thorough search for existing measures that have been used to assess the concept under investigation. Proven measures can be identified through reviewing other studies in related areas. Analysts save resources, improve the quality of research, and make their findings more generalizable by reviewing and incorporating data collection instruments used in relevant past investigations.

Proven measures are also obtained from a variety of commercial or academic sources. Many standardized collection instruments have been developed for measuring administrative, political, psychological, social, and educational concepts; specific tests of reliability are often reported with these tests. Useful noncommercial sources of measures are discussed in the chapter on survey research, Chapter 8.

Use multiple-item indicators and scales.   Scales and indexes are used to provide more reliable measurement than can be obtained through single-item indicators. When multiple items are used, the degree of overall error attributable to a random error on one item is reduced through the accumulation of accurate measurements across other items.

Reliable measures should accurately reflect the actual value of a research concept. Statistical tests of reliability are frequently applied to test the reliability of the indicators that constitute a scale. A common test is checking the items of a scale to determine whether they vary together from observation to observation (i.e., whether they are correlated). If a particular item is not sufficiently correlated with other items, this indicates that changes in its value are random with respect to the systematic change found in other items. The item is consequently unreliable and should be discarded from the scale.[3]

A different approach used to assess the reliability of a scale is to repeat applications to the same population over time (e.g., the same people taking a personality inventory at different times). The same respondents are tested twice (or more), and their performance on each application is compared. Using this procedure, known as a test-retest reliability, the scores obtained by each individual on the initial administration of the testing instrument are compared to that individual's scores on the second testing, producing a correlation coefficient. A high coefficient suggests the testing instrument is consistently measuring stable and enduring characteristics of respondents, rather than measuring variable and transitory influences. Test-retest reliability checks may be influenced by practice (becoming testwise) and memory, and by events occurring between testing dates (mood, motivation, fatigue).[4]

Pretest measuring instruments.   A trial run of measuring instruments provides advance notification of sources of error in these tools. Pretesting is particularly important when proven measures are unavailable and analysts design their instruments, such as a questionnaire. In a questionnaire, pretesting identifies vague and ambiguous questions in the survey instrument. Vague questions, for instance, permit error to creep in because respondents interpret questions differently. Such interpretations may tend to be random, increasing error and decreasing reliability.

Unreliable measurement renders research findings suspect. The noise created by random fluctuations frustrates attempts to find meaningful patterns in data. While every research problem poses its own difficulties, analysts should identify the appropriate mix of approaches to increase reliability in measurement.

IMPROVING MEASUREMENT QUALITY: VALIDITY

Technically, validity is a determination of whether an indicator truly measures the concept it is intended to measure; for example, whether an IQ test measures intelligence, or whether asking persons if they voted in an election is a true indicator of voter turnout. Within this technical definition, an indicator is valid if it contains little systematic error. A measure is invalid to the extent that changes in its value are systematically related to some factor (e.g., motivation and fatigue when taking an IQ test) other than the concept itself.

In policy research, validity is ultimately defined in terms of the utility of research information in decision making. Here the basic question is one of usefulness—of "whether the measures have been so arrived at that they can serve effectively as means to the given end" (Kaplan, 1964:198). This definition of validity incorporates criteria such as the timeliness, completeness, and relevance of information.

Timeliness is making information available to stakeholders before it loses its capacity to influence decisions. Sometimes the capacity of information to influence decisions is fleeting, as in dealing with immediate crises such as fires and police actions. In other contexts, such as long-range planning activities, the timeliness of research-based information may be measured in months and years.

Timeliness is a characteristic of relevancy. If information is unavailable when needed, its use is limited and consequently lacks relevancy. Timeliness alone does not make findings relevant, but a lack of timeliness depletes information of value it might otherwise have possessed. Pressures of time often enter into the analyst's determination of how to measure concepts and often require tradeoffs with respect to the quality and quantity of information that can be gathered.

The *completeness* of information is another criterion of validity in research. Completeness implies nothing is left out of the information that is necessary in ensuring it adequately reflects real-world conditions. Assessments of completeness are always relative; no research effort examines every nuance of complex concepts. Costs and feasibility alone place boundaries on any such attempt. As with timeliness, completeness is linked to relevance. If important information is missing, the relevance of that information is reduced. Completeness alone, just as timeliness, does not ensure information is relevant.

The relevance of information goes beyond timely and complete data. It means that research information bears a logical and useful relationship to the concept under investigation—that the measures used are logically connected and important to the matter at hand. Relevant information makes a difference in a decision situation by helping users form impressions about past, present, and future events, or by confirming or correcting earlier beliefs.

Because of its complexity, no single technique exists to establish objectively and definitively the validity of a measure. Several approaches are commonly used. To assess *face validity,* consumers first evaluate the adequacy of the working definition of the concept (e.g., how the effectiveness of recreation services is defined), and second, assess whether indicators and data sources used in gathering information adequately portray that concept. In some situations, such assessments of face validity are elusive, particularly when "(1) there is no consensus about the definition of the concept to be measured; (2) the concept is a multidimensional one consisting of several subconcepts; (3) the measure is lengthy and complex" (Bailey, 1982:70). Face validity is maximized when analysts and users agree on the meaning(s) of important concepts and when they agree on indicators and data sources used in obtaining empirical snapshots of those concepts.

Although face validity assessments are ultimately a matter of judgment, they are critically important in policy research. If stakeholders do not believe that concepts have been well defined or that measures used inadequately reflect concepts, the relevance and usability of the information is diminished.

Agreement on face validity is enhanced through using measures that have been connected with concepts in previous research efforts. To what extent do dimensions and indicators reflect and build on past efforts? An initial step in any measurement strategy is to evaluate relevant literature to search out and improve measurement approaches used in prior investigations.

The process of achieving face validity for policy research information also requires analysts to work closely with policymakers and interested parties. In the early stages of the authors' evaluation of the California Political Reform Act, numerous hours were spent in group meetings to clarify study objectives and to identify dimensions and indicators that would be useful to the Fair Political Practices Commission and its staff.

Another approach to validation focuses on uses of indicators to *predict* future events. Indicators have *predictive validity* when they accurately forecast specific events. Tests of predictive validity are empirical. If indicators do not forecast relevant future events at a desired level of precision, they lack validity for that purpose.

The Index of Leading Economic Indicators, described earlier in this chapter, is intended to foreshadow trends in the economy. However, the predictive validity of the measure has been publicly challenged. An article in the *New York Times* (9/28/84:29) reported that critics "question the value of the index as a predictor. They have found it to provide very short, if any, advance notice of recovery from the trough of recession, and say it warns of downturns too long in advance to be of much use."

In other words, experience with the index has not demonstrated sufficiently relevant predictions to convince its critics to use it to make decisions. An economist with a leading New York investment adviser was quoted as saying, "We decided the Government series was providing little or no insight" (*New York Times,* 9/28/84:29).

Of course, other economists disagree. While recognizing prediction is far from perfect, they find the index sufficiently valid to consider in making decisions about the future. These supporters point out that no single index is sufficient in forecasting, and other data must be considered. A statement by another banking economist summarizes the point. "It's worth attention, but I think we have to be very careful in looking at other information as well" (*New York Times,* 9/28/84:29). This statement underscores a fundamental point. The use of multiple and overlapping measures is a powerful method of improving validity in policy research. Introduction of this strategy— termed triangulation—concludes the discussion of improving measurement quality.

IMPROVING MEASUREMENT QUALITY: TRIANGULATION

Errors of reliability and validity are reduced through using multiple and overlapping measurement strategies in the study of a policy concept. The resulting measurement plan incorporates a combination of approaches in the study of a single policy concept.

Underlying the need for triangulation is the premise that any single measure carries with it its own characteristic sources of error (Sechrest, 1979:2). When findings have been supported by two or more different measures, the uncertainty of their validity is reduced, adding to the clarity and usefulness of information. More powerful evidence is provided because results have been confirmed through multiple and overlapping measures. Denzin (1970:301–8) views triangulation as a comprehensive research strategy incorporating multiple data sources, investigators, and theory, as well as multiple methods of data collection.

Data Triangulation leads analysts to search for varied data sources relevant to the concept. If the effectiveness of public mass transit is being examined, data sources may include:

- Users of mass transit
- Nonusers (to ascertain reasons for not riding mass transit)
- Public officials
- Transportation authorities
- Bus drivers
- Complaint files
- Accident reports (to determine the frequency and severity of traffic accidents)
- Crime incident reports (to determine the frequency of on-board crimes)
- Related studies and documents

Multiple data sources provide a comprehensive and in-depth portrait of a concept such as the effectiveness of public mass transit. They enhance the usability of findings because they tap a variety of information sources relevant to stakeholders. Varied data sources allow analysts to compare results, see what they share in common, and provide a better-supported empirical basis for findings, conclusions, and recommendations.

Investigator Triangulation is the use of multiple observers to the same research event. If the comfort or cleanliness of public mass transit is being evaluated visually, triangulating observers reduces potential bias coming from any single observer in his or her assessment, providing a reliability check on data quality. This strategy works to the degree skilled observers are used:

Most investigations in fact do employ multiple observers, although all of them may not occupy equally prominent roles in the actual observational process. What Roth . . . has termed hired-hand research represents an inappropriate use of multiple observers: the act of making observations is delegated to persons who lack the skill and knowledge of the primary investigator. The use of undergraduates as coders, graduate students and housewives as interviewers, and computer specialists as data analysts represents a delegation of responsibility that places the least well-prepared persons in crucial role positions. When multiple observers are used, the most skilled observers should be placed closest to the data. (Denzin, 1970:303)

Theoretical Triangulation directs analysts to generate information incorporating multiple definitions, perspectives, and meanings of a policy concept. The effectiveness of public mass transit is a candidate for theoretical triangulation: it is a concept subject to varying meanings and interpretations. Effectiveness for some reflects convenience and reliability; for others, comfort or safety or economic health or environmental impacts such as air and noise pollution. Instead of formulating a single empirical definition of effectiveness, analysts work with competing and complementary definitions. Each definition examines a different dimension of effectiveness; each directs attention to different data sources; each calls for a different mix of research methods. Theoretical triangulation minimizes the likelihood that analysts present research findings and recommendations in which alternative or contradictory perspectives are ignored or unexamined.

Methodological Triangulation is achieved through combining two or more information collection methods in the study of a single concept. The assumption supporting this practice is that any research method, whether obtrusive or unobtrusive, reflects differing strengths and limitations. The use of only in-person surveys, for example, creates sources of error due to their obtrusiveness. Errors created by obtrusive methods are counterbalanced by using measures that do not require direct interaction with people; still, these unobtrusive methods generate their own characteristic errors. Documentary analysis (Chapter 9), for instance, depends on available materials as sources of data. Yet missing documents, deliberate original distortion of records, and selective recording of events may influence the trustworthiness of resulting data.

Since any single method creates its own sources of error, using multiple methods serves to cancel typical errors arising from a particular measurement procedure. When analysts use multiple methods in collecting data and when these methods produce complementary findings, the information then contains a degree of integrity and credibility unattainable by a single-method approach. An examination of the effectiveness of public mass transit through the use of different methods such as surveys of people (users, nonusers, transportation authorities) and documentary analysis of relevant records (accident reports, complaint files, past evaluations) adds clarity, support, and credibility to findings, and reduces sources of error inherent in the use of any single method.

Triangulation in Policy Research

Triangulation requires the simultaneous use of multiple and overlapping measurements in a single study. A fully triangulated measurement strategy incorporates in a single investigation multiple data sources, observers, theories, and methods.

Few if any policy studies achieve the goal of a fully triangulated measurement strategy. Time and expense rule out such an approach. Even in the absence of resource constraints, access to critical data sources may be limited by ethical, legal, and other restrictions. In many investigations, extensive triangulation is unnecessary in achieving information needs.

Analysis and interpretations of findings are a difficult task in a triangulated measurement strategy. Difficulties are encountered in comparing varied empirical findings across dissimilar methods, data sources, observers, and perspectives. All components of a triangulated approach may not merit equal weight in developing findings, since some procedures may be more accurate and relevant than others, complicating analysis and interpretation of data.

Such obstacles do not diminish the value of triangulation in improving measurement quality. Using multiple observers may not be possible, but multiple data sources may be available and accessible. It may not be possible to employ multiple methods; but within a single method, other forms of triangulation—perspectives, observers, data sources—can be used. Any policy study can be designed incorporating useful triangulation strategies. In the changeable and fluid reality of policy analysis, composed of competing perspectives, attitudes, and values, the question is not whether to triangulate, but the extent of triangulation possible, given constraints of circumstance.

CONCLUDING COMMENTS

Measurement is concerned with the how of obtaining quality information. It is a process of developing systematic (repeatable) procedures for linking concepts to real-world events of interest to stakeholders.

As a process, measurement requires that policy analysts exercise an array of technical skills. The initial steps in measurement require the development of working definitions, including their dimensions and empirical indicators. In policy research this initial step of defining concepts often involves meetings with stakeholders to develop agreed-on definitions and indicators. Working definitions specify the empirical counterparts of a concept, serving as a manual of instructions in collecting real-world observations.

In developing methods of collecting information, analysts consider the implications of a given approach for data quality. Obtrusive data collection methods, such as in-person interviews, introduce problems of bias; unobtrusive methods may only partially and indirectly reflect the concept of interest.

Decisions about levels of measurement also have important implications in policy research. The purposes of measurement in implementing public policy are often nominal—to differentiate cases (e.g., applicants for benefits) into clear groups (e.g., eligible or ineligible). Higher levels of measurement, i.e., ordinal and interval, commonly result in greater precision, providing more refined information. Higher levels of measurement also allow the use of more sophisticated statistical analyses.

When complex unidimensional or multidimensional concepts must be translated into single measures, policy analysts use a number of measurement techniques. Scales are appropriate to unidimensional concepts composed of multiple empirical indicators; indexes are appropriate to multidimensional concepts.

Measurement bias is a continuing concern of analysts. Errors emerge in all stages of research. These errors may be systematic, affecting the validity of findings, or random, affecting the reliability of results. Improving the quality of information means improving the validity and reliability of measures used to obtain empirical snapshots.

Validity in policy research is defined in terms of the usefulness of findings for decision making. This definition of validity incorporates concerns such as the timeliness, completeness, and relevancy of research information in policy making.

Triangulation, a measurement strategy designed to improve the validity and reliability of empirical findings, advocates multiple and overlapping research procedures in the study of a single concept. Underlying the need for triangulation is the premise that any single measurement procedure carries with it its own characteristic sources of error. Using overlapping measures in the study of a single concept counterbalances characteristic errors arising from particular measurement approaches. When findings have empirical support from multiple measures, more powerful evidence is provided since they have been confirmed through multiple processes.

Few policy studies achieve a fully triangulated measurement strategy. Limitations of time and money, a lack of access to critical data sources and difficulties in analysis, comparison and interpretation of diverse data foreclose such attempts. But any investigation can be designed incorporating triangulation strategies, improving the quality of decision-relevant information in the process. Triangulation is well suited to the fuzzy and variable world of public policy.

In sum, measurement strategies provide the glue bonding concepts to specific, empirical observations. The skill and care with which policy analysts fashion these fundamental building blocks of empirical research have strong implications for the nature of subsequent analysis, and for the degree to which subsequent information is accurate and useful to consumers.

NOTES

1. Publications are available that guide users in selecting statistical techniques based on levels of measurement. These include Andrews et al. (1974) and Siegel (1956).
2. For a comprehensive discussion of techniques for scale construction, see Shaw and Wright (1967) and Miller (1977).
3. Reference Kidder (1981:126–129) for more detail.
4. A variety of procedures are used to determine the degree of intercorrelation of scale items. A common method for rating the reliability of a scale is the split-half technique. The analyst determines consistency by splitting a test into two halves (usually odd-numbered and even-numbered items) and correlating the scores obtained by each person on one half with those obtained by each person on the other. Yielding an estimate called the split-half reliability coefficient, this procedure provides a statistical determination as to what degree the halves of a test are measuring the same quality, and how precisely the characteristic is being measured. Again, a high split-half correlation coefficient provides evidence of reliability and substantiates claims of validity through providing consistent, stable information.

REFERENCES

Andrews, Frank M., Laura Klem, Terence N. Davidson, Patrick M. O'Malley, and Willard L. Rodgers. 1974. *A Guide for Selecting Statistical Techniques for Analyzing Social Science Data.* Ann Arbor, MI: The Institute for Social Research, University of Michigan.

Bailey, Kenneth D. 1982. *Methods of Social Research,* 2d ed. New York: Free Press.

Denzin, Norman K. 1970. *The Research Act: A Theoretical Introduction to Sociological Methods.* Chicago: Aldine.

Hatry, Harry P., Louis H. Blair, Donald M. Fisk, John M. Greiner, John R. Hall, Jr., and Philip S. Schaenman. 1977. *How Effective Are Your Community Services?* Washington, DC: Urban Institute.

Hiele, Gene. 1981. "Client Effectiveness in Independent Living Centers: A Working Paper." Sacramento, CA: California Department of Rehabilitation, Independent Living Research Study.

Kaplan, Abraham. 1964. *The Conduct of Inquiry: Methodology for Behavioral Science.* San Francisco: Chandler Publishing.

Kerlinger, Fred N. 1973. *Foundations of Behavioral Research,* 2d ed. New York: Holt, Rinehart & Winston.

Kidder, Louise H. 1981. *Research Methods in Social Relations,* 4d ed. New York: Holt, Rinehart & Winston.

Lerner, Allan W., and John Wanat. 1983. "Fuzziness and Bureaucracy," *Public Administration Review* 43:500–9.

Meier, Kenneth J., and Jeffrey L. Brudney. 1981. *Applied Statistics for Public Administration.* Boston: Duxbury Press.

Miller, Delbert C. 1977. *Handbook of Research Design and Social Measurement,* 3d ed. New York: Longman.

Sechrest, Lee, ed. 1979. *New Directions for Methodology of Behavioral Science: Unobtrusive Measurement Today.* San Francisco: Jossey-Bass Publishers.

Selltiz, Claire, Lawrence S. Wrightsman, and Stuart W. Cook. 1966. *Research Methods in Social Relations,* 2d ed. New York: Holt, Rinehart & Winston.

Shaw, Marvin E., and Jack M. Wright. 1967. *Scales for the Measurement of Attitudes.* New York: McGraw-Hill.

Siegel, Sidney. 1956. *Nonparametric Statistics for the Behavioral Sciences.* New York: McGraw-Hill.

Springer, J. Fred, Joël L. Phillips, and Lynne Cannady. 1985. *Selective Prosecution: Lessons from Career Criminal Programs.* Sacramento, CA: EMT Associates.

Springer, J. Fred, and Allen D. Putt. 1977. "Impact of the Political Reform Act of 1974: A Questionnaire Survey." Sacramento, CA: The State of California.

Webb, Eugene J., Donald T. Campbell, Richard D. Schwartz, and Lee Sechrest. 1966. *Unobtrusive Measures: Nonreactive Research in the Social Sciences.* Chicago: Rand McNally.

6

Techniques for Direct Data Collection

Interviews and Observation

As information needs and measurement requirements are specified, policy analysts confront the task of collecting data. Careful and skillful data collection is central to effective policy research; conclusions and recommendations are only as good as the accuracy and usefulness of the empirical evidence supporting them.

The four chapters in Part IV introduce major methods of information collection for policy research. The discussion includes methods for collecting information from people (in-depth interviews and survey research), for collecting information from available documents and records, and for making direct observations of events.

Discussion of data collection for policy research may raise expectations of highly technical scientific techniques. Systematic techniques for collecting statistical data on large numbers of cases do play an important role in policy analysis, a role detailed in subsequent chapters. But the informational core of much policy research comes from more direct means such as conversations with knowledgeable persons or seeing events take place in person. Interviewing and observation are basic information collection skills used in policy research.

While strategies for interviewing and direct observation take many forms, they share the characteristic of "firsthand involvement" (Mann, 1970: 119–131). Talking to program administrators and staff, program clients, involved legislators, and other stakeholders offers opportunities to gather insights and detail not possible in the standardized questionnaires of survey research. Direct observation of program activities or other events provides the opportunity to examine what actually happens in the setting rather than relying on secondhand reports or agency records. As argued by sociologist John Lofland (1971:6), "The bedrock of human understanding is face-to-face contact."

Interviews and observation have distinct advantages and limitations as methods of research. Skilled analysts carefully consider information needs and decide what data collection tool or mix of tools are most appropriate to those needs. As stated by Martin Trow (1970:143), "Different kinds of information . . . are gathered most fully and economically in different ways, and . . . the problem under investigation properly dictates the methods of investigation."

This chapter identifies uses of interview and observation techniques in policy research. The discussion covers several major topics. First, policy research tasks best addressed through interviews or observation are discussed. Second, the chapter identifies alternative approaches to interviewing and observation and details particular applications suited to each. Finally, the discussion identifies challenges facing analysts in using these tools and offers approaches to overcoming them.

INTERVIEWS: GAINING KNOWLEDGE FROM PEOPLE

Interviews are in-person conversations in which analysts "elicit information or expressions of opinions or belief from another person" (Maccoby and Maccoby, 1954:499). The interview

> is probably man's oldest and most often used device for obtaining information. . . . When used with a well-conceived schedule, an interview can obtain a great deal of information; it is flexible and adaptable to individual situations, and it can often be used when no other method is possible or adequate. . . . Questions about hopes, aspirations, and anxieties can be asked in such a way as to elicit accurate information. Most important, perhaps, the interview permits probing into the context of, and reasons for, answers to questions. (Kerlinger, 1964:467)

Because of their flexibility, interviews come in many forms. Some interviews are highly structured and highly standardized. They ask the same questions of all respondents and often ask respondents to choose between a limited number of listed responses worked out in advance by analysts.

These structured interviews are the tools of surveys and polls discussed in Chapter 9.

This chapter focuses on less structured interviews—variously referred to as investigative, unstructured, exploratory, in-depth, semi-structured, nonstandardized, journalistic, elite, or intensive. While all these labels reflect the nature of less structured interviews, "intensive" will be used here.

> The label of "intensive" interviewing captures the thoroughness of the approach and the concerted effort required, not only to gather quality information, but also to collect lively quotations and interesting anecdotes. (Murphy, 1980:75)

Why Interview?

Policy analysts select data collection techniques based on their appropriateness for research questions being investigated, the available resources, and the uses to which the information will be put. Interviews are not appropriate to all questions facing policy analysts. Intensive interviews are not suited for gathering data on large numbers of respondents. They would be excessively time consuming and costly, yielding nonstandardized information difficult to analyze for purposes of describing group results. However, intensive interviews are particularly suited to several types of information need commonly encountered by policy analysts.

EXPLORATORY INFORMATION NEEDS

Previous chapters identified the need for exploratory information in policy research. In the early stages of policy formulation, a primary need is to develop initial understandings of the dimensions, scope, and magnitude of the policy issue. Intensive interviewing, properly conducted, is a useful approach in fulfilling exploratory information needs.

Dexter observes that the appropriate role of an analyst conducting an intensive interview is "to let the interviewee teach him what the problem, the question, the situation, is. . . . " (Dexter, 1970:5). Exploratory interviewing operates on the assumption that interviewees know more about the issue than do analysts, suggesting an approach that

- stresses interviewees' definition of the situation;

- encourages interviewees to structure their account of the situation; and

- lets interviewees introduce their notions of what they regard as relevant, instead of relying on investigators' notions of relevance.

When implemented with these objectives, intensive interviewing is a central tool for meeting exploratory information needs.

PROCESS INFORMATION NEEDS

Organizations rarely run completely by stated procedures. Program processes and procedures are shaped and reshaped as the program evolves. Intensive interviewing of program managers and staff is an important means of documenting current procedures used in organizational processes. Interviews also provide insight into the conditions that affect these procedures and the ways in which they have evolved.

The utility of the interview for identifying what is done in programs makes it a central data collection tool for process evaluations of public programs. In conducting process evaluations of career criminal prosecution programs, analysts used intensive interviews with past and current program directors to document changes in the procedures used to prosecute habitual offenders. Deputy prosecutors were interviewed to identify the points in the criminal justice system at which decisions about cases are made and what criteria are applied in making those decisions (e.g., who decides whether a defendant is a career criminal, at what point, and using what criteria?).

EXPLANATORY INFORMATION NEEDS

Intensive interviewing allows analysts to explore respondents' explanations for events. If respondents are being queried about decisions or actions they participated in, interviewers ask them to explain why those decisions or actions were taken. For example, identifying approaches prosecutors use to influence convictions and sentencing was a major objective for a process evaluation of career criminal programs (Springer, Phillips, and Cannady, 1984). Deputy prosecutors were interviewed to identify what actions they took to strengthen their case, under what conditions, and for what purpose when dealing with career criminals. The result was a description of distinctive prosecution approaches and the reasons they were used.

In a larger sense, respondents can be asked their perceptions of the causes and consequences of events occurring around them. Questioning about the circumstances that surround events or the conditions under which particular outcomes occur makes an important contribution to understanding program operations. Of course, asking respondents about causes is not definitive in establishing cause-and-effect relations. An analyst can use interviews alone to gain insight into causes "so long as one recognizes that whatever account or explanation he develops is conjecture" (Lofland, 1971:62).

PERCEPTUAL INFORMATION NEEDS

In-person interviews are an ideal vehicle for getting to know other persons. "In order to feel that one understands what is 'going on' with others, most people try to put themselves in the other person's shoes. They try to imagine or discern how the other person thinks, acts, and feels" (Lofland, 1971:2). Intensive interviews allow analysts to probe for the perceptions of respondents, to learn what events mean to them, how events impact their lives, why events have value and significance.

Policymakers often make decisions impacting the lives of citizens they know little about—individuals facing life situations different from those of decision makers themselves. Policymakers' ability to understand the concerns and needs of citizens is improved through direct information aimed at uncovering the ways in which citizens see events. Information developed through intensive interviewing helps sensitize decision makers to the ways in which policy impacts stakeholders in differing circumstances. An example illustrates the point.

Analysts in a federal program designed to aid the visually impaired were asked to assess client satisfaction with the program and to identify factors influencing satisfaction (California Technical Assistance Associates, 1978). Reasoning from a review of relevant literature, the analysts anticipated that factors influencing satisfaction would vary with the circumstances of the individual. Persons blind from birth, for instance, may have a program experience different from those who lost their sight at a later age.

The program helped train and place blind clients as managers of food vending and food service (cafeterias) in federal, state, and local government buildings. Intensive interviews were conducted with a sample of blind vendors. The interviews were designed to elicit the respondents' perceptions of their employment opportunity: What importance did it play in their lives? Why? How did it affect their future? Responses indicated that the meaning and implications of program services for clients varied with their life circumstances.

Younger clients, many of whom were blind from birth or childhood, placed primary value on the opportunities the program offered for learning job skills, earning a living, and eventually moving into other career opportunities. Opportunities for moving to more challenging and lucrative locations (particularly major cafeterias) were central concerns. The major meaning of the program in their lives was linked to building a career and to providing for self and family.

For clients who had lost their sight later in life, career and family concerns were often secondary. For many, families were grown and a first career was behind them. For these clients, blindness brought isolation and loneliness. The opportunity to get out, to meet people, and to establish friendships was central to their concerns. The preferred placements for these clients were often the smaller vending stands that provided sundries and food items to building employees. Convenience, stability, and a more intimate location were valued over opportunities for upward mobility. In this case, interview-based information provided program managers with perceptual data concerning placement and services to clients in differing life circumstances.

QUICK ANALYSIS INFORMATION NEEDS

Jerome Murphy (1980:3) introduces his fieldwork guide for policy analysts with the following observation. "Policymakers need facts. . . . To get the facts, they dispatch staffers with simple instructions: 'find out what's going on' they say, and report back quickly.'" Faced with this charge, carefully selected intensive interviews become an indispensable tool for gathering information quickly.

Intensive interviews are inefficient in gathering information about a broad range of attitudes or events from numerous respondents, but they do provide an important shortcut to getting the facts. If analysts can conveniently gain access to knowledgeable persons, the major dimensions of a policy issue can be learned in a few well-selected interviews. Individuals who know an issue area well can provide facts on the history of policy in the area, on current conditions, and on the limitations and opportunities for future action. Knowledgeable informants may also provide direction to appropriate records, literature, and other persons who should be interviewed. Differing perspectives on an issue are consciously sought to capture balanced and trustworthy information.

The preceding discussion suggests the range of contributions intensive interviews make to policy research. Their flexibility and openness to the perspectives of respondents make them invaluable for exploration and issue definition. Their adaptability to identifying issues of process and the reasons for program evolution make them a central tool for process evaluations. Their utility for allowing analysts to understand life circumstances and meanings of events for stakeholders make them important for ascertaining the human impacts of public action. The ability to gather in-depth information from knowledgeable persons makes interviews essential to quick analysis. Skills in intensive interviewing are an integral component of policy research. Following sections present a series of steps for successfully using intensive interviews in fulfilling information needs.

Getting Ready to Interview

Intensive interviewing involves a significant commitment of resources to one method of collecting information. Getting the most out of each encounter requires getting ready in several ways. First, analysts gain preliminary knowledge of the policy terrain. Going into interviews unprepared leads to inefficient use of time and costs the goodwill of respondents. Second, analysts identify appropriate persons to interview and develop plans for gaining access to these persons. Third, analysts develop a plan for the interview itself, including questions and the degree of structure that is appropriate to information needs. Each of these three tasks is discussed in following sections.

LEARNING ABOUT THE POLICY SETTING

Often, interviewers are outsiders to the policy issue being investigated. Gaining a preliminary understanding of the context of the issue is essential for identifying information objectives, asking productive questions, and providing useful information. A basic familiarity with the policy terrain provides analysts with knowledge of formal program organization and procedures, major issues and controversies marking the policy setting, and a basic introduction to the orientations of the stakeholders they will be interviewing.

Analysts gain an initial feel for the issue area through a combination of reading relevant literature and engaging in conversations with selected people. At the outset, reading may be relatively indiscriminate; anything potentially relevant is examined. Often, initial sources are suggested or supplied by policymakers asking for the analysis. As time goes on, reading focuses increasingly on material central to study purposes.

In beginning the evaluation of the federal program for placing blind clients in vending locations, analysts struggled through a never-ending stream of written materials.

- From the state agency housing the program they obtained program regulations, employee and client handbooks, copies of all applications, evaluations, or request forms used in program management, printouts from the program's management information system, copies of annual reports, and a number of program audits conducted by state and federal control agencies.
- From the state law library they obtained copies of federal and state enabling legislation, amendments, and committee reports.
- From the U.S. Department of Health and Human Services they acquired several studies of similar programs in other states.

- Through a computerized library search they found a number of journal articles and monographs that studied the program.

This initial reading familarized analysts with major program characteristics prior to interviewing. In a descriptive sense, the documents conveyed program organization and procedure. The analysts knew how the program was staffed, where employees were located, what their duties were. They understood the formal objectives of the program, how it had been established, and its major services to clients. They learned basic information about the numbers of clients, how clients entered the program, and how long they remained. This information provided a framework within which to identify potential respondents and to plan interview activities.

Analysts also gleaned initial indications of major controversies or issues that marked the program. They kept notes on differing assessments of the program and jotted down questions that might be explored further. As they worked through the material, patterns began to emerge. For the vending program, many issues revolved around a central management problem. To what extent should managers and staff emphasize sheltered employment for the blind clients as compared to emphasizing competitive business practices? Understanding this issue helped analysts structure interviews that clarified the implications of the different orientations for the program and helped them avoid asking questions insensitive to differences of opinion on the issue.

Of course, preliminary interviews with persons who are knowledgeable about the issue help in gaining initial understandings, but the major task of selecting respondents and conducting field interviews waits until analysts develop a basic familiarity with the program and its issues, and with the policy community.

A basic familiarity with the policy terrain is also important for establishing rapport with respondents. If the interview conversation makes it clear that the interviewer is an outsider—lacks knowledge of the policy terrain—suspicions and reluctance may arise in respondents. Learning the language of respondents is an important aid to effective interviewing.

> Any social group, to the extent that it is a distinctive unit, will have ... a somewhat different set of common understandings around which action is organized, and these differences will find expression in a language whose nuances are peculiar to that group and fully understood only by its members. (Becker and Greer, 1957:28)

Analysts learn the concepts, terminology, and points of view common to potential respondents to increase the chances of cooperative and informative responses. Rapport begins with the sharing of a common language.

SELECTING RESPONDENTS TO INTERVIEW

Each intensive interview necessitates an investment of time and resources, particularly when conducted in person at the respondent's location. In evaluating the blind vendors program, for example, analysts were doing well to complete four field interviews per day per analyst. A careful selection of respondents is important to the efficient use of research resources.

Murphy (1980) identifies two types of individuals that analysts seek to interview—"key informants" and "regular interviewees." Key informants are central figures in a study.

> Such individuals are quite familiar with the program and its environment; they know the key figures, the problems, the successes, the norms and the traditions. They are also reliable observers who have the time and the inclination to meet with you. (Murphy, 1980:78)

Key informants may be former program officials who have moved elsewhere, making them more candid and willing. They may also be present high-placed program officials, concerned legislators, academics who have studied the program, and knowledgeable staff analysts.

Key informants make important contributions throughout a study. They help analysts get oriented to a program, identifying important contacts and providing inside knowledge perhaps otherwise not available. They help analysts develop strategies for conducting the study, help in interpreting findings, and provide advice on how to make study information products more accurate and useful. A key informant strategically placed in an agency helps develop the interest and commitment important to utilization-focused studies.

Regular interviewees are those respondents providing the bulk of interview information in many policy studies. The relation between analysts and interviewees is more formal than with key informants, and analysts maintain more control over the encounter, using a more structured and standardized interview format. The selection of regular interviewees depends upon the information objectives in a study, but several categories of respondents are frequent participants.

Managers and staff in organizations involved in a policy issue are valuable information sources. "Program staff people are important sources of data for evaluations. . . . [T]hey are the most likely to know how well a program is managed and how well the program runs on a day-to-day basis" (Posavac and Carey, 1980:50).

Different organizational personnel are required for different information needs. Top managers are not the best source of information on day-to-day procedures in delivering an agency's services; nor are service delivery staff necessarily informed about interactions between their agency and other units of government. Staff know most about their areas of responsibility.

Citizens who are the recipients of public programs provide another source of respondents. These program participants are particularly important in evaluation studies. Those on the receiving end of public programs are in a unique position for providing information such as satisfaction with the way in which services are delivered. Program clients are aware of how a program impacts their own feelings, attitudes, and life conditions. However, clients are not a good source for assessing all types of program performance. For example, recipients of public health services may report on the convenience, courtesy, or speed of services. They are not an adequate source for assessing the medical sophistication of those services.

Regular interviewees may be selected from a variety of other groups, depending on information objectives. In programs designed to improve the health or independent living skills of patients, for example, family members have been used as a source of information about outpatient behavior (Posavac and Carey, 1980:51). Selection of respondents is guided by what they are likely to know and by what analysts need to know to meet information needs.

Analysts are aware that interview respondents frequently have a particular interest or point of view regarding the issue. Program staff can typically be expected to reflect a favorable orientation to their program; program clients to maintaining or enhancing services. Selecting respondents reflecting a single point of view produces incomplete and biased research information.

To guard against tunnel vision resulting from relying on limited points of view, analysts use the principle of triangulation in selecting interview respondents. Respondents are selected to represent different social, economic, organizational, or political perspectives on an issue, and to represent different views of self-interest on an issue. Key informants are useful in identifying various perspectives that should be represented among interview respondents. Individuals in positions requiring a broad view of an issue area—such as legislative staff members, advisers to high-level administrators, or program analysts—are important in developing a triangulated interview strategy and in producing balanced, relevant information.

Structuring the Interview

In the preparation phase, analysts are getting ready to engage in "a special form of face-to-face interaction" (Denzin, 1970:139). As with any conversation, intensive interviewing involves give-and-take between the participants. However, the roles of interviewer and respondent differ. Interviewers have a purpose—to elicit information—and this purpose requires that, to varying degrees, interviewers control or manage the conversation. Analysts desiring different degrees of control will introduce more or less structure into their questions.

Preparation of interview questions ranges from an unstructured format in which the interviewer determines question order and content in the context of each interview encounter, to standardized schedules in which each respondent is asked identical questions in an established order. The interviewer may work with a variety of formats falling between, such as a checklist or outline of information to be obtained without specific question wording. The appropriate degree of structure depends upon several considerations, discussed next.

LESS STRUCTURED INTERVIEWS

The degree of structure depends upon the specificity and standardization of the information analysts are seeking. Unstructured formats are well suited for exploratory analysis (Maccoby and Maccoby, 1954:499). Unstructured interviews minimize the necessity for analysts to pursue their understanding of issues through predeveloped questions, allowing interviewers to solicit the respondents' definitions of what is important. Interviews in which analysts are attempting to identify respondents' definitions of the situation or to tap respondents' unique expertise are typically unstructured.

Less structured interview formats are also useful when the information sought is confined to very few respondents. Thus, interviews with key respondents are frequently free-flowing but purposeful conversations. Similarly, interviews with people in unique positions (e.g., an agency head) are designed to allow interviewers to tap the knowledge and experience of respondents and to pursue unanticipated insights.

Previous sections stressed the importance of adequate preparation before interviewing. Unstructured interviews are no exception. While analysts occasionally go into interviews with the topics they want to cover only briefly considered, it is more typical to prepare some form of written interview guide. In unstructured interviews, this guide may simply be an outline or list of topics that interviewers want to be sure to cover. An excerpt from the guide used in conducting relatively unstructured interviews with regulated lobbyists provides an example. Topics that needed to be covered in those interviews included:

- Sources of information about reporting requirements
  —Adequacy of sources mentioned
  —Suggestions for improvement
- Problems with compliance

—Record keeping
—Prohibitions on behavior
—Expenditure limitations

A guide of this type does not specify the way in which questions are asked, nor does it constrain interviewers in following up on unanticipated responses. It simply helps interviewers organize thoughts and serves to provide a checklist to ensure that important information needs are covered.

MORE STRUCTURED INTERVIEWS

When information needs are more specific and standardized, more structured interview formats are used. The need for more defined question order and content arises in several circumstances. When analysts want specific types of information from interviews—such as a description of procedures within an agency—predetermined questions help ensure that the necessary information is solicited. Standardized formats are developed when a study involves more than one site, e.g., several local offices implementing a program. Standardization is also important when similar information is being sought from many respondents.

In all of these situations, the interview conversation dictates a more structured approach. The advantages of the structured interview also carry costs. Standardized question wording assumes respondents share a common vocabulary and that question wording can be developed to convey the same meaning to each (Richardson, Dohrenwend, and Klein, 1965:40–43). To ensure that these assumptions are warranted, the task of preparation prior to interviewing is increased. Structured interview schedules typically go through several revisions to refine the questions. Analysts typically have early drafts reviewed by colleagues, key informants, or clients themselves; in some instances, a few pilot interviews may be conducted to test question content, wording, and sequence (Chapter 8).

Although intensive interviews vary in the degree to which questions are standardized, question wording remains open-ended, rather general. Questions in intensive interviews typically use language that is somewhat nonspecific "so the interviewee can interpret them in his own terms and out of his own experience" (Dexter, 1970:55). Intensive interviews are an essential tool in gathering detail and nuance analysts cannot fully anticipate in advance.

Clearly, the degree of structure in intensive interviews is related to the particular research situation in which they are applied. Indeed, many interview situations require an interview approach falling between the unstructured and structured extremes. Interviewers conducting the career criminal prosecution interviews, for instance, occasionally altered wording or pursued unanticipated comments to improve rapport in the interviews and to improve the quality of information. Interview schedules may combine specific questions and less specified follow-up questions. A significant advantage of intensive interviewing is its flexibility; the degree of structure is one component of adapting interviews to particular information needs.

Conducting the Interview

Effective interviewing requires preparation, but preparation alone does not guarantee success. Intensive interviews are a "conversation with a purpose" (Murphy, 1980:75). The degree to which conversation is successful depends in part on the human relations skills (Mann, 1970) of interviewers. Skillful interviewers have the ability to gain access to respondents, to set them at ease, and to elicit the information respondents can provide while respecting their dignity and privacy. Accomplishing a successful interview is not simply a matter of having the right questions. It requires asking the right questions, in the right way, at the right time, while maintaining a professional, responsive, courteous approach to respondents.

ARRANGING THE INTERVIEW

Intensive interviews in policy research are often conducted in the work setting with managers, staff members, program clients, and other informed stakeholders. Gaining access to these respondents presents difficult problems of scheduling. In some organizations, potential respondents may be uncertain about their freedom to grant an interview. Analysts use a number of ways to arrange interviews with potential respondents.

In some circumstances, analysts may be able simply to walk into a respondent's office, introduce themselves, and conduct the interviews. More often, analysts arrange a time and place for the interview in advance. A telephone request and a willingness to schedule the interview at the respondent's convenience are often sufficient.

When multiple interviews will be conducted in an agency, it is important to gain the assistance and support of high-level managers in the agency (Mann, 1970:123). This is particularly important if interviews are to be conducted in a limited site visit. In evaluating career criminal programs, analysts worked closely with unit directors in the seven jurisdictions involved in the study. The directors received letters well ahead of each site visit. The letters identified the dates the evaluation team would be visiting and requested assistance in arranging interviews with specified staff members. The request was confirmed in direct telephone calls from the team leader. The active support of unit directors was essential to the efficient use of scarce time on site.

In most circumstances, it is desirable to interview respondents in their choice of settings (Murphy, 1980:83). It usually is more convenient for the respondent and puts the respondent at ease. In some circumstances, however, respondents may feel freer to respond away from the office.

INTRODUCTIONS IN INTERVIEWING

Initial moments of an interview are important to establishing rapport. Interviewers accomplish several objectives during this introduction phase. For example, they convey the purposes of the interview and the respondent's contribution to it (Denzin, 1970:139). At this point they attempt to establish trust with respondents, and attempt to establish their own credentials and concern in conducting the study. Introductory comments convey the identity of the interviewer, the general purpose of the research and the uses of the information, and, where appropriate, the identity of the organization sponsoring the study.

Respondents may ask questions about the interviewer's background and qualifications to conduct the study. Establishing one's qualifications is particularly important for interviews with high-level officials or in circumstances in which the interviewee is uneasy about the purpose of the study. It is helpful for interviewers to offer a business card to confirm that they are a staff member for Senator Smith or a health analyst in a department of health.

Establishing qualifications is one part of gaining the confidence of respondents. Developing a comfortable and open atmosphere for the interview can be more important. An effective means of establishing rapport, such as genuinely reflecting a desire to learn about the interviewee's experiences and perceptions, puts respondents at ease.

Other indications of the attitude of the interviewer help gain respondents' trust and encourage them to participate. Effective interviewers convey genuine enthusiasm and interest in respondents' comments. They are good listeners. Further, they are "sincerely appreciative of the subject's time and effort. After all, answering questions can be hard work, and time spent in an interview could be spent elsewhere. The subject deserves a genuine thank you and other expressions of appreciation" (Murphy, 1980:91).

QUESTIONING AND PROBING IN INTERVIEW

Interview questions do two things—solicit information and involve respondents in the interview. Questions are asked in ways that get respondents interested, get them to think about their answers, and keep their attention. Since people are different, interviewers using less structured formats adapt their questioning according to the way respondents react. Some respondents thrive on general questions and provide thorough and insightful responses with little prompting. Others want more direction and require more specific questions with follow-up probes and encouraging comments.

Responses to the rather general questions that typify intensive interviews would be incomplete without effective follow-up questions, or "probes." Probes may be developed ahead of time as part of the interview guide (Lofland, 1971:82). Frequently, however, interviewers insert probes in response to the progress of a particular interview.

Murphy (1980) identifies uses of probes for intensive interviews. The first use of probes is for clarification. Probes for clarification are used to lead the subject to explain points that are vague, ambiguous, or briefly communicated. A second use of probes encourages respondents to elaborate on potentially important points. Probes may ask the respondent to be more specific about facts—the "what, when or where" (Murphy, 1980:98) of a statement. They may also ask the respondent to specify the reasons behind an observation or event, or to provide specific evidence for a statement: "Are you thinking of any particular example?"

Another type of probe identified by Murphy (1980:98) is the silent probe. As in any conversation, a respondent's comments may be interrupted by moments of silence. Interviewers may be tempted to close this gap immediately with another question. But often, it is beneficial to remain silent to allow respondents to gather their thoughts before continuing. Allowing this time produces insights and clarifications missed when interviewers interrupt. The general rule in phrasing interview questions is to query the respondent in a nonthreatening and nonjudgmental fashion.

In sum, effective questioning and probing requires analysts to be attentive to information needs and to the interpersonal dynamics occurring between interviewer and respondent. The direct and flexible character of the intensive interview is its greatest strength as a method for collecting information; its success, however, requires skillful implementation of the interview encounter. "Successful interviewing is not unlike carrying on unthreatening, self-controlled, supportive, polite, and cordial interaction in everyday life. If one can do that, one already has the main interpersonal skills necessary to interviewing" (Lofland, 1971:90).

Recording and Analyzing Interview Data

Analysis of intensive interview data is a continuous process culminating in the reporting of major findings, alternatives, conclusions, and recommendations. Analysis is ultimately a creative process that "entails drawing inferences about what the data show, mean, explain, and imply" (Murphy, 1980:131). This process is emphasized at the point of preparing the final report, but decisions made in planning, recording, and managing interview data lay the foundation for subsequent analysis.

Experts on interviewing procedures voice little agreement on the best way to record the substance of respondent comments. Some argue that verbatim preservation of the interview is essential. "For all intents and purposes it is imperative that one tape record or otherwise preserve the interview itself" (Lofland, 1971:88). The freedom from taking copious notes, it is argued, allows interviewers to be more attentive and to ask more fruitful questions. Verbatim recording preserves the nuances of the discussion and reveals the subtle ways in which the interviewer may have led the respondent (Dexter, 1970:59).

On the other hand, critics argue that tape recording is an obtrusive and distracting form of recording information that puts respondents on guard and diverts attention of interviewers (Dexter, 1970:59). Simply jotting notes, sometimes sparingly, will allow a freer, more open and candid interaction between interviewer and respondent.

The resolution of these differing points of view is a matter of personal preference, the circumstances of the interview, and the potential uses of the information. In some instances, e.g., where respondents are comfortable (such as public officials who have become accustomed to recording devices) and their attention is devoted to the interview, tape recording is appropriate. In other circumstances, when the interview is sensitive or the session is constantly interrupted, recording may be less appropriate. Another consideration is time and resources. Transcribing tapes is a costly process not justified in many instances (Bucher, Fritz, and Quarantelli, 1956). Adept note taking may be the most efficient way to extract what is important from some interviews.

Notes are taken in a variety of styles. Some interviewers take copious notes to preserve the detail of responses and to demonstrate involvement in the session. Others find this distracting or impossible, given the pace of discussion, and prefer to rely on abbreviations and brief symbols. These brief notes may be used to indicate specific nuances that recall themes and the respondent orientations (Dexter, 1970:57).

Whatever the note-taking style, notes are organized and expanded as soon after the interview as possible. In the study of lobbyist regulation, a coffee shop across from the implementing agency became a favorite spot for clarifying and organizing interview notes before returning to the office. These periods of reflection on fresh interviews are important for recalling detail and for identifying general themes. Particularly significant comments are recorded or paraphrased for later use to enrich the realness of study findings. At the same time, general insights can be recorded and related to the specifics of the interview.

Developing categories of interview responses is fundamental to the process of analyzing information collected through intensive interviews. Once interview notes have been elaborated and rewritten, analysis is facilitated by filing relevant comments by different respondents under the appropriate category. One set of completed interview notes may be filed by respondent—chronologically, alphabetically, or according to position. These intact interviews preserve the context of a respondent's specific comments. A second set of files is analytic (Lofland, 1971:119). These files may consist of a series of folders labeled by various categories of interview content, e.g., case processing procedures. Relevant comments from each interview may be drawn from a copy of the completed notes and placed in the appropriate folder. Reviewing the analytic files allows analysts easy access to all interview materials on the topic of interest.

As the analysis proceeds, analysts combine, subdivide, or alter the file categories to reflect emerging patterns or insights. Evaluators in the career criminal study, for example, identified two subcategories within the "case processing procedures" category (Springer, Phillips, and Cannady, 1984:19).

Respondents in one group of programs reported systems of formal rules that specified the circumstances under which prosecuting attorneys could take specific actions in prosecuting a career criminal case. In one program, for example, cases charged as residential burglaries could not offer probation in return for a guilty plea—a very common plea bargain in most circumstances. Programs with formal rules about prosecutors' decisions were categorized as applying a procedural case processing policy.

Respondents in other programs reported no specific rules constraining the prosecutor's decisions. These programs provided experienced attorneys with additional resources to prosecute serious habitual offenders, but did not dictate the attorney's decisions. These programs were categorized as applying a discretionary case processing policy. This distinction in procedural policy turned out to be important in explaining the types of implementation problems experienced in the programs. The use of categorized files to organize interview material is an effective tool for facilitating analysis.

Data Quality Considerations Using Intensive Interviews

Intensive interviews typically produce nonquantitative information not easily translated into formalized, statistical tests of data accuracy. Analysts assess the probable truthfulness and accuracy of interview responses in other ways.

Triangulating data sources provides an important means of checking the quality of interview responses. Responses from interviewees in different positions are compared for similarities. Where consistency is high, confidence that the situation is accurately portrayed is higher. Information provided by regular respondents may be compared with those of key informants as another indicator of the trustworthiness of interview information. "Checking out against alternative accounts" (Douglas, 1976:148) is one method of assessing the quality of interview information.

The quality of interview data is also assessed through "checking out against direct observations of 'hard facts'" (Douglas, 1976:147). When respondents cover topics documented in agency records or in other documents, factual interview responses are checked against established records.

Analysts also consider the nature of the interview material itself in assessing information quality. If a respondent's comments are internally inconsistent, analysts are wary in assuming their validity (Murphy, 1980:69). If the account lacks detail or concrete examples, it may indicate that the respondent lacks in-depth knowledge of the area (Murphy, 1980:70). Similarly, responses based on secondhand or hearsay information are more questionable than those based on direct observation and experience (Murphy, 1980:70).

In practical terms, ensuring the quality of information gathered through intensive interviews is a matter of applying "tough-minded suspicion" (Douglas, 1976:147) to both interview content and procedure. Experienced analysts assess information against other interviews and other data sources. Responses are evaluated for consistency, plausibility, and detail. The successful use of intensive interviewing as a data collection method demands analysts be open to unexpected insights offered by individual respondents, while simultaneously maintaining guards against accepting inaccurate or biased reports.

OBSERVATION: GAINING KNOWLEDGE FROM EVENTS

"Seeing is believing." People place credence in direct experience with events and situations as a route to understanding and knowledge. Indeed, "direct experience seems to be the most pervasive, fundamental test of truth" (Douglas, 1976:5).

Despite the common reliance on direct experience for personal knowledge, direct observation has been often neglected as a method of data collection for policy research. A major reason for relying on other, less direct methods stems from the nature of direct observation. Direct observation requires being at the scene of the events being studied, and, if systematic, requires substantial time to collect a limited amount of data. Additionally, policy research may require information on programs affecting large populations; it often requires information about past events. Direct observation of policy issues is often not feasible in meeting these information needs.

Nevertheless, direct observation has important and increasingly recognized (McCall, 1984) advantages for policy research. Direct observation provides a complement to other methods of data collection in triangulated research strategies. It provides a potential means for analysts to assess information quality reported by others. "If you want to know what actually is occurring, there is no better way to find out than to observe it yourself, rather than rely on the potentially unreliable reports of others" (Murphy, 1980:113).

Some analysts argue that direct observation helps increase the usefulness of research information because concrete information observed on site is more acceptable to decision makers.

> A major contributor to nonuse of evaluation data is the practice of limiting . . . evaluations to examination of administrator's perceptions of program operation instead of actual observation of program observation. Evaluations typically monitor program execution through interviews, checklists, surveys, and questionnaires. While these methods are economical . . . , they sacrifice the advantages of observation of actual program activity. Consequently, the evaluations are viewed as only partly relevant. (Turner, Nielson, and Murray, 1983:374)

In some circumstances, direct observation provides a means of collecting unobtrusive information. When respondents are asked to report on issues affecting them, their self-interest may affect their responses. For example, cities in the frost belt allocate road repair dollars to fill potholes appearing in city streets each year. Relying on the reports of citizens concerning the need for repair on their streets could be expected occasionally to produce self-serving results; some would report poor conditions in anticipation of increasing the chances for repair.

To produce an unobtrusive measure of street condition, cities regularly conduct pothole surveys by sending employees throughout the city to rate streets according to the number and size of potholes. Maintenance is scheduled according to priorities established through this information gained by using direct observation. The direct observation of physical conditions provides information concerning the need for services as well as the effectiveness of past services.

Direct observation, then, has important informational roles in policy research. Following sections discuss two major observation techniques. First are *transient observations*. These largely unstructured observations typically complement other methods of data collection (Murphy, 1980:112). Second are more structured instruments for a method termed *systematic observation* (McCall, 1984).

Transient Observation

If intensive interviews are conversations with a purpose, observation is "watching with a purpose." Transient observation has typically been applied in studies by sociologists and anthropologists who immerse themselves in group cultures over extended periods of time. The time requirements of this technique and the difficulty of generalizing findings have limited its use in policy research.

Direct, unstructured observation is, however, a useful complement to interviews, document analysis, and other data collection techniques. While visiting a study site, an analyst frequently acts as a transient observer who "observes without disguise, is clearly an outsider, and is faced with tight time constraints" (Murphy, 1980:122). Transient observers combine observation with other research activities. They observe physical surroundings, events, and interpersonal interactions as they conduct interviews or work in agency offices while fulfilling other research activities. Transient observers take advantage of opportunities to be present at meetings or other relevant events which occur while they are on site.

Transient observation serves useful purposes in policy research. It is a prime method for evaluating interview information. The evaluation of the federal program placing visually impaired clients as food services managers provides an example. Interviews with program staff indicated that physical arrangements and appearances of merchandise in locations were a major factor distinguishing successful from unsuccessful managers. While on site interviewing vendors at their place of business, analysts assessed this assertion by noting physical arrangements and appearances of merchandise in stands of varying success. These observations were useful in confirming the comments and explanations provided by program staff.

Transient observation also provides analysts with enriched understandings of the climate and context of the setting being studied, helping them gain a flavor of events often important in structuring analysis. In the career criminal prosecution study, respondents told analysts about techniques of early case intervention through which police officers informally consulted with attorneys to strengthen their investigations. The analysts' understanding of this process was enhanced by observing consultations that occurred while they were in the room. These transient observations also provided a basis for generating ideas and avenues for further study and analysis.

Note taking for transient observation is similar to that for intensive interviews. Analysts typically jot brief reminders of the salient aspects of interpersonal interaction, individual behavior, and physical setting, and write more complete field notes at the earliest opportunity. Notes may often be incorporated into the analytic files created from intensive interviews.

Information based on transient observation is interpreted with care. Analysts may infer incorrect meanings to events and behaviors if they are not complemented with other knowledge of the setting, e.g., interview responses. Experienced analysts take care to cross-check data and assess the representativeness of the observations. But used in the proper context, "observations can be among the best sources of information because you collected the data directly" (Murphy, 1980:121).

Systematic Observation

Analysts also use more structured forms of observation in policy research. "Observation is systematic to the degree that plans for selection, provocation, recording, and encoding are both explicit and preset, rather than either implicit or emergent" (McCall, 1984:265). Systematic observation incorporates planned sampling of events or objects to be observed, explicit instructions for how to make and record observations, and a system for recording data in a standardized (usually numeric) form. Systematic observation is appropriate when analysts need explicit information in a known population of events.

APPLICATIONS OF SYSTEMATIC OBSERVATION: TWO EXAMPLES

Systematic observation has been an effectively used method in policy research. McCall (1984:266) comments that "systematic field research is more often a tool of applied than of academic research. . . . [A]pplied research usually means policy research."

Systematic observation is used when evaluating classroom teaching performance. Policies concerning teaching performance may be adopted by school boards and educational supervisors, but they have no impact unless they are implemented—that is, unless they are reflected in interactions between teachers and pupils in classrooms. "A program can appear to be ineffective when, in fact, it never happened" (Kerr et al., 1985:461).

The use of systematic observation for assessing performance is applied in policy areas other than education. In the health area, observation has been used to assess emergency room treatment behaviors (Douglas, 1976). In the criminal justice system, observation has been used to study the performance of lawyers, judges, and police (McCall, 1978).

The systematic observation of physical objects or conditions has also contributed to policy research. The pothole survey, introduced earlier, is an example of systematic observation of physical conditions. Also, trained inspectors have been used to rate the cleanliness of streets and alleys before and after implementation of city cleanup programs (Hatry, Winnie, and Fisk, 1981:99ff.). Local and state planning agencies use direct observation of housing units to assess the condition of housing in their jurisdictions.

Whatever the specific application, analysts using systematic observation develop rules that specify what events or objects are to be observed, how observations will be selected, and how data are to be recorded and scored. The following examples demonstrate major steps in systematic observation.

Evaluating classroom implementation. Educational policy is frequently designed to accomplish pedagogical or behavioral objectives. The comprehensive educational program in this example was designed to improve instructional methods with the objective of increasing student skills, opportunities, and rewards for learning in the classroom (Hawkins and Weiss, 1980). In a pilot project, program staff randomly selected and trained teachers in six schools nationwide. Project teachers were extensively trained in three approaches to classroom instruction:

1. *Interactive Teaching.* Teachers were trained in developing a sequence of lessons building on skills learned at each step. Teachers check progress and adjust lessons according to demonstrated progress. Students receive continuous feedback through teacher interaction.
2. *Student Team Learning.* Teachers assign students of different ability to teams that compete in academic improvement contests. Teachers monitor and advise while students teach and learn from each other.
3. *Proactive Classroom Management.* Teachers were taught techniques to manage disruptive classroom behavior. Specific direction, praise, and decreased opportunity for misbehavior were emphasized among these techniques.

The academic and social performance of students in project classrooms and students in control classrooms using conventional teaching was monitored through records and interviews. Direct observation was used to evaluate the extent to which the three teaching strategies were actually implemented in the project classrooms and to assess differences in teaching behavior between project and control classrooms. Observational measures of the strength of classroom implementation could then be related to improvements in student performance and behavior.

Trained observers scored teaching behavior in the study classrooms for three semesters following program implementation. Using the observation instrument displayed in Figure 6.1, observers scored teaching behavior during randomly selected classroom periods (50 or 60 minutes).

Teacher behavior was rated according to "conformity" ($\checkmark$) or "nonconformity" ($\times$) with the eleven categories of teaching behavior described in Figure 6.2. Behavior was scored on a minute-by-minute basis throughout the teaching period. Brief descriptive notes for later reference were written in the right-hand columns of the form. Categories 2, 4, 5, 6, 7, 8, and 10 represent teaching activities in which teachers were trained—"project activities." Categories 1, 3, 9, and 11 represent alternative teaching practices, or "normal classroom practices."

Observers were trained using a training and coding manual that described the teacher-coding categories in detail. Numerous examples were provided to familiarize the observer with conforming and nonconforming behaviors in each category. Completed observation forms were transformed into summary implementation scores for each class period that was reserved. Basically, each minute of teaching behavior that conformed to project activities was scored $+1$; each minute of behavior that violated project practices was scored -1, and normal teaching or poorly implemented proj-

Min.	Assessment	Mental Set/ Objectives	Input	Modeling	Guided Practice/ Check for Understanding	Groups	Procedures/ Directions	Reactive Management	Praise	Sponge/ Enrichment	No Task Defined # Off Task	Interactive Teaching Map
												Date _____ Teacher _____ Period _____ Observer _____ Total # of Students _____ 'X' = Alternative Teaching Practice '√' = Effective Implementation
0.												0.
1.												1.
2.												2.
3.												3.
4.												4.
5.												5.
6.												6.
7.												7.
8.												8.
9.												9.
10.												10.
11.												11.
12.												12.
13.												13.
14.												14.
15.												15.
16.												16.
17.												17.
18.												18.
19.												19.
20.												20.
21.												21.
22.												22.
23.												23.
24.												24.
25.												25.
26.												26.

FIGURE 6.1   The Interactive Teaching Map: Observation Form. (*Source:* Douglas M. Kerr, Lori Kent, and Tony C. M. Lam, "Measuring Program Implementation with a Classroom Observation Instrument: The Interactive Teaching Map," *Evaluation Review,* 1985, 9(4), p. 466. Copyright 1985 by Sage Publications, Inc. Reprinted by permission of Sage Publications, Inc.)

ect activities were scored zero. The overall implementation score for each class period was the sum of minute-by-minute scores.

The interactive teaching map is an example of a detailed system for recording direct observations of teaching behavior. The system proved an accurate and useful means for identifying differences in strength of implementation in classrooms. Stronger implementation was found to contribute to improved student performance and behavior. The information produced was used by program supervisors "to identify program strengths and weaknesses, meet staff training and development needs, and monitor changing implementation in the classroom" (Kerr, Kent, and Lam, 1985:480).

(1) Assessment/written work: This coding category includes all written tests, quizzes, worksheets, and other written assignments that inform teachers of students' comprehension of material and their mastery of learning objectives.

(2) Mental set/objectives: In presentations at the beginning of class, teachers specify what students will learn by the end of the lesson and what students must do to demonstrate their learning. Teachers also relate new material to old material and to topics that interest students.

(3) Input: This category includes all presentations and explanations of material through lecture, film, or discussion.

(4) Modeling: Demonstrations, examples worked out on the board, and step-by-step explanations of how to solve a problem, perform an experiment, complete a report, or carry out an assignment are included under this coding category.

(5) Guided practice/check for understanding: This coding category records instances in which teachers, during class, interactively monitor students' understanding of material. It includes oral question-and-answer sequences as well as supervised seatwork and verbal quizzes.

(6) Groups: This category records collaborative work among students, both in formal Student-Team-Learning groups and in informal, unstructured groups. The use of formal Student-Team-Learning groups is recorded at the top of the form.

(7) Procedures/directions: Administrative tasks, collecting and passing out papers, books, and tests, scheduling special events, instruction informing students what activity to do next and how to do it are coded as procedures/directions.

(8) Reactive management: All disciplinary actions taken to deal with misbehavior or inattention constitute reactive management.

(9) Praise: Each instance of positive encouragement and approval of students is recorded as praise.

(10) Sponge/enrichment: Sponge and enrichment activities fill classroom time that might otherwise be wasted or encourage misbehavior. Sponge activities are brief educational exercises that engage students in learning while they wait for roll to be taken, for late students to arrive, or for the bell to ring at the end of class. Enrichments are extra credit or extension activities for students who complete regular assignments before the rest of the class.

(11) No task defined: This category records all classroom time during which no learning activity is specified. Interruptions by public announcements or visitors are also coded "no task defined."

FIGURE 6.2   The Interactive Teaching Map: Code Category Definitions. (*Source:* Douglas M. Kerr, Lori Kent, and Tony C. M. Lam, "Measuring Program Implementation with a Classroom Observation Instrument: The Interactive Teaching Map," *Evaluation Review,* 1985, 9(4), p. 467. Copyright 1985 by Sage Publications, Inc. Reprinted by permission of Sage Publications, Inc.)

Assessing housing condition.   The U.S. Bureau of the Census began widespread collection of information on housing condition in 1940. In that year, census enumerators were instructed to observe the structure and to rate it as needing major repairs when parts of the structure such as floors, roof, walls, or foundation needed major repair or replacement. Under pressure from census users, particularly those concerned with urban renewal, the bureau made efforts to develop more refined measures of housing condition in succeeding censuses. By 1960, census personnel were rating housing condition by three categories—sound, deteriorating, or dilapidated.

In the 1960 census, enumerators determined the condition of housing units through direct observation. During the course of the census interview, enumerators rated the unit according to its extent or degree of visible defects. Observation was meant to identify defects associated with inadequate construction, hazards to occupants, weather tightness, and disrepair. Defects were defined as slight, intermediate, or critical. For example, enumerator instructions defined critical defects in the following way.

> Critical defects result from continued neglect or lack of repair, or indicate serious damage to the structure. Examples of critical defects are: Holes, open cracks, or rotted, loose or missing material (clapboard siding, shingles, bricks, concrete tile, plaster, or floorboards) over a large area of the foundation, outside walls, roof, chimney, or inside walls, floors or ceilings; substantial sagging of floors, walls, or roof; and extensive damage by storm, fire, or flood. (U.S. Department of Commerce, 1967:12)

Similar definitions were provided for slight and intermediate defects, and for inadequate original construction.

Once enumerators observed a housing unit for defects and for the quality of original construction, they used their observations to make a summary judgment about whether the dwelling was sound, dilapidated, or deteriorating. Criteria were also provided for making this decision. For example,

> *dilapidated housing* does not provide safe and adequate shelter and in its present condition endangers the health, safety, or well-being of the occupants. Such housing has one or more critical defects; or has a combination of intermediate defects in sufficient number or extent to require considerable repair or rebuilding; or is of inadequate original construction. The defects are so critical or so widespread that the structure should be extensively repaired, rebuilt, or torn down. (U.S. Department of Commerce, 1967:12)

Thus, the decision to classify a structure as dilapidated could be based on varying combinations of observed defects.

Following the completion of the 1960 census, the Bureau of the Census established a task force to assess the quality of housing condition data produced through enumerator observations. Following an extensive analysis, which included reliability tests involving rating the same housing units by several different enumerators, the task force reached the following conclusion:

> The statistics are unreliable. Our best estimate is that if another group of enumerators had been sent back to rate the housing units of the United States, only about one-third of the units rated as dilapidated or deteriorating by either group of enumerators would have been rated the same by both groups of enumerators. (U.S. Department of Commerce, 1967:5)

The task force went on to conclude that, given the categories and definitions used to rate housing condition in the 1960 census, "there does not appear to be any feasible method of improving the quality of enumerator ratings" (U.S. Department of Commerce, 1967:6). The Bureau of the Census did not attempt to collect observational data on housing condition in 1970 or 1980.

SYSTEMATIC OBSERVATION AND DATA QUALITY

The interactive teaching map provided educational policymakers with accurate and useful information, while the 1960 census produced inaccurate data on housing conditions. The factors that contribute to reliable observational data are related to the coding instrument, the observers themselves, and the setting in which observations are made.

The coding instrument.   Systematic observations are guided by coding instruments which provide observers instructions on what to watch, how to make decisions about scoring observations, and how to record their observations. Coding instructions used in the census housing condition observations were a major factor in producing unreliable results.

A major deficiency in the census rating procedures was the lack of sufficiently specific operational definitions (U.S. Department of Commerce, 1967:23). Terms describing extent of defects (e.g., "small," "slight," "large areas") were not precisely defined, so that different observers made different decisions concerning what a "small" defect was. Similarly, rules for making coding decisions were imprecise, e.g., "several," "some." Finally, observers were asked to make judgments about conditions without concrete guidance—e.g., "so serious that the structure should be torn down or rebuilt."

The accuracy and reliability of observational data is improved through precise operational definitions of what to observe and through devising precise scoring rules. The interactive teaching map specified observations through requiring minute-by-minute scores and providing clear, specific definitions of behavior that would be classified in each category. The precision of the observation instrument helped produce useful results.

The observer.   A second source of poor data quality is observers themselves. The census uses thousands of enumerators. The typical enumerator in the 1960 census was "a housewife in her thirties or forties with no particular experience in architecture, building construction, or any other line of endeavor relevant to the rating process" (U.S. Department of Commerce, 1967:24). Training on housing condition was limited to thirty minutes, less than 10 percent of total training time for census enumerators. It is predictable that relatively untrained observers would interpret vague terms in their coding instructions in varying ways.

Observers who applied the interactive teaching map represent an opposite extreme. Two of the three observers used in the study made observations in all six sites; the third observer was a local. All observers were thoroughly trained before going into the field, including pilot observations in actual classroom settings. In this instance, data quality benefited through collection by a limited number of well-trained and experienced observers.

The setting.   The setting in which observations are made impacts data quality. The errors in rating housing condition in the 1960 census were probably affected by two aspects of the environment in which observations were conducted. First, the conditions under which census enumerators worked did not encourage careful observation. The piecemeal rate of pay encouraged rapid data collection. It was estimated that the typical enumerator spent less than two minutes in determining housing condition. It is also probable that the characteristics of particular neighborhoods and communities may have influenced ratings. In particular, enumerators may have had a tendency to search for distinctions in quality by making harsher judgments when housing quality was uniformly high, and more lenient judgments when quality was low (U.S. Department of Commerce, 1967:24).

Precise instruments and careful training help overcome rating bias attributable to the setting. However, experienced analysts are aware of the importance of the environment in which observations are made. When known observers are in the classroom, for example, teachers may alter their normal behavior since they are aware their performance is being assessed. This danger increases to the extent that the subject has control over what occurs in the setting. In the interactive teaching example, it was not likely that teachers could control the complex interaction between teacher and students that was the subject of observation.

The data quality problems encountered in the 1960 census indicate some of the limitations of systematic observation as a method for collecting information. Rating housing condition on the basis of visible defects requires complex judgments. The census data collection process did not allow the investment of time nor the detailed scoring of specific structural components necessary to rate housing condition with reasonable accuracy. Given the constraints inherent to the census process, direct observation was not an appropriate means for collecting the desired information.

On the other hand, the interactive teaching map exemplifies a situation in which systematic observation provides accurate information. Assessments of the reliability in coding classroom behavior by three different coders confirmed that coding decisions demonstrated high inter-rater reliability (Kerr et al., 1985:471). When instruments are precise and operational, scoring methods are explicit, observers are well-trained, and the setting is conducive to this method of data collection, systematic observation plays an important role in producing useful information for stakeholders.

CONCLUDING COMMENTS

Direct experience gained through in-person interaction or through observing events illustrates basic ways of gaining knowledge in day-to-day life. This chapter identified the roles of intensive interviews and direct observation in producing information for policy-making.

Intensive interviews, ubiquitous in policy research, are useful in meeting a variety of information needs. They are well suited to exploratory data collection when analysts are seeking to develop an understanding of an issue area. They provide an efficient procedure for gaining information about program procedures and processes. They allow respondents to explain the reasons for their actions and to convey the meaning of events to them. They provide quick and efficient means of gaining information possessed by others. These advantages give intensive interviewing a place in much policy research.

Intensive interviewing has been characterized as a conversation with a purpose. As in any conversation, successful interviewers elicit desired information in ways that keep respondents interested, motivated, and cooperative, and that at all times respect respondents' dignity and privacy. To accomplish this mix, analysts prepare themselves for interviews by familiarizing themselves with the policy issue and with the policy terrain in which respondents work. Respondents are selected to represent various perspectives on the issues at hand, and questions are given various degrees of structure reflecting information needs. Where relatively standardized information is being elicited from different respondents, interview schedules are more structured.

No matter how thorough the preparation, intensive interviewing requires analysts to be flexible and responsive in the course of the interview. The initial minutes of an interview are important to establishing mutual expectations between interviewer and respondent, and to establishing trust and rapport. Probes may be used for guiding interviews. Probes elicit clarification of responses, prompt respondents to elaborate important points, and encourage respondents to continue providing helpful information.

Interviews are recorded in a variety of ways ranging from tape recording to minimal jotting of notes. Whatever the method, effective management and organization of interview notes facilitate subsequent analysis and report preparation. Notes should be clarified and written up as soon as feasible following the interview. Organizing notes from different interviews according to analytic categories helps identify patterns and themes in the data and contributes to efficient report writing. In sum, the intensive interview is a method frequently used in policy analysis. Well-honed interview skills are the key to effectively fulfilling information needs.

Direct observation of events also makes important contributions to producing policy-relevant information. Transient observation provides an important complement to information provided through interviews or other methods. If analysts are careful to avoid misinterpretations or unrepresentative inferences from such data, relatively unstructured observations provide a check on other information, generate ideas and hunches for further exploration, and enrich research findings through concrete examples and detail.

Systematic observation is preplanned observation of specified events. Systematic observation is constrained and guided by a manual of instructions that specifies what will be observed, where and when observations will occur, and how data are recorded. Physical objects and conditions are observed to provide indications of service need or effectiveness. Observations of behavior are particularly useful in studying "behaviors that most people cannot accurately describe, . . . and events that subjects may be motivated to distort or omit in reporting" (McCall, 1984:266).

To produce reliable information, systematic observation is guided by coding instruments and instructions that are specific, detailed, and operational. The selection and training of observers and the characteristics of the observation setting also have consequences for data quality. As with all data collection methods, systematic observation must be matched to appropriate information needs and to research resources if useful data are to be produced.

Experienced analysts are aware that some observational approaches raise ethical dilemmas. They avoid concealing their identities or observing persons under false pretenses. When gathering data, the analyst's interpretation of events becomes critical because those observed do not have the opportunity to explain their behavior or to comment on the meaning of what is reported about them.

Analysts reporting observational data provide clear and detailed descriptions of the events they observed and how observations were recorded. The basis for data interpretations is made explicit to facilitate data quality and usability assessments.

While direct methods of data collection seem basic and straightforward, their importance for useful policy research cannot be overemphasized. Policy analysis emerges in response to concrete issues and problems, and information collected close to those concerns provides an important basis for developing policy-relevant information.

REFERENCES

Becker, Howard S., and Blanche Greer. 1957. "Participant Observation and Interviewing: A Comparison," in *Human Organization* 16:28–32.

Bucher, R., C. E. Fritz, and E. L. Quarantelli. 1956. "Tape Recorded Research: Some Field and Data Processing Problems," in *Public Opinion Quarterly* 20:427–39.

Denzin, Norman K. 1970. *The Research Act: A Theoretical Introduction to Sociological Methods.* Chicago: Aldine.

Dexter, Lewis Anthony. 1970. *Elite and Specialized Interviewing.* Evanston, IL: Northwestern University Press.

Douglas, Jack D. 1976. *Investigative Social Research: Individual and Team Field Research.* Beverly Hills, CA: Sage Publications.

Hatry, Harry P., Richard E. Winnie, and Donald M. Fisk. 1981. *Practical Program Evaluation for State and Local Governments.* Washington, DC: Urban Institute.

Hawkins, J. D., and J. G. Weiss. 1980. *The Social Development Model: An Integrated Approach to Delinquency Prevention.* Washington, DC: Government Printing Office.

Kerlinger, Fred N. 1964. *Foundations of Behavioral Research.* New York: Holt, Rinehart and Winston.

Kerr, Douglas M., Lori Kent, and Tony C. M. Lam. 1985. "Measuring Program Implementation with a Classroom Observation Instrument: The Interactive Teaching Map," *Evaluation Review* 9, 4:461–82.

Lofland, John. 1971. *Analyzing Social Settings.* Belmont, CA: Wadsworth.

Maccoby, Eleanor, and Norman Maccoby. 1954. "The Interview: A Tool of Social Science," in G. Lindzey, ed., *Handbook of Social Psychology,* vol. 1. Cambridge, MA: Addison-Wesley, pp. 449–87.

Mann, Floyd C. 1970. "Human Relations Skills in Social Research," in W. J. Filstead, ed., *Qualitative Sociology: Firsthand Involvement with the Social World.* Chicago: Markham Publishing.

McCall, George J. 1984. "Systematic Field Observation," in *American Review of Sociology,* 10:263–82.

———. 1978. *Observing the Law: Field Methods in the Study of Crime and the Criminal Justice System.* New York: Free Press.

Murphy, Jerome T. 1980. *Getting the Facts: A Fieldwork Guide for Evaluators and Policy Analysts.* Santa Monica, CA: Goodyear Publishing.

Posavac, Emil J., and Raymond G. Carey. 1980. *Program Evaluation: Methods and Case Studies.* Englewood Cliffs, NJ: Prentice-Hall.

Place, Dorothy M. 1986. *Housing Condition Survey Training Manual.* Sacramento, CA: The Real Estate and Land Use Institute, California State Unversity.

Putt, Allen D., and J. Fred Springer. 1978. *Evaluation of the Political Reform Act of 1974.* Sacramento, CA: Evaluation Research Associates.

Richardson, Stephan, Barbara Dohrenwend, and David Klein. 1965. *Interviewing: Its Forms and Functions.* New York: Basic Books.

Springer, J. Fred, Joel L. Phillips, and Lynne Cannady. 1984. *Evaluation of the National Career Criminal Program.* Sacramento, CA: EMT Associates.

Trow, Martin. 1970. "Comment on Participant Observation and Interviewing: A Comparison," in William J. Filstead, ed., *Qualitative Sociology: Firsthand Involvement with the Social World.* Chicago: Markham Publishing.

Turner, Susan D., Lori Nielson, and Mildred Murray. 1983. "Observation Systems in Program Evaluation," *Evaluation Review* 7:373–83.

U.S. Department of Commerce. 1967. *Measuring the Quality of Housing: An Appraisal of Census Statistics and Methods.* Working Paper No. 25, Washington, DC: U.S. Department of Commerce.

7

Sampling in Policy Research

Public policies frequently have widespread effects. Changes in the availability of federal student loan guarantees affect the educational opportunities of students across the nation. Regulations promulgated by the Occupational Safety and Health Administration affect the operations of hundreds of thousands of organizations. Decisions to initiate user fees at city parks affect the recreational opportunities of citizens, particularly low income citizens.

In these situations, policymakers need information about the individuals and groups experiencing policy impacts. Sampling is an essential tool for this purpose. This chapter provides an overview of sampling methods and procedures frequently used in policy research.

The use of sampling in policy research is widespread: political polls, public health surveys, studies of public opinion and attitudes, surveys of production and consumption of goods and services all employ sampling. Sampling allows analysts to collect information economically and quickly. Representative samples, for instance, may be less than 1 percent of the size of a population, yet accurately and precisely reflect characteristics of that population. Savings in costs and time are compelling, as evidenced in the following case study.

DETERMINING THE EXTENT OF CREATIVE
FINANCING IN CALIFORNIA'S HOUSING MARKET:
A CASE STUDY IN SAMPLING

In the early 1980s, the Commerce Committee of the California State Assembly conducted hearings on the state's real estate industry. Following a decade of demand and increasing values, the high interest rates of the early 1980s had brought housing sales in the state to a virtual standstill. A national news magazine, in discussing the California housing market, declared that "only the advent of 'seller financing' . . . has kept the market from crashing completely" (*Newsweek*, September 21, 1981:85).

In testimony before the Commerce Committee, realtors and other industry representatives urged the legislature to take steps to assist home buyers in returning to traditional financial mechanisms, e.g., thirty-year mortgages at a fixed interest rate. The existing seller-financing practice was characterized as a time bomb because the typical loan from a seller would come due in full in from three to five years, requiring buyers to acquire new mortgage loans. Industry representatives argued that the increased demand for mortgage money at that time, combined with the normal demand for new mortgage money, would swamp existing mortgage markets and drive interest rates even higher.

Several committee members were concerned about industry fears. If these witnesses were correct, there would be serious implications for the state's economy. But they wanted more information. Statements by witnesses were based mainly on real estate industry perceptions, which in turn were based on personal observations—conversations with prospective buyers, calls to real estate brokers, word of mouth.

While personal experience is valuable in identifying seller financing as a possible public issue, it does not provide systematic and precise information. Word of mouth cannot precisely indicate the actual percentage of home sales in California that were seller assisted, or the typical contract terms of seller-assisted sales. It was this descriptive type of information committee members believed they needed before assessing whether public action was warranted. Since no systematic data of this type were available, policy analysts were asked to produce it.

The information desired by Commerce Committee members seemed straightforward. They wanted answers to three basic questions:

1. What percentage of current residential housing sales depends on seller-assisted financing?
2. How are home sellers assisting home buyers, e.g., first or second mortgages?
3. What are typical contract terms sellers are offering, e.g., amount of the loan, interest rates, duration of the loan?

The information objectives seemed clear; there was no need for a long process of problem clarification. Also, measurement seemed direct: per-

with producing that information. Tradeoffs and compromises are normal in developing sampling plans in policy research.

The housing study highlights the fact that resource limitations forced analysts to employ sampling procedures departing from the ideal, e.g., limiting the working population to seven urban counties and to the largest escrow firms. The point is this: Analysts need a solid understanding of sampling because ideal procedures are seldom fully applicable to actual policy research settings. When analysts must depart from ideal sampling plans, however, the implications of these departures must be known if they and policymakers are to assess realistically the quality of findings.

Findings generated in the housing study included the following:

- Fifty-six percent of the residential housing sales in the sample involved seller-assisted financing—most often (78 percent) in the form of a second mortgage.
- The average interest rate for seller-assisted loans was lower in comparison to banks or savings and loans (5 percent lower for second mortgages, 2.5 percent for first mortgages).
- Most (88 percent) seller-assisted loans were payable in full in eight years (4.7 years average for seconds, eight years for firsts).
- $37,396 was the average amount of seller-assisted loans for second mortgages; $65,551 for first mortgages.

The study results provided the legislature with concrete estimates of the explosiveness of the real estate time bomb. The accuracy of the estimates was dependent on the sampling strategy that produced them and in this case required considerable qualification. The following discussion describes basic sampling procedures employed by policy analysts in achieving information objectives.

CONSTRUCTING SAMPLING FRAMES

Identifying Target Populations

Before developing sampling frames, analysts first identify the target population. The target population in the preceding case was residential housing sales in California in the summer of 1981. Williams (1978:27) explains that target populations assume multiple forms:

> The entire United States adult population is frequently the target population for studies conducted by the various national opinion polls. In other surveys, the target population consists only of those persons living in a certain state, or city. Target populations do not have to consist of people. A day's produc-

centage rates of seller-assisted financing, type of mortgages, dollar amounts of mortgages, years of the loan, and so forth. There was no need for an analysis of causes or consequences; only descriptive information was requested. The major challenge became sampling—how to identify and select an adequate number of sample observations to provide an accurate descriptive picture of housing transactions in the state. It was challenge enough.

An initial task of policy analysts was to *identify the target population,* a process requiring them to clarify and define key concepts in the sampling plan. In this case, the legislature wanted to know about "residential housing sales in California during Summer, 1981." While seemingly clear, analysts had to resolve a variety of questions to be sure they understood just what they would be describing. Is the legislature interested only in single-family residences, only new homes, or both? Such questions were resolved through relating them to the issue generating the study—the potential pressure on future financial markets created by seller-assisted loans to buyers. Since these loans could be for new or old housing, single-family or multi-family dwellings—even condominiums—the target population would include all these housing variations as "residential housing sales."

Residential real estate sales in "California during Summer, 1981" also required clarification. Residential sales may take months to complete: how can it be determined when those sales occurred? To make "California during Summer, 1981" precise and to accommodate the request for timely information by the legislature, analysts further specified the target population as residential sales closing between June 1 and August 20, 1981.

Another major task was to determine what data sources would be used to collect information about this target population. Obviously, houses were sold in the state during the summer. The difficulty was in locating information sources that would represent "residential housing sales in the summer of 1981" as defined by the analysts. Somewhere, records of residential housing sales must exist. Once those sales transactions were located, a sample could be drawn.

Analysts had earlier considered other sources of information. What about obtaining a list of participants in housing transactions—buyers, sellers, agents—and then selecting a sample to interview about the financing of residential sales? Not likely. Agents are scattered through real estate offices throughout the state. They may not have the kind of detailed and systematic data required by the study's information needs. To get a complete list of buyers and sellers for all sales transactions in the state, which would number in the many thousands, was unrealistic. Even if it was possible, buyers and sellers might be unable or unwilling to divulge the financing details that information needs required. Therefore, buyers, sellers, and agents—as primary sources of information—were ruled out for these reasons.

A likely source of the needed information would be written records of housing sales. Did such records exist? One possibility was official records of deeds in the offices of County Recorders. Upon checking, analysts learned that to prevent commercial exploitation, these records were open only to owners and other select few. Also, the records were incomplete in terms of the detailed financial data required by information objectives.

After further inquiry, analysts found the needed information was located in escrow sheets which recorded financial data on real estate transactions. They subsequently decided that escrow records would serve as the set of identifiable sources of information—the "sampling frame"—for learning about residential housing sales in California. Escrow services are legally required; every sales transaction would have to have one. Files of these transactions are maintained on a continuing basis. The major problem with escrow records as a sampling frame was getting access to them; escrow services are dispersed in the state, and files are geographically scattered through the state in local offices. Still, escrow records were the single most complete and accessible documents of real estate transactions.

The sampling frame of escrow records necessitated changing the target population that could accurately be represented on a modest project budget. Clearly, obtaining escrow sheets throughout the state's fifty-eight counties was financially impossible. Accordingly, data collection was limited to seven counties, all metropolitan. These counties accounted for 60 percent of all housing units in the state. Even then, it was not possible to obtain information on all of the hundreds of escrow services operating in the seven counties. Using information provided by the statewide association of escrow services, the analysts contacted the largest firms (those handling the most residential transactions) in the seven counties. Most firms agreed to participate in the study and to allow access to files of housing transactions located in their local offices. In all, fourteen companies and seventy-three branch offices participated in the study. These offices accounted for 40–60 percent of all escrows registered in the seven metropolitan counties.

Consider the modifications made to the original target population due to the availability of information sources and to resource constraints. Although committee members wanted to know about residential housing sales in California, the actual sampling frame from which a sample would be drawn was more limited. The legislature would learn only about a sample of escrow services provided by fourteen of the state's largest escrow firms located in seven metropolitan counties. This reduced population is referred to as the "working population." The working population is represented by the specific, concrete, actual sampling frame which is employed in drawing the sample, e.g., escrow records in fourteen large escrow firms in seven metropolitan counties. If proper sampling procedures are used, information gained from the working population will apply to "residential housing sales in California"—the more abstract "target population."

Technically, results of the study tell policymakers nothing about housing transactions occurring in rural counties. Since none were included in the sampling frame, they had no chance of being represented when drawing

the sample. Technically, the study is silent on transactions that wer[e] in smaller escrow companies. They too were not represented in the w[orking] population. As a practical matter, decision makers will draw inf[erences] from the results of the limited sample to the more general target [popula]tion. The role of analysts in this process is to report the specific sou[rces of] information used in constructing sampling frames, and to report f[ully the] limitations of the findings when generalizing beyond sample findi[ngs].

To this point, analysts had identified the target population; [decided] on a major information source that would in important ways ref[lect the] target population; and constructed a sampling frame from which t[he sam]ple would be drawn. Sampling tasks remained, including a major [one:] specifying methods of drawing the sample—how to select specific [escrow] sheets. How would the escrow sheets be selected from the sampling [frame?] "Random" selection methods were a possibility. These methods allo[w infor]mation gained from the sample to be applied to the working pop[ulation] with statistically specified levels of accuracy and precision, providi[ng means] of assessing the large applicability of findings. Data obtained throu[gh "non]random" selection methods, in contrast, cannot be statistically ass[essed in] terms of their probable accuracy and precision when making ge[neraliza]tions. Random selection methods were chosen, based on the need t[o gener]alize sample findings.

In using random selection methods, analysts determine the [total] number of observations to be included in the sample—the sample s[ize. Sam]ple size directly relates to the accuracy and precision of study resu[lts when] statistically generalized to the working population. Although ther[e are es]tablished procedures for determining the size of a sample, budget c[onsider]ations again predominated. Sufficient resources existed to sample o[ne thou]sand housing transactions.

Even then analysts had to decide how many escrow sheets w[ould be] selected in each county and in each office. They eventually determi[ned that] the sample size of one thousand escrow sheets would be proportio[nately dis]tributed among counties according to the number of housing unit[s located] in each county. If a county contained 15 percent of the total nu[mber of] housing units in all seven counties, 150 transactions would be sa[mpled in] that county (.15 × 1000 = 150). Escrow sheets were randomly selec[ted from] the files of branch offices in these counties until the allotted nu[mber in] each county was reached.

This illustration demonstrates the multiple tasks and deci[sions re]quired in sampling for policy research. Sampling plans may be less [or more] complex in other research situations, but major tasks remain simi[lar. Deci]sions made at each phase directly influence the accuracy, precis[ion, and] usability of resulting information. Sampling requires thought and c[are] about the information needs of the study in relation to the costs a[nd]

tion of transistors, or all telephone calls made during a day are also possible target populations. . . . [V]irtually any group can become the target population of a sampling study. The possibilities are endless.

How the target population is defined is dependent on what policymakers need to know, on information needs. Proper identification of the target population is a first step in producing useful information and in developing adequate sampling plans.

Identifying target populations also serves to limit generalizations made from research findings. They place limits—boundaries on the scope and applicability of information. The findings developed in the housing study were limited to the state of California (as reflected in the sampling frame) during the summer of 1981. No empirical basis existed for applying findings beyond that population since no other states or times were represented in the sampling strategy.

Developing Information Sources

Once a target population has been identified, the search is on for sources of information yielding data on that population. The sources employed ultimately constitute working populations, which serve as sampling frames for the drawing of samples, e.g., escrow documents.

A sampling frame, in the most concrete sense, is a list of all members of a working population from which sample members will be drawn. The sampling frame does not have to be a list on paper, e.g., a personnel roster in an organization or a telephone book. Indeed, escrow sheets filed chronologically in file cabinets constituted the list in the housing study.

In drawing representative samples, a principal concern is that every unit of observation, whether an escrow sheet or a person, is included in the sampling frame. If not, information generated will be unrepresentative of those excluded from possible sample selection. Listing units of observation more than once increases the probability of selection, thus resulting in the overrepresentation of those units. Either way, unrepresentative samples occur, distorting sample findings.

Developing accurate, complete, and current data sources for use as sampling frames is a necessary but sometimes frustrating task. For example, telephone directories are a historically popular sampling frame for general population studies. Yet phone books underrepresent low-income groups. They exclude groups choosing not to list their numbers, e.g., professors, police officers, single women, the affluent. Persons with unlisted numbers may share characteristics; for example, single women or the more affluent may be more likely to request unlisted numbers. People new to the area will be excluded from the directory. Since excluded persons may constitute homogeneous groups (the poor or affluent, newcomers, single women), the use of telephone directories as a sampling frame may yield unrepresentative data when information about these groups is needed.

In the case of other policy studies, developing lists to serve as sampling frames may be easier. If personnel analysts are interested in assessing job satisfaction in some organization, for example, listings of employees for sampling frames can be developed from data sources such as personnel and payroll rosters. Census data, tax rolls, listings of registered voters, property and automobile owners, welfare recipients, permit and license holders all serve as sources for creating sampling frames. In developing lists, what should be considered is, first, the fit between the sampling frame and the target population, and second, the degree to which a list of members is complete, current, and accurate.

Few lists fully meet these criteria. Personnel rosters exclude recent personnel changes. Tax rolls underrepresent low-income groups. Many people do not vote. Sampling frames developed from listings of property owners overrepresent the affluent while underrepresenting the poor. Most listings are developed for nonsurvey purposes and do not match ideal requirements of the sampling analyst. In the final analysis, most complex sampling frames possess inadequacies. The role of analysts is to minimize the inadequacies as much as is feasible and to state any limitations when generalizing sample findings.

DEVELOPING SELECTION PROCEDURES

Once analysts have developed sampling frames, procedures are created to determine how members of those frames are selected for analysis. There are two basic types of sample selection: random and nonrandom. Random selection procedures allow information developed from a sample to be generalized to a working population using statistically specified levels of accuracy and precision (termed "sampling error"). Stakeholders then have a numeric basis for evaluating the quality of findings. Sample data obtained through nonrandom selection procedures, in contrast, cannot be statistically assessed for accuracy and precision when applied to a working population.

The ability to state empirical generalizations with specified levels of confidence gives random sampling great appeal. Jessen (1978:17) has noted that "statisticians generally prefer random or probability samples, because a well-established theory [using probability statistics] is available to aid them in understanding the behavior of such samples."

In policy research, preferences yield to concerns of information needs, costs, and time constraints. The choice of random and nonrandom samples reflects compromises among these considerations. Policy studies frequently include a combination of both types of samples, each discussed below.

Random Selection Procedures

The basic characteristic of a random sample is that it is *representative* of the working population. It is representative in the sense that all units of observation, e.g., escrow sheets in the working population, have a known probability of being selected for the sample. Therefore, if a sufficient number of observations are randomly selected, their characteristics should not significantly differ from the working population. To maximize representativeness, "randomization" is employed:

> The basic assumption of randomization is that every element, or some combination of elements, in the [working] population has a specified chance of being included in the sample. Additionally it is assumed that by drawing a random sample any differences between the sample and the population will be randomly, or normally distributed. (Denzin, 1970:85)

Even with the use of randomization procedures, samples do not perfectly represent working populations. Incomplete, dated, and inaccurate sampling frames, for instance, result in unrepresentative sample findings. Nonetheless, random sampling does decrease the likelihood of producing misleading sample findings. It provides a well-tested basis of generalizing results to a working population and offers the ability to specify the degree of sampling error likely in generalizing findings. It yields an important indication of the quality of sample data generated in a policy study.

To realize the advantages of random sampling, care is exercised in developing sampling procedures. Random samples are not attained without conformity to basic rules in selecting cases from sampling frames. Several variations of random selection procedures (simple random, systematic random, and stratified random) are frequently used in policy research.

SIMPLE RANDOM SAMPLING

The most straightforward selection procedure is "simple random sampling." Its basic feature is that every unit of observation in a working population has an equal chance of being included in the sampling frame. If a complete, current, and accurate list exists (a big "if"), drawing a simple random sample is direct. Each member in the sampling frame is assigned a unique identifying number from which sample members are drawn. Several procedures are available at this point for random selection from the sampling frame. For example, computer facilities—and even hand-held calculators—have programs to generate random digits. In the case of smaller sample sizes, a table of random numbers is commonly used for selecting sample members. Discussing the use of a table of random numbers illustrates the rule-bound process of random selection.

A table of random numbers (Table 7.1) is descriptive of its title; it is a tabular presentation containing numbers computer-generated in a random fashion. Tables of random numbers are commonly reproduced in books on statistics.

In order to illustrate the use of a table of random numbers, assume analysts need to select randomly a sample of 100 respondents from a working population of 400 persons. The following procedures are employed in drawing a simple random sample of 100 respondents.

1. Number all members of the study population; in this illustration, from 1 to 400.
2. Determine the number of digits needed for the random numbers to be selected. In the present illustration 400 members are in the working population; consequently, three-digit random numbers are used to give each member an equal chance of sample selection. If the study population was 4,000, a four-digit number would be used, if 40,000, a five-digit number, and so on.
3. Using the table of random numbers (Table 7.1), decide which of the five-digit numbers will be used for drawing the sample. The example calls for a three-digit number; agree that only the first three digits will be used in the five digits available (the last three or the middle three could be used). If a number is 14190, for example, it is read as 141; the last two digits are ignored.
4. Decide how to read the table. This is an arbitrary decision; move through the table in any pattern, but be consistent once the pattern is selected. One may, for example, read down the columns, up the columns, across from left to right or right to left, and so forth. For the purposes of this illustration, agree to read down the columns. When

TABLE 7.1   Excerpt from a Table of Random Numbers

ROW NUMBER

1	14190	30130	86772	48700
2	77517	00586	17275	33333
3	14101	19888	90328	60975
4	21795	51746	01451	95240
5	00120	70121	21769	24449
6	41075	68170	51260	15548
7	89367	91817	01101	79102

one column is completed, start again from the top of the following column.

5. Select a starting point. The starting point can be anywhere, e.g., upper left-hand column, third column line 2, lower right-hand column. Agree to start in the upper left-hand column.

6. Select the sample. Using Table 7.1, start at the upper left-hand column and read the first 3 digits only. A sample size of 100 is needed out of the sampling frame of 400 members. The task is to locate the first 100 numbers that fall in the range of 1–400. Starting with the first number, 14190, the first three digits are 141. Case number 141 is the first to be selected for the sample. The next number is 775(17); since that falls beyond the range of 1 to 400, ignore it. If a number previously selected comes up again, e.g., 141(01), that too is ignored. Continue the process of selecting relevant numbers until a total of 100 randomly selected members is reached.

The point about this detailed procedure is the general principle it represents, i.e, the rule-bound nature of the process. Somewhat ironically, achieving randomization requires very systematic methods. Selecting people on a street corner to interview is not random despite the appearance of chance. Only those persons on that corner at that time are selected, and they are likely to be there for reasons making them different from the general population, e.g., their place of employment.

Simple random samples require control of the selection procedure through which members of the working population enter the sample so that each member has an equal chance of selection. Such a process better ensures that sample members are drawn in an objective, unbiased fashion. It ensures that human judgment has in no way influenced the selection of sample members.

SYSTEMATIC RANDOM SAMPLING

A variation on the simple random sample is "systematic random sampling." The technique is particularly useful when a sampling frame is in the form of an actual list.

Suppose a personnel list of 400 employees is to serve as a sampling frame. Resources allow a sample of 100 of these employees. To utilize systematic selection, analysts first calculate the "sampling interval," which is simply the ratio of population size to sample size. In this case, 400/100 = 4, which becomes the sampling interval. Every fourth name on the list will be selected. Next, to begin the process, analysts randomly generate a number between one and four. This number becomes the "random start"—the initial observation selected into the sample. To complete the sample, analysts simply move down the list, selecting every fourth name on the list.

Systematic random sampling can be less cumbersome than simple random sampling. Systematic sampling incorporates the positive features of a simple random sample; the accuracy and precision of sample results are easily determined.

Because systematic sampling moves through an established list in a designated manner, the structure of the list can adversely affect the representativeness of the sample. For example, a list can be so arranged that it contains "periodic fluctuations." This is a particular problem when lists are compiled chronologically. Leege and Francis (1974:123) describe an example of periodicity in early attempts to examine social status in the United States. In one study, the researchers

> sampled marriage announcements in the June issues of *The New York Times* Sunday edition from 1932 to 1942. Finding that only Protestant marriages were described, they concluded "the upper-upper social class of New York City was preponderantly Protestant." Rival hypotheses immediately suggest themselves: e.g., the *Times* has a religious bias. However, one rival hypothesis—namely, that the finding was a result of periodicity—quickly found substantiation. Cahnman pointed out that "Jewish marriages happen for ceremonial reasons not to be performed in June," and a sampling of *Times* issues at other points in time disclosed a proportionate number of Jewish marriages.

At other times, the internal structure of a list is an advantage in systematic sampling. If, for example, a personnel list is arranged according to civil service rank, the sampling frame will yield a sample stratified by rank. It ensures proportional representation of persons of different ranks within the sample. Its advantages are clarified in the following discussion.

STRATIFIED RANDOM SAMPLING

"Stratified random sampling" divides a working population into categories or strata based on characteristics of interest, such as gender, age, income, education. Random samples are then selected from each category, or stratum. Unlike simple random and systematic random sampling, where members are selected from the total working population of members, stratified sampling draws sampling members from specified subgroups of the working population.

Stratified sampling procedures guarantee the representation of important subgroups in the sample. If analysts are conducting a citizen survey and a variety of ethnic groups reside in the community, stratification by ethnicity better ensures that each subgroup appears in numbers representative of its proportion in the community. In comparison, if simple random selection procedures are used, small but important subgroups may be underrepresented in sample findings simply because of their small numbers or because of chance factors in drawing sample members. Jessen (1978:184–85) comments that "there is little intuitional appeal in the rather haphazard way that random sampling permits any part of the ... [working population] to be represented." Small samples may exclude subgroup members completely. The basic function of stratification, then, is to realize a more representative sample through dividing the working population into subgroups and drawing randomly from each.

To illustrate the process of developing a stratified sample, assume analysts have been asked to evaluate the effectiveness of an educational program designed to increase reading skills in a junior high school. The working population is seventh-, eighth-, and ninth-grade students who receive one or two periods of reading instruction each day. Since gender may be related to enhanced reading effectiveness, analysts decide to stratify the working population into boys and girls; in effect, now there are two sampling frames. Since reading effectiveness may also be associated with the amount of reading instruction, analysts consequently divide the two subgroups into one period or two periods of reading instruction representing different levels of instructional support. This subdivision yields four separate sampling frames (Table 7.2).

Stratifying the working population into separate and distinct subgroups can continue indefinitely, depending on sample size. Analysts may want each grade represented by further dividing the working population into the seventh, eighth, and ninth grades, resulting in twelve sampling frames. As stratification continues, members in these smaller samples share more characteristics in common, e.g., ninth-grade girls with two periods of reading instruction per day. The working population, with its diverse characteristics of seventh-, eighth-, and ninth-grade boys and girls with one or two periods of reading per day, has become twelve smaller sampling frames, each of which shares internal characteristics important to assessing the effectiveness of the experimental educational reading program. Random samples from these groups logically yield more representative samples and more precise and accurate information. The haphazard component of random samples is minimized in stratified sampling because analysts have increased control over the composition of the final sample.

Stratified random sampling facilitates the analysis and generalizability

TABLE 7.2 Levels of Instructional Support

GENDER	ONE PERIOD	TWO PERIODS
Boys	Boys with one reading period per day	Boys with two reading periods per day
Girls	Girls with one reading period per day	Girls with two reading periods per day

of subgroup findings. Because the information resulting from the analysis is more controlled in comparison to simple random selection procedures, stratified sampling is well regarded by sampling analysts.

The use of stratified sampling assumes analysts have information on the stratified variables before subsamples are drawn, e.g., the number of members in each subgroup and important shared characteristics such as age, gender, income. Further, stratified sampling is advantageous only if analysts have reason to believe that the stratified variables are important to information needs. If, for example, a review of relevant research indicates that gender makes no difference in response to reading effectiveness programs, there is no advantage to stratifying the sample by gender. When detailed knowledge of subpopulations is needed and prior knowledge of subgroups exists, stratified random sampling is a powerful and economical design.

Accuracy and Precision in Random Sampling

When every member of a target population is included in a study, i.e., when a census has been conducted, statistics used to describe that population are straightforward. No statistical estimates of the generalizability of results (sampling error) are appropriate since every member of the target population has been observed. Random sampling, however, results in estimates. When the sample has been correctly drawn, an estimate of what the results would have been had all members been surveyed is possible. Since all members were not surveyed, the assumption is that there will be some sampling error existing in the estimates.

The expected amount of sampling error can be controlled by selecting an appropriate sample size. As the size of a sample relative to the total size of the working population increases, estimates are made with greater statistical assurance that sample results reflect actual characteristics of the working population.

Accuracy and precision requirements are dominant factors influencing sample size. The specific requirements in regard to sample size depend on the uses to be made of the research information. If analysts need to predict the outcome of a close election and must ensure that the prediction is highly precise and accurate, then the sample size must be increased to satisfy users of the information. If only a rough idea of the election outcome is needed, then lower levels of accuracy and precision can be accepted, and sample sizes are reduced. In policy research, accuracy and precision requirements of information are determined through consultation between analysts and stakeholders.

Accuracy and precision levels are expressed in "confidence levels" (accuracy) and "confidence intervals" (precision). Confidence levels provide a measure of how *certain*—how confident—analysts can be of sample results when statistically generalized to a working population. Analysts can never be 100 percent certain of the accuracy of the results unless the entire population of members is surveyed, i.e., a census is conducted. They can make statistical estimates of the degree of confidence or certainty users can place in sample results, e.g., 99 percent, 95 percent, 90 percent confidence. Again, the uses of the information determine acceptable confidence levels.

Confidence intervals yield a measure of the precision of sample results when generalized to the working population. If the results of a random sample indicate that 40 percent of employees favor a compressed workweek (four 10-hour days), the most precise estimate that can be made is that 40 percent of the working population favor a compressed workweek. Because a random sample only imperfectly mirrors a working population, analysts specify, for purposes of determining sample size, the margin of error (confidence interval) acceptable in the estimate.

If, returning to the example, a margin of error of plus or minus 4 percent is acceptable, the most precise estimate that can be made is that between 36–44 percent of all employees favor a compressed workweek. Assuming a confidence level of 95 percent had been specified, analysts would be 95 percent certain that between 36–44 percent of employees in the working population favor a four-day workweek. As in the above example, confidence levels and confidence intervals, i.e., sampling error, are combined in reporting the findings of sample data.

A number of guides are available to assist analysts in selecting sample sizes.[1] Tables 7.3 through 7.5 provide an example of such guides (McCall, 1982:329–32). The three guides yield appropriate sample sizes at varying levels of confidence (90 percent, 95 percent, and 99 percent) and at varying confidence intervals (plus or minus 1–5 percent).

To illustrate the use of one of these guides (Table 7.3), suppose an analyst needs to ask a random sample of employees if they approve of some policy change proposed by management. Assume accuracy and precision requirements are established at a 90 percent confidence level and a 5 percent confidence interval. If there are 2,000 employees in the working population, a sample size of 238 employees would be needed to achieve this degree of accuracy and precision in generalizing sample results; if 10,000 employees, a sample size of 263 would be required.

Deciding on an appropriate sample size is a key to producing accurate and precise generalizable information. Yet statistical criteria are not the sole considerations influencing sample size in policy research. Resources loom as a limiting factor, particularly in costly labor-intensive activities such as in-person interviews. Stakeholders should be informed of what can be accomplished within available time and cost restrictions, including sample size considerations.

Statistical Significance and Decision Making

Only random selection procedures statistically ensure sample findings approach a true picture of a working population through a determination

TABLE 7.3 Appropriate Sizes of Simple Random Samples for Specific Permissible Errors Expressed as Absolute Proportions when the True Proportion in the Population Is 0.50 and the Confidence Level Is 90 Percent

POPULATION SIZE	SAMPLE SIZE FOR PERMISSIBLE ERROR (PROPORTION)				
	0.05	0.04	0.03	0.02	0.01
100	73	81	88	94	99
200	115	136	158	179	194
300	142	175	214	255	287
400	161	206	261	323	378
500	176	229	300	386	466
600	186	248	334	443	551
700	195	264	362	495	634
800	202	277	388	543	715
900	208	288	410	587	794
1,000	213	297	429	628	871
2,000	238	349	546	916	1,544
3,000	248	371	601	1,082	2,078
4,000	253	382	633	1,189	2,514
5,000	257	390	653	1,264	2,875
6,000	259	395	668	1,319	3,180
7,000	261	399	679	1,362	3,440
8,000	262	402	687	1,396	3,665
9,000	263	404	694	1,424	3,862
10,000	263	406	699	1,447	4,035
15,000	266	411	716	1,520	4,662
20,000	267	414	724	1,559	5,055
25,000	268	416	730	1,584	5,324
30,000	268	417	733	1,601	5,520
40,000	269	418	738	1,623	5,786
50,000	269	419	741	1,636	5,959
75,000	270	420	744	1,654	6,205
100,000	270	421	746	1,663	6,336
500,000	270	422	751	1,686	6,675
1,000,000	271	423	751	1,688	6,720
2,000,000	271	423	751	1,690	6,742

Source: Reprinted by permission from *Sampling and Statistics Handbook for Research* by C. H. McCall, Jr., pp. 329–332, © 1982 by Iowa State University, Ames, Iowa.

of sampling error. However, sampling error is not the sole gauge of information quality. Other errors not reflected in statistical estimates reduce the quality of results; these are termed "nonsampling errors." Following are two major sources of nonsampling errors influencing the quality of findings generated from random samples.

TABLE 7.4 Appropriate Sizes of Simple Random Samples for Specific Permissible Errors Expressed as Absolute Proportions when the True Proportion in the Population Is 0.50 and the Confidence Level Is 95 Percent

POPULATION SIZE	SAMPLE SIZE FOR PERMISSIBLE ERROR (PROPORTION)				
	0.05	0.04	0.03	0.02	0.01
100	79	86	91	96	99
200	132	150	168	185	196
300	168	200	234	267	291
400	196	240	291	343	384
500	217	273	340	414	475
600	234	300	384	480	565
700	248	323	423	542	652
800	260	343	457	600	738
900	269	360	488	655	823
1,000	278	375	516	706	906
2,000	322	462	696	1,091	1,655
3,000	341	500	787	1,334	2,286
4,000	350	522	842	1,500	2,824
5,000	357	536	879	1,622	3,288
6,000	361	546	906	1,715	3,693
7,000	364	553	926	1,788	4,049
8,000	367	558	942	1,847	4,364
9,000	368	563	954	1,895	4,646
10,000	370	566	964	1,936	4,899
15,000	375	577	996	2,070	5,855
20,000	377	583	1,013	2,144	6,488
25,000	378	586	1,023	2,191	6,938
30,000	379	588	1,030	2,223	7,275
40,000	381	591	1,039	2,265	7,745
50,000	381	593	1,045	2,291	8,056
75,000	382	595	1,052	2,327	8,514
100,000	383	597	1,056	2,345	8,762
500,000	384	600	1,065	2,390	9,423
1,000,000	384	600	1,066	2,395	9,513
2,000,000	384	600	1,067	2,398	9,558

Source: Reprinted by permission from *Sampling and Statistics Handbook for Research* by C. H. McCall, Jr., pp. 329–332, © 1982 by Iowa State University, Ames, Iowa.

INADEQUATE SAMPLING FRAMES

A common source of error is using incomplete, outdated, and inaccurate sampling frames in selecting sample members. An oft-cited illustration of the consequences of this error is the 1936 presidential poll conducted by *Literary Digest* and used to predict whether candidates Franklin D. Roosevelt

TABLE 7.5 Appropriate Sizes of Simple Random Samples for Specific Permissible Errors Expressed as Absolute Proportions when the True Proportion in the Population Is 0.50 and the Confidence Level Is 99 Percent

POPULATION SIZE	SAMPLE SIZE FOR PERMISSIBLE ERROR (PROPORTION)				
	0.05	0.04	0.03	0.02	0.01
100	87	91	95	98	99
200	154	168	180	191	198
300	207	233	258	280	295
400	250	289	329	365	391
500	285	337	393	446	485
600	315	380	453	524	579
700	341	418	507	599	672
800	363	452	558	671	763
900	382	482	605	740	854
1,000	399	509	648	806	943
2,000	498	683	959	1,349	1,785
3,000	543	771	1,142	1,741	2,541
4,000	569	823	1,262	2,036	3,223
5,000	586	859	1,347	2,267	3,842
6,000	597	884	1,410	2,452	4,406
7,000	606	903	1,459	2,604	4,923
8,000	613	918	1,498	2,731	5,397
9,000	618	930	1,530	2,839	5,835
10,000	622	939	1,556	2,932	6,239
15,000	635	970	1,642	3,249	7,877
20,000	642	986	1,688	3,435	9,068
25,000	646	996	1,717	3,557	9,972
30,000	649	1,002	1,737	3,644	10,682
40,000	653	1,011	1,762	3,758	11,726
50,000	655	1,016	1,778	3,830	12,456
75,000	658	1,023	1,799	3,930	13,585
100,000	659	1,026	1,810	3,982	14,229
500,000	663	1,035	1,837	4,113	16,057
1,000,000	663	1,036	1,840	4,130	16,319
2,000,000	663	1,036	1,842	4,139	16,453

Source: Reprinted by permission from *Sampling and Statistics Handbook for Research* by C. H. McCall, Jr., pp. 329–332, © 1982 by Iowa State University, Ames, Iowa.

or Alf Landon would win. Since analysts did not have available a list of all registered voters in the United States, they conducted a mail survey using sampling frames developed from telephone directories and automobile registrations. Questionnaires were sent to ten million adults who owned a phone or an automobile. Based on more than two million responses, the prediction was that Landon, the Republican candidate, would win by a virtual landslide, a prediction that proved embarrassingly incorrect.

Only 40 percent of homes in the United States had telephones at the time; only a slim majority owned cars (Williamson et al., 1982:115–16). The sample was consequently slanted in favor of higher socioeconomic groupings who tend to vote Republican. Voters not having telephones or automobiles were excluded; however, they carried the day by voting Roosevelt into office. Random selection procedures assume—sometimes incorrectly—the use of complete, current, and accurate sampling frames in selecting sample members.

NONRESPONSE

Errors arising from nonresponse present an ongoing threat to the quality of sample findings. In mail surveys, only a small number of sample respondents may complete and return the questionnaire. In household surveys, respondents may not be at home, even after repeated attempts to interview them. Nonresponse strikes at the very core of random sampling—the representativeness of sample findings in generalizing results to the working population.

Reasons for nonresponse vary. In a mail survey, questionnaires may have the wrong address. Respondents may refuse to participate because of the nature of the questions or because they are too busy or for innumerable other reasons. In a household survey, reasons for nonresponse include refusals to participate and those not at home. Some of those contacted may be incapable of responding due to language barriers or psychosocial and physical reasons. A number of techniques are employed to assess the effects of nonresponse on the representativeness of random sample results.[2]

A common method is to conduct a follow-up survey of nonrespondents. Telephone, mail, and in-person surveys are all used in obtaining information from individuals not initially responding. The resulting information is then compared to the original sample results to assess whether the two samples differ or are similar in responses given. The chi-square test, a simple statistical tool, is often employed to assess the similarity of responses in respect to important questions in the survey between respondents and nonrespondents.

Other techniques are available to evaluate the representativeness of a sample. For a random sample of employees in an organization, comparisons of sample findings can be made to personnel records, e.g., age, gender, educational level, length of employment, income levels. Census data are frequently used as a basis for assessing the representativeness of sample respondents in surveys involving a geographic component. In addition, sample results can be compared to results from similar research studies. Again, similarities in response patterns can be an indication of the representativeness of sample information.

The combined impact of nonsampling errors, such as inadequate sampling frames and nonresponse, causes sample findings to mirror inaccurately the working population, regardless of accuracy and precision estimates. For this reason, sampling error alone is an incomplete and possibly misleading basis for assessing data quality. Any complete evaluation of data quality includes an assessment of sampling and nonsampling errors.

Random selection procedures assume representative sampling frames; any lack of representativeness due to inadequate sampling frames and nonresponse is not reflected in estimates of sampling error. Consequently, reporting the nature of sampling frames used in research studies and reporting the size, sources, and implications of nonresponse permit stakeholders to assess better the quality and usability of findings. Such reporting is standard practice for better research studies.

Nonrandom Selection Procedures

Nonrandom samples yield useful information in policy research. Conditions may be that a random sample is not necessary, given information needs, or cannot be obtained at affordable cost or is too time consuming to do, perhaps due to the difficulty of developing adequate sampling frames. Resource and technical constraints may leave little choice but to employ nonrandom selection methods.

Nonrandom samples should not simply be viewed as a substitute for random samples; they fulfill useful informational roles in policy research. For instance, they are used to obtain ideas and insights into a working population before conducting a random survey. Such preliminary, or pilot, studies may be used for a number of reasons: estimating variability in a population for sample size considerations, pretesting survey wording and order of questions, testing coding and analysis plans, and so forth.

Another situation requiring nonrandom sampling is when selecting a small number of observations to represent diverse or large populations. In a national evaluation of career criminal programs, a telephone survey identified eighty-seven operating programs across the nation. Seven were selected as sites for detailed research. Analysts selected the seven sites based on criteria designed to select programs that manifested great diversity in jurisdiction size, geographic location, and program approach. Differences—not similarities—were sought among programs. The objective was to document how career criminal programs function over the range of their diversity. A random sample may not have produced the diversity of programs needed for information objectives. In other situations, analysts may need to select the most typical cases for analysis, e.g., typical midwestern cities or typical career criminal programs.

Numerable methods of nonrandom sampling are employed in policy research. The following are among the more common.

OPPORTUNITY SAMPLING

Opportunity sampling is best illustrated through "eyewitness reports" seen on television and heard on radio, where respondents are selected because of their immediate availability and convenience. If analysts walk out on the street and interview the first 10 citizens they meet, this practice results in an opportunity sample of a locale's inhabitants. Opportunity samples are accidental. Actual observations are determined by the day and time respondents were interviewed, places selected to interview respondents, weather conditions, and so on. Opportunity samples are used to gain an initial sense of a population. They are employed in pretesting questionnaires and pretesting data collection and analysis plans.

Another application of opportunity sampling is in conducting exploratory research. Detailed statistical samples require extensive prior knowledge of the population of interest. When the research task is exploratory— when analysts have little prior knowledge concerning the issue—opportunity samples are appropriate. They allow analysts to explore the diversity of a problem with relative ease and efficiency.

PURPOSIVE SAMPLING

Purposive sampling uses judgment and expertise in selecting sample members. Judgment, not chance, determines the composition of the sample. Purposive sampling is used by experts in judgmentally picking typical cases for study, e.g., selecting typical state agencies to represent state government or selecting typical cities to represent a national urban population.

Purposive sampling has important applications in policy research. The choice of the seven career criminal programs described earlier was purposive. Criteria were established for determining potentially important distinctions among programs, and jurisdictions were picked to represent the range of distinctly different programs, yielding seven diverse career criminal programs.

Purposive sampling is frequently employed by analysts preparing descriptions of public program procedures and policies. In the career criminals evaluation, knowledgeable attorneys, judges, law enforcement personnel, and other persons close to the programs were purposively selected for lengthy in-depth interviews. The information objective of the interviews was to describe program organization, formal policies, and the ways in which these policies are implemented in prosecuting cases. These information needs would not be met using random selection methods.

"Snowball" sampling represents another variation of purposive selection methods. This procedure requires analysts to ask initially identified members of a population to expand the sample size by naming additional members. In a study of influential persons likely to wield power in policy decisions by a local planning commission, initial interviewees were asked to name three persons they felt would affect planning decisions in the area. Names that were mentioned by at least three persons were selected into the sample.

Purposive samples are important in policy research as long as they are directed at appropriate information needs. They are not designed to provide precise and accurate statistical estimates. They depend on judgment, and "experts often hold differing views on the best way to choose representative specimens, or to decide which are the most representative units" (Kish, 1965:19). Often, expert judgment is combined with additional sources of information (census data, past studies) in selecting typical or atypical units of observation. Even then, statistical determinations of the applicability of these findings are not possible, given the nonrandom selection process.

QUOTA SAMPLING

Quota sampling is sometimes used in governmental and commercial survey organizations. In quota sampling, sample members are selected because they fit a pattern of prespecified characteristics; they fit a predesignated profile. Frequently, the attempt is made to ensure that sample characteristics (e.g., age, socioeconomic standing, political affiliation, gender) reflect relative proportions existing in the target population. In this way, the method parallels that of stratified sampling, but selection procedures are not random.

To draw a quota sample, analysts proceed by classifying the target population on important characteristics serving as predictors of behavior and attitudes. If gender is important, sample members should contain the gender proportion reflective of their proportion in the target population. The same process is followed for other characteristics important to information needs. The proportion of the target population possessing each characteristic is usually confirmed through documentary sources such as census reports and organizational records or through exploratory studies.

Once the population has been stratified and relative proportions determined, interviewers are given a specified quota of types of people to be interviewed. An interviewer may need to fill a quota of five females, 35–45 years old, who are in an income range of $30,000–$40,000; seven unemployed males, 25–35 years old, and so on. Differences exist in how much discretion the interviewer is allowed in selecting respondents, e.g., choosing the place and time of interviews.

Quota sampling is sometimes used in an attempt to enhance the generalizability of results at a reduced survey cost. Problems emerge, however, in statistically generalizing findings from a quota sample to a larger population, i.e., in treating quota sampling as a method of random selection.

> Few, if any, of the procedures [in quota sampling] provide equal (or even known) probabilities of selection to each person in the universe belonging to the quota class. Because of this lack of positive control on the selection, biases usually result. Most users of this method make an attempt to remove these biases through adjustments in the estimates. But this is not an easy task, and it is difficult to determine the precision of the estimate in any final sense. (Jessen, 1978:196)

In addition to selection errors, bias can be introduced by the interviewer. Quota sampling plans may give considerable latitude to interviewers in selecting respondents in quota classes. When selection depends in any manner on the judgment of the interviewer, an efficient interviewer, particularly if paid by the interview, will select the most readily accessible persons for the completion of quotas. Only the most dedicated will climb several flights of stairs, try to interview residents behind locked gates, or interview those with aggressive pets.

Recognizing the limitation of quota sampling in generalizing findings, some have suggested controls which would bring the process closer to random selection designs. Sudman (1967:6) calls these newer quota sampling approaches "probability sampling with quotas." This approach limits the discretion of interviewers. They are given quotas of types of people to be interviewed, are required to follow a specific travel plan, and are instructed to conduct interviews at specified hours. These plans further require the specification of neighborhood sampling locations and specified households for selection of respondents. Sudman reported that when such controls were incorporated, results similar to those obtained through random sampling were found. The cost for the improved quota sampling is high, but still may be less than the costs of standard random sampling designs.

SAMPLING AND TRIANGULATION IN POLICY RESEARCH

Choosing sampling strategies reflects considerations of information needs, resource limitations, and other contextual features. No best selection plan exists independent of context. Random sampling requires randomized selection. Its use culminates in statistically specified estimates of sampling error, providing an indication of the applicability of findings to working populations. When the purpose is statistically to generalize results or when randomization is easy to achieve, random sampling strategies may be preferred.

Even the best of random sampling plans do not yield error-free information. Sampling error alone is an incomplete, possibly biased indicator of data quality and usefulness. Nonsampling errors such as inadequate sampling frames and nonresponse distort the representativeness of sample findings. Conversely, if statistical generalizations are unnecessary, inappropriate to information needs, or too costly, sample members may be selected through nonrandom procedures. Contextual factors (purposes, resources) dictate choices of sampling plans in policy research.

Random and nonrandom sampling strategies have been discussed as if the choice is to use one or the other. In practice, the two are often combined, resulting in multiple and overlapping samples. Such a triangulated sampling strategy avoids the potential bias of restricting observations to a single data source represented in a sampling frame. The attempt is to sample several data sources through random and nonrandom selection procedures, thus increasing the chances that information is complete, accurate, and more useful. Multiple sampling provides a basis for comparing results among varying data sources and presents a convincing claim for the quality of the findings.

The evaluation of the California Political Reform Act, discussed at length in Chapter 9, provides a case in point. This study was intended to generate information that, in some instances, was likely to exhibit serious problems due to the sensitivity of the information required. One example was the desire to determine whether lobbyists' expenditures on "gifts" or "wining and dining" for legislators actually declined. The law prohibited expenditures of more than $10 per month for any single legislator by any single lobbbyist. For a number of reasons, no one data source was adequate to answer this question fully and accurately. Multiple samples of differing data sources were used such as:

- A *systematic random sample* (n = 450) of financial disclosure reports filed by lobbyists both before and after the law was implemented. These data revealed a significant decrease in reported budget for entertainment and gifts. The obvious shortcoming of this analysis is that it covers only reported expenditures; illegal expenditures would not be reported.
- A *systematic random sample* of registered lobbyists (n = 300). In a mail survey, the sample of lobbyists indicated reductions in their use of gifts and entertainment to improve access to legislators.
- A *purposive sample* of legislative staff (n = 167) who would be knowledgeable regarding lobbying activities (e.g., administrative assistants to legislators, senior committee consultants). Their responses corroborated the changes reported by lobbyists.
- A *purposive sample* of eighteen experienced lobbyists representing different interests (e.g., business, labor, public interest groups), and representing different types of lobbying (e.g., contract lobbyists with a variety of clients versus single-interest lobbyists). These lobbyists par-

ticipated in detailed face-to-face interviews. Their responses again paralleled those of the mail surveys.

On the basis of these triangulated samples, analysts were more confident that "gift" and "wining and dining" expenditures had become a less prominent facet of lobbying influence in the capitol. The fact that data sources were of different types (official records and unofficial perceptions) and that respondents held different perspectives (legislative staff and lobbyists from different interests) made the convergence of findings more convincing and useful.

CONCLUDING COMMENTS

This chapter provided an overview of sampling methods and procedures used in policy research. These sampling procedures are appropriate in sampling any population of interest, whether escrow records or persons.

Sampling strategies are not determined solely through sampling theory; they are first and foremost the consequence of specific information needs and resource constraints. The challenge is to develop a sampling strategy reflecting information needs, given the constraints of circumstance. There is no single best approach to sampling in policy research.

When random samples are needed to generalize findings, detailed planning is necessary. Adequate sampling frames must be constructed, random sampling procedures specified, and acceptable accuracy and precision levels established. The success of these efforts is evaluated through examining

- the clarity and specificity of target populations identified in the study;
- data sources employed in constructing sampling frames;
- procedures used in drawing random samples;
- the extent of sampling error when applied to the working populations; and
- the impacts of nonsampling errors on information quality.

Random selection procedures are used to generalize survey findings beyond the bounds of the immediate research situation. Their use generates statistical estimates of the accuracy and precision of sample findings, enhancing assessments of quality.

Estimates of sampling error, viewed alone, are incomplete guides in assessing information quality and usability. Nonsampling errors may distort sample findings. Inadequate sampling frames, nonresponse, and chance factors all serve to undermine the representativeness of sample findings, the core purpose of random selection.

Nonrandom sampling does not require the rule-bound procedures of random sampling. Sample members may be selected on the basis of convenience rather than on the basis of random probability. Interviewer discretion may be applied in the selection of respondents. The consequence of using nonrandom samples is the inability to provide statistical assessments of the generalizability of survey data.

However, unique and important purposes exist for nonrandom samples, such as gaining an initial understanding of a population, pretesting instruments (e.g., questionnaires), or selecting observations for a host of special information needs. Nonrandom samples are used when information objectives, time, cost, and situational considerations rule out or make random selection methods unneeded. Nonrandom samples are additionally used in triangulated studies to augment other data sources developed in a study.

In policy research, a mix of random and nonrandom strategies is common. These triangulated sampling plans avoid an overreliance on a single data source in generating information. As in any research, data needs are the dominant concern in designing sampling strategies. Experienced analysts use the full range of sampling options to produce policy-relevant information within available resources.

NOTES

1. See Portman, Mouradian, and Bruno (1975). For more specialized determinations of sample size, reference Kish (1965), Jessen (1978), Raj (1972), or Williams (1978).
2. Kish (1965:557–62) provides an excellent discussion of additional remedies for nonresponse.

REFERENCES

Denzin, Norman K. 1970. *The Research Act: A Theoretical Introduction to Sociological Methods.* Chicago: Aldine.
Jessen, Raymond J. 1978. *Statistical Survey Techniques.* New York: John Wiley & Sons.
Kish, Leslie. 1965. *Survey Sampling.* New York: John Wiley & Sons.
Leege, David C., and Wayne L. Francis. 1974. *Political Research: Design, Measurement and Analysis.* New York: Basic Books.
McCall, Chester. 1982. *Sampling and Statistics Handbook for Research.* Ames, IA: University Press.
Portman, Roger H., Robert A. Mouradian, and R. Richard Bruno. 1975. *Tables for Determining Sample Size and Sample Error.* Mission Viejo, CA: National Research Foundation Press.
Raj, Des. 1972. *The Design of Sample Surveys.* New York: John Wiley & Sons.
Sudman, Seymour. 1967. *Reducing the Costs of Surveys.* Chicago: Aldine-Atherton.
Williams, William. 1978. *A Sampler on Sampling.* New York: John Wiley & Sons.
Williamson, John B., David A. Karp, John R. Dalphin, Paul S. Gray. 1982. *The Research Craft: An Introduction to Social Research Methods.* 2d ed. Boston: Little, Brown.

8

Survey Research

To know what people are thinking, what they feel and believe, is often an advantage. If you are a candidate for a political office, you want to know how voters assess your qualifications—or if they recognize your name. If you are a city manager, you want to know if citizens are satisfied with public services provided by your city. If you are a social work administrator, you want to know if clients believe your program improved their life situation. If you are a personnel manager, you want to know employee attitudes toward personnel practices and policies. Survey research relies upon an approach to finding out what these citizens, clients, and employees think: ask them!

Survey research collects data through interaction with persons in a position to provide information. Survey analysts rely on having others tell them what they need to know. This self-report approach carries strong advantages. Survey research is a flexible method for collecting information in a variety of research situations. It is an essential data collection technique when representative information is desired from large and geographically dispersed populations. In addition to technical advantages, survey research has a special appeal to policymakers in a democratic political system. Advocates of citizen surveys, for instance, have noted such surveys go beyond helping to determine the adequacy of public services and helping to guide their improvement.

> Surveys can also be an effective channel for a kind of citizen participation in government. The ... survey gives citizens a chance to "talk" to city hall with anonymity. It permits citizens, at least those sampled, to make their preferences and displeasures known and in a way that can be constructively used by government. Citizens are likely to welcome the opportunity to voice their concerns, particularly when effective action follows the survey. (Weiss and Hatry, 1971:11)

As a means of communication between citizens and policymakers, survey research enhances democratic accountability and responsiveness in government.

Ironically, the very practice of relying on self-reports by respondents creates the greatest pitfalls in doing surveys. People are active and thinking. They have their own interests and priorities, their own sets of demands on their time, their own way of viewing the world. Thus, gathering information through surveys is not simply making observations; it is a process of social interaction. Respondents are not passively submitting to a sequence of questions. They are actively involved in figuring out what the survey is asking, figuring out if and how it affects them, figuring out whether it's worth their time to respond, and figuring out what they want to say or write.

The fact that survey research requires interaction with a large number of persons makes it a potentially problematic method for collecting information. Respondents can select themselves out of a study by refusing to be interviewed or by discarding a mailed questionnaire. They may misinterpret questions. They may not know what they feel or believe about an issue. They may try to please interviewers by giving an appropriate, socially acceptable response. They may get tired or bored and quit responding, or respond without thinking. A continuing challenge in survey research is getting respondents to participate in a survey and getting them to provide needed information accurately and candidly.

Fortunately, the technology of survey research provides analysts with numerous alternatives in devising a survey strategy maximizing respondent participation in providing accurate and useful information. The objectives of this chapter are to clarify strategies used by analysts in designing and conducting surveys, and to clarify how to make informed judgments about a survey's worth as a decision-making resource. The following discussion explores major alternative survey approaches available to analysts.

ALTERNATIVE SURVEY TECHNIQUES

Analysts contemplating a survey must decide whether to use in-person interviews, telephone interviews, or self-administered questionnaires. The fundamental distinction between these techniques is the extent to which respondents have contact with interviewers. In-person interviews require the physical presence of interviewers. Telephone surveys present respondents with only the voice of interviewers. Self-administered questionnaires, whether sent by mail or distributed in some other fashion, are given to a group of respondents to complete by themselves. Each of these techniques offers differing strengths and limitations. They differ in the quantity and quality of information each can provide. They differ in the resources and skills required to implement them. They differ in the speed with which information can be collected. Following sections examine the relative merits of the three basic survey approaches. A summary of the comparisons is provided in Table 8.1.

In-Person Interviews

Advantages and disadvantages accrue when using in-person, or personal, interviews. The greatest advantages relate to the quantity and quality of resulting information. The greatest disadvantages relate to high costs and to the exacting skills required of interviewers. The pluses and minuses of in-person interviews are discussed in following paragraphs.

In-person interviews accommodate a greater volume of information than any other survey technique. A twenty-minute telephone interview is a long interview; some believe thirty minutes represents a maximum time requirement for either telephone or self-administered surveys (Kidder, 1981:152). On the other hand, it is not unusual for personal interviews to last one hour or more. The greater duration of effective interview time can

TABLE 8.1. Relative Merits of Alternative Survey Techniques

EVALUATION MEASURES	IN-PERSON INTERVIEWS	TELEPHONE INTERVIEWS	SELF-ADMINIS- TERED QUES- TIONNAIRES
Response Rate	+ +	+ +	−
Avoidance of Interviewer Bias	−	+	+ +
Ability to Obtain Detailed, Complete Responses Through Clarification and Probing	+ +	+	−
Motivation of Respondent to Provide Information	+ +	+	−
Quantity of Information That Can Be Collected	+ +	+	−
Ability to Contact Widely Dispersed Populations	−	+ +	+ +
Simplicity of Administration	−	+	+ +
Speed of Collecting Information	−	+ +	+
Low Costs	−	+	+ +

Key: + + = good, + = fair, − = poor

be attributed to the richness of the social interaction developed in personal interviews. By maintaining a friendly, interested, nonjudgmental approach, in-person interviewers heighten respondents' motivation to participate in the survey. Being the object of interviewers' attention lends importance to respondents and promotes complete and considered responses.

A second advantage of in-person interviews is the ability to obtain detailed, clear responses through clarification and probing. When a question is not understood, an interviewer can repeat it or offer alternate standardized explanations of the question's meaning. In a self-administered questionnaire, respondents might simply skip a troublesome question. Further, the quality of responses is improved by probing. Probing stimulates further discussion so more detailed information is obtained. If respondents give incomplete or unclear responses, interviewers may counter with neutral probes, e.g.: "Could you tell me a bit more about that?" "Why do you think that is so?" "Are you thinking of a specific example?" The skillful use of probes allows interviewers to secure complete, detailed, and understandable data. Once the interview is complete, the opportunity to clarify or augment information is lost.

The positive influence of establishing personal contact with respondents is evidenced in the high response rates typical of in-person surveys. Well-planned surveys using skilled interviewers frequently obtain responses from 80 to 90 percent of all individuals contacted. This high rate of response strengthens the likelihood of obtaining information which accurately represents the population of individuals under study. If 90 percent of those contacted are willing to share information with the interviewer—as opposed to the 20–30 percent who respond to many mail surveys—analysts and users are more assured that responses accurately reflect the views of the population they represent.

There are multiple reasons for the high response rates typical of in-person interviews. Respondents unable to read and write can still verbally respond to questions. Of more importance, persons insufficiently motivated to write out responses to written questionnaires may be willing to respond verbally. Many people are more confident of their speaking skills than they are of their writing skills. In brief, some of the strongest advantages of in-person surveys reside in the relative lack of barriers to participation. Indeed, personal interviews provide a degree of social inducement to participate. Most people enjoy talking to someone genuinely interested in what they have to say.

The very richness of the social interaction characterizing personal interviews is also the basis for limitations regarding the quality of information gathered through this technique. Whenever people interact, an individual's behavior is influenced by another person's presence and demeanor. The interviewer's appearance, manner, and behavior, method of recording responses, and other factors may bias information collected in the interview.

Behavior as simple as arching an eyebrow or smiling at an individual's response can influence a respondent's subsequent answers. If the interviewer's clothing and appearance significantly depart from those of the respondents, answers may be tailored to the image projected by the interviewer. Consequently, the advantages of in-person interviews are largely dependent on a major qualification—the skills of the interviewers in dealing with respondents.

An example demonstrates the difficulty of the interpersonal situations which often confront interviewers. In studying the attitudes of local citizens regarding mass transit, policymakers wanted to evaluate preferences regarding additional tax support for public buses. Interviewers asked respondents the following question: "Public transportation is partly supported by local taxes. Would you vote for or against an additional local tax to support expanded public transit services, or are you unsure of how you would vote?" If respondents indicated they would vote for additional taxes, interviewers asked a follow-up question: "What kind of local tax would you support?" Interviewers were then instructed to record up to three kinds of local tax volunteered by respondents.

In asking this question, interviewers experienced a problem. Many respondents did not understand what was being asked. They were insufficiently aware of public revenue mechanisms to volunteer the kinds of taxes most acceptable to them. Not infrequently they would ask interviewers what was meant by the question. Since no standardized language had been developed for clarifying the question, interviewers were faced with a dilemma. If they did not clarify the question, they jeopardized their hard-won rapport with respondents. Interviewers who took this approach reported respondents sometimes became self-conscious, felt embarrassed over their inability to respond, and seemed to withdraw from active interest in the interview.

On the other hand, ad-lib attempts to clarify the question carried great potential for compromising the accuracy of responses. One interviewer, for example, gave in to the empathy she felt for the embarrassed respondents and attempted to help them out by providing some examples of different kinds of taxes. When presented with examples such as sales tax or property tax, respondents would often, with obvious relief, select one or more of the examples as their response. The trade-off facing interviewers in this situation was a difficult one. On the one hand was the danger of losing rapport with the respondent; on the other hand was the danger of putting words into the respondent's mouth and destroying the accuracy of results. Reducing these potential sources of error in personal interviews is discussed later in this chapter.

Personal interviews are the most costly way in which to gather survey information. Interviewers must be recruited, trained, and compensated. Significant costs are involved in traveling to interview sites (e.g., respondents' homes and offices) and in making call-backs when respondents are not there. Attempts to cut costs—such as minimizing training, using volunteer interviewers, or eliminating call-backs—have adverse effects on data quality. The use of personal interviews in collecting information requires the commitment of significant resources.

Telephone Interviews

Traditionally, in-person interviews, compared to telephone interviews, have been preferred by policy analysts. However, this preference toward in-person interviews is increasingly being eroded by studies demonstrating the accuracy and usefulness of telephone surveys and by the high costs of in-person interviews. Indeed, telephone surveys maintain many of the data quality advantages of personal interviews while contributing further advantages of their own.

One advantage of telephone surveys lies in the speed of collecting information. Polling organizations conduct national telephone surveys of voter preferences in the waning hours of elections to give almost immediate feedback to candidates and citizens. Telephone surveys are the dominant method used by mass media in their coverage of fast-breaking events of public interest. Policy analysts are increasingly recognizing the benefits of telephone surveys in obtaining timely information for decision making. In-person interviews or mailed questionnaires may take weeks to collect information needs, telephone surveys only days.

A second advantage of telephone surveys is the ability to interview over a broad geographic area at minimal cost. Backstrom and Hursh-Cesar (1981:21) explain this advantage:

> It is far easier and cheaper to conduct national surveys by phone than to maintain a national field staff [of interviewers] or to assemble one for a single survey. Moreover, local, regional, and national interviewing can be conducted simultaneously, and the results can be analyzed and made available at the same time, without even a day's delay. Individual personal interviews may be scattered over a large area, and the interviewer may be able to complete only one per day; phoners let their fingers do the walking.

The relative efficiency of telephone surveys, which require fewer interviewers than in-person surveys, makes them a less costly technique.

The preceding quotation from Backstrom and Hursh-Cesar reveals a third advantage of telephone interviews—their relative simplicity of administration. Unlike personal interviews, which take place in dispersed locations, telephone interviews are frequently conducted in centralized locations. This physical proximity of the interview activity enhances the ability of the interview supervisor to monitor the course of the interviews and to take appropriate actions to ensure quality control. For example, a principal source of bias in telephone interviews is the interviewer's voice and the image conveyed by it. A decided lack of enthusiasm in the interviewer's tone of voice reduces respondents' motivation to participate. If a telephone interviewer's verbal communications to respondents show potential for influencing their answers, the interview supervisor can provide instant feedback to correct the situation. Such instant feedback in monitoring interviewer behavior is lacking in personal interviews.

Contrary to early assumptions regarding telephone interviews, experience has demonstrated their capacity to produce accurate information. Telephone interviews do not offer as many possibilities for interviewer bias as do in-person interviews. Interviewers' clothing, appearance, and body language are hidden from respondents and do not influence their responses. The high quality of information collected through telephone surveys has been documented through studies comparing in-person and telephone survey methods. For example, research comparing telephone and personal interviews has found little difference in the completeness and validity of responses (Groves and Kahn, 1979; Jordan, Marcus, and Reeder, 1980).

Thus, telephone surveys are capable of rendering quality information, are cost efficient, and carry administrative advantages. There is an important limitation of telephone interviews when used to survey the general population. Anyone in the population who does not have access to a telephone cannot be reached. Although a great majority of United States households have access to a telephone (90 percent plus), telephone surveys underrepresent groups such as the poor, the elderly, and persons in transit. For many policy purposes, underrepresentation of these groups may bias findings since these groups were not included in the sampling frame.

Further, in general population surveys the selection of telephone numbers may become problematic. Telephone books provide a sampling frame for the selection of numbers, but the exclusion of all persons with unlisted numbers means that a sample drawn from the phone book will be unrepresentative. Perhaps 15–30 percent of those with telephones do not list their numbers—even more in some urban areas. It is probable that these individuals constitute homogeneous groups, differing in attitudes, age, socioeconomic status, and so forth, from those who publicly list their names.

One way to overcome this potential bias is to employ "random digit dialing" (RDD). Through this technique, random sequences of numbers are dialed from a study area's working exchanges, i.e., all prefixes in a given geographic area. RDD includes in its sampling frame households having unlisted numbers, thereby eliminating a potential source of bias in telephone surveys.

One approach to generating telephone numbers in RDD is to select four-digit numbers randomly and add them to the three-digit exchange prefixes in the study's geographic area. The four-digit numbers may be generated through the use of a table of random numbers or, in the case of larger studies, may be computer generated. Returning to the table of random numbers in Table 7.1 in the previous chapter and using 451- as a sample prefix, the first number dialed is 451-1419, the second 451-7751, and so on. A single, four-digit number may be used once or it may be added to all prefixes existing in the geographic area. A difficulty with this technique of random digit dialing is that a disheartening number of calls are unused, disconnected phones.

Wimmer and Dominick (1983:63) suggest an alternate RDD method which reduces the number of incomplete calls. Analysts add one or two digits to a telephone number randomly selected from a directory. If, for example, the number is 451-8124, a table of random numbers is used to produce add-ons. If the add-on digit is 3, the next telephone number dialed is 451-8127, the following 451-8130, and so on. Since many telephone companies distribute numbers in series, e.g., the 81-series, the probability that a phone number in the same series will be operational is increased and the number of incomplete calls decreased. A survey using random digit dialing gives all working numbers in a sampled area an equal chance of being selected, improving the representativeness of the information.

Another consideration in telephone surveys concerns the motivation of respondents to participate in the survey. Telephone interviewing is a form of social interaction which carries less social inducement to participate than does in-person interviewing; it is easier to hang up the phone than to ask someone to leave. Reduced motivation to participate is reflected in the shorter effective length of telephone interviews when compared to personal interviews.

But research findings comparing the techniques suggest that differences in motivation do not necessarily reduce response rates. While some analysts have reported lower response rates for telephone interviews, others have found telephone response rates "usually no worse, and often better than completion of in-person samples" (Kidder, 1981:152). Experience has shown that well-designed telephone surveys result in response rates comparable to the 80 to 90 percent rates characteristic of in-person interviews.

Telephone interviewing presents an advantageous mix of information quality, ease of administration, and relatively low cost. Technological advances promise to make the technique more efficient. Babbie (1982:154) portrays current technology in computer-assisted telephone interviewing:

> The interviewer sits in front of a computer terminal and its video screen. The central computer randomly selects a telephone number and dials it on behalf of the telephone headset the interviewer is wearing. On the video screen is an introduction and the first question to be asked. The respondent answers the phone, and the interviewer says hello and introduces him or herself and the study. Then the interviewer reads the first question displayed on the screen and types the respondent's answer into the computer terminal. The respondent's answer is immediately stored within the central computer.

Self-Administered Questionnaires

Self-administered questionnaires differ significantly from in-person and telephone interviews. They are designed to be completed by respondents without assistance. Respondents read the question and answer by checking, circling, writing out, or in some way recording their response. No interviewer is present to motivate respondents to participate or to guide them through the survey.

Important benefits are realized using this survey approach. Self-administered surveys are simple to administer. They are the least expensive technique for collecting information from people. The costly process of recruiting, training, and deploying interviewers is replaced by the lesser expense of mailing questionnaires. Given identical research resources, more persons can be contacted using self-administered questionnaires than through in-person and telephone interviews.

The absence of interviewers has beneficial implications for the quality of information collected. For example, the possibility of interviewer bias is eliminated; respondents are not influenced by an interviewer's appearance, body language, demeanor, or voice. Since there is no direct physical or verbal contact, errors arising from the interview situation itself are avoided.

The fact that respondents answer the survey at their leisure, rather than within the time constraints of an interview, is advantageous. A questionnaire allows respondents to take their time in completing the survey. When personal historical data are being requested, for instance, respondents have an opportunity to consult their records before answering. In interviews, pressure on respondents for immediate answers can produce ill-considered responses. When pressures are less immediate, as in mailed questionnaires, respondents may consider each question carefully rather than answer with the first thought that comes to mind.

While the absence of interviewers can be advantageous, the lack of in-person or verbal interaction with respondents reduces their motivation to participate in the survey. This lack of interaction and the additional burden of reading and responding to the questionnaire contribute to the relatively low response rates characteristic of mail surveys. Rates of completed returns can be less than 5 percent for surveys with particularly low motivation for respondents, e.g., questionnaires in bills sent out by telephone and utility companies. Such response rates undercut data quality, particularly if the attempt is to gain systematic and dependable information on an entire population. Regardless of how skillfully mailed surveys are planned and conducted, response rates infrequently exceed 70–75 percent.

Given that response rates lower than 70 percent are characteristic of mail surveys, how representative is the resulting information? Is there a difference between those who do respond and those who do not? Bailey (1982:157) answers in the affirmative:

The respondents who do not answer are generally not a random selection of the sample but have some biasing characteristics. For example, the elderly are more likely to be ill and unable to respond. The more mobile are less likely to have a current address and thus are less likely to receive a questionnaire. The poorly educated are unable to read the questionnaire and write answers. Even many highly educated people feel that they can express themselves better through speaking than through writing, or are simply too lazy to write lengthy paragraphs, or feel that their grammar or spelling is not adequate given their educational level, and thus feel embarrassed to tender a response.

The possibility of "nonresponse bias" is a major concern of analysts using mail surveys. Low response rates may yield unrepresentative survey findings, a misleading decision resource. The problem is particularly acute in policy research because low response rates raise questions regarding the credibility of the resulting information as a basis for action. Analysts combat the problem of nonresponse in two ways. First, procedures exist which are used to increase response rates. Carefully applied, they make return rates in the 70-percent range attainable for many mail surveys. Second, there are methods for ascertaining if nonresponse bias has influenced survey findings, discussed in Chapter 7.

Nonresponse is not the sole limitation of self-administered questionnaires. The absence of an interviewer and the consequent reliance on reading and writing skills hinder the ability to obtain complete, detailed survey information. For example, interviewers can probe for more detailed information from respondents than is possible in a questionnaire. Further, if respondents do not understand a question, interviewers can provide specified alternative wordings of the question for purposes of clarification. Alternative wording is not common in mail surveys, primarily because it increases questionnaire length. Increased questionnaire length requires more effort and more time from respondents, decreasing response rates. The constraints of questionnaire length mean self-administered questionnaires cannot gather the quantity of information possible through personal or telephone interviews.

Because the form of interaction with respondents is so different from that of personal or telephone interviews, the self-administered questionnaire provides its own set of potential barriers to participation by respondents. But these limitations can be minimized, and the mailed survey offers strong advantages in administration and cost. Self-administered questionnaires provide a useful technique in the research strategies of policy analysts.

DESIGNING SURVEY INSTRUMENTS

Regardless of the survey technique(s) selected to fulfill information needs, decisions must be made on the content and phrasing of questions to be asked of respondents. Designing questions is where analysts get down to detail in eliciting the information needed. The set of questions (also called items) respondents are asked to reply to in an interview is conventionally termed an interview "schedule"; for self-administered surveys the set of questions is called a "questionnaire." In referring to both questionnaires and interview schedules, the term "survey instrument" is used. This section introduces major considerations confronting analysts in designing survey instruments. To provide some continuity and familiarity to the discussion, frequent reference is made to a citizen survey concerning mass transit.

The survey was conducted in Lake Tahoe—one of the West's most popular vacation spots (California Technical Assistance Associates, Inc., 1982). High astride the California-Nevada border along the crest of the Sierra Nevada mountains, Lake Tahoe is one of the world's scenic wonders. More than two thousand campsites, extensive outdoor recreational facilities, world-class ski resorts, and gambling casinos make Lake Tahoe a magnet for visitors and residents alike.

The popularity of Lake Tahoe is taking its toll on the environmental quality of the area. The growing gambling industry on the Nevada border, an avalanche of condominium and hotel construction, and a parade of automobile traffic have tainted the clean air and threatened the clear waters of the area. As part of an attempt to protect the lake's environment, the Tahoe Regional Planning Agency (a regional environmental protection commission) embarked on an aggressive program to improve mass transit facilities in the area and to relieve the community from the polluting crush of automobile traffic.

A successful transit system attracts riders; it meets the needs and expectations of citizens. Thus, an important part of the planning process for improving and expanding Lake Tahoe's transit system was to assess people's attitudes toward their mass transit systems and to determine their unmet transit needs. A survey of citizens was one of the chosen mechanisms for gathering the information. The analysts conducting the survey were charged with the task of designing and implementing a study to accomplish these objectives. The choices that analysts encountered in devising specific questions for the survey provide a basis for discussing issues of question design.

A fundamental choice facing analysts designing the survey was whether to use free (open ended) or fixed (closed ended) question formats. In the mass transit study, one information need was to ascertain citizens' motivations for riding public buses. Both free and fixed response questions were considered in responding to this information need. In free response questions, no alternatives are provided; respondents answer in any way they choose.

The central characteristic of free response questions is that respondents are invited to compose their own answers. They are not restricted by preestablished response categories. Respondents follow their own logic unencumbered by a prepared set of replies. Their ideas are obtained in

---

Different people have different reasons for riding the bus. What are your reasons for riding the bus rather than using other forms of transportation such as automobiles?

1._____
2._____
3._____
4._____

---

their own language, expressed spontaneously. Their responses provide quotable quotes, lending color, authenticity, and credibility to research findings.

In fixed response questions, respondents are offered preestablished response categories from which they circle their views:

Why do you ride the bus instead of using other forms of transportation such as automobiles?

No driver's license/can't drive...1
Personal transportation unavailable..2
Economy of bus...3
Dislike driving in traffic..4
Parking difficult/unavailable 5
Prefer convenience of bus..6

The major characteristic of fixed response questions is that respondents answer only in terms of response categories which have been developed in advance by analysts.

Choosing between free and fixed formats is in the final analysis a judgment made by analysts who weigh multiple considerations. These considerations regarding question format can frequently be classified into two major categories. The first category represents substantive considerations—which format will most effectively elicit needed information? The second category of concerns is procedural—which format is most suitable, given resources available for the survey, the survey techniques being used, and the resulting quality of the information obtained?

The major advantage of free response questions is substantive. Certain kinds of information are not easily gathered through fixed response questions. For example, in the fixed format response question provided above, a respondent may prefer the convenience of the bus, but analysts can only speculate why respondents think it is more convenient. A free response question is better for capturing the unique reasoning of respondents and for gathering unique in-depth information from individuals. Free response questions are needed when analysts do not have a clear idea of the range of possible responses to a question. Devising a complete and accurate set of fixed responses requires a well-developed prior knowledge of how respondents will answer the question.

While they are necessary to the purposes of intensive interviewing (discussed in Chapter 6), free response questions carry limitations for survey research purposes. A major drawback is lodged in the analysis of such questions. Using the question above as an illustration, respondents will offer a wide variety of reasons for riding public buses. It is meaningless simply to list every reason given; analysts organize responses into a manageable number of response categories. Too few categories of responses eliminate or distort the more subtle meanings and distinctions between respondent answers. Too many categories divide respondents into too many small groups and hinder attempts to generalize about types of people holding particular views. Numerous hours are consumed in developing nonoverlapping, accurate categories of responses. Analyzing and interpreting free response questions is difficult and time consuming.

Free response questions pose problems in interviews and self-administered questionnaires. In survey interviews, open-ended questions are unwieldy because interviewers should record responses verbatim. Respondents may "run with" the question, going on and on and digressing into areas unrelated to the topic at hand. Keeping respondents on track in a respectful and courteous manner can be a difficult task. Open-ended questions are particularly problematic for self-administered questionnaires. Their use requires adequate writing skills and demands more of the respondent's time, lowering response rates. They require more space, limiting the number of questions that can be asked and increasing the overall length of the questionnaire. Indirect methods of controlling the quantity of writing, such as limiting the number of lines provided to write responses, must be relied on to indicate the desired length or detail of the response.

In comparison, closed-ended or fixed format questions provide numerous procedural advantages. They are easier to process and analyze because responses are simply checked or circled, making them easily tabulated. Closed-ended questions require no writing; they are easier and quicker to answer; and they shorten the time required to complete the interview or questionnaire, resulting in increased response rates. An important benefit of using fixed response questions is reduced cost and greater speed in producing results.

However, there is a loss of spontaneity and expressiveness in using closed-ended questions. Respondents may feel frustrated because there is no opportunity to clarify or qualify their responses, or because they believe that response categories inadequately reflect their views. Attaining quality information is always a matter of making reasonable trade-offs between a variety of sources of bias and distortion. Analysts weigh potential losses of detail against other types of loss, such as the potential increase in nonresponse to a given question because it requires a written answer, or potential interviewer bias if there are not sufficient resources to train interviewers thoroughly.

In the final analysis, decisions on question format hinge on the research context. A major consideration is: Will the format—whether free, fixed, or a combination of the two—produce accurate and useful information? Most surveys contain a mix of free and fixed response questions. When using open-ended questions in a mail survey, analysts regulate the amount respondents write by limiting the space provided for answering. Reasonable space should be given to obtain complete responses and to discourage respondents from writing in the margins and on the back of questionnaires.

Question Wording

Unclear questions generate unclear responses. If respondents have to ponder the real meaning of questions, their individual responses will reflect their individual interpretations of what is real. The following example of a vague question is drawn from a transportation survey:

How many vehicles in working condition are available for use by members of your household?
_____Number of Vehicles

This question is vague in the sense that vehicle has multiple meanings. For example, respondents may or may not include in their response such vehicles as bicycles, motorized bikes, mopeds, and leased or company-owned vehicles. They may wonder if the question includes both registered and unregistered vehicles. The number of vehicles given in a response depends on how each respondent interprets the term vehicle. Questions more exact in their meaning, e.g., specifying what is meant by vehicles in the question, are easier to answer and result in more dependable data than those which are incomplete or imprecise.

Sometimes two or more questions are combined in a single item. How should respondents answer the following question when their agency provides individual transportation services for senior citizens but not for disabled persons?

Does your agency currently provide individual transportation services for senior citizens and for disabled persons?
_____Yes
_____No

A yes response implies that both groups are provided individual transportation services; a no response, that neither group is afforded those services. In "double-barreled" questions such as this, accuracy is decreased because it is impossible to know which part of the question "yes" responses reference. Questionnaire items containing the words *or* and *and* should be examined to see if they consist of combined questions with only one response expected. Double-barreled questions confuse respondents and distort answers, resulting in less trustworthy and useful survey results.

To the extent possible, question wording should mean the same thing to all respondents. Words that lie outside a respondent's knowledge and experience result in random and less useful responses. The extremes of vocabulary should be avoided, such as technical jargon familiar only to those with specialized training and slang terms which mean different things to different respondents. The objective is to keep the wording simple, direct, and familiar to all respondents.

In part, question wording depends on the educational level of respondents plus their experience and knowledge of the survey topic. Talking down to respondents should be avoided. Yet analysts should remember they are close to the subject matter involved, and respondents may not share their familiarity and concern with the issue. Experienced analysts choose words understood by respondents at varying educational levels yet avoid coming across as patronizing.

A question is "loaded" when its wording is not neutral, but suggests to respondents that one response is more desirable than another.

Public schools have their own bus system for students. In order to save taxpayers' money, it has been suggested school buses be discontinued and local bus services expanded to provide transportation to and from schools. What do you think of this idea?

This question is loaded because it says taxpayers' money is saved by discontinuing school bus services. It is safe to assume respondents want to "save taxpayers' money." Such a question is slanted, emphasizing one side of an issue, suggesting only one reasonable and intelligent response to the question. Analysts constantly guard against loading questions with the use of emotionally charged words such as "saving taxpayers' money," "free enterprise," "bureaucracy," "big business," "big labor," and so on. Questions should be stated in neutral terms.

A related form of question wording that pushes respondents in the direction of a certain response is a "leading question." Questions beginning with phrases such as "Wouldn't you say ..." or "Most people agree ..." or "Would you agree ..." lead respondents to agree. Another way of leading respondents is to cite an authority, such as "Major transportation authorities believe. . . ." Surveys containing leading questions slant responses and come across as trying to prove a point rather than trying to collect unbiased information.

Survey questions sometimes ask respondents to tell personal things about themselves—their income, political preferences, religion—that they might not quickly reveal to friends and associates. In part, respondents provide this information because of promises of confidentiality: analysts promise that respondents' names and individual answers will not be revealed. In larger part, it is expected that people want to be honest in their responses. Survey research is based on the general assumption that respondents will not misrepresent facts or their opinions in responding to questions. (For a criticism of this assumption, see Douglas, 1976.)

Analysts avoid question wording which discourages honest responses. Questions of an embarrassing and sensitive nature poorly handled by analysts lead to suspect information. Some respondents will refuse to answer such questions. Others invent or distort answers because, for example, they do not wish to appear uninformed. For them, it is better to guess than to profess ignorance about a subject.

A study by the newspaper *Der Speigel* illustrates this reaction. The paper published results of an opinion poll showing the favorability rating of cabinet ministers in the Federal Republic of Germany. The pollsters included the name of a fictitious minister on the list. He came in sixth in favorability, ahead of ten other names (Lewis and Schneider, 1982:44).

In another study, researchers at the University of Cincinnati (Lewis and Schneider, 1982:43) asked a sample of that city's residents about a fictitious "1975 Public Affairs Act." When the following question was asked: "Some people say that the 1975 Public Affairs Act should be repealed. Do you agree or disagree with this idea?" one-third of the respondents expressed an opinion (16 percent agreed, 18 percent disagreed). The *Los Angeles Times* gave the respondent the option of saying "don't know" to the same question and found 9 percent still giving their opinion on the nonexistent 1975 Public Affairs Act (4 percent agreed, 5 percent disagreed).

Misreporting by respondents is reduced by considering all questions for their potential embarrassment, by minimizing the number of personal questions asked and by providing face-saving alternatives in question wording. For example, asking, "Did you vote in the city election last week?" places some nonvoting respondents in what they perceive is an embarrassing position and leads to survey results showing a higher percentage of voters than there actually were. A version of this same question with a face-saving alternative is, "Did you have the opportunity to vote in the city elections last week?" followed up with (if yes) "Did you vote in last week's elections?"

Respondents will always answer questions based on their individual understanding, regardless of analysts' best intentions. But for every improvement made in question wording, attendant benefits are realized in obtaining higher quality information for decision making.

Additional Design Considerations: Filter Questions and Question Order

The design of survey instruments is more than question format and question wording. Completeness and accuracy of survey results are also affected by the overall flow and sequencing of the items. If respondents become confused about the relevance of questions for them or are put off by questions at the beginning of the survey, they may withdraw or misreport information. Two prominent concerns in the sequencing of questions are addressed below.

FILTER QUESTIONS

Some questions may be applicable only to a subgroup of respondents. Asking, "How close to your destination can you usually get using the bus?" is only relevant to respondents who ride buses. For nonusers, this question is confusing because it does not apply to them. It may encourage misreporting by those who feel they should use public transportation but don't. Filter questions provide a solution to this problem:

Do you ride the bus at Lake Tahoe at least once a month?
No..1
Yes...2

    If YES, how close can you usually get to
    where you're going using the bus?
        1–4 blocks...1
        5–8 blocks...2
        9–16 blocks..3
        Over 16 blocks..4
        Varies...5
        Don't know...9

In a filter question, the first item determines whether the respondent is qualified to answer the subsequent item. If not qualified, the respondent (or interviewer) moves without interruption to subsequent questions which are applicable. Well-designed filter questions enhance the flow of items, minimize confusion and misreporting, and facilitate coding and analysis of responses.

QUESTION ORDER

The sequence of questions is another consideration in designing survey instruments. If beginning questions are personal in nature, e.g., asking income or age, respondents may feel an invasion of their privacy and refuse to participate. People are more willing to provide personal information after trust has been established. Early questions should arouse the respondent's interest in the survey and instill confidence by demonstrating a desire for information the respondent can provide. The first question after the introduction in the Tahoe transit study eased the respondent into the survey with the following language: "We're interested in getting your impressions of public transportation in your area. Have you happened to travel by public transit in the past month?"

Questions fulfilling major information needs of the survey usually follow introductory questions. These questions, which may require considered thought on the part of respondents, should be asked while motivation and mental energy are high. Core questions in the Tahoe survey included those identifying attitudes of users and nonusers of public buses, and their thoughts for improving public transit in the Tahoe area.

The concluding section of the instrument typically includes questions of a demographic or personal nature, e.g., age, years of education, gender, income. These items come late in the questionnaire for two reasons. First, they ask for information well known to respondents; therefore, accuracy is less affected by boredom or fatigue. Second, if positioned earlier in the instrument, respondents may feel these questions are embarrassing, inappropriate, none of the analyst's business.

Because each survey produces its own problems of question order, the final ordering is determined by the research situation. In personal or telephone interviews, for instance, free response questions may be desirable for early questions. They allow respondents to speak freely and to become comfortable with the interview. Yet free response questions placed early in a mail survey may discourage respondents.

However ordered, questions should be organized so they flow from one topic to another in a coherent and logically sequenced fashion. When shifting from one topic to another, "transitional" statements are used. Toward the end of the Tahoe survey, interviewers used the following language:

Now a few final questions . . . First, how many automobiles are usually available for use at your household?

The brief transitional statement let respondents know that there was a change in the topic of questioning and also that the interview was coming to a completion. Transitional statements are an important part of effective communication with respondents.

IMPLEMENTING SURVEYS

Analysts conducting the Tahoe transit survey confronted a demanding time schedule, not unusual in policy research. The entire study, from clarifying research objectives to submitting the final draft report, consumed fifteen weeks. The high costs of locating in the expensive resort environment of Lake Tahoe meant that research staff had to get in, get the interviews done, and get back to the office as quickly as possible. Information was gathered by telephone interviews (for a general population survey) and by self-administered questionnaires passed out by analysts to bus riders on selected routes (for a daily users survey). Six interviewers had to conduct six hundred interviews within two weeks, and bus riders were surveyed during a one-day period. Responses were coded, edited, and computer analyzed within a fifteen-day time period. Two weeks after data analysis, a completed draft report was given to the project monitor.

The fact that surveys can provide quick information makes careful planning and implementation important. Once interviewers are in the field, there is no time to stop and rethink problems of wording in the interview schedule. Analysts having to distribute questionnaires on their assigned buses throughout the Tahoe basin had to react in standardized ways to unusual contingencies, e.g., respondents who had already filled out the instrument on another route. They could not talk it out. The statistical analyst did not have the luxury of sitting down and determining what charts and tables would be appropriate once analysis was under way. All of these activities had to be thoroughly planned in advance. While all research requires planning and coordination, these activities are particularly relevant to surveys. The following discussion considers strategies for adequate planning and adequate quality control during the implementation of surveys.

Initial Planning of Surveys

The initial planning stage for a survey includes phases characterizing early stages of other research efforts. Information objectives are clarified and translated into specific information needs (discussed in prior chapters). However, there are issues particularly important to the planning of surveys.

First, since surveys depend on contact with people to gather information, the nature of the target population demands careful thought. The Tahoe transit survey provides a case in point. Did the objectives of the study require a survey of bus riders, or a survey of the general population in the

Tahoe area, or both? Should the large number of visitors and vacationers frequenting the lake be included in the survey? Thorough consideration of information needs led to the conclusion that both the general population and daily riders should be surveyed as separate but overlapping target populations. A reliance on the general population alone would produce too few regular bus riders to gain generalizable information on such concerns as the quality of service and how to improve that service. Reliance on riders alone would not allow an examination of those who do not ride buses and why they do not use public buses. Both target populations had to be surveyed. Analysts also decided that attempts to survey visitors as another target population would yield only low priority information and would be a difficult and costly endeavor. Visitors were consequently excluded from the target populations of the survey.

Considerations of target populations should address their ability to provide information. Relevant factors include their interest in the survey, their familiarity with public transit, their educational levels, and other characteristics. These characteristics of the target population(s) influence the design and implementation of the survey. For instance, the population of bus riders in the transit survey were likely to be familiar with bus service, to have moderate interest in the topic, to be of varied educational levels, to have a disproportionate number of the young and elderly, to be in a situation of limited time, and to be answering the questionnaire on a moving bus. Asking free response questions under these circumstances would present respondents (and analysts) with a difficult task.

Second, analysts planning a survey are particularly sensitive to prior surveys of a similar type. In planning the Tahoe transit survey, analysts conducted a thorough search, reviewing numerous survey instruments and survey reports on mass transit studies conducted in other locales. This review proved invaluable in considering the variety of questions that could be asked, the question formats that could be used, and problems that had been encountered in prior studies.

In recent years, a number of reference works containing previously used questionnaires have been published. The Urban Institute and the International City Managers' Association, for example, have published a work entitled *How Effective Are Your Community Services?* (Harry et al., 1977). This reference provides methods by which public officials can regularly obtain information on the effectiveness and quality of their services. It includes survey instruments for assessing the following basic services commonly provided by governmental units:

- Crime control
- Recreation services
- Library services

- Fire protection
- Transportation services
- Public mass transit
- Solid waste collection and disposal
- Water supply

Another two-volume series by the Urban Institute (Millar, Hatry, and Koss, 1977) includes questionnaires for evaluating the effectiveness of social services. These survey instruments measure improvement in client condition, client satisfaction with social services, and unmet needs, i.e., those individuals and groups requiring but not obtaining needs for social services.

These and other compendiums of existing questionnaire items (see Robinson, Athanasion, and Head, 1973; Robinson, Rusk, and Head, 1973; Robinson and Schaver, 1973) yield field-tested questions relevant to many information needs. The use of these standard questions increases the comparability of surveys and allows analysts to benefit from one another's efforts in grappling with similar information objectives.

It is particularly important that survey analysts think through the intended analysis of the data during the planning stages. Surveys, by their nature, produce standardized information over a large number of observations. To be understandable, this data must be clearly summarized in an appropriate format. In the Tahoe study, the actual tables to be presented in the research report were determined during the planning process. This determination provided concrete guidance for deciding exactly what information needed to be presented and highlighted, and for designing analysis procedures. Methods of data analysis are decided upon in the planning stages of the survey, not after data are collected.

GETTING READY TO SURVEY

In survey research, analysts are thoroughly prepared before going to the field. Once survey materials have been designed and printed, making changes is costly and impractical. An important component of adequate preparation is *pretesting*—conducting a trial run or field test of survey instruments on smaller samples of target populations. In the Tahoe transit survey, over thirty telephone interviews were conducted using procedures planned for the full-scale survey. The pretest identified questions that were vague, difficult, and time consuming for respondents. It revealed problems with the random digit dialing technique. In telephone prefixes with relatively few numbers in use, interviewers became frustrated by the large number of dialings necessary before reaching working numbers. This inefficient access to working numbers was also costly. Based on the pretest, analysts negotiated with the planning agency to drop a low density prefix from the study. Failure to do so would lock analysts into a sampling plan that would prove costly and would damage interviewer morale for a minor improvement in the representativeness of findings.

Several principles guide the use of a pretest. Procedures and instruments employed should be exactly as planned for the full-scale survey. Instruments should be, in the best judgment of analysts, ready for use in the field. Staff for the pretest should be the staff who will administer the actual survey. Complete notes should be kept of all problems experienced in the pretest. The results of the pretest should be analyzed according to the planned analysis of the total survey, including the preparation of tables.

Pretesting suggests important changes in instrument design. Some response categories, for example, may be unused, suggesting their deletion or that they need to be reworded. Pretesting provides a basis for improving the wording, form, and sequencing of questions, and for assessing their value in yielding accurate and useful information for decision making. In larger surveys, multiple pretests may be necessary to refine instruments and survey procedures.

Another task in getting ready to survey is particularly important for in-person and telephone surveys. For these surveys, interviewer skill is a key to information quality; adequate training is essential. A thrust of training programs is to increase interviewers' awareness of how their own personality and mannerisms influence respondents, thus distorting information. Role playing is often an effective training device. Interviewers pair up to act out interview situations using instruments and procedures designed for the study. Their performance is observed and discussed by other participants, and another pair takes over. The value of role playing as a feedback device is further enhanced by videotaping the sessions for instant replay and analysis. Other elements of a quality training program include:

- thoroughly informing interviewers about the study, including survey objectives and potential uses of the information;
- familiarizing interviewers with specific purposes of each question;
- emphasizing the interviewer's role in collecting quality data;
- reaching agreement on procedures to be followed in the field, e.g., ways of recording comments, callback timing and method; and
- explaining conditions of employment, e.g., payment, breaks.

GAINING ACCESS TO RESPONDENTS

Policy analysts using survey research are keenly aware they are imposing on respondents. Respondents are asked to drop what they are doing, listen or read, think, formulate responses, and answer questions perhaps of little interest or value to them. Typically, the only rewards are the opportunity to express their opinion and the opportunity to participate in a study. In a very real sense, survey analysts are getting something for nothing. This imposition on respondents carries a responsibility for analysts to respect them as individuals who have their own concerns, responsibilities, pressures, and feelings. An unswerving premise of survey research is: The respondent merits respect.

It follows that respondents must not be lied to, misled, pressured, made to feel guilty or obligated, manipulated, or otherwise treated as less than a full partner in an effort to create information for improving public policy. Gaining access to respondents and getting them to participate in the survey is essential in achieving a successful survey, but the task is approached in a way which places the autonomy and dignity of respondents first.

In gaining access, the nature of initial contact with respondents is crucial. In personal or telephone interviews, introductory statements inform respondents of the objectives and uses of the survey information and encourage their participation. Introductory statements should be clear and brief, yet provide an adequate explanation.

> Hello, my name is . . . We have been asked by the Regional Planning Agency at Lake Tahoe to conduct a survey of citizen attitudes toward public transportation at the lake. The information will be used to improve public transportation in Lake Tahoe. The interview will last about ten minutes. Is this a convenient time to talk with you?

The problem of gaining and maintaining access to the respondent is most critical with respect to self-administered surveys. Indeed, bias due to nonresponse is such an important potential source of error in mail surveys that analysts pay special attention to methods of maximizing questionnaire returns. The most important of these strategies are summarized in Figure 8.1.

Even when these steps have been taken, the planning of mail surveys should include a nonresponse test. As noted in the chapter on sampling, the purpose of this test is to assess the effects of nonresponse on the representativeness of sample findings. If necessary, analysts then add appropriate qualifications in the interpretation of survey results.

Skilled analysts are aware that survey techniques such as in-person and telephone surveys are obtrusive collection methods, meaning data quality remains a prime concern in producing dependable and useful information. Using multiple and overlapping measurement techniques—triangulation—minimizes errors and produces a powerful approach to improving data quality.

In the Lake Tahoe transportation study, analysts triangulated data sources, perspectives and interpretations, and data collection methods to better ensure high-quality information.

- Prepare a cover letter which justifies the study and the importance of each respondent to the success of the study. Use a letterhead and a signature which lend prestige and official status to the survey (Jones, 1979). Include a self-addressed, stamped envelope for the respondent.
- Protect the privacy of the individual respondent. Assurances of anonymity have a positive effect on response rates, particularly among higher income and more highly educated groups (Jones, 1979).
- Make the questionnaire attractive and eye-catching. It should present an uncluttered, neat appearance. Special formats such as a pamphlet are desirable for lengthy questionnaires.
- Ask the minimum number of questions needed to fulfill information needs. Response rates decrease as questionnaire length increases.
- Be courteous in question wording. Use words such as "please" and "would you mind." Thank respondents for participating in the survey.
- Mail the questionnaire as first-class, stamped mail. Questionnaires which arrive looking like junk mail are more likely to be discarded.
- Employ follow-up procedures. Mail a reminder postcard one week after the original mailing. After three weeks, follow through with a letter (and another questionnaire) emphasizing the importance of a response.

FIGURE 8.1. Guidelines for Increasing Response Rates in Mailed, Self-Administered Questionnaires

- Varied data sources, such as users and nonusers of public buses, bus drivers, public officials, transportation authorities, complaint files, crime incident reports, and accident reports, were studied to provide an in-depth yet comprehensive evaluation of the effectiveness of public mass transit in the Lake Tahoe basin.
- Incorporating multiple perspectives and interpretations of the meaning of the "effectiveness" of public mass transit, e.g., convenience, dependability, comfort, safety of buses, minimized the possibility that study findings would be less useful because they excluded important perspectives as to what is meant by effectiveness.
- Using multiple data collection methods such as intensive interviews, surveys, and documentary analysis in evaluating effectiveness provided better-supported and persuasive findings since similar evidence had been generated through multiple and overlapping data collection methods.

Triangulation reduces the uncertainty of findings and adds to the clarity, comprehensiveness, credibility, and usefulness of information as a decision resource.

CONCLUDING COMMENTS

This chapter clarified strategies used by analysts in designing and conducting surveys. The discussion of surveys has revealed a set of research techniques with broad appeal. Survey research is perhaps the most flexible data collection method for collecting information systematically. It is adaptable to a wide variety of information needs of concern to policymakers. It is particularly useful when information is desired from large populations, given its capacity to generalize findings from a relatively small representative sample to a working population.

However, any method used alone carries its own limitations. Policy analysts do not automatically succumb to the appeal of simply asking people to gain information. Consumers of policy research carefully assess information produced through surveys with an eye to the appropriateness of these data methods for collecting the information they need. They also evaluate those steps taken by analysts to ensure data quality, including the use of multiple and overlapping measurement techniques.

A characteristic of surveys is that information is collected by asking people, rather than directly observing them or analyzing documentary evidence. Surveys produce information in the form of verbal or written self-reports. This self-report approach assumes respondents are able and willing to provide the desired information. These assumptions may be unjustified for a variety of reasons.

Respondents may be unable to provide the desired information because they have not thought about the matter or do not know about the matter: it may be unimportant to them. If respondents are asked about something that occurred in the past, they may simply have forgotten. They may not understand questions, or they may be unable to communicate their responses. Numerous ways exist in which the ability of respondents to provide information is compromised by poor question wording or by questions which suggest appropriate responses. The ability to respond cannot be lightly assumed.

The willingness of respondents to answer questions can also be problematic. Some barriers to willing participation are general; some people simply do not wish to have their privacy disturbed. Others are specific; people may be unwilling to offer certain types of information.

Willingness to answer truthfully is a concern in some policy research studies. Since survey information may be used to make decisions which affect respondents' lives, they may orient their responses to encourage the policy decisions they desire. Some citizens who would like to have a new bus route near their homes, but would use it only when the car was unavailable, might tell an interviewer they would be frequent users if the new route was initiated. When survey information is used to evaluate the effectiveness of a program, respondents receiving benefits from the program, or working in it, may have a strong incentive to make things look good.

Analysts should not assume that survey research is an inexpensive method of collecting information. When information needs are straightforward and respondents easy to target and contact, surveys are cost effective. But when populations are large or difficult to target, and when information requirements are complex or sensitive, surveys become costly.

These limitations do not cancel the appeal of surveys as a research approach; they do acknowledge that no single research method provides a panacea for collecting information for decision making. No single method yields error-free portraits of issues under study. Skilled policy analysts consider surveys as one means of collecting information which may be replaced or supplemented by other approaches, depending on information needs and resource constraints.

REFERENCES

Babbie, Earl R. 1982. *Social Research for Consumers.* Belmont, CA: Wadsworth.

Backstrom, Charles H., and Gerald Hursh-Cesar. 1981. *Survey Research,* 2d ed. New York: John Wiley & Sons.

Bailey, Kenneth D. 1982. *Methods of Social Research,* 2d ed. New York: Free Press.

California Technical Assistance Associates, Inc. 1982. *Utilization and Assessment of Public Transportation in the Tahoe Basin.* South Lake Tahoe, CA: Tahoe Regional Planning Agency.

Douglas, Jack D. 1976. *Investigative Social Research: Individual and Team Field Research.* Beverly Hills, CA: Sage Publications.

Groves, Robert M., and Robert L. Kahn. 1979. *Surveys by Telephone: A National Comparison with Personal Interviews.* New York: Academic Press.

Hatry, Harry P., Louis H. Blair, Donald M. Fisk, John M. Greiner, John R. Hall, Jr., and Philip Schaenman. 1977. *How Effective Are Your Community Services?* Washington, DC: Urban Institute and International City Managers' Association.

Jones, Wesley H. 1979. "Generalizing Mail Survey Inducement Methods: Population Interactions with Anonymity and Sponsorship," *Public Opinion Quarterly* 43:102–11.

Jordan, Lawrence, Alfred C. Marcus, and Leo G. Reeder, 1980. "Response Styles in Telephone and Household Interviewing: A Field Experiment," *Public Opinion Quarterly* 44:210–22.

Kidder, Louise H. 1981. *Research Methods in Social Relations,* 4th ed. New York: Holt, Rinehart & Winston.

Lewis, I. A., and William Schneider. 1982. "Is the Public Lying to the Pollsters?" *Public Opinion Quarterly* 5:42–47.

Millar, Annie, Harry P. Hatry, and Margo Koss. 1977. *Monitoring the Outcomes of Social Services,* 2 vols. Washington, DC: Urban Institute.

Robinson, John P., Robert Athanasion, and Kendra B. Head. 1973. *Measures of Occupational Attitudes and Occupational Characteristics.* Ann Arbor, MI: Survey Research Institute.

Robinson, John P., Jerrold G. Rusk, and Kendra B. Head. 1973. *Measures of Political Attitudes.* Ann Arbor, MI: Survey Research Institute.

Robinson, John P., and Phillip R. Schaver, 1973. *Measures of Social Psychological Attitudes.* Ann Arbor, MI: Survey Research Institute.

Weiss, Carol H., and Harry P. Hatry. 1971. *An Introduction to Sample Surveys for Government Managers.* Washington, DC: Urban Institute.

Wimmer, Roger D., and Joseph R. Dominick. 1983. *Mass Media Research: An Introduction.* Belmont, CA: Wadsworth.

9

Documentary Research

Collecting Information from Available Data

Budget documents, client records, minutes of meetings, staff reports, annual reports, speeches, statistical reports, legal rulings, legislation, regulations, past studies, journals, periodicals, books, and newspapers share a common use in policy research. All serve as sources of information for analysts. They also represent information collected or recorded by individuals or organizations for their own purposes. Adapting these materials to research purposes is a core information collection skill for policy analysts.

Available data are a rich information resource used for multiple purposes in policy research. They help analysts define issues and determine what, if any, new information is needed to address those issues. Available data provide depth and insight in beginning and exploratory stages of a research project, allowing analysts to build and improve on past efforts. Existing data are used to cross-check newly collected information to compare the complementarity of findings and conclusions. In many instances, available data provide the most direct response to fulfilling major information needs.

From a project management perspective, available data assume particular importance in helping analysts get the most out of a research budget. Accessing existing materials requires a minimal investment of time and money; most are readily obtainable on a free or low-cost basis.

This chapter explores uses of available documents and records by pol-

icy analysts. The discussion reflects several objectives. First types and sources of available data are introduced. Second, advantages and limitations of these sources in conducting policy research are discussed. Third, methods for using available data to accomplish differing research objectives are identified; content analysis is highlighted as a particularly systematic technique for analyzing documentary information. Finally, methods for assessing and improving the quality of documentary information are identified.

TYPES OF AVAILABLE DATA

The generation and dissemination of information continues at an accelerating, spiraling rate of growth. While past eras were labeled the Machine Age or the Atomic Age, the present period is best characterized as the Information Age. One result of the information explosion is that a vast quantity of materials produced and consumed by organizations and individuals exists for research purposes.

The beginning paragraph in this chapter lists a few examples of the range of information sources available to policy analysts. All of these sources share the characteristic of capturing past or ongoing events on paper, or increasingly on electronic storage media. These sources represent a number of differing types of available information collected or produced for distinctive purposes.

Internal Sources of Available Data

Documentary information emanates from sources both internal and external to an organization. Public agencies routinely collect, record, and store information for internal management purposes. These agency documents and records take several forms reflecting the specific uses of the information in the program.

LEGAL AND PROCEDURAL DOCUMENTS

Public organizations and programs operate according to legal responsibilities set by legislation authorizing their activities, by administrative rules and regulations that make these responsibilities specific (e.g., through specifying procedures and criteria for decisions), and by procedural handbooks and manuals describing standard operating procedures governing staff activities.

These documents provide the legal and procedural structure of an organization or program, and are an important source of information about the mission of an organization and its implementation activities. Such

information frequently helps analysts identify goals and objectives of organizations (though they are by no means the sole source of information for this purpose). These documents also state how an organization intends to carry out its mandate. Legal and procedural documents are central to understanding the formal structure of public programs.

MANAGEMENT RECORDS

Organizations accumulate records of their resource needs and expenditures—in terms of dollars, personnel, or material resources. For managers, this documentation provides a basis for making budget requests, for hiring, for purchasing, and for monitoring the functions of the organization. For analysts, it provides a basis for describing and assessing the agency's activities and for addressing questions of efficiency.

Available data 'on fiscal matters include annual budgets and accounting records. Personnel records include job descriptions, performance appraisal guidelines and reports, records of staff qualifications and experience, and much more.

Other, less standardized sources also serve management purposes in organizations. Minutes of meetings, hearings, and so on, document the history of organizational activity and the issues that have been addressed. Memorandums provide a look into the inner workings of organizations. Murphy (1980:124) comments:

> Memos are particularly useful in revealing pressing issues, the arguments behind different positions, and who stands where. Their distribution lists also indicate who seems to count in making particular decisions (and whom you should see for additional information). These internal documents usually portray program operations more realistically than public relations material [such as newsletters, annual reports, and program brochures].[1]

CLIENT RECORDS

For many policy research needs, client records are a particularly important source of information. Social services agencies keep a variety of records on the numbers and characteristics of the persons they serve, the nature and quantity of services that are delivered, and the outcomes of those services for clients. These records are collected and recorded in a variety of forms, including eligibility or entrance forms, records of program visits or receipts of services, and exit records.

Records may be objective (e.g., age, gender, or other characteristics of the client; number of program visits; identity of service provider), or they may be more subjective (e.g., narrative notations of the progress of clients in a substance abuse program). In the former case, data will tend to be uniform and are likely to be accurate; in the latter, accuracy and interpretation are more problematic. Because of their direct relation to service delivery and effectiveness, client records are a major data source for policy analysts, although privacy and confidentiality restrictions may limit access.

STUDIES AND REPORTS

Organizations produce numerous studies and reports on policy issues. These reports may be prepared for internal consumption, such as a study of time management designed to improve productivity in an organization. They may also be prepared for external consumption, such as annual reports that represent the organization to the public. In any case, policy analysts consider the purposes of studies and reports as part of evaluating the information they present.

These and other internal records and documents stored by individual agencies serve diverse purposes in policy research. Sources such as annual reports, newsletters, and budget justifications "provide general background material as well as project the images that officials would like others to view. These documents, prepared primarily for public consumption, are usually accurate on basic facts, but are uncritical of program practices" (Murphy, 1980:124).

Standard operating procedures, staff reports, organization charts, personnel actions, minutes of meetings, and memoranda disclose the workings of the agency. Other internal sources of information, such as program effectiveness studies, complaint files, and records of these served by the program, provide data concerning agency performance in achieving its statutory responsibilities.

External Sources of Available Data

In comparison to internal data, the diversity and quantity of external secondary data sources seem endless. Massive amounts of information are routinely gathered and published by government, professional, and commercial sources. These data are stored in various locations—public and academic libraries, governmental units, professional and trade associations, corporations, and so forth.

Analysts search for external data frequently in combination with their search for internal data bases. They may find that other governmental units have published materials relevant to an agency's responsibilities, activities, and performance. These external government sources include reports and

statistics published by units in the executive branch such as the central budget office, the chief executive's office, or the audit agency; other branches
of government (the courts, legislative appropriations committees); and
other levels of government—local, state, and federal. External sources often
provide perspectives different from information produced by the units responsible for the program.

Government organizations are a rewarding source of policy-relevant
data. Much information published by these agencies is carefully gathered,
with fully documented and time-tested procedures for attaining factual accuracy. A familiar example is the *Census of Population,* compiled every ten
years (in years ending in zero). This source, published by the Bureau of the
Census, provides data regarding population characteristics of states, counties, urbanized areas, areas of more than one thousand or more inhabitants,
and other census-designated places. Demographics include age, ethnicity,
gender, marital status, family composition, national origins, employment,
income, level of education, citizenship status, and others. The *Current Population Report,* published annually, updates information in the *Census of Population.*

The *Census of Population* is one of innumerable documents and records
produced by federal agencies. In addition to information published
through federal outlets, state and local government agencies yield useful
sources of data. Most states publish, for example, economic models and
forecasts. Cities and counties have planning agencies producing information about their population, economy, transportation, and so on. State and
local data are produced to suit their respective needs; they may be more
current compared with similar federal government data.

Academic institutions, interest groups, trade associations, private research organizations, and other sources outside government produce and
store data relevant to policy analysis. Newspaper articles, a commercial
source of data, serve as a frequent information source. Books, magazines,
and articles in academic, professional, and trade journals provide general
information about policy issues and are helpful in developing alternative
approaches to their resolution.

The discussion to this point has focused on written documents. But
the search for relevant sources—external and internal—is not limited to
written communications.

> As we know from the Nixon tapes of the White House Oval Office, documen-
> tary evidence doesn't come just in the form of the written word. Tape record-
> ings, slides, photographs, diagrams, plot plans, blueprints, models, drawings,
> cartoons, and charts all can provide important data. While working on a proj-
> ect examining the safety of fish processing plants, I came across some photo-
> graphs of bug-infested work environments. These photos provided excellent
> documentation of unsanitary conditions. (Murphy, 1980:127)

USING AVAILABLE DATA IN POLICY RESEARCH

Because available data have been generated for the purposes of others, research challenges emerge that are not encountered in creating new, original data. Analysts first have to determine the appropriate role of available data in their research. Second, analysts search for available data closely matching present study needs. Since available data has been created by others, it is not obvious what is available, who has generated it, or why. Finally, analysts assess the quality of available data to determine the degree of reliance it warrants in research results. Benefits of using available data in policy studies follow.

Benefits of Available Data

Time Effective.   Research information is more rapidly generated through an analysis of existing data than through the drawn-out process of designing, implementing, analyzing, and reporting the results of primary research. Collecting original data can be so time-consuming as to be impractical for decision-making needs.

Cost Effective.   Similarly, collecting available data is less costly than primary data collection, a benefit of vital importance to any sponsor. The major costs of research are those associated with data collection; the collection of available records and documents is inexpensive in comparison to primary data collection methods such as surveys. "There is also a societal benefit in the sense that the primary investigators use only a part of the data collected at such great expense, and storing or discarding the original data wastes societal, organizational, and intellectual resources" (Chadwick, Bahr, Albrecht, 1984:261).

Unobtrusive.   In studying human populations, analyzing available data is less intrusive than tapping primary sources through, for example, interviews and surveys. There is less invasion of privacy, and the goodwill of potential respondents is not jeopardized. Analyzing available data increases the likelihood that a previous intrusion was worthwhile—that the time respondents devoted to previous surveys, for example, yielded expanded research benefits.

Credibility of Research Results.   Existing information serves as a basis for research findings. Citing directly from records and documents counteracts charges of analyst bias. Guba and Lincoln (1983:232) add that records and documents as a source of evidence "constitute a legally unassailable base from which to defend oneself against allegations, misinterpretations, and libel. The best defense in a challenge to an evaluation report [or any policy study] is for the evaluator to be able to show that he did in fact tell the truth, and the best evidence for truth is often the public record."

Uses of Available Data

Given the benefits of available data, it comes as no surprise that they are used in a variety of ways in generating information. An obvious example of their use is in demography, a field which studies characteristics of human populations, such as size, growth, density, distribution, and vital statistics. Demographers employ official statistics, frequently census data, and use them to explain and predict population shifts, fertility and mortality patterns, changes in the composition of the labor force, migration rates, and so on. The demographers' use of official statistics plays an important role in policy planning by meeting needs for estimation information.

The official statistics, frequently produced by administrative agencies for their unique policy concerns, can be analyzed for information purposes different from those intended by governmental entities collecting the data. The extent and variety of available data make them amenable to a variety of policy research applications. The following discussion introduces the contributions of available data to policy research tasks.

RECOGNIZING AND CLARIFYING POLICY ISSUES

Public issues represent problems, threats, needs, and opportunities which are dealt with through public action. But issues must be recognized before being acted upon. Available data serve as a catalyst for the recognition of issues by individuals and organizations. Newspapers and periodicals, for example, provide information about many such issues: alcohol and drug abuse, toxic waste disposal, solid waste disposal, unemployment, child abuse, political reform, mismanagement of public resources, crime trends, and so forth.

A constant monitoring of relevant available data provides the impetus for issue recognition. The term "strategic environmental monitoring" has been coined to mean the search for and processing of information about changes in an organization's environment, developed through analysis of external information sources. The monitoring process, incorporating an ongoing review of key information sources, is used in initiating policy and in adjusting existing policy.

Available data are also helpful in clarifying and defining policy issues, making them more specific and amenable to analysis. Analysts use available data to explore central components of a concept, to gain depth and insight into its dimensions, to assess how others have viewed and defined it. A major use of available data is in exploratory research where analysts are attempting to outline major dimensions of an issue.

Research procedures invariably call for literature reviews to learn how past efforts can contribute to present information needs. It is wasted effort to reinvent the wheel every time a new information need is discerned. Past attempts at gathering information are essential resources for policy analysts.

DESIGNING AND IMPLEMENTING POLICY STUDIES

The uses of available data extend beyond the phases of issue recognition and clarification. Once understandings have been achieved on key concepts and dimensions underlying the issue, existing data provide information in designing and implementing empirical data collection efforts.

An examination of how previous studies were conducted yields insights into data sources, sampling approaches, analysis plans, measurement techniques, and data collection strategies. Analysts then design their research plans by building on past efforts, avoiding pitfalls encountered by those who investigated similar issues.

Available data may serve as the sole data collection technique in a research study. Indeed, they constitute the only practical source for determining historical trends. Past events cannot be directly observed. For example, during the evaluation of the Political Reform Act, newspaper articles were used to analyze trends in the quantity and content of PRA-related stories appearing in California's newspapers over a two and one-half year period. Although survey research could be used to sample informed observers familiar with the history of the PRA, observer responses would be subject to errors caused by memory lapses and individual bias. Any time data requirements call for information of a historical or longitudinal nature, or data on inaccessible subjects (e.g., deceased, missing), existing sources may serve as the sole or prime data source.

Available data are used to document a variety of specific facts and figures relevant to study purposes. Official statistics and reports include numerous references, such as the number of unemployed black females in New York City in 1988, current rates of return on municipal bonds, or the number of registered voters in Fairfax County, Virginia.

Available data are employed to check the representativeness of sample data. If the analyst has drawn a random sample of households in a community to survey residents, the representativeness of the sample in mirroring the community is evaluated by comparing demographic features of the sample (e.g., age, income, education, gender, ethnicity) with the most recent census data for the community.

Available data such as census data, license registration, and voting lists are also used to draw samples for surveys. "Though none of these sources is perfect, since records are kept for different purposes, with different degrees of accuracy, by people of different levels of competence, they are much better sources of samples than the informed hunches of investigators" (Kerlinger, 1973:523).

Available data are further employed to compare and evaluate results generated from primary data collection techniques. In a large study based on interviews with state prison inmates, for example, the RAND Corporation asked respondents about their past arrests and checked their responses against official law enforcement records (Peterson et al., 1982). The degree of correspondence provided one indicator of the dependability of information gathered in the interviews.

GENERATING ALTERNATIVES AND RECOMMENDATIONS IN POLICY STUDIES

For analysts, the experiences of others, as documented in available data, are essential in designing and implementing quality policy research. This statement equally applies when a research objective is to recommend alternatives as possible solutions to a policy concern.

Using available data allows analysts to identify alternative approaches to similar issues researched in prior studies. Such studies frequently suggest alternatives useful in resolving a policy issue. The number and diversity of approaches help analysts compare alternatives, estimate costs and benefits of varying options, and rank options when making recommendations. In fortunate cases, available information may be sufficient in and of itself to generate feasible alternatives. Collecting original empirical data may be unnecessary.

The preceding overview of the benefits and uses of available data demonstrates its value throughout policy research phases. Although its uses entail difficulties detailed in later discussions, experienced analysts routinely assess existing information before proceeding to the active collection of original data.

RETRIEVING AVAILABLE DATA

Available data come in many forms, are produced by numerous organizations, and reside in disparate forms and locations. This section introduces strategies for retrieving existing information useful in policy analysis. The discussion addresses internal and external sources separately.

Retrieving Internal Data

Internal data sources are retrieved using manual, on-line, or some combination of the two data search approaches. Manual searches are often necessary in retrieving relevant internally based information since many agencies do not have comprehensive computerized data bases.

Manual searches require analysts to ask agency officials what relevant documents and records are available. Analysts ask the same of others having an interest in the program—legislators and legislative aides, program clients, lobbyists, news reporters, industry representatives. When available, reviews of agency library holdings or materials produced by internal publication offices may prove informative.

A manual search may yield more than official program records and documents. Individually maintained, informal materials such as personal correspondence, notes on meetings, memos for the record, and field notes may also be collected.

> Officials often like to maintain their own records for posterity, not to mention for self-protection on sensitive matters. These materials are often unavailable, but if you can get access they can be invaluable in understanding an individual's perspective and in getting an unofficial view of what happened and why. Personal records can provide revealing contrasts to documents prepared for public consumption. (Murphy, 1980:126–27)

Developments in computer technology are having an impact on retrieving available data, including internal data. Computer-based management information systems (MIS) store, organize, and produce information for decision-relevant purposes. Data from units of an agency (personnel, planning, accounting, and so forth) are stored in a computer system and become accessible to policymakers and analysts through terminals or through their own personal computers. Sometimes, the MIS in an agency not only sorts and distributes internally collected information, but also supplements it with relevant external data.

Management information systems are not limited to simply storing and retrieving information in standardized formats. Through a computer terminal, decision makers and analysts alike ask questions of the data and receive answers quickly—most of the time! In studying career criminals, analysts updated records on each offender in the study sample by querying computerized criminal justice information systems and by requesting individual arrest and court records.

Since data bases are compiled using standardized reporting formats, policy analysts apply statistical procedures to establish trends, diagnose relationships, and so forth. In a study of a national program that places blind business persons in food service facilities for government buildings (the Business Enterprises Program), analysts used data from the program's fiscal information system for statistical analysis. Their analysis identified sales volume, profit margins, and return on investment for different types of food services. Findings provided a basis for program planning to improve benefits for program clients and for the organizations that were contracting for food services (California Technical Assistance Associates, Inc., 1978).

Computer-based information systems provide a wealth of program-related data useful in fulfilling information needs. Their increasing employment by public entities ensures that analysts will automatically tap these on-line information sources in seeking relevant internal data.

From the standpoint of thoroughness, some combination of manual and on-line methods is desirable to ensure comprehensive retrieval of pertinent sources. On-line services exclude nonrecurring information such as special reports, complaints, or memos. These sources are retrievable only through manual search. On-line services exclude the possibility of obtaining personally maintained records and documents. Unless updated frequently, data may not represent the most current situation. A comprehensive search frequently necessitates the use of both manual and on-line data retrieval methods.

Retrieving External Data

External data sources are also retrieved using manual and computerized searches. Familiar manual retrieval methods require the physical and frequently laborious task of examining research guides and bibliographies, indexes, statistical sources, dictionaries and encyclopedias, government publications, media reports, legal materials, books and journals, and other materials frequently maintained in public and academic libraries.[2]

Computer technology is increasingly easing burdens associated with time-consuming manual retrieval of library-based materials. Sitting in front of a console, analysts command a computer to do the searching. The card catalog is a computer terminal. The search process, compared with manual retrieval efforts, is faster, more thorough, more cost effective.

Computer-assisted literature searching is becoming an efficient and effective method of retrieving external data. Wholesalers of computerized collections of information sources (called data bases) presently exist. These wholesalers (called data base distributors or vendors) access multiple data bases made available by information producers in government, academic institutions, and commercial organizations, and then market access time to decision makers and analysts needing the information.

Lockheed Corporation, a major data base distributor, illustrates the process. Lockheed markets an on-line data base called "Environline." This source provides abstracts of literature on the environment from special reports, conference proceedings, and several thousand international journals. Another Lockheed data base, NTIS (U.S. National Technical Information

Service), provides citations and abstracts of unrestricted technical reports from federally sponsored research and development projects. LEXIS, distributed by the Mead Corporation, allows users access to legal information covering federal law, the U.S. codes, the Code of Federal Regulations, the Federal Register, briefs, and case laws. NEXIS, another data base marketed by the Mead Corporation, offers the full text of major newspapers including the *New York Times, Washington Post,* and *Christian Science Monitor,* in addition to indexing magazines, newsletters, and wire services. Its coverage is international, and the data base is updated daily.[3]

To retrieve information from these on-line data bases, or electronic libraries, appropriate computer software is needed. Users then subscribe to the data base, much like subscribing to a magazine or newspaper. Computer search techniques are changing available data retrieval and analysis methods, whether internally or externally generated. On the horizon, videocassettes, reel-to-reel videotape, and videodiscs will provide important new data sources. Transmitting and receiving information via coaxial cable, telephone lines, microwave, and satellite are opening new information sources for policy analysts.

As with internal data retrieval methods, manual and computerized searches will frequently be required since relevant information may not be accessible through on-line services. For the immediate future, data bases are cost-effective sources for information after a manual search has been conducted and when

- the issue being researched is known by numerous synonyms, making a manual search impractical and time-consuming;
- the subject term is one not found in subject indexes;
- information objectives require multidisciplinary or international coverage of available data; or
- the information is too recent to appear in printed sources.

ASSESSING THE USEFULNESS OF AVAILABLE DATA

Ultimately, the contribution of available data to policy studies depends on two considerations. First, how closely does existing data fit present information needs (applicability)? Second, how much confidence is warranted in the integrity of the data (data quality)?

Data Applicability

Analysts evaluate the relevancy of available materials in relation to current information needs. Evaluating the applicability of existing data includes the following assessments:

- *Timeliness.* Are the data timely? Information becomes outdated; and since the purpose of many policy studies is to gather current data, prior data must correspond to present needs. Data gathered five years ago may not be pertinent to present information needs.
- *Scope of Coverage.* Are relevant variables included in existing information sources? Analysts depend on data being available that reflect current data needs. More likely, sources will yield only partial information, covering only some of the necessary variables in differing levels of detail.
- *Definitions.* Are definitions and operational meanings of key concepts consistent with present data needs? The appropriateness of operational definitions and dimensions and indicators attached to those definitions are of importance in assessing applicability.

The cost effectiveness and easy availability of sources can entice analysts into relying on available data inadequately meeting these criteria. An evaluation of the activities of the "M-2 Sponsors Program," a state-level volunteer program, provides an illustration (Phillips, Cannady, and Springer, 1985). M-2 sponsors volunteers to make monthly visits to state prison inmates not receiving regular visits from friends or relatives. Program objectives include improving inmate adjustment to long-term institutionalization and reducing behavioral problems in the institution. With a restricted budget and facing difficult problems of primary data collection within high-security prisons, analysts evaluating the program relied primarily on institutional records (inmate files) as a data source.

The indicators of institutional behavior available in inmate files were formal incident reports filled out by prison officials when an inmate broke prison rules. The report recorded serious incidents such as fights, thefts, and stabbings; and minor infractions such as tardiness or absence from work assignments. As indicators of institutional behavior relevant to evaluating the impact of the M-2 sponsors' program, these records had serious shortcomings.

First, the scope of the behavior they measured was too restricted to reflect the range of effects sponsors had on inmates. The reports did not contain information on the institutional adjustment of inmates—loneliness, morale, or plans for the outside. Incident reports did not reflect any of these behaviors and therefore contained inadequate scope for the objectives of the study.

Second, the operational definition of institutional behavior implicit in the reports reflected the institution's security concerns—violence and rule infractions. More appropriate operational definitions may have emphasized more positive behaviors, such as attending self-improvement or educational programs. Indeed, interview results suggested that the types of behaviors represented in available records may be the most difficult for a once-a-month volunteer program to influence, but that more subtle effects were likely. Since quantitative data collection was restricted to inmate files, it is not surprising that the evaluation did not find a significant relation between program involvement and institutional behavior.

Data Quality

In addition to the applicability of existing information, data quality is a central concern when using available information sources. The reason is analysts have no control over information objectives and data collection procedures producing the original findings, hence no control over data quality. As a result, analysts assess research objectives and research procedures when evaluating available data quality.

- *Research Objectives.* A concern of any analyst assessing existing sources is the purposes for which the data were produced, i.e., the study may have been conducted for purposes dictating a particular orientation or flavor. Program documents and records may be misleading in presenting a balanced picture of program performance because data are designed to justify the program, not to reveal its flaws. Research conducted by others may be slanted to support the point of view of sponsors commissioning the study. The purposes of data generation and the persons responsible for it provide clues in evaluating available data quality.
- *Research Procedures.* Evaluating data quality involves a critical assessment of research procedures used in generating data. What mix of obtrusive and unobtrusive methods was employed in collecting the original data? Were findings based on small samples or large populations? Were samples representative? Were validity and reliability checks conducted? Were data sources adequate? All too often, insufficient information is reported about research procedures to enable an adequate determination of data quality. In this situation, indicators of data quality depend, for example, on a close internal analysis of the study. Where possible, findings are cross-checked with other sources of information. The reputation of the individuals and organizations gathering the original data provide indirect evidence of data quality.

Incident reports used in the study of the M-2 sponsors program are also vulnerable to criticism on data quality grounds. Incident reports are generated by prison guards and other officials, and reflect individual or institutional bias in documenting events. Inmates labeled troublemakers, for instance, may be watched more closely, accruing a number of reports that do not truly represent their behavior relative to other inmates.

Evaluations of the applicability and quality of available sources determine their roles in policy research. Some sources will be rejected as too remote from study objectives, outdated, or of questionable value. Others will serve as sole sources of information in a study. Still others will be incorporated into triangulated data strategies that include a variety of data sources and perspectives. Existing data searches should routinely be conducted, particularly before primary data collection procedures are designed and implemented.

While available data serve multiple purposes in research, methods for extracting systematic and quantitative data from these sources frequently employ a form of documentary research called "content analysis." This term is an umbrella label for a number of systematic techniques used in generating information from recorded sources. The following case study provides an example of the use of content analysis and introduces its application and limitations in policy analysis.

NEWSPAPER REPORTING ON THE POLITICAL REFORM ACT OF 1974: GENERATING INFORMATION FROM PRINTED SOURCES

California's Political Reform Act (PRA) was a product of widespread citizen indignation following the Watergate revelations during the Nixon presidency (Springer and Putt, 1979). The PRA became state law through California's direct democracy provisions, appearing as an initiative (Proposition 9) on the ballot in the primary elections of June, 1974.

Approved by nearly 70 percent of the voters, the Political Reform Act included detailed requirements for reporting campaign contributions, along with strict limitations on the use of money by lobbyists and strict financial disclosure requirements for public officials. The creators of Proposition 9 attempted to ensure effective implementation of the reforms by creating the Fair Political Practices Commission, an independent state agency with an operating budget protected from legislative cuts.

In 1977, two years following the implementation of the Political Reform Act, analysts contracted with the Fair Political Practices Commission (FPPC) to perform an evaluation study of the impact and implementation of the campaign and lobbying disclosure provisions of the PRA (Putt and Springer, 1977). The purpose of the evaluation was to provide an information base for improving the implementation and the administration of the act. One of the more important objectives of the act was to disseminate information to the voting public about the sources and uses of money in politics. Accordingly, documenting the amount and type of information getting to the public was a major objective of the study.

The Research Approach

The evaluators considered a number of methods in collecting the needed information. A statewide citizen survey was one possible approach. Citizens could be asked directly about their awareness of PRA-generated information and about the communication channels through which they received that information.

This option was rejected. First, the survey would exceed resources available to gather the information. Statewide surveys are expensive. Second, the survey would have to contact many uninformed respondents before gaining detailed responses on content and sources of PRA-generated information, making the use of this method inefficient. Finally, the survey approach would be obtrusive, possibly leading to distorted data. Desiring to represent themselves as good citizens, respondents might indicate more awareness and attention to political information than was in fact the case.

The use of available data, newspapers in this case, provided an alternative. Newspapers are a major medium for conveying political information to the public. They serve as an ongoing forum for the public discussion of the act and its effects on political processes. The printed media are well-suited to the type of information frequently disseminated by the Fair Political Practices Commission, e.g., long lists of campaign contributors and the amounts they donate to specific candidates and causes. Newspapers provide a major arena for debate and comment on the way in which the act is implemented and on the way in which the act affects the play of California politics.

An analysis of printed media seemed well suited as a major data source for documenting the degree to which the FPPC had fulfilled its responsibility to make disclosure information available to the voting public. It also offered an opportunity to document external commentary and assessments of the act's implementation and impacts.

Further, raw data for analysis of newspaper coverage were readily available. The Fair Political Practices Commission maintained a printed media file containing a continuous record of California newspaper articles pertaining to the Political Reform Act from January 1, 1975 (when the PRA was implemented) to the time of analysis. The stories were collected by a newspaper clipping service in San Francisco and forwarded to the commission. The clipping service extracts articles from all newspapers and tabloids regularly published in California—over 1,200 publications. Discussions with company representatives confirmed the thoroughness and accuracy of their search procedures. Based on previous studies of their service, between 85 and 95 percent of the PRA-related articles appearing in the state are likely recovered by their search procedures.

A total of 5,480 newspaper articles—the entire contents of the Fair Political Practices Commision's printed media file—were evaluated for their applicability to information needs. Not all articles in the file were applicable to research objectives. Articles were excluded, for example, if they

- did not mention the Political Reform Act or the Fair Political Practices Commission (some articles only made reference to political reform in general or to political reform in other states);
- contained only an incidental, brief mention of the PRA or the FPPC (one paragraph or less in an article on another topic);
- referenced provisions of the Political Reform Act that were not being evaluated; for example, conflict-of-interest provisions;
- appeared in monthly or irregular publications; or
- were illegible or incomplete.

Approximately half of the 5,480 articles were excluded from the content analysis based on the preceding criteria. The remainder were included in the study.

The working population of relevant newspaper stories had been identified; but before analysis could begin, analysts had to specify in detail the information to be collected from the articles. Instructions had to be developed to guide coders who would actually read the newspaper articles and record information from them. Development of the instructions involved (a) clarifying concretely the information objectives of the content analysis, and (b) exploring the content of the articles to gain a preliminary understanding of the kinds of information the articles could provide.

Two primary information objectives guided the analysis of newspaper articles:

1. Analysis would document the *extent* of coverage of the campaign disclosure and lobbying provisions of the Political Reform Act. The extent of newspaper coverage in the state is an important indicator of the availability of information to the public. The extent of coverage depends in turn on such factors as the circulation of the newspapers, the prominence given PRA-related articles within the newspaper, and the geographic areas of the state (urban, suburban, rural) in which articles appeared.

2. Analysis would document the *content* of information conveyed to California's newspaper audience through PRA-related articles. This task included documenting the number of articles using actual disclosure information, identifying how this information was used in articles, recording assessments of the Political Reform Act on California politics as reported in newspapers, and recording assessments of the performance of the Fair Political Practices Commission in implementing provisions of the Political Reform Act.

These primary information objectives serving as guides, analysts randomly selected a sample of fifty articles, reading them in detail. As they read, they developed categories to record the content of articles as they related to information objectives, e.g., geographic location of newspaper, circulation figures. When the first reading was complete, analysts constructed an initial set of categories and coding instructions. Coders would use these instructions in categorizing the content of newspaper articles.

With the help of coders, the analysts used these instructions to conduct a pre-study of the articles. The research team coded a random sample of 150 articles, carefully noting problems in coding information, recording relevant information that was not picked up in the first reading of fifty articles, and developing an ongoing list of suggestions for improving the coding process. Revisions followed, and the content analysis instrument (coding instructions and data collection forms) was ready for full field application.

Coding categories and their instructions determine the quality and usefulness of data generated through a content analysis. A simple example illustrates the point. Using an industry listing of newspaper circulation figures, coders were instructed to record the number of daily copies sold by the newspaper in which the article they were coding appeared. The instructions specified the use of the following subdivisions in categorizing articles:

1. Circulation of less than 1,000
2. Circulation of 1,000 to 4,999
3. Circulation of 5,000 to 9,999
4. Circulation of 10,000 to 24,999
5. Circulation of 25,000 to 49,999
6. Circulation of 50,000 to 99,999
7. Circulation of 100,000 to 199,999
8. Circulation of 200,000 to 499,999
9. Circulation of more than 500,000
0. Circulation unknown

In another example, coders were instructed to determine the prominence of the headline featuring the article by measuring its height (with a ruler) using the following category subdivisions:

1. Less than 4/16 of an inch
2. 4/16 to 5/16 inch
3. 6/16 to 7/16 inch
4. 8/16 to 9/16 inch
5. Greater than 9/16 inch

Such instructions provided precise, clear-cut guides in categorizing article content. Minimal coder judgment was required in determining circulation or the prominence of the headline. Instructions for coding less obvious, more complex content—such as assessments of the act's impact on California politics or the identification of the reasons for these assessments—required more judgment on the part of coders, creating data quality problems discussed later in the chapter.

Armed with pretested and refined coding instructions and trained in their use, the project team analyzed newspaper coverage of the PRA. Because of the diversity of the contents of the articles, analysts read and recorded the contents of 50 percent of the articles, every other article in the file. The large sample size ensured a high degree of accuracy and precision in portraying newspaper coverage in the state. Procedures were developed to ensure that information was consistently recorded using understood coding instructions. Frequent discussions of the criteria for making decisions about categorizing contents were held among analysts. Coding problems encountered by any one analyst were conveyed to other members.

As a more formal check on the reliability of coding decisions, forty articles (eight for each of the five coders) were reassigned to different analysts and coded again. Comparisons of first and second coding typically revealed an acceptable degree of coding uniformity, showing coders were consistent in coding information from articles. Where reliability was not satisfactory, problematic information was reanalyzed and reconciled. Coded data were entered into the computer for statistical analyses.

Findings

The content analysis of newspaper articles was one of several research approaches contributing to the triangulated evaluation study of the Political Reform Act. Major findings of the content analysis follow.

Newspaper coverage of the political reform act. An average of 22 articles containing information generated by the PRA were published in California newspapers each week during the two and one-half year study period. Over half (55 percent) appeared in newspapers published in urban areas (50,000 or over), half of these in cities of over 350,000 inhabitants. Another one-fourth of the articles were published in suburban areas; the remaining 19 percent in rural areas of the state.

Another indication of the visibility of PRA-related news is the prominence given articles within newspapers. Information was recorded on the size of headlines to assess this aspect of coverage. The majority of PRA-related stories were not prominent. Nearly one-fifth (19 percent) were headlined in letters less than one-quarter inch in height; another 50 percent carried headlines of four- or five-sixteenths inch. Still, nearly one-third (31 percent) of the articles held headlines of some prominence, some 10 per-cent of them having an additional subtitle or banner. If these are considered relatively major headlines, 230 major stories had been published in Califor-nia newspapers during the period of the study.

Content of newspaper articles on the political reform act.   Approxi-mately 29 percent of the sample (379 articles) conveyed assessments of the consequences of the PRA for California politics, either through editorial comment or through reporting the statements of others. Nearly two-thirds of these evaluative judgments (64 percent) conveyed a negative assessment of the impact of the act to the reader; one-fourth (25 percent) were positive in their assessments of the consequences of the PRA for California politics. The remaining 10 percent cited pros and cons equally. Reasons for assess-ments were also coded. Reasons for negative assessments emphasized the difficulties individuals or officials experienced in meeting the requirements of the act (complexity of reporting forms, the confusing requirements of the act). Other negative assessments focused on specific provisions of the act (e.g., criticisms of lobbying provisions stressed the view that lobbyists with fewer resources would find it more difficult to comply with reporting requirements of the act), or singled out loopholes in certain provisions. Ad-ditional reasons for negative assessments were general, e.g., the act limits political expression and participation and discourages qualified persons from seeking office. While critics of the PRA frequently cited immediate and specific problems of implementing and complying with the act, sup-porters emphasized the intended objectives of the PRA; for example, claim-ing it limits the influence of money in politics, increases faith in govern-ment, and has a positive impact on legislative decision making.

The content analysis produced many findings beyond these, providing feedback information to the Fair Political Practices Commission. It docu-mented the extent to which the state's newspapers used the campaign fi-nance reports disseminated by the FPPC. While the technique did not docu-ment how many voters read the information, it did demonstrate that use of FPPC information had become a regular part of political reporting. The analysis of article content could not claim to be the best or only indicator of the success of the FPPC in achieving the act's intentions in disseminating information, but it did provide one measure of the commission's perfor-mance in communicating disclosure information to the public.

USING CONTENT ANALYSIS IN RESEARCHING AVAILABLE DATA

Content analysis refers to any systematic approach designed to collect data from recorded information sources such as newspaper articles. "Instead of observing people's behavior directly, or asking them to respond to scales, or interviewing them, the investigator takes the communications that people have produced and asks questions of the communications" (Kerlinger, 1973:525).

Any research effort depends on careful readings of relevant documents and records, whether used to gain insight and context, to see how others have gathered data, or to compare research findings. Content analysis, as a research technique, is distinguished from these less structured uses through its *systematic* and *quantitative* orientation to information collection.

Content analysis is *systematic* in the sense of being a rule-guided process: categorizing data such as newspaper articles is based on standardized coding procedures and instructions. Once procedures are developed, checks are made to ensure that coders are consistently applying these instructions to each piece of content, as illustrated in the analysis of newspaper articles. Within acceptable bounds, the findings of a content analysis should be the same if repeated by other analysts; it should be replicable.

The rule-bound nature of the method enhances the dependability of findings given its emphasis on coding uniformity, and maximizes chances that findings reflect contents, not individual judgments and predispositions of individual coders. Content analysis is particularly useful whenever a problem requires precise and replicable methods for analyzing attributes of documents which may escape casual scrutiny (Holsti, 1969:19–20).

The results of a content analysis are *quantitative*. Observations are coded in numerical form. The result is a data set that allows a quantitative description of the content of the documents under study. Appropriately drawn samples of documents allow analysts to generalize findings with specified degrees of accuracy and precision to working populations, as was done in the content analysis of newspapers.

The standardized format of the data allows precise comparisons to be made between the content of different groups of observations. In the case study, for example, the number of articles appearing in different parts of the state or in different time periods following implementation of the PRA could be charted, providing information on trends. The quantitative and systematic orientations of content analysis in collecting information serve to distinguish it from other less rigorous uses of available data. Using content analysis to capture relevant information requires careful development of appropriate categories to guide data coding and analysis.

Constructing Categories in Content Analysis

Content analysis allows a numerical description of collections of documents. However, it only allows description in terms of how the categories were structured to capture data. The heart of any content analysis resides in the categories used to code data from available sources such as newspapers. It is from these categories that information relevant to study objectives is drawn: "Content analysis stands or falls by its categories. Particular studies have been productive to the extent that the categories were clearly formulated and well adapted to the problem and to the content" (Berelson, 1971:147).

In constructing coding categories for the analysis of newspaper articles, a primary concern was that proposed categories adequately and accurately capture information needs of the study. Many hours were devoted to detailing specific categories of data to be drawn from the analysis of newspaper articles, and discussing the categories with users of the study results. Studies of a like nature were consulted for guidance, and a pre-study of newspaper articles was conducted to assess the range of information about PRA-related articles appearing in the state's newspapers.

The task then became one of refining categories: deleting less relevant ones, adding more meaningful ones, combining those that overlapped or duplicated one another, and deciding on the level of specificity—the number of subdivisions—needed within the categories. Deciding on questions of specificity varied with information needs. For instance, one purpose of the analysis was to determine the extent of newspaper coverage of the Political Reform Act in different areas of the state. To document this information, articles were coded on the basis of their geographic region of publication. The coding category and subdivisions follow:

VARIABLE 004: GEOGRAPHIC REGION OF PUBLICATION

0. Southeast
1. North Coast
2. Sacramento Valley
3. Mountain
4. San Francisco Bay
5. Central Coast
6. San Joaquin Valley
7. Santa Barbara-Ventura
8. Los Angeles-Long Beach Metropolitan Area
9. San Diego Metropolitan Area

Each of these regions was defined by the counties it encompassed, and coders referred to a list of publications within each area to categorize newspaper articles. Finer distinctions could easily be made within this category; the state could have been subdivided into twenty geographic areas instead of ten. These additional subdivisions would produce more specific information.

Adding subdivisions within categories (or adding more categories) permits analysts to make more comparisons and facilitates more explicit statements of finding. But increased detail comes at a cost. Creating many subdivisions within categories increases research costs since coders must make increasingly finer judgments in categorizing raw data. Errors in categorizing content increase as coders are required to make more detailed judgments in classifying data. Using too many subdivisions limits the ability to generalize findings statistically due to small sample sizes within the subdivisions. "Every advantage of using more and narrower categories is counterbalanced by some costs. Ultimately, the choice can be made only in terms of the problem at hand" (Holsti, 1969:98).

Whatever the number of categories and their subdivisions, coders, following written instructions, should be able to classify all relevant raw data such as newspaper articles into appropriate categories. Categories should be precise in meaning, unambiguous, complete (able to code all possible responses) and not overlap or duplicate one another. These rules of effective category construction are unevenly met in practice.

To illustrate, categorizing newspaper articles on the basis of their geographic region of publication met the preceding conditions of effective category construction. Each relevant article, on the basis of its geographic origin, was easily placed into one of the ten subdivisions making up the category. Subdivisions themselves were distinct, clear in meaning, unambiguous, complete, ensuring that coders could accurately and quickly place the geographic location of the newspaper articles in the appropriate subdivision of the category.

More complex information needs created problems in constructing adequate categories. Newspaper articles were coded to determine the degree to which reporters made or reported overall evaluations of the Political Reform Act in reference to its impacts on California politics. The purpose was to capture the ways in which the state's newspapers reported positive and negative consequences of the PRA. The coding category follows, and the written instructions used to obtain the evaluations appear on page 246.

**VARIABLE 20: SUMMARY ASSESSMENTS
OF THE IMPACT OF POLITICAL REFORM ACT**

1. Positive
2. Ambivalent/leaning positive
3. Ambivalent
4. Ambivalent/leaning negative
5. Negative
6. Argumentative/leaning positive
7. Argumentative
8. Argumentative/leaning negative

Coding Instructions for Summary Assessments

Code only those articles making specific overall evaluations, e.g., an article reporting on the contents of reports received from lobbyists does not itself constitute an assessment. If the article also includes judgments about "increased access to legislators," "excessive costs of compliance, etc.," it is an assessment. A positive or negative assessment requires that the article contains evaluative judgments *only* in the positive or negative direction. Ambivalent assessment refers to mixed evaluative statements, e.g., favorable and unfavorable judgments of differing provisions of the act, qualifying assessments. An argumentative judgment refers to overall evaluations which include a variety of conflicting points of view.

Unlike coding articles based on the "geographic region of publication," coders found it elusive, time consuming, and tedious to classify articles using the subdivisions established to obtain summary assessments of the impact of the PRA. Distinguishing ambivalent from argumentative articles, for instance, was sometimes a difficult judgment. The fact that assessments take a great variety of forms, unlike geographic location, made clearcut placement of the contents of articles problematic, increasing the error rate of coding judgments. Subdivisions were less distinct in specific meaning, less clear and more ambiguous in comparison to coding the geographic region of publication. Extensive training, including numerous examples of articles containing assessments, was necessary to prepare research assistants for coding summary assessments.

Despite the difficulty of coding this aspect of article content, detailed information concerning summary assessments of the impact of the Political Reform Act was of great interest to the Fair Political Practices Commission. Thus, information on this aspect of reporting became a central information need. Fewer, less complex subdivisions could have been used in coding content, e.g., positive, negative, and ambivalent evaluations, but important differences and shades of meaning would be lost in distinguishing among assessments. For users, the precision and relevancy of the resulting information would be diminished. Determining the proper balance between category simplification (for maximal coder and category reliability), and differentiation (for capturing meaningful differences in the data) is a subtle but significant determination in developing categories to capture information needs.

IMPROVING DATA QUALITY IN CONTENT ANALYSIS

The quality of results generated from a content analysis depends in part on the consistency of the categories developed to code information. When categories are clearly specified, complete, and mutually exclusive, the trustworthiness of the coded results is maximized. Five coders classifying the contents of identical newspaper articles using identical categories and written instructions should generate common results. To the extent results differ, reliability suffers, setting limits to the usefulness of the information in providing accurate descriptions, drawing inferences, supporting findings, and making recommendations.

Reliability in content analysis is frequently a function of coder judgment. Unless a neutral instrument such as a computer is used for coding, analysts rely upon the judgments of coders in classifying content. Coders' skill, insight, training, and experience then becomes an important variable in assessing the reliability of coding decisions. "Even if they possess skills necessary to make the judgmental tasks required of them, training is usually necessary to ensure that coders are relying upon the same aspects of their experience in their decisions" (Holsti, 1969:135).

Training begins with an explanation of the purposes of the analysis, including the categories to be used in classifying data. Practice follows, employing actual coding instruments. The materials coded should be those coded in the research project. During these sessions, training is leisurely, relaxed. Coders are encouraged to ask questions and to raise concerns and suggestions as they code sample data. At times their concerns reflect inexperience with the classification system. At times their concerns reflect the existence of ambiguous and unworkable categories and subdivisions that need revision and clarification. Training sessions enhance intercoder reliability through correcting misperceptions, while improving category reliability through refining classification schemes.

During the training period, analysts statistically identify coders consistently deviating from others in placing data in categories. A common approach is to tabulate the percentage of agreement between every pair of individual coders after they have categorized identical sample materials. Dissenting coders—those with consistently low agreement percentages—may need additional instructions or may in fact be sensitive to significant distinctions in the data to which others are unaware. Whatever the reasons, refinements at this stage enhance reliability, better assuring the trustworthiness of coded results.

While training is essential to increasing coder reliability, pretesting categories is essential to increasing category reliability. Pretesting proposed categories on a sample of the documents to be coded enables analysts to determine which categories need reworking. Analysts modify coding categories that unnecessarily require coders to make fine distinctions among subdivisions, or that contain categories that overlap one another or are incomplete, or that do not capture important aspects of the data under analysis. Multiple pretests may be necessary before categories are finalized.

Testing the dependability of categories and coder judgments continues beyond the pretesting and training phases of the content analysis. After the main body of data are coded, a subsample of the coded material is analyzed by different coders in order to calculate intercoder reliability figures, which represent levels of agreement by different coders in categorizing identical data.

What level of agreement is necessary to qualify the coded information as "reliable"? No set answer exists.

> This question depends on the research context and the type of information coded. There are instances where little coder judgment is needed to place units into categories and coding becomes a mechanical or clerical task, such as counting the number of words per sentence in a newspaper story or tabulating the number of times a network correpondent contributes a story to the evening news. In this context, one would expect a fairly high degree of reliability, perhaps approaching 100%, since coder disagreements would probably be the result only of carelessness and fatigue. If, however, a certain amount of interpretation is involved [as in coding summary assessments of the impact of the Political Reform Act in the case study] reliability estimates are typically lower. In general, the greater the amount of judgmental leeway given to coders, the lower the reliability coefficients will be. (Wimmer and Dominick, 1983:156)

Other techniques of assessing intercoder reliability are provided by Krippendorff (1980:133–46), Holsti (1969:137–42), and Budd, Thorp, and Donohew (1969:66–68).

The significance of the information sought, in addition to the type of data coded, determines acceptable levels of reliability. In the case study, the content analysis of newspaper articles yielded information not easily generated from other sources, and consequently served as a primary basis for some findings and recommendations of the evaluation study. Consequently, substantial resources were expended to ensure an adequate level of reliability in results.

The Lake Tahoe transportation study, introduced in an earlier chapter, provides a contrasting example of a less systematic content analysis. In its beginning stages, the study included a content analysis of complaint files maintained by a transit agency.

A total of 138 complaints made by bus riders over an eight-year period were analyzed and categorized according to their contents. The information objective was to gain insights into frequent complaints expressed by users and observers of public transit in the Lake Tahoe basin. The results of the content analysis served as one input in the development of relevant questions for two major surveys: a random telephone survey of users and non-users of public transit in Lake Tahoe, and an on-board survey of transit riders. Other sources such as past transportation surveys and suggestions by transportation specialists and public officials served as more important inputs for the two surveys.

Because the intent of the analysis was simply to identify major areas of complaint that could be probed further in surveys, only one day's work by one analyst was devoted to the content analysis, reflecting its minor information role in the transportation study. Frequent complaints by transit patrons revealed by the brief analysis included bus drivers not stopping for waiting passengers, rude or discourteous behavior on the part of the drivers, and drivers operating the bus in a careless, unsafe manner. Questions regarding these oft-cited complaints were incorporated in the on-board and telephone surveys of Lake Tahoe residents.

Defining an acceptable level of reliability in content analysis, then, is a contextual issue. Relevant considerations include the significance of the coded information in contributing to study objectives, the subtlety of the data to be coded, and resource constraints. As a general rule in establishing a meaningful level of reliability, Krippendorff (1980:147) suggests, "Where possible, *standards for data reliability* should not be adopted *ad hoc*. They *must be related to the validity requirements imposed upon research results, specifically to the costs of drawing wrong conclusions*." Adequate reliability involves a determination of how the inconsistencies encountered in category development and coding influence the findings and potential usefulness of study results.

The reliability of results in a content analysis is not solely a function of high levels of category and coder agreement. Issues of reliability extend to all parts of a study—sampling, counting, interpreting, as well as coder and category reliability. For this reason, research reports include information on reliability checks made during the course of the study. Incorporating such information allows decision makers to assess better the dependability of data generated through a content analysis.

Dependable results are a necessary but insufficient basis for assuming information is useful to decision makers. A high level of coder agreement reflects that data have been consistently categorized; it provides no indication that the choice of categories or the documents analyzed are relevant to information needs.

> The importance of validation lies in the assurance it provides that research findings ought to be taken seriously in constructing scientific theories or in making decisions on practical issues. Such assurances are particularly desirable when content analysis results ... are intended to have policy implications, when they are meant to aid government or industry, when they are proposed as evidence in court, or when they affect individual human beings. In such situations, wrong conclusions may have costly consequences. (Krippendorff, 1980:155)

A number of approaches are used by analysts in improving the validity of content analysis studies. Triangulating information sources and data collection methods, comparing study findings with past studies, working closely with stakeholders through the course of the study—all increase research usage.

Data quality in content analysis also depends on the merit of available materials selected for analysis. In determining whether to use these materials, analysts assess their quality and their applicability for present purposes. Making this determination involves a search for relevant available data and an assessment of their value for current study purposes.

CONCLUDING COMMENTS

This chapter discussed uses and constraints of available data—information gathered and recorded by others for their purposes. Available data are in great supply and are employed by analysts in varying phases of policy analysis.

Available data are produced by sources internal or external to an organization. Public agencies routinely collect information describing their statutory and legal basis, operations, and impact. External information sources seem boundless. Massive quantities of information are compiled and published by government, academic institutions, professional and trade associations, corporations, and commercial sources. These data are often stored in libraries, government units, and commercial repositories. To maximize retrieval of pertinent information, manual and computerized searches may be undertaken.

Analysts assume an ethical and legal responsibility in retrieving and using documents and records, particularly those personal, private, or classified in nature. State law, as well as the Federal Freedom of Information Act and privacy acts, provide guidance as to which data are available to private citizens and which are not. Policy analysts may encounter choices in deciding what information can be ethically used in research undertakings. Actions such as asking an insider for confidential records or documents violate acceptable behavior. Ends do not justify means of acquiring information through illegal, deceptive, or unprofessional practices.

Available data carry limitations in their usefulness for policy research. Because existing materials are gathered by others for their purposes, analysts evaluate the timeliness of sources, their scope of coverage, and their operational definitions of key concepts. These criteria determine their applicability to current information needs.

Data quality is also evaluated since analysts had no control over information objectives and research procedures employed by original investigators. Assessing data collection procedures used in generating information, comparing findings using different data sources, and determining the reputation of the individuals and organizations producing data provide evidence of data quality. Evaluations of the applicability and data quality of existing information sources determine their significance in policy research. Data searches of available data are routinely conducted before primary data collection procedures are structured and initiated.

One of the more systematic and quantitative methods used in researching existing materials is content analysis, a rule-guided approach designed to collect data from recorded information sources. The foundation of any content analysis is the categories used to collect information. It is through these data-capturing categories that detailed information relevant to study objectives is collected. To the extent feasible, categories should be well defined, complete, and not overlap or duplicate one another.

The dependability of results generated from a content analysis depends in large measure on coder and category reliability. Coder reliability checks provide indications of the reliability of coding decisions. Establishing an acceptable level of reliability is contextual, depending on the significance of the information for study objectives, the complexity of information needs, and resources allotted to the analysis.

Content analysis represents one of many uses of available sources of information in policy research. Analyzing data produced by others conserves financial resources; it is unobtrusive as a research approach; and it provides supporting evidence, enhancing the credibility of findings and recommendations. Available data are often used in recognizing and clarifying policy issues, in designing and implementing policy studies, and in generating alternatives and recommendations for policy-making. In multiple ways, any policy analysis benefits from the recorded experiences of others.

NOTES

1. Murphy comments that with increasing access to public records through public information laws like the Federal Freedom of Information Act, more government business "transpires orally and even internal documents are being written with an eye toward their eventual public consumption" (1980:195).
2. Captor (1979) provides guidelines for manually identifying and locating information in libraries on public policy issues.
3. Those interested in learning what on-line services are available can consult the *Directory of Online Databases,* updated quarterly by Cuadra Associates, Santa Monica, CA; the *Directory of On-line Information Sources,* CSG Press, Rockville, MD; the *Encyclopedia of Information Systems and Services,* edited by Anthony T. Kruzas and published annually by Gale Research Company, Detroit, MI; and the *NTIS Directory of Computerized Files, Software, and Related Technical Reports,* National Technical Information Service, Arlington, VA.

REFERENCES

Berelson, Bernard. 1971. *Content Analysis in Communication Research.* New York: Hafner Publishing.

Budd, Richard W., Robert K. Thorp, and Lewis Donohew. 1969. *Content Analysis of Communications.* New York: Macmillan.

California Technical Assistance Associates, Inc. 1979. *The California Business Enterprise Program For the Blind: Performance and Prospects of a State-Administered Business.* Sacramento, CA: California Department of Rehabilitation.

Captor, Renée. 1979. *Library Research for the Analysis of Public Policy.* Croton-on-Hudson, NY: Policy Studies Associates.

Chadwick, Bruce A., Howard M. Bahr, and Stan L. Albrecht. 1984. *Social Science Research Methods.* Englewood Cliffs, NJ: Prentice-Hall.

Directory of Online Databases. Santa Monica, CA.: Cuadra Associates.

Directory of On-Line Information Sources. Rockville, MD: CSG Press.

Guba, Egon G., and Yvonna S. Lincoln. 1983. *Effective Evaluation: Improving the Usefulness of Evaluation Results Through Responsive and Naturalistic Approaches.* San Francisco: Jossey-Bass Publishers.

Holsti, Ole R. 1969. *Content Analysis for the Social Sciences and Humanities.* Reading, MA: Addison-Wesley.

Kerlinger, Fred N. 1973. *Foundations of Behavioral Research,* 2d ed. New York: Holt, Rinehart & Winston.

Krippendorf, Klaus. 1980. *Content Analysis: An Introduction to Its Methodology.* Beverly Hills, CA: Sage Publications.

Kruzas, Anthony T., ed. *Encyclopedia of Information Systems and Services.* Detroit, MI: Gale Research Company.

Murphy, Jerome T. 1980. *Getting the Facts: A Fieldwork Guide for Evaluators and Policy Analysts.* Santa Monica, CA: Goodyear Publishing.

NTIS Directory of Computerized Files, Software, and Related Technical Reports. Arlington, VA: National Technical Information Service.

Peterson, Mark, Jan Chaiken, Patricia Ebener, and Paul Honig. 1982. *Survey of Prison and Jail Inmates: Background and Method.* Santa Monica, CA: RAND.

Phillips, Joël L., Lynne P. Cannady, and J. Fred Springer. 1985. *Evaluation of the M-2 Sponsors Program: Impacts on Institutional Behavior.* Sacramento, CA: EMT Associates.

Putt, Allen D., and J. Fred Springer. 1977. *Impacts of Campaign Disclosure and Lobbying Provisions of the Political Reform Act of 1974: A Final Report to the California Fair Political Practices Commission.* Sacramento, CA: The State of California.

Springer, J. Fred, and Allen D. Putt. 1979. *Regulating Campaign Finance: The California Experience.* Davis, CA: Institute of Governmental Affairs, University of California.

Wimmer, Roger D., and Joseph R. Dominick. 1983. *Mass Media Research: An Introduction.* Belmont, CA: Wadsworth.

10

Making Data Understandable
Statistical Analysis and Displays

The information collection skills described in Part IV provide the informational grist for policy research. The chapters in Part V discuss analytic skills that allow policy analysts to make sense of data, to find answers to research questions, and to effectively communicate their findings to stakeholders. The chapters are organized to describe several distinctive approaches to analysis commonly applied in policy research.

Chapter 10 discusses the application of basic techniques of statistical analysis to policy problems. Statistical measures provide the basis for interpretation and communication of data sets necessary to informing many policy decisions. Chapter 11 provides an overview of experimental approaches to organizing and interpreting information. These designs are prominent tools for meeting causal information needs in policy research. Chapter 12 introduces major approaches to assessing the costs related to designing and implementing public responses to social problems. Chapter 13 provides guidelines and techniques for conducting quick analysis useful when time and other resources are in limited supply.

STATISTICS AND POLICY RESEARCH

The Constitution, in the first article, requires the federal government to collect statistics in a decennial census. In the founding of the United States government, framers recognized that "a government works better if it has reliable and impartial information" (Kruskal, 1977:3) concerning the conditions of its population. Presently, the federal government gathers and publishes a broad range of statistical information through agencies such as the Bureau of the Census and the Bureau of Labor Statistics. States and localities add to the store of statistical data. Often, the term *statistics* refers to these bodies of facts and figures aggregating aspects of a community's social, economic, and political condition.

But statistics are more than collections of numerical information. Statistics are also a "body of methods for obtaining and analyzing data in order to base decisions on them" (Kruskal, 1977:4). Statistics, both as numbers (data) and as a body of methods (analysis techniques) cut across all aspects of policy research, providing essential quantitative information to decision makers. Thus, statistics permeate policy research, and developing statistical skills is central to becoming competent producers and consumers of policy information.

This chapter acquaints readers with basic applications of descriptive statistics in policy research. The discussion emphasizes the opportunities and limitations statistical analysis presents to producers and users. The focus is on how statistical analysis is used to provide the kinds of information policymakers need to know.

Statistical analysis sometimes suffers from a credibility gap. The view is that anyone can lie with statistics and that, properly manipulated, statistics can be made to support any argument. There is truth to these criticisms, but statistical awareness protects stakeholders from these dangers. Consumers of statistics need to cast a jaundiced eye at the numbers that come before them; they should question the quality of the conclusions presented to them. A major purpose of this chapter is to provide consumers of statistical information with basic guidelines for assessing the quality of statistical information.

Information presented in numbers serves worthwhile purposes. For example, statistics serve the fundamental purpose of describing (summarizing) the information conveyed by a large number of empirical observations. They serve to abstract trends and relationships from data, expressing findings in precise numerical terms. The contribution of this descriptive function of statistics is discussed, and basic descriptive techniques are presented in later sections.

Visual displays of statistical findings are an important tool for conveying policy research findings. The importance of clear and accurate representation of findings is stressed throughout the following discussion, and methods of displaying statistical information are presented. Statistical analysis plays an important role in answering questions of explanation and estimation. Regression analysis is discussed as a key tool in producing information relevant to these questions. This chapter, then, presents descriptive statistics as a crucial linchpin in developing findings of policy research.

COMMUNICATING STATISTICAL INFORMATION: DESCRIBING SINGLE VARIABLES

One of the most difficult tasks facing policy analysts is communicating findings to decision makers. Numerical data are not self-explanatory. They must be analyzed, summarized, and communicated in concise, understandable ways. Consider the following data representing the numbers of daily flu shots given by a county health clinic in the month of December.

77	45	14	22	67	36	55	44	48	39
27	33	62	72	61	59	55	88	17	21
28	57	43	62	70	83				

Presented in the above format, this information does not tell health administrators or county supervisors much about flu protection in the county. Raw quantitative data require organization and clear presentation to make them understandable and useful for decision making. Descriptive statistics are used to summarize data sets and to make them understandable.

Describing Single Variables

A basic objective in presenting statistical information is to describe clearly the *distribution* of the numeric values of a single variable such as the number of flu shots administered daily. Table 10.1 organizes and presents a frequency distribution for the raw data on numbers of flu shots given daily.

TABLE 10.1   Number of Influenza Vaccinations per Day: Green County Health Clinic (December)

NUMBER OF VACCINATIONS	NUMBER OF DAYS	PERCENTAGE OF DAYS
25 or Less	4	15.4
26–50	9	34.6
51–75	10	38.5
More than 75	3	11.5
Total	26	100.0

A previously unintelligible group of numbers now has been organized and displayed to convey more clearly the quantity of vaccinations given in a 26-day period. A "frequency distribution" is a table that displays numbers of observations (e.g., days) grouped according to numerical values (e.g., numbers of vaccinations).

Table 10.1 incorporates several guidelines for clear communication of statistical information (Welch and Comer, 1983:82–83).

- *Descriptive Title.* Clear communication begins with telling users specifically what information is being presented. A clear table title conveys the type of data being displayed (number of vaccinations per day) and where it was collected (location and time).
- *Clear Labels.* Rows and columns in effective tables are clearly labeled so that readers understand what numbers mean (e.g., number of days) and what categories mean (e.g., number of vaccinations).
- *Meaningful Categories.* Tables are a means of organizing and summarizing raw data. Proper organization requires analysts to evaluate how best to achieve the purposes for which the data have been collected. For frequency distributions, categories should be established to reflect clearly the relevant information contained in the data. Generally, "each category should have some entries in it, yet categories should not be so large as to obscure the range and variation in the data" (Welch and Comer, 1983:82).
- *Numbers and Percentages.* Effective presentations of frequency distributions include both numbers of observations and percentages (the number of observations [days] in each category divided by the total number of observations in the table [26 days in Table 10.1]). Percentages clearly indicate the relative numbers of observations found in each category. Since percentages more clearly indicate the relations between categories, category numbers are often omitted from tables with only the total number of observations (N) being presented.

Frequency distributions used to display basic data are common in presenting information in policy studies. Frequency distributions and other associated summary statistics provide research consumers with a basic descriptive picture of the events, attitudes, behaviors, and so on that are under study. This basic picture has several components.

First, frequency distributions identify what events are typical—what events occur with greatest frequency. Table 10.1 demonstrates that, of the four categories in the table, the health clinic gives from 51 to 75 inoculations most often (on 38 percent, or 10, of the days that month). For categorized data, the category of greatest frequency, or occurrence, is called the modal category and provides a simple indicator of central tendency, of what single value tends to occur most often in the distribution.

Second, frequency distributions provide an indication of the degree of variation, or dispersion, among the observations in a data set. In Table 10.1, for example, the modal category contained only 38.5 percent of the observations in the distribution, meaning that 61.5 percent of the observations are spread among the other categories. Indeed, 26 to 50 shots were given on nearly as many days (34.6 percent) as the modal category; in other words, that category was nearly as typical. On 15.4 percent of the days (4 days) the clinic delivered 25 or fewer shots, and on 11.5 percent of the days (3 days) the clinic delivered more than 75 shots. This information is important because it indicates the degree of day-to-day fluctuation in the demand for shots.

Third, frequency distributions provide information on the shape or pattern of the events being described. Table 10.1 represents a distribution with most of the observations in the middle two categories and with fewer observations in the end categories. A very different pattern would be pictured if, for instance, 38.5 percent of the observations were found in the 25 or less category, and 15.4 percent in the 51 to 75 range. This change would depict a distribution that was asymmetrical, skewed to the lower end; days with more than 50 shots would be relatively rare.

Summary Statistics: Central Tendency and Dispersion

Table 10.1 organizes the raw data on flu inoculations and presents it in a way that is understandable. However, by taking the raw numbers of inoculations and collapsing them into four categories, analysts have discarded information. In essense, an interval level measure (numbers of shots) has been reduced to an ordinal level measure (categories of higher and lower numbers of shots). From Table 10.1, users learn that on the 9 days in the 26–50 category more shots were delivered than on the 4 days in the 25 or less category. However, the table cannot indicate exactly how many more shots were delivered on those days. This detail has been lost in the process of collapsing the data into a categorized frequency distribution.

Making statistical information clear and understandable means reducing detail existing in the original data set. Categorized frequency distributions are one means of accomplishing this goal, but analysts also use statistical measures to summarize the characteristics of data sets. These summary statistics describe distributions in different ways, and thereby they discard detail in different ways. While these statistics are essential to making large data sets understandable, consumers of statistical reports need to be aware that they simplify raw data, discarding information in the process.

WHAT IS TYPICAL IN A DISTRIBUTION?

Frequency distributions describe what is typical, or characteristic, of a given set of events or observations. The manager of the county health clinic may need to know, for instance, "How many flu shots can I expect to give on an 'average' day?" Table 10.1 does not provide a precise answer to this question, i.e., a specific number. Analysts most often use one of two summary statistics to provide this average—the "median" or the "mean."

Median.   The median is a measure of what is typical in a distribution. It is the middle point in the distribution—that point which has half of the observations above it and half below. The median number of flu shots given by the clinic is determined by ranking all observed daily inoculations from low to high as follows.

14	17	21	22	27	28	33	36	39	43
44	45	48	©	55	55	57	59	61	62
62	67	70	72	77	83	88			

Since there are 26 observations (days) in the distribution, the median value—the midpoint—is that which has 13 days below and 13 days above. This value (marked by the ©) lies between 48 and 55 because the distribution has an even number of observations. It is calculated by halving the difference between the value of the observation above the median and that below ($55 - 48 = 7, 7/2 = 3.5, 48 + 3.5 = 51.5$). Thus, the median number of shots given at the clinic was 51.5. (If the number of observations is odd, the median is simply the value of the middle observation.)

Mean.   The most familiar measure of central tendency is the mean, which corresponds to the common sense notion of average. The mean is calculated by adding the values of all observations in a distribution and dividing by the number of observations in the distribution. Thus, for the health clinic, the mean number of daily shots in December was

$$(77 + 45 + 14 + 22 + 67 + 36 + 55 + 44 + 48 + 39 + 27 + 33 + 62 + 72 + 61 + 59 + 55 + 88 + 17 + 21 + 28 + 57 + 43 + 62 + 70 + 83) = 1,285$$

and

$$1,285/26 = 49.4$$

In this case, the two measures of what is typical are very similar. The median is 51.5 and the mean is 49.4. They tell the manager that on the average the clinic gave approximately fifty flu shots a day in the month of December.

Know your data!   Some consumers of statistics might conclude that an average is an average, and means and medians are the same thing. This is a potentially misleading conclusion. Means and medians are calculated in different ways, and they reveal different characteristics of data sets or frequency distributions. In the first place, means use addition and division in their calculation, and therefore assume the distribution being summarized is measured at the interval level. However, the differences in the measures go beyond this distinction, as the following example illustrates.

An eastern city has a housing service that helps potential residents search for housing suitable to their needs and resources. An analyst in that agency wants to describe typical costs of housing in different city neighborhoods. One neighborhood has half of its houses valued at $70,000 or below. However, one block at the top of the hill has several historic mansions valued between $350,000 and $500,000. When the mean value of housing in the neighborhood is calculated, it yields an average of $123,000. However, this summary statistic reflects the fact that a minority of neighborhood houses are extremely expensive.

The median value, reflecting the fact that half of the neighborhood's houses are valued below $70,000, is $70,000. In this instance, there is a significant discrepancy between median ($70,000) and mean ($123,000). The reason is technical but has significant implications. The mean "averages in" the high value of a relatively few but expensive historic mansions in the neighborhood.

The housing service analyst would paint a different picture of the neighborhood depending on whether the mean or the median is used in describing the typical cost of a house. To decide which is most appropriate, two questions need to be asked. First, what is the purpose of the statistical summary? Second, does the summary measure reflect the characteristics of the data most appropriate to this purpose? In the housing case, the purpose of the summary is to provide an indicator of the availability of housing at a given price. Since the median indicates that half of the housing in the neighborhood is valued at less than $70,000, it would be the more informative summary in this case.

The general point behind this discussion is that consumers of statistics need to be sensitive to the fact that statistical analyses are a simplification of reality, and consumers must be wary of accepting summaries that mask important details relevant for their purposes. The similarity of mean and median in the distribution of flu shots reflected that there were no extreme, atypical cases in which the clinic gave either unusually high or unusually low numbers of shots. When observations are distributed fairly evenly on both sides of the distribution (i.e., when the data set is symmetrical), the mean and median will be similar. When observations are extreme on one side of the distribution (i.e., when the distribution is asymetrical), the mean will be drawn toward those extreme scores. In skewed distributions, the median is often a more meaningful measure of central tendency. In other cases, depending on the uses of the information, both summary statistics might be presented in reporting results.

WHAT ARE THE DIFFERENCES IN A DISTRIBUTION?

Averages provide information on what a typical value is; they do not provide information on just how typical the observations in the distribution are. Consider the following example. Table 10.2 presents information on numbers of shots given on five days in two different health clinics. Each clinic, on the average (mean), gave 50 shots per day during the week. However, the work load pattern facing the administrators of the two clinics is . very different. In Brown County, the numbers of shots vary little from day to day. The least number of inoculations given on any one day was 40; the highest was 60. In other words, the demand for shots is fairly stable for the period observed, and the manager can plan on allocating resources for approximately 50 shots a day barring unexpected events.

Despite the identical number of daily shots on the average, the situation in Green County is different. The number of shots given on individual days ranges from a low of 20 to a high of 80; the demand for shots on the busiest day is four times that of the slowest day. In Green County, the demand for flu shots fluctuates significantly, and it will be harder for the clinic administrator to allocate resources accurately for meeting daily needs.

The difference between the distribution of daily shots in Green and Brown Counties is a difference in the dispersion or variability of observations—the pattern of differences between observations in the data set. This information is important in describing a distribution. Information on dispersion augments averages by identifying how closely the distribution clusters around an average or typical value. In Brown County, the mean is a useful indication of how many shots can be anticipated on a given day; in Green County the mean is a less useful indicator of daily demand. Analysts

TABLE 10.2   Number of Influenza Inoculations per Day: Green County and Brown County Health Clinics (Week of December 15)

	GREEN COUNTY (NUMBER OF SHOTS)	BROWN COUNTY (NUMBER OF SHOTS)
Monday	80	60
Tuesday	20	50
Wednesday	50	55
Thursday	70	40
Friday	30	45
Average (mean)	50	50

use several measures to describe the dispersion of observations in frequency distributions.

Range, midspread, and hinge.   The range is a starting point for describing the dispersion of values in a distribution; it equals the highest minus the lowest score in a distribution. In Table 10.2, the range of values for Green County is 20 to 80 (range = 60), and that for Brown County is 40 to 60 (range = 20). The range identifies the outer limits of a distribution. As with any summary measure, however, it can be misleading. In the housing example, the high end of the range would identify the very atypical value of the most expensive mansion on the hill.

To provide a more detailed measure of dispersion, analysts use measures associated with the median. The upper hinge is the score that has one-fourth of the values in the distribution above it (Hartwig and Dearing, 1979). To identify the upper hinge for daily flu shots in Green County, refer to the ordered distribution of values for the county (page 258). The upper hinge is the value halfway between the median and the highest value, or 62 (the seventh value above the median). The lower hinge is 33, the value halfway between the median and the lowest value. The midspread is the range between the hinges (33 to 62 = 47.5).

These measures indicate that on one-half of the days of the month the clinic gave between 33 and 62 shots; on one-fourth of the days there were fewer than 33 and on one-fourth of the days there were more than 62. The combination of median, midspread, and range provides a detailed summary of the shape of a distribution.

Standard deviation.   A commonly used measure of dispersion is the standard deviation. This measure is calculated through the following steps (Welch and Comer, 1983:101).

1. Calculate the mean of the distribution.
2. Subtract the mean value from each value in the distribution. (For example, for the flu shots: $14 - 49.4 = -35.4$; $17 - 49.4 = -32.4$; and so on for each value in the distribution.)
3. Square each resulting value, e.g. -35.4 squared $= 1253.16$; and so on for each value. This procedure eliminates negative values.
4. Add all the squared values.
5. Divide this sum by the number of observations in the distribution (e.g., 26).
6. Take the square root of the product of the division. The resulting value is the standard deviation of the distribution.

The steps required for calculating the standard deviation indicate that the statistic is only appropriate for variables measured at the interval level; subtraction, addition, multiplication, and division are all used in the procedure. The calculation indicates the standard deviation is a more complex summary than the range or midspread. Indeed, to describe the meaning of the calculations in words is difficult. It is frequently defined as the "square root of the average squared deviation from the mean" in the distribution, but this description may not be much help to consumers of statistics who are not well versed in the technique.

The point is that statistics should be selected for their understandability to users whenever possible. The standard deviation is an important tool for statistical analysis because it (and other closely associated measures) is a central component of advanced statistical procedures. But just because it is an important measure does not mean it should automatically be used to convey information to stakeholders. The range, median, and midspread will often accomplish this purpose more effectively. In statistical analysis, considerations of users and the purposes of the analysis guide the selection of techniques.

Communicating Frequency Distributions Through Visual Displays

When using statistics, analysts are confronted with the challenge of clear analysis and communication. The previous section emphasized the importance of the correct selection of summary measures. This section introduces the use of visual displays—graphs and charts—as a crucial aid to clear statistical communication.

> Often the most effective way to describe, explore, and summarize a set of numbers—even a large set—is to look at pictures of those numbers. Furthermore, of all methods for analyzing and communicating statistical information, well-designed data graphics are usually the simplest and at the same time the most powerful. (Tufte, 1983:9)

The effective and creative use of charts and graphs—visual displays—is significant for clear communication of policy research findings. Visual displays assist users in understanding information, in highlighting important data, and in saving time. The following examples provide an introduction to the usefulness of graphics in communicating quantitative information.

LINE GRAPHS

Line graphs are a form of visual display suited to representing information over time—trends. Line graphs include single or multiple lines representing one or more events. Figure 10.1, a single-line graph, is adapted from data presented in a newspaper story concerning the rising cost of government in New York State (*New York Times,* February 1, 1976:iv–6).

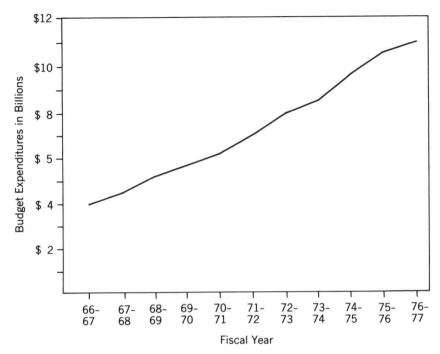

FIGURE 10.1   New York State Total Budget Expenditures (in billions of dollars, fiscal 1966–1976). (*Source:* Adapted with permission from Edward Tufte, *The Visual Display of Quantitative Information* (Cheshire, CT: Graphics Press, 1983), pp. 66–68).

The line graph portrays a constant increase in total dollar expenditures in the New York State budget. Expenditures increased from $4 billion in fiscal 1966–1967 to $10.8 billion ten years later. The line graph visually reinforces this interpretation by displaying variations among fiscal years and by showing an overall trend conveying conclusions that New York State has experienced a substantial and continuous increase in spending.

But the graph is conveying a false impression.

> Two statistical lapses ... bias the chart. First, during the years shown, the state's population increased by 1.7 million people, or 10 percent. Part of the budget growth simply paralleled population growth. Second, the period was a time of substantial inflation; those goods that cost state and local governments $1.00 to purchase in 1967 cost $2.03 by 1977. By not deflating, the graphic mixes up changes in the value of money with changes in the budget. (Tufte, 1983:68)

Figure 10.2 displays the same ten-year budgetary trend in per capita expenditures (which standardizes for population growth) of constant dollars (which adjusts for inflation). The conclusion conveyed in this graphic

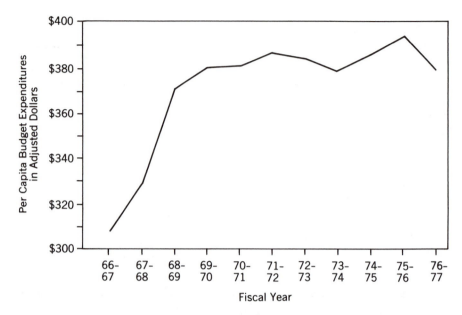

FIGURE 10.2   New York State Total Budget Expenditures (per capita expenditures in constant dollars per capita, fiscal 1967–1977). (*Source:* Adapted with permission from Edward Tufte, *The Visual Display of Quantitative Information* (Cheshire, CT: Graphics Press, 1983), p. 68.)

is that budgetary expenditures increased substantially between 1967 and 1970 (about 20 percent) and have remained relatively constant after 1970. Indeed, there was a substantial decline between 1976 and 1977.

The preceding example of misleading visual impressions underscores a general principle in the communication of statistical information. Visual displays efficiently convey conclusions about data, but they must be carefully designed to reveal the truth about data. Line graphs are powerful tools for displaying trends and other information, but the numbers being graphed must be calculated so that they accurately and fairly portray the concern.

PIE CHARTS

Pie charts are a common technique for displaying proportions or percentages, and are particularly useful when the distribution contains a relatively small number of categories (three to seven). Pie charts are often used to display budgetary information (percentage of the budget devoted to different categories of expenditure). In constructing pie charts, the largest part is presented first (starting at 12 o'clock) with decreasingly smaller parts following. Pie charts are easily adapted to many applications displaying the portions of some whole that fall into specific categories.

Figure 10.3 provides an example. The Guam Visitors Bureau was interested in bolstering the contribution of tourism to the island's economy. As part of its planning process, the bureau conducted a survey of Japanese visitors to the island during the winter months. Figure 10.3 displays the relative portion of visitor expenditures on hotel, gifts, food and beverage, optional tours, entertainment, and transportation. The pie chart does not add any information beyond a simple frequency distribution, but it displays the information in a way that is clear and understandable.

BAR GRAPHS

Another common technique for visually displaying and comparing quantities is the bar graph. The length of the bars indicates relative quantities. Bars are vertically or horizontally displayed. Bar graphs are particularly useful for making comparisons between occurrences. Figure 10.4 displays bar graphs of responses to four questions asked in a survey of 407 registered voters on the island of Guam. The purpose of the survey was to assess the attitudes of voters regarding several provisions of a proposed Commonwealth Act that would make important changes in the status of Guam as a protectorate of the United States. The intended use of the survey was to provide a basis for (a) making changes in the proposed act, and (b) planning a public information campaign prior to a referendum on the act.

FIGURE 10.3   Average Expenditures by Japanese Visitors to Guam: December–February. (*Source:* Jay R. Merrill and E. Vance Merrill, *Guam Japanese Tourism Survey* (Agana, Guam: Merrill and Associates, 1986), p. 14.)

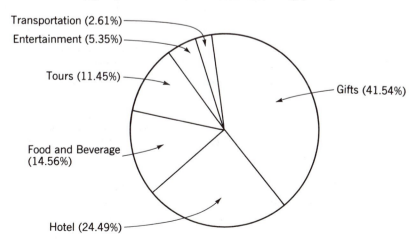

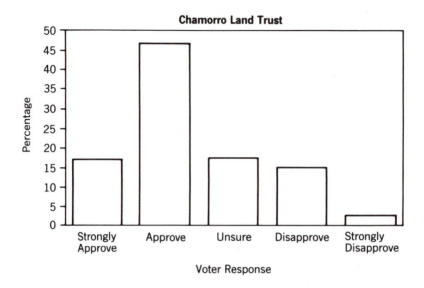

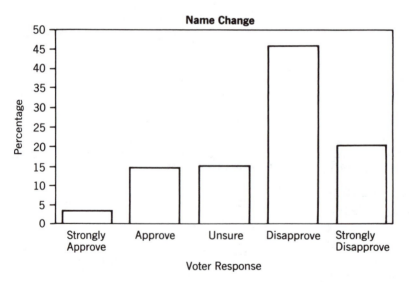

FIGURE 10.4   Voter Reponses to Four Provisions of the Proposed Guam Commonwealth Act. N = 407 voters. (*Source:* J. Fred Springer, E. Vance Merrill, and Jay R. Merrill, *Guam Commonwealth Survey* (Agana, Guam: Merrill and Associates, 1985), p. 24.)

The graphs depict four distinct patterns of voter attitudes. The first provision would establish a land trust for the indigenous Chamorro peoples of Guam. The graph clearly indicates a pattern of approval for setting aside certain public lands for use by Chamorros—nearly two-thirds of the voters (64.1 percent) approved; 18 percent disapproved.

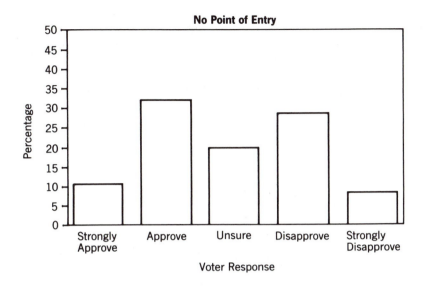

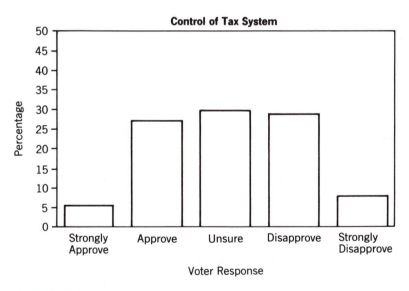

FIGURE 10.4 Continued

The second graph depicts the opposite pattern—strong disapproval. Two-thirds (66.3 percent) of the survey respondents disapproved of a proposal to change the name of Guam to the traditional Polynesian name Guahan. Only 20 percent expressed approval. This contrast between approval and disapproval is clearly and quickly conveyed by comparing the bar graphs.

The third graph displays a pattern of relative polarization in voter attitudes. When asked whether Guam should no longer serve as a point of entry for immigrants desiring to establish residence leading to U.S. citizenship, 43 percent approved and 37.3 percent disapproved. The graph depicts this polarization through the near equal height of bars on either side of the graph. Finally, the fourth graph depicts a pattern of relative uncertainty among voters. Thirty percent of the voters were unsure about whether the local government of Guam should take control of the tax system from the United States government.

Consider the relevant information that the Guam Commonwealth Commission, who sponsored the survey, could quickly glean from the bar graphs in Figure 10.4. The strong support for the land trust and the strong opposition to the name change are immediately evident. Given the opposition according to this survey, the commission may consider dropping the proposed name change from the act. The land trust provision may well be emphasized in the public information campaign. The polarization and uncertainty regarding the immigration and tax provisions warrant careful attention. The commission may desire further analysis of attitudes and beliefs concerning these provisions.

COMMUNICATING STATISTICAL INFORMATION: DESCRIBING STATISTICAL RELATIONSHIPS

The preceding section demonstrated how simple descriptions and visual displays of single variables provide useful information to stakeholders. At other times, however, consumers of policy research require information on the joint distribution of two (or more) variables. This section presents basic techniques for analyzing and displaying the relation (joint distribution) between two variables. Techniques for analyzing relations between three or more variables are discussed in other works on statistical analysis (Hyman, 1955; Jones, 1984).

There are two primary reasons policymakers require information on joint frequency distributions. First, they may simply want more descriptive detail in profiling events or observations. For example, the Guam Visitors Bureau may want to profile visitors by age, gender, and combinations of age and gender (e.g., among visitors in the 20–30-year age range, how many are female and how many male?). This information has implications for advertising and promotion, development of new tourist services, and designing tours, for example.

Second, decision makers may be interested in the degree to which one variable is associated with the occurrence of another. A local chief of police may want to know if crime rates are lower in precincts with officers assigned to foot patrol than in precincts with officers assigned to foot patrol than in

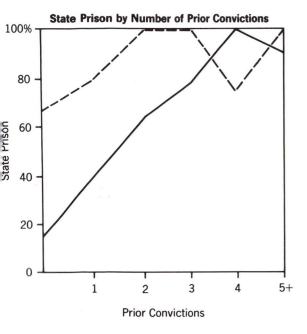

State Prison by Number of Prior Convictions

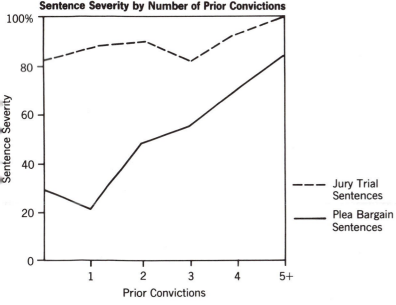

Sentence Severity by Number of Prior Convictions

— — Jury Trial Sentences

——— Plea Bargain Sentences

FIGURE 10.6   Line Graph for Relation Between Number of Prior Convictions and Sentence Severity. (*Source:* Ronald A. Harris and J. Fred Springer, "Plea Bargaining as a Game: An Empirical Analysis of Plea Negotiations in California," *Policy Studies Review* 4:255. Reprinted with permission.)

precincts without foot patrol. The following section discusses contingency tables as a method of displaying and analyzing the relation between two variables.

Communicating Relationships: Contingency Tables

The Guam Commonwealth Commission wanted to use the information generated by its survey of registered voters to help plan a strategy for designing and promoting a Commonwealth Act that would meet approval of the majority of Guam's voters. The survey indicated that, on several issues, the island voters were divided. Nearly equal numbers of voters, for instance, approved of and disapproved of the proposal to eliminate Guam's status as a point of entry for aliens seeking to meet residence requirements for becoming U.S. citizens (Figure. 10.4).

Given the division of opinion on the issue, more detailed analysis was desirable. Specifically, analysts conducting the survey sought to give the commission information concerning who approved and disapproved. Knowledge about who took the supporting and opposing points of view could provide insight into the reasons for approving and disapproving, and help the commission develop a strategy for resolving disagreements.

The survey analysts were particularly interested in the potential effects of ethnic membership on voter attitudes. The island population is composed of two large ethnic groups—Chamorros and Filipinos—and a number of less sizable ethnic communities. Table 10.3 displays the ethnic distribution of the survey sample.

Analysts reasoned that the interests of different ethnic groups may differ substantially with respect to the immigration issue. Chamorros are the indigenous group who may desire to limit immigration to the island, thereby reducing competition for jobs and land. Other groups, particularly Filipinos, tend to be recent immigrants themselves and may desire to bring additional friends and family to the island. In short, ethnic status may be related to whether a voter approves or disapproves of the no point of entry provision.

To assess this potential relationship, analysts examined the joint distri-

TABLE 10.3   Ethnic Distribution of Survey Respondents: Guam Commonwealth Survey. *N* = 407 Voters

ETHNICITY	NUMBER	PERCENTAGE
Chamorro	240	59.0
Filipino	104	25.6
Other	63	15.4
Totals	407	100.00

bution of ethnic grouping and support of the provision. In this analysis, support for the provision is the "dependent" variable, the variable that is being influenced by another variable or variables, e.g., ethnicity. The dependent variable is the effect in a cause-effect relationship, i.e., the variable being influenced by independent variables. Ethnicity is the "independent" variable, the variable expected to have an influence on support for the provision. The independent variable is the cause in a cause-effect relationship. Identification of which is the independent and which is the dependent variable comes from the statement of the research question—e.g., what is the effect of ethnicity, the independent variable, *on* support for the immigration provision, the dependent variable? Table 10.4 provides information on this question.

Table 10.4 presents the joint frequency distribution between ethnicity and approval ratings for the no point of entry provision. The effect of ethnicity on support becomes clear. Chamorros are three times more likely than Filipinos to support the no point of entry provision. Filipinos are more than three times as likely to disapprove (68.3 percent versus 21.7 percent). These findings provide support for the conclusion that the no point of entry provision is influenced by voter ethnicity.

The above example demonstrates the basic mechanics of calculating and displaying the relationship between two variables. In interpreting statistical findings presented in the form of contingency tables, experienced users carefully consider the presentation of the table and whether the presentation clearly and fairly represents the information most relevant to their purposes.

Visual Displays of Relationships

Charts and graphs are also useful in communicating information about relationships between variables. Figure 10.5 provides an example of the use of a shaded bar chart to provide descriptive information about the joint distribution of age and gender among visitors to Guam. The figure displays the preponderance of 20–29-year-olds and the tendency toward more females among younger visitors and more males among older visitors.

Figure 10.6 uses multiple line graphs to provide a visual display of a more complex relation. The graph indicates the relation between the number of prior felony convictions for defendants and two measures of the de-

TABLE 10.4 Ethnicity by No Point of Entry Provision. N = 407 Voters

ETHNICITY	APPROVE	UNSURE	DISAPPROVE	TOTAL N
Chamorro	56.6%	21.7	21.7	240
Filipino	18.3%	13.5	68.2	104
Other	31.7%	22.2	46.1	63

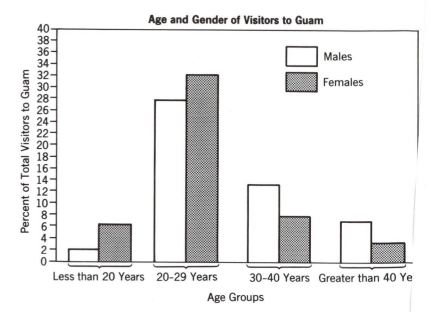

FIGURE 10.5 Bar Graph of Joint Frequency Distribution: Age and Gender of V Guam. (*Source:* Jay R. Merrill and E. Vance Merrill, *Guam Japanes Survey* (Agana, Guam: Merrill and Associates, 1986), p. 18.)

pendent variable sentence severity. The top graph compares the between prior convictions and the percentage of convictions that tenced to state prison for both jury trial convictions and plea ba convictions (all convictions were for burglary or robbery). The secon indicates the same set of relations with the dependent measure per of maximum legal sentence.

The graphs display important findings. First, the gap betw trial and plea bargained outcomes at the left side of the graph i that offenders who plea bargain with no prior felony convictions receive sentences less severe than first-time offenders who choose jury trial. However, this gap steadily narrows as the lines move to right. When offenders have four or five prior felony convictions, little difference between sentences in jury trial convictions and gained convictions. Offenders with long criminal histories do not g of a break when they plea bargain. The visual display in Figure 10.6 this information more succinctly and more quickly than a series o ical tables.

REGRESSION ANALYSIS

Contingency table analysis is appropriate for nominal and ordinal tion. However, interval data that take on a range of discrete valu

easily analyzed and displayed in this way (unless the data are categorized and information made less refined). Figure 10.7 portrays a hypothetical "scattergram" which visually displays the relation between an interval level independent variable (the daily price of gasoline) and a dependent variable (daily ridership on the Bi-State Transit Agency).

Each data point on the scattergram represents two scores for each observation—the intersection of the average cost of gasoline (the horizontal axis) and the number of riders on Bi-State buses (the vertical axis) on a particular day. A staff analyst in the agency suspects that the recent increases in ridership at Bi-State are largely due to increased commuting costs associated with recent hikes in gasoline prices. The raw data presented in Figure 10.7 would seem to support this expectation; days with higher average gas prices tend to have high ridership also. Regression analysis provides a variety of statistics, discussed below, that summarize the relation portrayed in the scattergram.

Bivariate Regression

Bivariate linear regression is based upon the assumption that "the relationship between two variables can be summarized by a line" (Meier and Brudney, 1981:279). The computations for linear regression identify the location of the straight line that minimizes the total squared vertical distance of each of the data points in the scattergram from the straight line. This type of regression is known as ordinary least squares. Figure 10.8 portrays the location of the linear regression line summarizing the relation between

FIGURE 10.7   Scattergram of the Relation Between Daily Gas Price and Daily Ridership

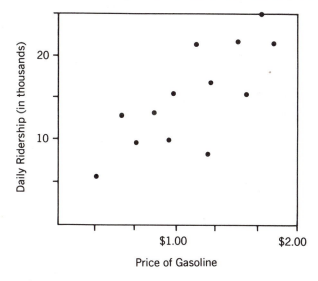

daily gasoline price (the independent variable) and daily bus ridership (the dependent variable).

Regression analysis produces a number of summary statistical measures. One group of these measures describes the location of the regression line and provides a basis for predicting a value of the dependent variable for a particular value of the independent variable. The next section discusses the predictive equation that accomplishes this purpose. The second group of summary measures describes the "goodness of fit" of the regression line or the accuracy of the predictions that are produced by the equation. A subsequent section will discuss one of these measures.

THE REGRESSION EQUATION

Any line can be located by two points, and regression statistics describe the regression line by providing a basis for specifying two points in the space represented by a scattergram. The first point is located by what is called the intercept. The intercept identifies the value of the dependent variable (on average) at the point that the regression line intersects the vertical axis of the scattergram—the point designated by "a" in Figure 10.8.

The second point is located through application of what is called the regression coefficient, or "b." The regression coefficient is the ratio of changes in the dependent variable (Y) over changes in the independent variable (X) as reflected in the regression line. For Figure 10.8, the regression coefficient would summarize the amount of increase in daily bus ridership that would accompany each penny rise in the cost of gas.

FIGURE 10.8 Linear Regression Line for Relationship Between Daily Gas Price and Daily Ridership

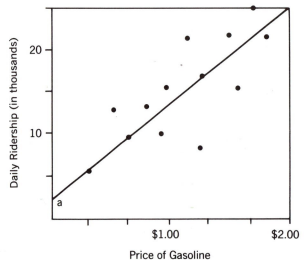

$$b = \frac{\text{change in dependent variable}}{\text{change in independent variable}}$$

The intercept and the regression coefficient are components in the regression equation that provide a basis for predicting values of the dependent variable when values of the independent variable are known. The regression equation takes the following general form.

$$Y = a + b(X)$$

Y is the symbol for the values of the dependent variable that are predicted by the equation. That prediction is produced by beginning with the value of the intercept and adding the amount of increase in the value of the dependent variable that would accompany a specific value of the independent variable (X). The equation will identify the value of Y on the regression line that intersects with any value of X.

For the data displayed in Figure 10.8, assume that the regression equation is (Meier and Brudney, 1981:300)

$$Y = 212 + 187X$$

In other words, the expected ridership for a given day would be 212 plus the product of the price of gas that day (in cents) multiplied by 187. On a day in which the price of gas is 69 cents, expected ridership would be

$$212 + 187(69) = 13,115.$$

A 50-cent increase in gas price would produce the following increase in ridership.

$$212 + 187(119) = 22,465$$

The ability to predict or estimate the value of a dependent variable (e.g., ridership) with information about an independent variable (e.g., gas price) often makes regression analysis a useful tool in policy research.

GOODNESS OF FIT

A regression equation can be developed to assess the relationship between any two interval variables. The closer the scatter of dots around the regression line, the stronger the relation between the variables and the more accurate the resulting predictions. Statisticians use the coefficient of determination (r^2) as a summary meaure of the degree of "fit" between the regression line and the cluster of dots.

The coefficient of determination indicates the percentage of the variance in the dependent variable that is "explained" by the independent variable; accordingly, it varies between 0 and 1.00. If r^2 equals 0, there is no relation between the independent and dependent variables, e.g., no relationship between gasoline prices and ridership. If r^2 equals 1.00, the independent and dependent variables would be perfectly related, e.g., perfect association between gasoline prices and ridership. All of the dots in the scattergram would fall *on* the regression line, and values of the dependent variable would be hypothetically predicted with complete accuracy. If the equation for predicting daily ridership has an r^2 value of .85, the agency could expect that predictions based on the equation would be highly accurate. If the value were .30, predictions would be prone to significant error.

The regression equation is a powerful summary statistic applicable to a variety of estimation and explanatory problems. The power of regression equations can be improved by including more than one independent variable in the analysis, a technique known as multiple regression. While further exploration of statistics exceeds the purpose of this text, analysts and users alike benefit from a basic understanding of this statistical measure.

CONCLUDING COMMENTS

Statistics and statistical analysis are fundamental to policy research. Statistical tools provide means for organizing, summarizing, and communicating information about populations of interest. This type of analysis is integral to analytic methods discussed in this text. This chapter presented basic principles in the use of statistics, providing examples of common statistical tools.

Producers and consumers of statistical information constantly balance the need to summarize complex data and the need for detail. Descriptive statistics organize and summarize data, but they exclude detail in the process. Even the simple statistics that describe central tendency and dispersion in frequency distributions of single variables can be misleading. Consumers are appropriately cautious in accepting statistical summaries at face value.

Clear communication of statistical results poses a challenge to analysts. To be useful, statistical data must be made understandable—effectively organized, summarized, and displayed. Clear and focused tables are a necessity. Graphs, charts, and other visual displays play an important role in effectively communicating statistical information.

Many users lack skills in understanding statistical communications.

Statistical analysts have a special responsibility to present statistical information fully and accurately. This chapter demonstrated that statistical results are not self-evident or self-explanatory and can easily mislead and distort findings. Analysts clearly explain the strengths and the limitations of the analysis approaches and strive to present an accurate interpretation of data.

Excellence in statistical analysis requires that producers and consumers place substantive problems and purposes before technique. In policy research, the intended uses of information guide choices of techniques. More complex and esoteric analysis is not better analysis if it is not understood and if it is not used. Effective use of statistical analysis is an area in which the skilled policy analyst plays a crucial role linking the world of research and the world of information utilization.

REFERENCES

Harris, Ronald, A., and J. Fred Springer. 1985. "Plea Bargaining as a Game: An Empirical Analysis of Plea Negotiations in California," *Policy Studies Review* 4:245–58.

Hartwig, Frederick, and Brian E. Dearing. 1979. *Exploratory Data Analysis*. Beverly Hills, CA: Sage University Papers.

Hyman, Herbert. 1955. *Survey Design and Analysis*. New York: Free Press.

Jones, E. Terrence. 1984. *Conducting Political Research*, 2d ed. New York: Harper & Row.

Kruskal, William H. 1977. "Issues and Opportunities," in William B. Fairley and Frederick Mosteller, eds., *Statistics and Public Policy*. Reading, MA: Addison-Wesley Publishing.

Loether, Herman J., and Donald G. McTavish. 1974. *Descriptive Statistics for Sociologists: An Introduction*. Boston: Allyn and Bacon.

MacRae, Duncan, Jr., and James A. Wilde. 1979. *Policy Analysis for Public Decisions*. North Scituate, MA: Duxbury Press.

Meier, Kenneth J., and Jeffrey L. Brudney. 1981. *Applied Statistics for Public Administration*. Boston: Duxbury Press.

Merrill, Jay R., and E. Vance Merrill. 1986. *Guam Japanese Tourism Survey*. Agana, Guam: Merrill and Associates.

Springer, J. Fred. 1983. "Burglary and Robbery Plea Bargaining in California: An Organizational Perspective," *The Justice System Journal* 8, 2:157–58.

Springer, J. Fred, E. Vance Merrill, and Jay R. Merrill. 1985. *Guam Commonwealth Survey*. Agana, Guam: Merrill and Associates.

Tufte, Edward R. 1974. *Data Analysis for Politics and Policy*. Englewood Cliffs, NJ: Prentice-Hall.

Tufte, Edward R. 1983. *The Visual Display of Quantitative Information*. Cheshire, CT.: Graphics Press.

Tukey, John W. 1977. *Exploratory Data Analysis*. Reading, MA: Addison-Wesley Publishing.

Welch, Susan, and John C. Comer. 1983. *Quantitative Methods for Public Administration: Techniques and Applications*. Homewood, IL: Dorsey Press.

11

Evaluating Policy Outcomes Using Experimental Methods

Public policy is frequently intended to produce change in the conditions of society and the welfare of citizens. Prenatal health care programs are intended to reduce infant mortality rates and to improve the health of newborns; drug abuse prevention efforts are intended to reduce the extent of drug use and thereby alleviate the many problems attendant to it; the food stamp program is intended to ensure that the poor can attain adequate nutrition to sustain health. While there may be disagreement about the precise intentions for public policies, the intention to alter life conditions is a basic rationale for launching policy initiatives.

A major purpose of policy decisions, then, is to achieve policy objectives through controlling conditions and events. Controlling events means policymakers need information about the *cause(s)* of those events. "For exercising control over events, a causal relation must be assumed between the variables. To control events means to produce or inhibit them.... [C]ausal assumption[s] ... provide a basis for action, an intervention strategy, for achieving [policy] purposes" (Meehan, 1981:86–87).

Knowing about causes is relevant at all phases of the policy process. At the policy stimulation, clarification, and choice stages, information about causes of social problems guides decisions about what actions may alleviate them. Evidence that poor nutrition, alcohol use, or smoking during pregnancy contributes to infant mortality provides a basis for funding pre-natal care programs as an intervention strategy. Any actions designed to affect current conditions (e.g., health practices during pregnancy) to achieve a future objective (improved infant health) is based on causal as-sumptions. There is no doubt that if one seeks to produce change, knowl-edge about causes is an advantage.

Establishing causal linkages is the major purpose of impact evalua-tions which seek to determine whether policy actions work—whether they achieve desired objectives. To answer this question, impact evaluations seek to identify (a) whether intended changes in social conditions have occurred, and (b) whether those changes have actually been caused by policy initia-tives. "Ideally, we would like to compare what actually happened with what would have happened if the world had been exactly the same as it was, except that the program had not been implemented" (Hatry, Winnie, Fisk, 1981:25).

The interest in establishing causes in policy analysis has focused atten-tion on experimentation as a research methodology for producing informa-tion about causes. In common sense terms, experimenting is trying some-thing out to see if it works. For policy analysts, experiments are potentially useful approaches to evaluating whether certain factors or events cause given results.

This chapter examines the use of experimentally oriented techniques in policy research. It discusses the nature of experimental methods and the reasons they provide a well-accepted model for testing cause-effect linkages. The chapter also examines the feasibility of experimental methods in policy settings by discussing their relative merits and drawbacks.

EVALUATING OUTCOMES: TRUE EXPERIMENTS

A true experiment is a process of carefully controlled observation and infer-ence. Many think of experiments as being carried out in "laboratories" (arti-ficially created settings that isolate the experiment from extraneous events that may contaminate it). Indeed, laboratory experiments do contribute to policy information. More frequently, policy research experiments are con-ducted in field (natural) settings. Illustrations of laboratory and field experi-ments follow.

Good-Looking but Dangerous:
A Laboratory Experiment

Research investigating the consequences of physical attractiveness has shown that attractive people have significant advantages over less attractive counterparts. Whether fair or not, better-looking people are expected to have happier, more successful lives in store for themselves. In causal terms, attractiveness is expected to be a cause of desirable outcomes in people's lives.

As Sigall and Ostrove (1975) report, one hopes the influence of physical attractiveness occurs only when it is the sole source of information available. In other words, any unfair consequences of differences in looks should be canceled when more important information is known about the person.

Unfortunately, Sigall and Ostrove report that research evidence does not permit such consolation. In one study, adult subjects were presented with accounts of transgressions supposedly committed by children of varying physical attractiveness. When the transgression was severe, the offense was viewed less negatively when committed by a good-looking child than when the offender was less attractive. Further, subjects believed less attractive children were more likely to be involved in future offenses. Another earlier study suggested that attractive women are convicted less often of crimes of which they are accused than are less attractive women. From a policy point of view, these findings suggest that physical appearance represents a basis for discrimination, threatening equity in judicial sentencing decisions.

These and other findings indicating a tendency toward lenience for attractive offenders served as the basis of a laboratory experiment by Sigall and Ostrove. In their study, the attractiveness of a criminal defendant was varied along with the nature of the crime committed. They expected that when the crime was unrelated to attractiveness (e.g., burglary), subjects would assign more lenient sentences to attractive defendants. But, when the crime could be viewed as attractiveness-related (e.g., swindle, confidence game), attractive offenders would receive relatively harsh treatment compared with treatment afforded less attractive offenders. In this situation, good-looking offenders might be seen as taking advantage of their attractiveness, incurring animosity and severe judgments from their jury of peers.

EXPERIMENTAL PROCEDURES

Subjects participating in the experiment were sixty male and sixty female undergraduates. Each was presented with an account of a criminal case and asked to indicate an appropriate term of imprisonment as a sentence. One-third of the subjects were led to believe that the defendant was physically attractive, another third to believe she was unattractive. The remaining one-third received no information concerning attractiveness. Cross-cutting the attractiveness variable, one-half of the subjects were given a written account of an attractiveness-related crime, a swindle. The other half was given a written account of an attractiveness-unrelated crime, a burglary. The 120 undergraduates were randomly assigned to the groups receiving differing information on physical appearance.

When undergraduates arrived to participate in the study, each was shown to an individual room and given relevant material. The top sheet told them they would read a criminal case account and be given biographical information about the defendant. After considering the material they would be asked to respond to questions.

The criminal case account began on the second page. Attached to the page was a five-by-eight-inch card containing routine data which was identical in all conditions. In the attractive conditions, a photograph of an attractive female was included in the upper right corner of the card. The unattractive conditions included a relatively unattractive photograph of a female. No picture was presented in the control conditions. Subjects then read either the account of a burglary or a swindle. In both accounts, the information given left little doubt concerning the defendant's guilt.

On the final page of the booklet, subjects were asked to complete the following statement by circling a number between one and fifteen: "I sentence the defendant to (__) years of imprisonment." After sentencing had been completed, a second form was provided asking subjects to rate the seriousness of the crimes (burglary and swindle) and to rate the defendant on a physical attractiveness scale. A postexperimental interview followed at which time subjects were debriefed—informed about the nature of the experiment.

FINDINGS

Researchers' expectations were confirmed. When the offense was unrelated to attractiveness (burglary), the unattractive defendant was more severely punished than the attractive defendant. But when the offense was attractiveness-related (swindle), the attractive defendant was treated more harshly. Table 11.1 provides further detail. Since there were no differences in responses between males and females, gender was ignored in reporting results.

TABLE 11.1   Average Sentence Assigned in Years (N = 20 per condition)

	DEFENDANT CONDITION		
OFFENSE	ATTRACTIVE	UNATTRACTIVE	CONTROL
Swindle	5.45	4.35	4.35
Burglary	2.80	5.20	5.10

Based on the experiment, researchers concluded that when crimes are attractiveness-related, advantages otherwise held by good-looking defendants are lost. Further, the notion that good-looking people usually tend to be treated more leniently because they are viewed as less dangerous and more virtuous remains tenable. Sigall and Ostrove (1975:389) add that it

> is possible to derive a small bit of consolation from this outcome, if we speculate that only the very attractive receive special (favorable or unfavorable) treatment, and that others are treated similarly. This is a less frightening conclusion than one which would indicate that unattractiveness brings about active discrimination.

The Delaware Dislocated Worker Program: A Field Experiment

Dislocated workers—"persons who have lost long-term, stable jobs due to an increased international competition and/or changing technology" (Bloom, 1987:157)—have become an increasingly serious public problem in the modern economy. Needs estimates have placed the numbers of dislocated workers in the United States as high as two million persons. In response to the problem, the Job Training Partnership Act (JTPA) provided for grants-in-aid to fund state efforts to help dislocated workers reenter the job market.

The Delaware Department of Labor was an early recipient of JTPA funds. Because there was little track record in the area concerning how to design such a program, and little knowledge about what program activities might be effective, Delaware launched a six-month pilot program to generate experience and knowledge for designing an effective statewide program. The pilot program was designed as a field experiment that would provide services to 65 eligible workers. The objectives of the program were (a) to reduce participants' need for unemployment insurance (UI) benefits, and (b) to help increase their earnings.

EXPERIMENTAL PROCEDURES

Procedures for identifying subjects in the field experiment proceeded through several steps.

1. A pool of dislocated workers was identified through an outreach program to UI applicants receiving between seven and twelve weeks of benefits. Outreach efforts included cards to potentially eligible persons, announcements in UI offices, local media announcements, and the cooperation of UI staff. The effort produced a pool of 965 potential participants.

2. Members of the pool of applicants were screened to ensure they met study criteria. In addition to meeting the definition of a "displaced worker," eligible participants were required to have at least a tenth grade education, have access to transportation, and have no opportunity for recall by the former employer. Screening reduced the pool to 175 eligible applicants.
3. A lottery was used to randomly assign 65 eligible participants to the program. The remaining 110 eligibles became the control group to which program participants would be compared.

Once subjects were selected, they received four programmatic services. First, all participants attended four or five job-search workshops to assess their career goals and to develop skills for finding suitable jobs. Second, participants received ongoing individual counseling on their job-search activities. Trained counselors met them regularly and made suggestions for improving their efforts. Third, participants received job development assistance from a team of job developers who instituted searches for openings and contacted employers. Finally, thirteen of the participants most in need were provided with retraining in new job skills. The program provided these services for as long as they were needed or for up to six months.

FINDINGS

The purpose of the field experiment was to determine whether the pilot program achieved its basic purposes—to reduce UI benefits and to increase earnings. To answer this question, analysts "compare[d] the experience of participants with estimates of what their experience would have been without the program" (Bloom, 1987:163). The experience of the control group, those not receiving program services, provided this estimate. Accordingly, both program participants and the control group members were monitored for UI benefits and earnings at each of four quarters for a full year after random assignment.

When the results for each group were compared, evaluators found the following:

*   In the first quarter of follow-up, program participants received an average of $100 per month *more* in UI benefits than members of the control group; at six months there was no difference between the two groups; and by the third quarter participants were receiving slightly less ($10) than the control group. However, at one year the UI benefits to participants had returned to an average of $100 more than was received by the control group.
*   In the first quarter of follow-up, participants earned an average of $20

per month *less* than members of the control group. At six months the differential was −$260; at 9 months it was −$570; at a year it was −$220.

Based on these comparisons, the analysts concluded that "the program did not appear to improve participants' job prospects" (Bloom, 1987:166). While the conclusion of the experimental data was that the program, as implemented, did not work, the Department of Labor did learn from it. In particular, a close examination of the process for delivering services suggested ways in which they might be improved.

FEATURES OF TRUE EXPERIMENTS

Field and laboratory experiments represent two variations of true experimental research designs. The major difference between them is the setting in which they are conducted. Laboratory experiments are conducted in a highly controlled, artificially contrived setting—a characteristic often making it difficult to know how applicable findings are in the empirical world without further study. Field experiments are conducted in natural settings—a condition that minimizes concerns of artificiality, but makes it more difficult to isolate specific causal factors analysts are examining.

Nevertheless, both variations share certain characteristics that make them experiments. Their advantage resides in the ability to control extraneous factors, i.e., potentially rival explanations, while comparing relations between two or more selected variables, e.g., relations between physical attractiveness and sentencing judgments or relations between participation in a dislocated workers program and subsequent benefits. The increased ability to control nonprogram-related factors in an experiment means analysts and stakeholders have increased confidence in stating that policies and programs are achieving (or not achieving) intended effects.

To enhance knowledge about causal statements, true experiments— field and laboratory—reflect commonalities of procedure and process. The following sections discuss control, comparison, and assignment as common characteristics of true experiments.

Controlling Conditions

Analysts using experimental methods ask questions such as, "What are the effects of physical attractiveness on sentencing judgments?" or "What are the impacts of participation in a job-search program on future earnings?" These questions reflect conditions that can be varied. To analysts conducting the experiment, they are variables that can be manipulated—controlled—according to information purposes of the experiment. "Experimenters can control the variables they wish to study the effects of, or they can control who is exposed to those variables" (Kidder, 1981:17).

Analysts in the "good-looking but dangerous" case, for example, systematically varied information concerning attractiveness while holding other conditions constant, e.g., background of offenders. Evaluators of the dislocated workers program controlled the availability of program services to specific workers; some received program services, others did not. The ability to control relevant factors is a requirement of true experiments.

When analysts control experimental conditions (e.g., who enters a program), they can observe what happens after exposure to the experimental or treatment program. They can observe and measure the effect they are testing after the treatment (or experimental) group has received program services. In the dislocated workers example, evaluators measured levels of UI benefits and earnings at different time intervals after subjects were assigned to the program.

The ability to link treatment and subsequent levels of the condition expected to be affected does not guarantee that the treatment caused subsequent conditions to change. The level of earnings is affected by many factors, from individual ability and luck to the general condition of the economy. Simply observing earnings after participation in the program does not demonstrate that the program had any effect on those earnings. Higher earnings after program participation may have been produced by factors other than the program, such as a hike in legally required minimum wages. By the same token, lower earnings after participating in the program do not prove that the program was a failure; they may have been even lower if the program did not exist. The point is that factors other than the treatment program may have caused or produced the outcomes.

Campbell and Stanley (1966) have identified factors other than the treatment program that could explain changes in intended outcomes. These rival explanations challenge and undermine cause-effect relationships in experimental studies. Such threats to the accuracy of causal statements are categorized as threats to the "internal validity" of experiments.

Internal validity is concerned with whether the experimental stimuli (e.g., physically attractive and less-attractive offenders) made the difference in study results or whether findings resulted from uncontrolled extraneous factors. With respect to public programs, "the extent to which an experimental study has internal validity is the extent to which it determines that the program rather than some other factor 'caused' the impact on society" (Clark, 1976:8). A major source of rival explanations in assessing cause-effect relations is referred to as the effects of *history*. The history threat to the internal validity of findings takes four specific forms (Mohr, 1988:52–56).

1. *External Events.* Events occurring during the study might influence experimental subjects (beyond the experimental variable itself) and provide competing explanations for results. If the effects of video presentations in promoting healthful practices among the elderly are being studied, the advent of a flu epidemic in the community rather than the video presentations may cause experimental subjects to change their health practices. "The longer the time lapse between preprogram and postprogram measurements, the higher the probability that historical events will become potential rival hypotheses" (Nachmias, 1979:25). External events are a particular problem in field experiments where subjects are exposed to a variety of influences in the natural environment.

2. *Maturation Processes.* Biological and psychological changes in subjects occurring during the course of the experiment may influence their responses, e.g., fatigue, motivation, physical and intellectual growth. Experimental subjects may perform better or worse, not because of program effects, but because of reduced interest, weariness, and other factors, thereby producing competing explanations for observed changes.

3. *Testing.* Experimenters often conduct a pretest of subjects to provide a baseline against which change between pretest and post-test scores can be measured. However, differences between preprogram and postprogram scores may be due to experience gained in preprogram testing, not to program effects. A program designed to improve English-language proficiency could incorrectly report improvement if the same test was used in the pretest and post-test phases since subjects may have become "testwise."

4. *Attrition.* Some subjects may leave the experiment before it is over, and their post-test scores will not be available. This is a problem if those who leave the program would be affected by the experiment in a systematically different way than those who stay. For example, if children who move out of a school midway in a reading experiment are lower achievers, the results of the experiment would be biased toward success.

To minimize potential rival explanations of changes in subjects exposed to the experimental condition (e.g., program services), analysts compare changes on the variable of interest in those who have received the treatment with those who have not received the treatment. The assumption underlying this comparison is that control group subjects have been influenced by essentially similar historical and maturation factors that also influence experimental subjects. If true, differences between the amount of change experienced by experimental subjects and change experienced by control subjects is attributable to the treatment program and not extraneous factors.

Comparison of Conditions

Comparision is inherent to experiments. In the laboratory experiment, the attractiveness of offenders and the nature of sentencing judgments made against them were compared among experimental and control groups. In the field experiment, UI benefits and earnings were compared among experimental and control groups. Comparison is used to analyze the joint occurrence of program services and outcomes.

> A comparison is made of a group that was introduced to the policy with one that was not, or of the group's scores on the target variables before and after implementation of the policy. In the former case, an experimental group is compared with a comparison group; in the latter, an experimental group is compared with itself. (Nachmias, 1979:23)

Comparison in itself is insufficient in establishing causal relationships. Campbell and Stanley (1966) identify threats to the quality of information when making comparisons.

- *Selection Bias.* Making comparisons between groups incorrectly believed to be equivalent is a factor adversely affecting internal validity. If analysts evaluating alternate programs for reducing drug usage in high schools decide to implement the program at one school and use students at another school as a comparison group, experimental findings are susceptible to selection bias if students attending one school have different attitudes toward drugs from those at the other. In other words, differences in results may be due to differences in the attitudes of students in the two schools rather than to program effects. Consequently, the two groups are not equivalent, producing invalid comparisons.
- *Interaction of Selection with Other Factors.* Selection bias interacting with other factors (maturation, history, and so forth) contributes to problems of internal validity in experimentation. Even when experimental and control groups reflect similar preprogram scores, other differences such as ability and interest may result in one group achieving higher scores on postprogram measures. Given these effects of interaction, studies comparing volunteers with nonvolunteers, for example, should be skeptically viewed. Suppose sixty cocaine users are identified and thirty of them volunteer for a drug rehabilitation program. If the program reduces cocaine use in the volunteers and the control group experiences no reduction, it cannot be concluded that the program would be effective for nonvolunteers. Perhaps the volunteers were motivated to "get clean," and the program produced effects only because the volunteers were receptive and motivated.

To control these threats to the internal validity of findings, true experiments require analysts to randomly assign subjects to treatment and con-trol groups.

Random Assignment of Subjects

The objective of assigning subjects to receive an experimental treat-ment (e.g., to receive program services) or to be part of the control group is to produce two groups that are alike in all ways that might affect out-comes of the study. Policy studies using true experiments employ a specific method of achieving this equivalence among groups—random assignment (randomization).

The assignment process is central to true experiments. The procedure for random assignment is similar to random sampling discussed in a previ-ous chapter.

> Most often, a fairly large group of subjects is identified as the set of objects to be observed. This set is then sub-divided into experimental and control groups (or assigned to whatever treatments the experiment will investigate) by some random process, such as picking names out of a hat or employing a table of random numbers. (Mohr, 1988:45)

Because it requires control of which subjects are assigned to which group, randomization necessitates centralized assignment: an accessible pool of participating subjects must be identified prior to the assignment procedure. Thus, true experiments must be subject to a significant degree of control by analysts.

The result of random assignment is that every subject has an equal chance of being in the experimental or in the control group. Since no char-acteristic of the individual influenced which group that person is assigned to, it is probable the two groups are alike with respect to potential biasing characteristics. As with random sampling, the probability that there may be important chance differences between the groups decreases with increases in the number of subjects. Because it ensures equivalence in composition of experimental and control groups, randomization allows analysts to attri-bute postprogram differences between groups to program services rather than to differences in motivation, ability, growth, external events, and so forth.

DESIGNING TRUE EXPERIMENTS

Experimental methods are categorized based on the extent they incorporate fundamental features of true experiments: controlled comparison and ran-domization of subjects. Using these characteristics, three types of re-search designs can be identified based on how well they control sources of invalidity: true experiments, quasi experiments, and pre-experiments. Sub-sequent sections of this chapter discuss each of these experimental techniques, identifying their strengths and limitations in generating accurate and useful policy information.

True Experimental Designs

True experiments share basic features of controlled comparison and random assignment of subjects to treatment and control groups and consequently are superior in controlling extraneous sources of invalidity. These basic features are applied through a variety of specific formats or designs, each of which arranges treatment (experimental) and control groups in such a way as to reduce specific threats to the internal validity of findings. The following examples illustrate common designs used in true experiments.

PRETEST/POST-TEST CONTROL GROUP DESIGN

This classic experimental design contains at least one experimental group and at least one control group. As in all true experimental designs, assignment to the groups is random. Pretreatment and post-treatment (e.g., before and after receiving program services) measurements are made for the experimental group; parallel measurements are made for the control group. The difference between pre- and postmeasurement scores provides a measure of change occurring during the experimental period for each group. Since the design ensures that the experimental and the control group are essentially equivalent, differences in change between the experimental and the control group can more persuasively be attributed to the effects of the treatment (e.g., program services). Table 11.2 provides a visual summary of the Pretest/Post-test Control Group Design.

POST-TEST ONLY CONTROL GROUP DESIGN

The post-test only control group design (Table 11.3) deletes pretested groups altogether. Subjects are randomly assigned to one of the two groups. The experimental group receives the treatment and a post-treatment test. The control group receives the post-treatment test alone.

TABLE 11.2   The Pretest/Post-test Control Group Design

SUBJECTS	PRETESTED	EXPOSED TO TREATMENT	POST-TESTED
Experimental Group	Yes	Yes	Yes
Control Group	Yes	No	Yes

TABLE 11.3   The Post-test Only Control Group Design

SUBJECTS	PRETESTED	EXPOSED TO TREATMENT	POST-TESTED
Experimental Group	No	Yes	Yes
Control Group	No	No	Yes

This design has appeal because of its relative ease of implementation; no pretesting is required. For analysts expected to evaluate program impacts after programs have been implemented, this is an appealing benefit. Furthermore, the design retains many of the analytic qualities of true experiments. The fact that subjects are randomly assigned provides assurance that whatever differences do exist are randomly distributed between the two groups, alleviating problems of selection and selection interaction. With no pretesting, factors of testing are removed as sources of rival explanations. These sources of invalid information become irrelevant since initial measures are not taken of experimental and control groups. However, the lack of a pretest means that the amount of change attributable to the experimental treatment can not be directly measured. Denzin (1970:153) cautions that analysts "must still be sensitive to the fact that there is no substitute for before measures when the true and complete effects of experimental treatments are to be determined. . . ."

Limitations and Uses of True Experiments in Policy Analysis

The benefit of true experimental designs is their approach to eliminating threats to the internal validity of conclusions about causal links between programs and outcomes. The random assignment of subjects to experimental and control groups and the controlled comparison of groups allow analysts and users to be more certain that observed improvements in outcomes are attributable to program-related factors and not to nonprogram factors. According to one survey, policymakers and legislative staff believe true experiments yield persuasive evidence for program planning and policy-making purposes (Caplan, 1977:68–78).

But true experiments, like any other research approach, reflect limitations in policy research applications. The following sections discuss limitations of experimental research in fulfilling information needs.

ARTIFICIALITY

The artificiality of true experiments, particularly laboratory experiments, has been an oft-cited limitation of this approach. The argument is that analysts attempt to control too many conditions, making findings sterile, ungeneralizable, inapplicable to real-life settings and real-life people. The criticism that these experiments are poor representations of natural processes gains increased credibility as analysts strive to control more and more conditions in the study.

The artificiality of experiments can have effects on study results. Experimental subjects may respond differently to a program if they are aware they are a part of a study. The problem is that "individuals may not respond to the experimental manipulation as such, but to their interpretation of what responses these manipulations are supposed to elicit from them" (Nachmias, 1979:36).

Conversely, artificiality is advantageous under some circumstances. By establishing an artificial setting, analysts "attempt to create a situation in which the operation of variables will be clearly seen under special identified and defined conditions" (Festinger, 1971:10). In this fashion, analysts find how experimental variables affect attitudes and behaviors under pure conditions. But a following task is to

> find out how these variables interact with other variables. The possibility of application to a real-life situation rises when one knows enough about these relationships to be able to make predictions concerning a real-life situation after measurement and diagnosis of the state of affairs there. (Festinger, 1971:10)

Artificiality is consequently useful, given certain information needs. Nevertheless, the gap between experimental settings and settings in which findings are applied frequently raises questions about the usability of experimental information.

Because field experiments take place in action settings, they seem less artificial. But their major limitation is controlling extraneous variables; controlling sources of rival explanations in field experiments is typically not as complete and as successful as in laboratory experiments. Thus, the applicability of findings may be purchased at the cost of reduced confidence in the internal validity of results.

GENERALIZABILITY

A related concern about true experiments focuses on the generalizability of findings, often referred to as "external validity." Before discussing external validity, it should be emphasized that internal validity remains the principal concern of analysts conducting experiments. If analysts are unsure "that the experimental manipulations caused the results reported, then it makes little sense to worry about whether results can be generalized to other situations" (Clark, 1976:10). Also, many policy studies are idiosyncratic, context dependent, tailored to individual requirements of specific programs. Generalizing beyond these programs may be unnecessary from the perspective of decision makers.

External validity is concerned with the representativeness and generalizability of experimental findings, e.g., to what populations and settings can experimental results be applied? Even if a study confirms that program services resulted in improvements in program recipients, and even if the study seems internally valid, analysts and users may still need to determine whether such improvements can be expected in different settings, different conditions. External validity can be important to decision makers since it provides a basis for assessing whether a program can be applied elsewhere.

External validity then raises concerns of how relevant findings are beyond the confines of the experimental setting. To what extent, if any, can findings generated in the "good-looking but dangerous" laboratory experiment be generalized to sentencing judgments in diverse courtroom situations? To what extent can experimental results in Delaware be applied to different settings? In policy research, skilled users are alert to factors in the environment in which an experiment is conducted, and to the implications of the setting for the probable applicability of findings in their own communities.

SERVICE DELIVERY

Staff concerns for program delivery pose threats in conducting field experiments in agencies. Administrators may be understandably reluctant to assign subjects to control conditions because they believe their professional obligation is to serve all who qualify. Political pressures may make it impractical to provide a program to one group in the community and not to others. Weiss (1972:63) adds:

> The randomized assignment procedure of the experiment also creates problems. Practitioners generally want to assign people to "treatments" on the basis of their professional knowledge and experience. They want to decide who can most benefit from service and which kind of service is most suitable, and not to leave the process to chance.

Creating and maintaining experimental conditions and controlling for extraneous variables is a challenge for analysts conducting experiments in field settings. Approaches to meeting that challenge are examined in later sections.

ETHICAL CONCERNS

Limitations of true experiments arise from ethical and moral considerations. Objections to random assignments of persons on ethical grounds often emphasize the deprivation or risks believed to be sustained by control group participants (Boruch et al., 1985:168–69). Politicians and agency administrators may believe it morally wrong to provide a service to some and not to others in their jurisdiction. Or they may believe it ethically wrong "to provide a government service temporarily (during the experiment) when the service could cause clients to become dependent and make them worse off after the service is terminated" (Hatry, Winnie, and Fisk, 1981:45).

Countering these objections is the argument that if the program is ineffective, then it is wasteful and wrong to offer it to clients. Randomized tests provide strong proof of a program's effectiveness or ineffectiveness, and the use of true experiments "reflects the evaluator's ethical obligation to program clients: to obtain the least equivocal estimate of program costs and effects" (Boruch et al., 1985:168).

No fixed solutions exist to guide analysts and stakeholders in resolving ethical dilemmas associated with experimental procedures. In some situations, as when there is an oversupply of clients and an undersupply of program resources, random assignment may be ethically appropriate. In other situations, concerns of denying services to control groups may be moderated through testing a number of program variations instead of an all-or-nothing allocation of program services. In yet other cases, informing participants in advance of the nature of the experiment and debriefing them after the experiment may resolve concerns. In all situations, adherence to professional and community standards of conduct must remain the principal guideline in planning and implementing policy experiments.

Other limitations associated with experiments may be avoided or minimized through effective planning and implementation efforts. In the planning stages, attempts should be made to gain the endorsement of relevant parties to the experiment. Relevant parties include public officials and agency management, community groups, and others in the policy community. Continuing attention to controlling potential sources of extraneous variables is required as the design of the experiment evolves.

During implementation, managers of the experiment attempt to "maintain the integrity of the design while allowing a certain amount of flexibility in its detail to meet unanticipated occurrences (Nachmias, 1979:43). Since there will likely be some variation from the planned implementation of the study, analysts make adjustments and qualify their research findings accordingly.

Conditions Appropriate to True Experiments

Even considering their limitations and problems, experiments provide strong evidence concerning effects of policies and programs. Controlled, randomized experiments significantly strengthen conclusions and recommendations regarding policy outcomes. The following section presents situations when experiments may be particularly appropriate in policy and program analysis (Hatry, Winnie, and Fisk, 1981:107–15; Weiss, 1972:66–67).

- *When substantial doubt exists regarding program effectiveness.* The ability of experiments to provide persuasive cause-effect relationships makes them a useful approach in resolving uncertainties concerning program benefits. To the extent findings can be generalized to the larger population of clients and recipients, the results are of increased value to policymakers.

- *When financial resources are insufficient to provide service to all eligible persons.* When resources are few and eligible applicants many, the random assignment of applicants becomes more feasible. Of course, public officials ensure that priority clients are not denied needed services. Experiments are also useful when new programs are introduced over a period of time so that delayed recipients can serve as controls for those getting program services earlier. Costly new programs that may be particularly difficult to terminate or modify once implemented are also good candidates for experiments.

- *When experiments can be safely and ethically conducted.* If withholding program services from control groups means such action could cause them harm, place them in a situation potentially dangerous (e.g., withholding police or fire protection services while testing the effects of a new program), or raise legal and ethical issues, experiments become questionable. Should analysts and decision makers decide to proceed, it may be necessary for clients to give their written consent to experimental procedures. Those participating in the experiment should be made aware of the implications of their participation, and they should be debriefed at the conclusion of the experiment. During the study, personal information gathered on participants must be gathered legally and maintained in confidence. To the extent that analysts, decision makers, and other participants agree that withdrawing service or providing services at varying levels is not likely to have damaging effects, randomized experiments become more feasible.

- *When experimental conditions can be maintained during implementation.* For a large-scale experiment spanning an extended period of time (a year or longer), controlling sources of invalidity becomes a major challenge for analysts. Policymakers, program personnel, and other participants may want to deviate from original plans, introducing elements confounding the interpretation of effects. Some of these problems can be minimized through effective planning and management of the experiment. But experiments are feasible and desirable only when basic elements of random assignment and controlled comparison can be sustained during the experimental period.

EVALUATING OUTCOMES: QUASI EXPERIMENTS

Preceding discussions enumerated political, administrative, ethical, and resource limitations constraining the use of true experiments in policy analysis. Though a powerful and elegant approach to unraveling effects of policy, features of the action setting may prevent the use of true experiments in fulfilling information needs. When events preclude true experiments, quasi experiments may be used by policy analysts.

> This approach is characterized by an effort to use the logic of experimenta- tion in situations which are not truly experimental; in such situations the investigator cannot randomly assign individuals to groups and cannot control the administration of the treatment or stimulus. (Caporaso and Roos, Jr., 1973:xvii)

Quasi experiments, then, do not fulfill the strict requirements of true experiments. They lack the ability to randomly assign persons to experi- mental and control groups, and they frequently lack genuine control groups. Unlike true experiments that attempt to rule out effects of influ- ences other than exposure to program services, quasi experiments leave sources of invalidity (i.e., rival explanations) uncontrolled. The hope is that uncontrolled sources can be assessed for their effects through gathering additional information and through statistical manipulations.

Well-designed quasi experiments are capable of ruling out many threats to the validity of policy findings. Such designs provide useful evi- dence of program effectiveness or ineffectiveness, particularly when used in conjunction with other sources of evidence. The following discussion provides a case illustration of a quasi experiment evaluating the effective- ness of an anti-drug television campaign (Domino, 1982:163–71).

"Get High on Yourself": A Quasi Experiment

Drug abuse is clearly a problem of major proportions. How to deal with it is less clear. Although studies have been conducted examining the relative effectiveness of educationally oriented programs, for example, re- sults have been mixed. As Domino comments, "the beneficial effects of drug education are at the present not documented" (1982:163).

The quasi experiment presented here was conducted to test the effec- tiveness of an antidrug television campaign called "Get High on Yourself." The campaign, televised nationwide by the National Broadcasting Com- pany, involved an hour-long variety special featuring entertainers and sport celebrities, public service announcements, and several special programs. The week-long campaign received substantial media attention, with adver- tisements and preview stories appearing in major magazines and newspa- pers.

EXPERIMENTAL PROCEDURES

Subjects were drawn from three urban high schools in a large south- western city to test the effectiveness of the program. All were volunteers.

To obtain valid responses, questionnaires included as part of the experiment were administered in class and answered anonymously.

The three high schools selected differ from one another in student makeup. School A serves a predominantly lower middle class area having a large Hispanic population. Local authorities believe the high school has a substantial drug abuse problem. In this school students were informed of the upcoming television campaign and were urged to watch television that week. A number of classes then used the televised campaign as a focus of discussion.

School B serves a more diverse area, but again, the largest single minority is Hispanic. Drug abuse is also a concern at School B. In this school no mention was made of the television campaign. The intent was to use School B as a comparison group for any changes occurring in School A.

School C serves a middle to upper middle class area with minority student enrollment under 10 percent. According to local officials, drug abuse is not a particularly important problem. The intent here was to have School C serve as a control for socioeconomic level and the various factors (e.g., differences in watching television) that could accompany differing socioeconomic levels among the three schools.

In each school, experimental procedures were aided through the cooperation of student leaders and selected teachers whose classes provided a heterogeneous sampling of the school, e.g., English and Social Studies classes. The first session of the experiment took place ten days prior to the television campaign; the second four weeks later. The same classes were tested twice—before and after the campaign. Five questionnaires were administered at each school during class time. Instructions accompanying the five questionnaires stressed anonymity and the volunteer nature of the experiment. Two of the five questionnaires surveyed the self-esteem of participants, e.g., "I normally feel warm and happy toward myself," "I usually feel inferior to others." Two questionnaires more directly addressed drug use. One asked respondents to indicate for each of thirteen classes of drugs their pattern of usage in the last two weeks. The drug categories were beer, wine, hard liquor, caffeine, tobacco, cough syrup, marijuana, inhalants, ups, downs, tranquilizers, heroin, and other narcotics. The other questionnaire sought subject attitudes toward drug use, e.g., "People who are addicted to drugs are emotionally sick," "Some drugs can make you a better person." The fifth questionnaire, administered only at the post-treatment period, asked respondents how many hours of television per day they had watched over the past two weeks and if they had watched the "Get High on Yourself" special.

FINDINGS

The major focus of the experiment was to determine if a commercially produced televison program package whose primary message was "get high on yourself" would have an effect on the self-esteem, drug use, and drug attitudes of a sample of students at three urban high schools. Statistical analysis indicated the answer was that the campaign had no measurable effect.

For example, none of the changes in self-esteem, drug use, and drug attitudes from pre- to post-treatment in any of the three schools reached statistical significance, nor were any trends toward significance identified by the analyst. The actual effect of the hour-long special "was one of boredom, and many of the youths in this study clearly indicated this in both written comments and classroom discussion" (1982:169). In general the findings appeared to agree with the results of other studies. Domino (169–70) concludes with the observation, "At the same time, it is somewhat reassuring that the impact of television may not be as substantial as most parents fear."

DESIGNING QUASI EXPERIMENTS

The Get High on Yourself study reflects limitations of quasi experiments. The comparison groups, composed of volunteers from three urban high schools, were not randomly assigned and could have differed from one another in important ways. Differences between school populations could have explained any resulting differences in pre-post changes. Historical factors—events occurring between pretesting and post-testing phases—could have been different in the schools, accounting for differences in changes. Pretests given to experimental subjects at the three schools may have affected post-test responses. Finally, there is no reason to believe the three high schools selected were representative of American secondary education, in turn limiting the generalizability of findings.

Even considering such drawbacks, the use of comparison groups and the pre-post testing provided evidence on the effects of the program. The analysts also enhanced the accuracy and generalizability of findings through comparing their findings to additional sources of information, e.g., prior studies of the effects of television campaigns on drug usage. They found their results paralleled the results of similar studies, diminishing the criticisms of data accuracy and relevancy typical when using quasi experimental designs. The following quasi experimental designs include attempts to control for major sources of invalid information when true experimentation is not possible. To accomplish this partial control, they creatively use the principles of pre-post measurement and comparison with other groups.

Time Series Designs

Time series designs are quasi experiments frequently used by policy analysts. Their use involves a series of measurements at intervals before a program begins and after its introduction (Figure 11.1). "It thus becomes possible to see whether the measures immediately before and after the program are a continuation of earlier patterns or whether they mark a decisive change" (Weiss, 1972:68).

Time series designs are feasible when adequate historical data exists and when underlying trends are consistent and likely to remain so in the absence of new programs. They are also most appropriate when "the link between the program intervention and the outcomes being measured is close and direct so no other major events are likely to have had a significant influence . . ." (Hatry, Winnie, and Fisk, 1981:28).

A noted drawback to these designs is the difficulty in controlling for events that may parallel the program's introduction and affect measured differences (Campbell and Stanley, 1966:39). Happenings independent of the program and occurring during the experiment may cause observed changes. When analysts can account for such influences of history on findings, the credibility of results is enhanced.

Time series designs have several variations. One of the more important variations is "multiple time series designs," designs including at least one comparison group in the experiment. If analysts can locate similar comparison groups elsewhere and take periodic measures of these groups over the same time span, it becomes possible to test effects of history on findings, improving the validity of resulting information.

An example of multiple time series designs is the Connecticut crackdown on speeding program (Campbell and Ross, 1968:33–53). Analysts evaluated this program partly on its effectiveness in reducing the number of traffic fatalities per 100,000 population. Collecting reports of traffic fatalities for periods before and after the program was implemented, their examination indicated a reduction in deaths coinciding with the program's implementation. However, the possibility that nonprogram factors—weather

FIGURE 11.1 Time Series Design

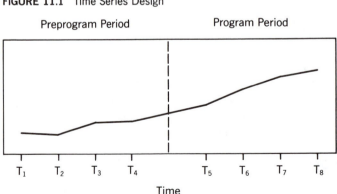

conditions, improved vehicle safety, national safety campaigns—might have resulted in the measured decline could not be excluded as rival explanations. To assess these possible sources of invalidity, analysts compared Connecticut's fatality rates with fatality rates in four neighboring states. Comparisons revealed that Connecticut's fatality rate declined relative to adjoining states, strengthening the conclusion that the speed enforcement program had some effect in reducing fatalities. A significant advantage of multiple time series design is the ability to rule out rival explanations for program effects, e.g., reduced traffic fatalities.

Nonequivalent Control Group Designs

In designs based on nonequivalent comparison groups, available population segments are used as comparison groups. Pre- and post-test measurements are made for the experimental and comparison segments, and results compared. If comparison groups do not reflect changes occurring in the experimental group, as in the Connecticut illustration, it becomes more convincing that program-related factors were responsible for observed outcomes.

Nonequivalent control group designs assume varied forms. They may compare a jurisdiction having the program with similar jurisdictions not having the program, evidenced in the Connecticut illustration. Or within jurisdictions, comparison groups may be population areas not served by the program.

> A state supervising a number of county programs, for example, might find important service delivery variations among them that should be compared. If some counties do not implement any version of the program, the no-program counties also can be compared with the counties with program variations. Local governments might compare program variations in different police, fire, or solid waste collection districts, or variations in library or recreational facilities. (Hatry, Winnie, and Fisk, 1981:36–37)

Nonequivalent control group designs are useful when comparison groups can be selected for which adequate statistical data are available and when groups are sufficiently similar to enable meaningful comparisons. Acquiring adequate statistical data and identifying similar comparison groups can prove difficult. Comparable data may be lacking or nonexistent. Even when statistics are collected, what is collected and how it is collected and maintained vary among and within jurisdictions, complicating data analysis and interpretation.

A major question introduced above in using these designs is how to make comparison segments similar to the experimental group. Lacking randomization procedures characteristic of true experiments, comparison groups may significantly differ in composition from experimental groups, e.g., in interest, motivation, socioeconomic status, and other aspects.

Sometimes analysts will attempt to make comparison more equivalent to experimental groups through "matching"—pairing experimental group members and comparison group members on variables believed to be particularly relevant for program effects. Evaluators of career criminal programs, for instance, have used comparison groups made up of noncareer criminal offenders who were matched with offenders in career criminal programs according to the type of crime they had committed (e.g., burglary with burglary, robbery with robbery). The crime committed is an important variable affecting program effects such as conviction rates and sentence length. The closer the match, the more powerful the nonequivalent control group design becomes in isolating program effects from extraneous factors. But for a number of reasons, matching is less satisfactory than random assignment.

> Not the least is that we often cannot define the characteristics on which people should be matched. That is, we don't know which characteristics will affect whether the person benefits from the program or not. We may have matched on age, sex, race, and IQ, when the important factor is motivation. As some wit has said, if we knew the key characteristics for matching, we wouldn't need the study. (Weiss, 1972:69–70)

The better matched the experimental and comparison groups are, the better this design will control for the effects of history, maturation, and other threats to internal validity. The main concern with nonequivalent control designs is selection bias and its interaction with other factors—making comparisons with groups incorrectly believed to be equivalent to one another. It remains a concern unless analysts are able to randomly assign persons to experimental and control conditions, or unless analysts provide additional sources of evidence, e.g., related studies, to minimize threats to information quality.

Patched-Up Designs

Quasi experimental designs are approximations of true experimental designs. In constructing quasi experiments for specific purposes, there are "no uniformly accepted standards for making many methodological choices" (Kohfeld and Springer, 1983:40).

In other words, flexibility of design is a significant feature of quasi experiments. The variations of quasi-experimental designs possible are limitless, allowing analysts to control sources of error likely to surface in a given research setting. Campbell and Stanley (1966) speak of a "patched-up design" which adds controls to minimize sources of competing explanations: "As part of this strategy, the experimenter must be alert to the rival interpretations . . . which the design leaves open and must look for analysis of the data, or feasible extensions of the data, which will rule these out" (227).

Patched-up designs are constructed to address particular threats to validity that may exist in assessing program effects. Patched-up designs explicitly recognize that quasi experiments do not offer a standardized approach to evaluating causal links. Quasi experiments are a "mixture of methods and judgement" (Cordray, 1986) requiring analysts to tailor study design to the particular information need.

LIMITATIONS AND USES OF QUASI EXPERIMENTS IN POLICY ANALYSIS

Quasi experiments incorporate the rationale of true experiments but lack the ability of controlled comparison and of randomly assigning subjects to experimental and control conditions. The consequences are that nonrandomized experiments may yield misleading information when evaluating program effects. Boruch et al. (1985:172) noted that when research experiments were run in parallel, results based on nonrandomized designs differed from those based on randomized designs:

> That there are exceptions where the results are the same, is also clear. The problem, however, is that one often cannot know in advance whether this will be true. The state of the art is well-developed enough to anticipate chronic threats to validity of analysis in nonrandomized experiments, but not sufficiently well-developed to predict them accurately and to accommodate them.

When true experiments are not possible in policy settings, quasi experiments enable analysts to rule out at least some threats to the validity of cause-effect relationships. Additional information sources and statistical analyses allow analysts to test for the effects of yet other possible rival interpretations. Being able to rule out some competing explanations for observed program effects is an improvement over not being able to rule out any. The point is that quasi experiments often have the overriding advantage of practicality and feasibility in policy research. Well-conceived and well-implemented quasi experiments yield findings useful for many information purposes, particularly when additional sources of information are employed in improving information quality.

EVALUATING OUTCOMES: PRE-EXPERIMENTS

In evaluating program effects, analysts may also use designs known as pre-experimental. The inherent weakness of pre-experimental designs is the lack of systematic pre-post and control comparisons. "In all cases, they leave considerable room for differing interpretations of how much change has occurred and how much of the observed changes was due to the operation of the program" (Weiss, 1972:74). To compensate for this weakness, supplementary data and statistical manipulations are used to strengthen findings. Three pre-experimental designs employed in policy analysis are the One-Shot Case Study, the One-Group Preprogram/Postprogram Design, and the Static-Group Comparison Design.

One-Shot Case Study Design

In this pre-experimental design, a program is implemented with the intention of producing specific effects. The effects on the group receiving program services are observed at some point after implementation. No measures are taken before program initiation.

Precisely understanding effects of program services is difficult without before measures. A basis of comparison is needed to assess differences before and after treatment. Consequently, analysts reconstruct preprogram measures through means such as referencing earlier research documenting the need for the program, conducting interviews with agency personnel and program recipients on their status prior to program implementation, and analyzing historical records containing preprogram data (typically personal and social information) on clients. Still, one-shot case study designs remain "vulnerable to many confounding effects (history, maturation, selective drop-outs, the particularities of program implementation), and the evaluator has to determine how relevant such factors are likely to be" (Weiss, 1972:76).

One-Group Preprogram/Postprogram Design

Unlike the one-shot case study design, this pre-experiment requires analysts to make at least two separate observations on identical groups. Participants are tested before program implementation, and after the delivery of program services the same participants are again tested. Differences in scores between the measurement periods are statistically examined to evaluate program effects. The One-Group Preprogram/Postprogram Design parallels the before and after true experiment, but lacks a control group.

The absence of a control group allows the intrusion of extraneous factors hampering the validity of findings. These factors create rival interpretations to the hypothesis that the program was responsible for observed differences. A major limitation is that changes other than the experimental program may have produced observed differences. The longer the time lapse between preprogram and postprogram measurements, the greater the chance that history becomes a credible rival interpretation in explaining findings.

This pre-experimental design is an improvement over the one-shot case study because it features repeated observations (before and after testing), but as Denzin (1970:169) observes, "Repeated observations raise problems that are best resolved by adding at least one comparison group." The One-Group Preprogram/Postprogram Design is applicable to policy settings in which programs are expected to produce immediate changes. Pre- and postquestionnaires, for example, can be used to measure the immediate effects of substance abuse prevention training on student attitudes.

Static-Group Comparison Design

This pre-experimental design relies on the use of two groups, both observed only at the postprogram phase. Here, experimental group members exposed to program services are compared with another group whose members have not been exposed to program treatment. Comparisons are made to evaluate effects, if any. The intent of analysts using the static-group comparison design is to make the two groups equivalent so valid comparisons are possible.

Since no before observations are collected, valid comparisons require that the two groups differ only in that one group was exposed to the program treatment and the other group was not. The basic concern associated with this design consequently is selection bias—the lack of equivalency between groups.

Several approaches are used in making groups more equivalent. Some have been discussed, such as reconstructing pretest measures through the use of program records and referencing prior background research on the problem. Matching the groups on relevant personal and social factors is yet another possibility. Of the three pre-experimental designs discussed, the static-group design is preferred because of its use of comparison groups.

LIMITATIONS AND USES OF PRE-EXPERIMENTS IN POLICY ANALYSIS

In comparison to quasi experiments, pre-experiments control fewer factors affecting information quality. Employing these techniques increases the chance of producing inconclusive information linking program services with effects on recipients.

But several approaches strengthen pre-experiments, e.g., developing additional sources of data, conducting statistical analyses. Further, in the absence of other alternatives, they take on added appeal. Pre-experiments may be used to

> provide a preliminary look at the effectiveness of a program. If, for example, before-and-after study (with all the contaminating effects of outside events, maturation, testing, and so on) finds little change in participants, then the program is probably having little effect. It may not be worthwhile to invest in more rigorous evaluation. (Weiss, 1972:74)

Pre-experiments may also be used when comparison groups are unavailable, when fast results are needed, and when analysts evaluate programs that have been in operation for a period of time. Pre-experiments occupy useful informational roles in policy research.

TRIANGULATION AND EVALUATING OUTCOMES

Experimental designs represent a particular approach to evaluating outcomes. The logic of experiments relies heavily on eliminating the possibility that observed changes might be attributable to some cause other than the experimental treatment—a given policy, program, or activity. In policy research, analysts frequently supplement experimental logic with additional information designed to provide increased evidence concerning the plausibility of causal links.

The reason is that policies and programs are complex, multifaceted, composed of many interacting components. They are "rarely so unidimensional that they warrant a single research methodology" (Sylvia, Meier, and Gunn, 1985:101). Employing multiple and overlapping measures—triangulation—is an effective approach to evaluating complex policies and programs in terms of their impacts. It is also effective in yielding information of increased accuracy and relevance, adding to its subsequent usability. More powerful evidence of program effects is provided when results are confirmed through multiple processes.

Triangulation assumes a variety of formats in assessing effects. Boruch (1976:43) discusses evaluating major components of a program using true experiments and assessing remaining components using quasi experiments:

> There is often ample justification . . . that components of a complex program (rather than the total program) should be tested using randomized experiments. The component evaluations can often be engineered nicely into a larger quasi experimental framework for assessment. And when conducted properly, they can help to identify how well microelements of a social program are working, even if political or ethical constraints prevent randomized tests of macroelements or of the complete program.

Triangulation methods are not limited to combining experimental techniques. Research methods discussed in prior chapters (participant observation, content analysis, surveys and interviews) enhance the persuasiveness of findings regarding program outcomes. Using additional methods, data sources, and so on, serves to cancel errors arising from a particular data gathering procedure, whether true experiments, quasi experiments, pre-experiments, or any other single approach to causal analysis. Multiple approaches allow analysts to compare results, seeing how they differ and what they share in common, providing a better-supported empirical basis for conclusions about program impacts. The diversity and complexity of public programs require analysts to use a range of skills in addressing information.

CONCLUDING COMMENTS

This chapter explored the use of experimental techniques when evaluating policy effects and outcomes. It introduced experimental methods employed by analysts studying program effectiveness and examined their usefulness in producing decision-relevant research information. Three experimental techniques have been identified: true experiments, quasi experiments, and pre-experiments. The three approaches can be placed on a continuum based on how adequately each controls sources of internal validity.

True experiments, occupying one extreme of the continuum, are the more powerful of the three approaches in assessing program effects, i.e., in controlling sources of rival explanations for observed programmatic outcomes. Whether conducted in a laboratory or field setting, true experiments interpret policy impacts through comparing changes in experimental and control groups. Their use better ensures that changes observed in experimental groups are due to program services, not to extraneous nonprogram influences. Their major features are controlled comparisons and the random assignment of subjects. The emphasis is on the control and manipulation of relevant variables, and on comparisons of outcomes between experimental and control groups. Two common types of true experimental designs are the pretest/post-test one control group design and the post-test only control group design. Both incorporate major features of true experiments.

Although true experiments provide strong evidence causally linking program services to effects on client groups, they are not without drawbacks. Findings may be distorted due to the obtrusive nature of experiments. Participants, recognizing they are part of an experiment, may respond differently to a program than would otherwise have been the case. Pretesting individuals may sensitize them to the nature of the experiment, affecting postprogram scores. Experimenters themselves may be a source of bias, unknowingly communicating effects they are looking for from subjects. Administrators may be reluctant to assign persons to control conditions, believing their professional obligation is to serve all who qualify. Randomly assigning individuals to experimental and control conditions may be objected to on ethical and moral grounds by agency personnel, public figures, and community groups.

Some of these limitations can be minimized through effective planning and implementation efforts, e.g., ongoing collaboration with users, gaining the endorsement of relevant parties. The results may justify the efforts: controlled, randomized experiments significantly strengthen findings, conclusions, and recommendations when assessing program effects.

Quasi experiments occupy a middle ground on the continuum linking the three experimental approaches. They lack the ability to randomly assign subjects to experimental and control conditions and consequently lack true control groups. They leave sources of invalidity uncontrolled—frequently selection and selection interaction remain problematic.

But when true experiments are not possible due to political, administrative, ethical, economic, and other reasons, quasi experiments possess the advantage of feasibility. Through gathering additional information, combined with using specialized statistical techniques, quasi experiments are capable of ruling out many threats to the validity of the resulting information. Some of the more frequently employed quasi experiments rely on time series designs and nonequivalent control group designs.

Quasi experiments incorporate the logic of true experiments but do not feature some of their primary characteristics such as controlled comparisons and randomization. The implications are that findings are more difficult to interpret in comparison to true experiments, and that quasi experiments when used alone increase the risk of producing inconclusive results. They are practical when true experiments are not; and they are flexible, allowing analysts to create designs responsive to sources of error likely to arise in a given experimental situation. If well planned and implemented, quasi experiments yield information useful in examining program outcomes.

Pre-experiments occupy the lesser position on the continuum. They are weaker than quasi experiments, unable to control for multiple sources of rival interpretations for observed effects. Analysts employing these techniques alone increase the likelihood of producing inconclusive information regarding policy impacts. Pre-experimental designs include the one-shot case study, the one-group preprogram/postprogram format, and the static-group comparison approach.

Pre-experimental findings are strengthened through incorporating additional data sources and through data analysis techniques. If true experiments and quasi experiments are not feasible, pre-experiments become more useful. They may be used to provide initial assessments of program performance, or used when comparison groups are unavailable or when quick results are needed by decision makers.

Whatever experimental techniques are used, conclusions about impacts are enhanced through employing multiple and overlapping approaches to measurement. Triangulation includes combining experimental techniques in a single study and incorporating additional information sources such as surveys and interviews, documentary analysis, and participant observation. These additional methods and data sources serve to cancel errors emanating from a single data gathering procedure, providing a better basis for comparing results and yielding better confirmed information assessing cause-effect relations.

The ongoing intent of experimental methods is to causally link program services to effects on target groups—to rule out sources of invalidity serving as competing explanations for observed changes. But a technically valid study provides no guarantee of its utility in decision making. Assuming research use occurs as a normal by-product of a technically sound experiment is inviting undervalued findings and recommendations. In policy research, issues of technical validity must be coupled with utilization issues if results are to make a difference in the life conditions of people.

REFERENCES

Bloom, Howard S. 1987. "Lessons from the Delaware Dislocated Worker Pilot Program," *Evaluation Review,* 11:157–77.

Boruch, Robert F. 1976. "Coupling Randomized Experiments and Approximations to Experiments in Social Program Evaluation," in Ilene N. Bernstein, ed., *Validity Issues in Evaluation Research.* Sage Contemporary Social Science Issues, no. 23. Beverly Hills, CA: Sage Publications.

Boruch, Robert F., David Rindskopf, Patricia S. Anderson, Imat R. Amidjaya, and Douglas M. Jansson. 1985. "Randomized Experiments for Evaluating and Planning Local Programs: A Summary on Appropriateness and Feasibility," pp. 165–75, in Eleanor Chelimsky, ed., *Program Evaluation: Patterns and Directions.* Washington, DC: American Society for Public Administration.

Campbell, Donald T., and H. Lawrence Ross. 1968. "The Connecticut Crackdown on Speeding: Time-Series Data in Quasi Experimental Analysis," in *Law Society and Review* 2:33–53.

Campbell, Donald T., and Julian C. Stanley. 1966. *Experimental and Quasi Experimental Designs for Research.* Chicago: Rand McNally.

Caplan, Nathan. 1977. "Social Research and National Policy: What Gets Used, by Whom, for What Purpose, and with What Effects?" in S. S. Nagel, ed., *Policy Studies Review Annual.* Beverly Hills, CA: Sage Publications.

Caporaso, James A., and Leslie L. Roos, Jr., eds. 1973. *Quasi Experimental Approaches: Testing Theory and Evaluating Policy.* Evanston, IL: Northwestern University Press.

Clark, Lawrence P. 1976. *Designs for Evaluating Social Programs.* Croton-on-Hudson, NY: Policy Studies Associates.

Cordray, David S. 1986. "Quasi Experimental Analysis: A Mixture of Methods and Judgement," in W. M. K. Trochim, ed., *Advances in Quasi Experimental Design and Analysis.* New Directions for Program Evaluation, no. 31 (Fall 1986). San Francisco: Jossey-Bass Publishers.

Denzin, Norman K. 1970. *The Research Act: A Theoretical Introduction to Sociological Methods.* New York: McGraw-Hill.

Domino, George. 1982. "'Get High on Yourself': The Effectiveness of a Television Campaign on Self-Esteem, Drug Use, and Drug Attitudes," *Journal of Drug Education* 12:2.

Festinger, Leon. 1971. "Laboratory Experiments," pp. 9–24, in William M. Evan, ed., *Organizational Experiments: Laboratory and Field Research.* New York: Harper & Row.

Hatry, Harry P., Richard E. Winnie, and Donald M. Fisk. 1981. *Practical Program Evaluation for State and Local Officials,* 2d ed. Washington, DC: Urban Institute.

Kidder, Louise H. 1981. *Research Methods in Social Relations,* 4th ed. New York: Holt, Rinehart & Winston.

Kohfeld, Carol W., and J. Fred Springer. 1983. "Evaluating Career Criminal Prosecution Units: Technical and Ethical Dilemmas in Quasi Experimental Design," in J. McDavid, F. Ricks, and W. Shera, eds., *Competing Perspectives in Evaluation.* Victoria, BC: Canadian Evaluation Society.

Nachmias, David. 1979. *Public Policy Evaluation: Approaches and Methods.* New York: St. Martin's Press.

Meehan, Eugene J. 1981. *Reasoned Argument in Social Science: Linking Research to Policy.* Westport, CT: Greenwood Press.

Mohr, Lawrence B. 1988. *Impact Analysis for Program Evaluation.* Chicago: Dorsey Press.

Sigall, Harold, and Nancy Ostrove. 1975. "Beautiful but Dangerous: Effects of Offender Attractiveness and Nature of the Crime on Juridic Judgment," *Journal of Personality and Social Psychology* 31:3.

Sylvia, Ronald, Kenneth J. Meier, and Elizabeth M. Gunn. 1985. *Program Planning and Evaluation for the Public Manager.* Monterey, CA: Brooks/Cole Publishing.

Weiss, Carol H. 1972. *Evaluation Research: Methods for Assessing Program Effectiveness.* Englewood Cliffs, NJ: Prentice-Hall.

12

Analysis of Costs in Policy Research

"There's no such thing as a free lunch." This often-repeated statement summarizes the common sense basis for including cost considerations in analyzing public policies. Decision makers operate in a context of scarcity, confronting hard-pressed competing demands for programs and services. Accomplishing policy goals requires expending resources—and foregoing the opportunity to use those resources to pursue other objectives.

Concerns about the efficient and effective application of scarce resources make cost and economic analyses important contributors to decisions throughout policy processes. At the policy clarification stage, decision makers are concerned about estimating the resource requirements of policy proposals. At the policy choice stage, decision makers are interested in which decisions provide the greatest public benefit for the dollar. At the implementation stage, managers are concerned about ways to improve program efficiency, the ratio of resources used to results accomplished. In evaluating programs, the cost of program accomplishments is a relevant input.

ECONOMIC ANALYSIS: A POINT OF VIEW

"To speak of an economic approach to policy inquiry is not to refer to the consideration of economic issues or questions in any narrow sense" (Paris

and Reynolds, 1983:79). Economic analysis is not the study of unemployment, inflation, or foreign trade; it is the application of a perspective to the
analysis of public policy. This perspective, or point of view, serves the roles
of

- explicitly identifying resources required by specific public policies;
- comparing alternative means of meeting policy objectives to identify
  those that are most efficient (require the fewest resources to produce
  desired outcomes); and
- assessing policy options to "figure out if the benefits of a program
  outweigh its costs" (Gramlich, 1981:4).

To provide the preceding information for stakeholders, policy analysts have
developed a variety of techniques. This chapter introduces basic tools used
in the economic analysis of public policies and programs, and clarifies them
through illustrations.

The remainder of the chapter discusses techniques of cost analysis in
three sections. The first section discusses methods for making the costs of
public programs explicit. Two tasks are involved: (1) identifying the full
range of resources required by a program, and (2) attaching dollar values
to those resources.

A second section introduces techniques used by policy analysts to compare the relative efficiency of alternative means for accomplishing a policy
objective. This section assumes the necessity or desirability of the policy
outcome and provides means of attaining desired outcomes with the least
expenditure of funds.

A third section focuses on cost-benefit analyses. This approach provides a framework for considering whether the public benefits of a program
or policy outweigh the cost to the public. Cost-benefit approaches take on
an ambitious objective—analyzing the ability of policies to generally improve the public welfare.

DETERMINING THE COSTS OF PUBLIC ACTION

The determination of costs is fundamental to economic analysis of public
policy. Analysts cannot pose questions of efficiency or net benefit in the
absence of reasonably accurate estimates of the resources required by a program. Despite their central importance, costs are sometimes inadequately considered in policy research. "Ignoring costs altogether" has been identified
as one of the most common pitfalls in analyzing policies (Bickner, 1980:57).
Reasons for this omission may be technical, e.g., training in analysis methodologies that ignore economic issues, or political, e.g., some policy objectives are seen as so important that cost is irrelevant.

Less obvious errors in cost analysis result from "counting only a portion of program costs" (Patton and Sawicki, 1986:146). In 1973, when Congress passed legislation providing financial support for patients in need of kidney dialysis, estimates of foreseeable program costs were in the low millions. By 1978, the program required $1 billion, half the total National Institute of Health budget. Five years later, costs climbed to $1.8 billion. "The failure to provide an accurate estimate of costs led to an unexpectedly large cost to the taxpayer and made it impossible to implement other programs also dealing with pressing health problems" (Posavac and Carey, 1984:262).

What is a Cost?

The costs of public programs may seem obvious. Costs might simply be equated with the cash outlays of government. Examples of cash outlay include salaries to personnel administering programs or providing services (e.g., administrators, physicians, and nurses in a rural health clinic); the cost of equipment required to provide services (e.g., medical instruments); the cost of resources consumed in providing services (e.g., vaccine, syringes, medical supplies); and the cost of physical space required by the program (e.g., leasing office space). However, cash outlays only partially reflect the costs that analysts identify for public programs. The reasons lie in basic principles of public sector economic analysis.

Government as Public Agent

In the logic of economic analysis, government is assigned a "special and circumscribed" role (Rothenberg, 1975:64). This role is defined within the context of the perceived benefits of a "free market" economy—an economy that allows production, consumption, and price to be determined through voluntary transactions between producers and consumers. Two basic assumptions about the operation of a free market are important to understanding the special role of government in this perspective.

1. Because decisions to buy and sell are seen as voluntary, each market transaction is "deemed to reveal an improvement for both partners to the transaction (else one or the other would not have entered upon it)" (Rothenberg, 1975:64).
2. In the typical case, buying and selling are assumed to directly affect only the well-being of the parties involved—the buyer and seller. The welfare of other persons—third parties—is assumed to be unaffected.

Given these assumptions (i.e., that buying and selling improves the welfare of partners to the transaction and leaves the welfare of others unchanged), individuals and firms are free to pursue their own self-interest in economic transactions. If their welfare improves and no one else suffers, the total welfare of society (seen as the sum of individual welfares) is assumed to rise.

The role of government is different. Democratic government is not a private consumer or producer operating within the assumptions of the market. The public has no individual welfare in itself, but "operates only as collective agent" of all private individuals in the society (Rothenberg, 1975:65). Public policy, from this perspective, should use public powers of production and regulation to increase the overall welfare to the greatest extent possible. A corollary to this justification is that public action should increase net individual benefit beyond what would result from private market transactions without public action.

The role of government as a collective agent is one reason cash outlays are an incomplete measure of cost in public programs. The social perspective defined for government means that costs of public action are conceived of as all costs required to carry out the policy. An example clarifies the point.

Under pressure of declining state funding, public universities have sought ways to cut back on costs. As a savings measure, one university discontinued the practice of mailing registration packets to students. The practice resulted in cash outlay savings; mail costs and packaging costs were reduced. Furthermore, it seemed probable that students who came to campus and picked up packets would be those most likely to attend; fewer packets would be wasted.

If the university was acting as a private agent, this savings would be seen as increasing the efficiency of university operations (assuming there was no significant loss of students as a result of the action). From a social perspective, however, the policy may well have been inefficient. Students individually used resources (fuel, time) to come to campus and wait to receive packets. These resources could have been used in other more productive activities or in activities that would have been more highly valued by the students. From the social perspective, this resource use is a "cost." If the value of this cost exceeds the cash savings to the university—and that seems likely—the policy was socially inefficient.

The relation between government action and social costs carries further implications. The assumptions behind free market decisions additionally suggest that individual transactions contribute to the welfare of all, i.e., they are socially efficient. However, when the assumptions fail, private transactions do not produce an improvement in social welfare. Many private economic decisions, for example, do affect the welfare of persons not immediately involved—third parties.

Air, water, and waste pollution produced by manufacturers provides an illustration. Pollution affects the health and quality of life of the public generally, yet private efficiency considerations dictate that the manufacturer reduce cash outlays on pollution control as much as possible. These third party effects, what economists call "external costs," are potential reasons for government intervention to protect the welfare of affected citizens. Later in this chapter, external costs are addressed as important considerations in cost-benefit analysis.

Another principle of public sector economic analysis posits that decision makers should consider the value of public expenditures in comparison to the value of other possible uses of those expenditures. In this view, "the value of the missed chances to do other things" (Whyte et al., 1980:297) is a cost associated with public programs. Policy analysts refer to these foregone possibilities as "opportunity costs."

Opportunity costs are incorporated into cost analyses in a variety of ways, depending on the particular problem under study. A number of studies have assessed the costs of college education. In addition to measuring direct expenditures on personnel, material, and facilities, analysts have included students' foregone opportunity to engage in productive employment. Not only does this represent a cost to them as individuals in the form of "lost" earnings, but it also represents a cost to society in terms of foregone production and tax contributions (Levin, 1975:98). The opportunity cost of productive employment is part of the total cost of higher education. Throughout this chapter, examples of the ways in which opportunity costs enter economic policy analysis will be evident.

In summary, if it is assumed that government should act as collective agent for all the people in economic decisions, the relevant costs for public action are of much greater scope than simple cash outlays. For public decisions, all resources used, public or private, are relevant costs.

Measuring Costs

Describing the finances of public programs presents a demanding challenge. Financing often comes from a number of different sources. Locally delivered social service programs may be funded by a combination of federal, state, and local governments. Also, public programs administered through nonprofit organizations may receive partial support from private or charitable sources (e.g., United Way). Volunteer workers and income from fees for service additionally complicate the funding picture and the process of measuring costs.

Further, records of financial resources (i.e., budgets) typically reflect only a portion of relevant program costs. The value of private resources consumed as a result of public programs (e.g., costs of compliance with environmental regulations or, less obvious, the costs of citizen time in taking advantage of services) are relevant costs from the public perspective. The value of these private costs is often difficult to measure. What is the value of the resources used by students to personally pick up their registration packets?

Developing more adequate cost information systems for public programs is an important long-term solution to gathering data on the cost of public policies. For now, policy analysts identify and estimate many program costs on a situational basis. The following section identifies techniques analysts use to meet the challenges of costing public policies.

TECHNIQUES FOR MEASURING POLICY COSTS

The "ingredients approach" represents a pragmatic method of assessing the costs of public programs (Levin, 1975:100). The technique involves two related tasks:

1. *List Cost Categories.* The first task is to identify and develop an exhaustive list of resources required by a program. The emphasis is on identifying obvious costs and those less obvious—those not explicitly recognized in budgets or program financial statements.
2. *Measure Costs.* Once the exhaustive list of resource categories has been completed, the second task is to identify or estimate a dollar cost for each. Total program cost is the sum of these component costs.

The ingredients approach has the advantage of focusing attention on appropriate cost components before assessing the availability of cost information. Going immediately to existing financial information may lead analysts to rely on what is available, overlooking important other cost considerations.

Listing Cost Categories

Estimating the costs of a program as a whole is not possible without breaking those costs into their component parts (Posavac and Carey, 1984:259). The diversity of public programs requires creating categories appropriate for each particular circumstance. Table 12.1 provides a hypothetical worksheet for listing the costs of a social service program (job training, health services, and so forth).

Cost categories listed at the left side of the worksheet represent conventional budget categories—personnel, facilities, materials and equipment, and miscellaneous expenditures. The columns across the top of the worksheet identify the various organizations or economic groups that may bear costs under a policy. The total cost of a public program requires specification of appropriate cost categories for all resources required by the policy, including all levels of government and private sources.

The categories listed in Table 12.1 are broad and need to be specified in the context of individual programs. The exact ways in which costs are identified and measured depend upon the nature of the program and the availability of cost information. Recognizing this situational nature of cost

TABLE 12.1   Cost Estimation Worksheet

	COST TO IMPLEMENTING AGENCY	COST TO OTHER GOVERNMENT LEVELS OR AGENCIES	CONTRIBUTED PRIVATE INPUTS	IMPOSED PRIVATE COSTS	TOTAL COST
Personnel					
_____					
_____					
Facilities					
_____					
_____					
Material and equipment					
_____					
_____					
Others (specify)					
_____					
Total					
User charges	−( )			+( )	
Other cash subsidies	−( )	+( )	+( )		
Net Total					

Source: Adapted from Henry M. Levin, "Cost-Effectiveness Analysis in Evaluation Research," in Marcia Guttentag and E. L. Struening, eds., *Handbook of Evaluation Research,* vol. 2 (Beverly Hills, CA: Sage Publications, 1975), p. 101. Copyright 1975 by Sage Publications, Inc. Reprinted by permission of Sage Publications, Inc.

analyses, the following discussion presents general considerations in identifying and measuring public program costs.

Costs to Government

Columns 1 and 2 in Table 12.1 represent costs incurred by governments. Column 1 accounts for costs directly applicable to the agency primarily responsible for carrying out program activities. Column 2 represents costs that may be borne by other government agencies as a result of the program. These costs for other agencies may be generated in different ways.

First, analysts count resources contributed by different levels of government. The cost of state services for vocational rehabilitation, for example, may include expenditures from the state treasury (e.g., the relevant portion of the state contribution to the state Department of Rehabilitation) as well as the federal contribution to the case service costs for individual clients. Many programs are funded through multiple contributions from federal, state, and local levels.

Second, programs implemented by one agency may generate costs for other public agencies. These costs may be substantial. An evaluation of a statewide career criminal prosecution program provides an illustration. One objective of the program was to increase the number of years convicted career criminals were sentenced to prison. Using a quasi-experimental design, analysts estimated that the program produced 2,022 additional years of sentence for offenders convicted in one year.

In assessing program costs, evaluators noted that the total budget for the prosecution program was $3,779,312 (state and local contribution). However, the state Department of Corrections estimated that the cost of incarcerating one prisoner for that year was $10,734. Therefore, the costs of incarceration attributable to the prosecution program were

$10,734 per year × 2,022 years = $21,704,148.

The analysts demonstrated that costs produced for the Department of Corrections for this program were almost six times the cost of the prosecution program itself (Springer and Phillips, 1982). The total costs of this program would be seriously underestimated without identifying costs generated for other government agencies.

PERSONNEL COSTS

For service programs, which are labor intensive, personnel costs are usually the largest component of government expenditures. Analysts include all relevant personnel costs such as benefits (e.g., health and life insurance contributions, retirement contributions) and other personnel-related costs (e.g., employer contributions to social security). When administrators or staff have responsibilities in more than one program, analysts count only the portion of their salary and benefits that applies to the program under study.

DIRECT AND INDIRECT COSTS

The distinction between direct costs and indirect costs (sometimes called "overhead") is important to identify fully the costs of a specific program. Direct costs are directly related to specific services provided by a program. For example, "the time a social worker spends helping a family obtain assistance from city agencies is a factor in direct costs" (Posavac and Carey, 1984:261).

Indirect costs or overhead stem from resources required to run the program, but not directly related to specific services provided to a client.

"Thus, the cost of secretarial assistance, as crucial as it is in maintaining a service, is not a direct cost but an indirect cost. The facility administrator's salary, telephone bills, amount paid for custodial service, and so forth are all indirect costs" (Posavac and Carey, 1984:261).

FACILITY AND EQUIPMENT COSTS

The cost of equipment (e.g., typewriters, copiers, automobiles) and facilities (e.g., office space) are components of indirect cost. The method of measuring these costs depends on the way in which equipment and facilities are acquired. In the simplest case, when facilities and equipment are rented, cost is simply the cost of rental. When facilities are shared with other programs or when they are purchased, other methods of estimating cost are necessary.

The facility and equipment costs of a program to improve the skills of grammar school students in science, for instance, must be disentangled from the cost of other programs sharing the school facilities and equipment. If some common basis for prorating costs (e.g., percent of total facility time or space used by each program) can be established, total facility costs can be allocated among programs sharing the facility. If this is not feasible, costs may be estimated by "imputing a rental value equal to the ... rental for comparable facilities" (Levin, 1975:103).

Estimating the annual cost of facilities purchased or constructed by government requires depreciating the cost of the facility over its usable period and considering the portion of that value that would apply to the period of use being studied, e.g., a year. Assume, for example, that a governmental unit constructs a $1 million building that is considered to have a forty-year life with no salvage value at the end of its useful life. The annual cost of the facility, assuming a constant rate of depreciation, would be one-fortieth of the cost, or $25,000.

Analysts also consider the opportunity costs attached to the resources invested in purchases of facilities. Opportunity costs are based on the potential value of nondepreciated costs if they are available for use in other ways—e.g., in private investment. For example, if the $1 million building was twenty years old, half its value would be used up. The analyst would, then, calculate the opportunity cost of $500,000. The costs of durable equipment are calculated analogously to facility costs, though periods of depreciation are shorter.

In addition to personnel, facility, and equipment costs, analysts include the cost of material (office supplies, fuel, and so forth) necessary for direct and indirect expenditures. The sum of these costs for all government agencies, plus any unique miscellaneous costs for a program, constitute governmental expenditures necessary to the program.

Private Costs

Columns 3 and 4 in Table 12.1 refer to private resources consumed in pursuing public action. These costs do not show up in government budgets or accounting systems but do represent costs to society in carrying out policy decisions. To calculate full program cost, analysts estimate the resource costs—contributed or imposed—that programs require of the private sector.

CONTRIBUTED PRIVATE COSTS

Some public elementary schools operate writing centers in which students compose, illustrate, and assemble original stories. Centers are staffed by volunteer parents who work with the children, type stories, and prepare materials used in the program. The schools offer a number of other special programs that use resources contributed by the community. Much of the equipment in schools' computer facilities, for instance, is contributed by national computer manufacturers.

Many educational, health, substance abuse, and other service programs use unpaid volunteers and contributed goods. If an agency uses voluntary workers (a "contributed private input"), the contributed time is typically valued at the rate that would be paid if the volunteers were employees. The cost of contributed equipment and material is calculated at market value.

IMPOSED PRIVATE COSTS

Government action often requires private parties—individuals or firms—to expend resources in complying with or taking advantage of public programs. A frequently overlooked cost is the value of client resources required to participate in a program. The cost of books and transportation, for example, are part of the cost of education or training programs. Health services may require clients or patients to wait for medical assistance.

> There is clearly a cost to the client or patient in terms of foregone work and other activities. For women the cost may be reflected in monetary outlays for child care. . . . Even when there are no direct monetary costs due to waiting, there is a sacrifice of other alternatives that would have been undertaken during that time. (Levin, 1975:99)

The value of client inputs is assessed according to actual outlays when they can be estimated (e.g., the average cost of books per course for students). Estimating the value of client time requires that time spent in acquiring service be estimated and a dollar value applied to that time.

Client inputs are only one imposed private cost of public policies. Policies that regulate business activities require expenditures to comply with pollution controls, safety requirements, fair employment requirements, and so forth. While government expenditures on the administration of regulatory programs constitute less than 1 percent of the federal budget, estimates of compliance costs to the private sector were as high as $100 billion in 1979 (Gramlich, 1981:202). As a result, analyses of the costs and benefits of regulatory programs focus primarily on imposed private costs to business.

User Charges, Subsidies, and Political Decisions

The discussion of costs has emphasized comprehensive identification of all resources consumed in carrying out a given public action. From the perspective of economic analysis, policymakers should consider costs at all levels of government, plus costs in the private sector, when determining the true cost of policy actions. In the political context of public decisions, however, policymakers are often not inclined or free to adopt the comprehensive perspective represented in Table 12.1. A few examples make the point.

The first major skirmish of the tax revolt of the late 1970s was California's Proposition 13—a statewide ballot initiative that reduced and limited property taxes in the state. Faced with reduced tax revenues, local governments sought ways to reduce their costs. One widely adopted savings measure was to transfer certain tax-supported activities to a fee, or user charge, basis. This transfer of costs from tax support to private fees ranged from new or higher fees for the use of parks and other recreational facilities to new sets of fees designed to pay for the development of city infrastructure.

Charges to housing developers are major examples of these efforts. After Proposition 13, many local governments levied fees for parks, schools, roads, water systems, sewer, flood control, and so forth, as requirements before building permits were issued (Springer, 1986:5). In many jurisdictions, these new fees added thousands of dollars to the private costs of development. As a result, the cost of housing in these jurisdictions increased, and the state's serious shortage of low- and moderate-priced housing was exacerbated. Local decision makers had solved a cost problem for local government by shifting tax-supported services to private producers and consumers (an "imposed private cost").

Changes in federal grants-in-aid provide another example. As part of the cost-cutting efforts of the 1980s, the federal government reduced grants to local jurisdictions for construction of sewage treatment plants. Despite the possible costs of water pollution to the larger public, the costs of sewage treatment were returned to local governments as a means of reducing the cost (i.e., cash outlays) of the federal government.

In each of these actions, policymakers were concerned primarily about "cost," as represented by cash outlays in one column of Table 12.1.

Local decision makers faced with revenue limitations reduced costs by shifting them to the private sector through user charges. Federal decision makers reduced sewage cash subsidies to local governments in the name of reducing the scope of government. The bottom rows of Table 12.1 illustrate the ways in which cash subsidies and user charges can reduce costs in one column (−) while increasing them in another (+). Implications for economic analysis and policy decisions can be drawn from these examples.

First, in many circumstances policymakers are less interested in the total costs of policy to society than in the specific costs to their agency, jurisdiction, or constituents. Terminating sewage treatment grants may demonstrate a cost-cutting attitude to constituents, regardless of total social costs. An agency director may stay within budget by reducing agency costs through user charges or by soliciting grants. Public decision makers often are held accountable in terms of cash outlays, and the cost information they desire from analysts may reflect this limited perspective.

Second, economic approaches to policy analysis carry assumptions and value positions that may not reflect the concerns or preferences of decision makers. The assumption that contributed and imposed private costs should be considered in determining the cost of public action, for instance, may contradict the value preferences of some policymakers. The fact that economic approaches embody a particular perspective raises questions about the scope of their usefulness in the multi-perspective world of stakeholders, a topic discussed in subsequent sections.

COST-EFFECTIVENESS ANALYSIS

The difference between cost-effectiveness analysis and the more general cost-benefit analysis (next section) is that cost-effectiveness techniques do not attempt to place a dollar value on outcomes. Cost-effectiveness analysis involves "a comparison of alternative courses of action in terms of their costs and their effectiveness in attaining some specific objective" (Quade, 1967:1). Costs are compared relative to measures of quantifiable outcomes, not to the value of those outcomes.

In policy analysis, the fact that outcomes do not have to be valued frequently makes cost-effectiveness an appealing approach to identifying efficient policy. The reasons are twofold. First, program objectives are frequently mandated, and the relevant question is how to achieve those objectives in the most cost-effective manner. Program implementers are often concerned with maximizing the attainment of mandated objectives; they are less often concerned with questioning whether attaining those objectives is worth the cost.

Second, there are many areas in which it is difficult to place a dollar value on outcomes. "A bomb could be rated in terms of the size of the hole it makes (expressed in cubic yards) divided by the dollar cost of the bomb. By comparing the two ratios, military planners can choose the bomb providing the bigger bang per buck" (Posavac and Carey, 1984:265). It is not possible to place a dollar value on the horrors of war, but when the objective is set, it is possible to identify cost-effective ways to achieve military goals. The nebulous value of national defense is one reason why cost-effectiveness techniques were pioneered in the Department of Defense.

The difficulty of valuing policy objectives also applies in many areas of domestic policy. "What is the market price that will help us assess the benefits of increase in self-concept, reading level, or music appreciation of a youngster?" (Levin, 1975:92). While economists have developed means of assigning monetary value to a wide range of program outcomes that have no evident market price (Sinden and Worrell, 1979), the assumptions necessary to make these estimates render analysis vulnerable to criticism in public discussion. When the results of policy alternatives can be measured in the same way, cost-effectiveness analysis is an appealing approach to policy analysis.

Cost-Effectiveness Comparisons

When policy alternatives are not expected to differ in effectiveness, e.g., when planners are attempting to select between alternative highway routes of identical mileage between two cities, total program cost is the relevant measure for cost comparison. The least expensive alternative is preferable if all else is equal. Frequently, program alternatives are not equal in their production of desired outcomes. Alternative policies for reducing polluting auto emissions, for example, may vary significantly in both cost and effects on pollution.

When the analyst's objective is to compare policies with differing costs and differing levels of performance, the appropriate basis for comparison is a measure that relates cost to the amount of desired policy outcome produced by each program. This section presents two common bases for this comparison—average cost per unit of outcome and marginal cost per unit of outcome.

AVERAGE COST

A straightforward method for relating cost to outcome is simply to calculate the average cost required to produce some standard unit of desirable outcome. A school district staff analyst, for instance, may be assigned responsibility for comparing the cost-effectiveness of two programs for increasing reading proficiency. One program, involving 500 randomly selected students, uses computer-assisted audiovisual instruction; the second, involving another 500 randomly selected students, uses small-group instruction through trained teacher aides.

An average cost per unit of effectiveness approach can be applied to the programs by measuring the effectiveness of each on a standard indicator of program effect—e.g., numbers of students surpassing mean reading achievement scores for their grade level. The analyst can then compare the programs according to average annual cost required for individual students surpassing mean reading achievement for their grade. Table 12.2 presents a hypothetical comparison between two programs.

The table provides several comparisons between the programs. Computer-assisted instruction for 500 students cost one-third more for the year of the experiment—$30,000 versus $20,000. Since the programs enrolled equal numbers of students, cost per student in the intensive-group program is also one-third less expensive. However, the relevant comparison for cost-effectiveness analysis is not simply the number of students served but the cost of achieving program objectives. The hypothetical data in Table 12.2 reveal that, in a program serving 500 students in a year, the computer-assisted approach would be slightly more efficient in terms of cost per student surpassing mean reading skills for his or her grade—$75 per unit of effectiveness versus $77.

MARGINAL COST

Average cost serves as a useful standard for comparing programs with different approaches to the same policy goal. But when the costs of providing service vary with the scale of the program, average cost can be misleading. The reasons are related to the mix of fixed versus variable costs in a particular policy approach. To illustrate, reconsider the example in Table 12.2.

Fixed costs "do not vary with the level of goods or services provided" (Weschler and Schunhoff, 1980:280). To enroll students in the computer-assisted audiovisual program, for example, a lab must be established with

TABLE 12.2   Cost-Effectiveness Comparison of Two Reading Programs

	COMPUTER-ASSISTED	INTENSIVE GROUPS
Students in program	500	500
Students above grade mean	400	260
Annual program cost	$30,000	$20,000
Cost per student served	$60	$40
Cost per student above mean	$75	$77

an audiovisual studio, computer equipment, appropriate software, and a trained technician. To a point, these costs will be fixed, whether one student uses the lab, two students, or more—up to the capacity of the lab. Variable costs are those costs that increase with the level of service—diskettes, energy, or teaching time required in the lab, for example.

When fixed costs for a given policy approach are high compared to variable costs, the average cost per unit of effectiveness will be high for small numbers of cases and will decline as the fixed costs are spread over a larger number of units of service. Economists call the incremental cost of providing additional units of service "marginal" costs—costs incurred at the margin of service. For programs with low fixed costs compared to variable costs, the marginal cost of providing the thousandth or ten thousandth unit of service does not differ markedly from the tenth or twentieth.

Figure 12.1 illustrates hypothetical average cost curves for the reading programs. Assuming that the intensive-group approach is composed entirely of variable costs—teacher aides' salary and materials necessary for each participating student—the cost per student success will remain at $77 per student no matter how many students are involved (assuming the rate of success is also constant). The cost curve for the computer-assisted alternative represents a program with $20,000 dollars in fixed costs and $10,000 in variable costs (or $25 per student in variable costs for the 400 program successes). Given this ratio of fixed to variable costs, the average cost per

Figure 12.1 Hypothetical Average Cost Curves for Alternative Reading Programs

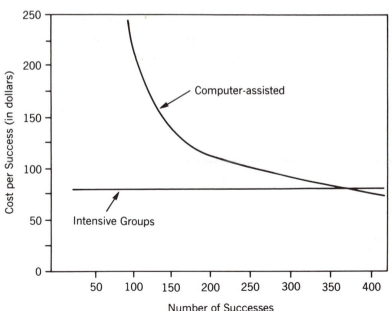

success is $225 for 100 successes, $112.5 for 200 successes, $91.67 for 300 successes, and $75 for 400 successes.

The general principle demonstrated in this example is that analysts need to be aware of the relation between program scale and efficiency. When different policy approaches reflect different proportions of fixed to variable costs, comparisons should consider the appropriate scale of the program. The marginal cost of additional units of service, then, are an important consideration in decision making.

Table 12.3 makes this point explicit with respect to the reading program example. If the scale of each program was increased to 1,000 students, the cost-effectiveness of the computer-assisted approach would become much more evident.

Since the intensive group approach does not require a fixed investment (to simplify the comparison, assume the physical requirements for the program are met through unutilized space in the classroom), the cost of servicing the second 500 students equals that of serving the first 500. If program performance remains constant, the marginal cost per success for the second 500 students will remain $77. Because the fixed costs of the computer-assisted programs are spread over more students, the marginal cost of a program success for the second 500 students is less than one-third the cost of a success for the intensive-group method. The computer-assisted approach is not only more effective in percentage of successes; it is more cost-effective per success.

Marginal cost comparisons help policymakers in a variety of decision situations. First, marginal cost analyses aid decision makers in fitting policy alternatives to the scale of the problem being addressed. High technology approaches to teaching students reading, for example, may be more cost-effective for large school districts with tens of thousands of students, but less cost-effective for small school districts.

Marginal analysis is also useful for allocating budget increases (or cutbacks) among programs (Schultze, 1969). Since these incremental program increases or decreases have their effects at the margin of services, decision makers may allocate increases where effects per unit cost are greatest, and decreases where effects per unit cost are least.

Distribution of Effects

Average and marginal cost measures provide average (mean) costs for program effects within the population receiving program services. These averages do not provide information on the distribution of service benefits between subgroups within the target population. Not all persons exposed to services benefit equally from them. In the reading program example, neither teaching approach brought all students to the national average for their grade level.

TABLE 12.3 Marginal Cost Comparisons of Reading Programs

	PROGRAM SIZE	FIXED COSTS	VARIABLE COSTS	TOTAL COSTS	AVERAGE COSTS (a)	MARGINAL COSTS (a)
Computer-Assisted	500	$20,000	$10,000	$30,000	$75	—
	1,000	$20,000	$20,000	$40,000	$50	$25
Intensive Groups	500	—	$20,000	$20,000	$77	—
	1,000	—	$40,000	$40,000	$77	$77

(a) Per student surpassing mean reading achievement for his or her grade level.

Policymakers concerned about equity in program services, or in compensatory programs that focus benefits on less advantaged students, want information on who benefits more or less from different program alternatives. To provide this information, analysts divide the recipient population into relevant subgroups (e.g., by gender, ethnicity, socioeconomic status, or other variables that may be related to differential program impact) and compare effectiveness measures between them.

The point is that differential distribution of policy benefits requires decision makers to go beyond criteria of cost-effectiveness or efficiency alone. In many social programs, the greatest effects can be achieved by focusing on those program participants who are easiest to serve. Job training programs, for instance, have frequently been criticized for ignoring the chronically unemployed and focusing service on those who already have some job skills and experience. Though it may be more cost-effective (i.e., provide more job placement and longer job retention per dollar spent) this practice of case "creaming" (Robertson, 1984) is counterproductive if the policy objective is to provide marketable job skills for the chronically unemployed. Cost-effectiveness is a single criterion for making policy decisions and must be balanced against competing criteria and values (e.g., equity or specific group benefits) in the policy process.

COST-BENEFIT ANALYSIS

The most ambitious and comprehensive applications of economic reasoning to policy research are referred to as cost-benefit analyses. The concept of comparing the monetary value of public expenditures to the monetary value of their benefits to society has a long history. "Sir William Petty found in London in 1667 that public health expenditures to combat the plague would achieve what we would now call a benefit-cost ratio of 84 to 1" (Thompson, 1980:1).

In the United States, the River Harbor and Flood Control Act of 1936 required that the Army Corps of Engineers justify projects by comparing costs and benefits. Cost-benefit techniques have since expanded far beyond the assessment of physical investments such as those of the Army Corps of Engineers. Human investment programs such as vocational rehabilitation, and social welfare programs such as food stamps, environmental and economic regulations, and more, have all been subjects for cost-benefit studies.

The spreading application of cost-benefit analysis reflects the appeal of the technique as a guide to decisions. By offering an explicit approach, cost-benefit analysis promises to offer a widely applicable guide to making policy choices. If the monetary value of policy costs and benefits can be calculated and compared, then the most desirable policy alternative (including no action) is that which provides the greatest net benefit (total benefits minus total costs).

Cost-benefit as a criterion for policy choice is appealing. There is a temptation to believe "that benefit-cost analysis is a mechanical substitute for common sense. Nothing could be further from the truth. Benefit-cost analysis is really a framework for organizing thoughts, for listing all the pros and cons, and for placing a value on each consideration" (Gramlich, 1981:5). The advantages of making costs and benefits explicit must be balanced by the realization that "the great disadvantage of cost-benefit analysis is that it is very hard to perform satisfactorily" (Quade, 1975:26).

Cost-benefit analysis incorporates the costing principles and techniques discussed in previous sections, but applies them in a more comprehensive approach to policy choice. The following discussion provides an overview of those aspects of economic analysis central to accomplishing, interpreting, and evaluating cost-benefit studies.

Value Assumptions and Limitations

Much economic study is concerned with the allocation of resources by individuals or firms so that individual preferences are maximized. Welfare economics, however,

> is that branch of economics that focuses on the question of how a society can allocate those scarce resources so as to maximize social welfare. Or, put differently, welfare economics is concerned with the formulation of criteria that will allow decisionmakers to distinguish between those activities, programs, or projects that would make society better off and those that would make it worse off. (Anderson and Settle, 1977:10–11)

As a guide to the allocation of society's resources, cost-benefit analysis is the application of welfare economics to policy actions.

Welfare economists have provided criteria for determining whether society is better or worse off, and these criteria provide the fundamental value premises behind decisions based upon cost-benefit analysis. One value criterion (the Pareto criterion) states that society is better off when a policy action "makes at least one person better off and no one worse off ('better off' and 'worse off' being defined solely in terms of the individual's ordinal preference schedule)" (Paris and Reynolds, 1983:96).

The advantage of the Pareto criterion is that it will not allow policy decisions that increase the welfare of some individuals at the expense of others. It also eliminates the need to determine whether one individual's gain is worth more or less than another's loss; no losses are allowed. But this criterion is restrictive. It is difficult to imagine public actions that do not result in making some individuals worse off (in terms of their own preferences).

The restrictive implications of the Pareto value criterion led welfare economists to develop an alternative—the Kaldor-Hicks criterion. This criterion posits that "an increase in general welfare occurs if those that are made better off from some change could, in principle, fully compensate those that are made worse off and still achieve an improvement in welfare" (Anderson and Settle, 1977:13). In other words, the Kaldor-Hicks criterion allows a policy that increases the welfare of some at the expense of others as long as the net benefit (value of the gains of some minus value of the losses of others) is positive. The greater the net benefit, the more desirable the policy.

This value criterion provides the basis for cost-benefit analysis. If the total benefits (increases in welfare) of a policy exceed the net costs, the general welfare has been improved. Cost-benefit analysis as a research technique seeks to identify all benefits and costs of a policy, determine their value, and calculate the difference between total costs and total benefits. Thus, the Kaldor-Hicks criterion allows the calculation of net benefit as an indicator of improvement in the welfare of society.

On the other hand, the fact that a net improvement in benefits allows the possibility of transfer payments to ensure that a policy makes no one worse off does not mean that these side payments will be made. In fact, policies that pass the test of cost-benefit analysis will typically decrease the welfare of some. The decision criteria behind the technique provide no guide to evaluating policies on the basis of distributional consequences—consequences on subgroups of the recipient population.

Policymakers concerned about these consequences must seek information on the distribution of net benefits (or net costs) among different subgroups in the affected population (as in the above discussion of distributional considerations in cost-effectiveness analysis). Policymakers pursuing the values of equity or redistribution will frequently prefer policy choices other than those indicated by the dominant criteria of cost-benefit analysis. If policy analysts are to provide useful information for decision makers with differing values, the distribution of costs and benefits must be made explicit.

Technical Assumptions and Limitations

The basic tasks of cost-benefit analysis seem straightforward:

- Identify all costs and all benefits of a policy (program) or of alternative policies.
- Determine the value of total costs and total benefits (in monetary terms so that they are comparable).
- Calculate the net benefits (positive or negative) of the policy (policies) so that cost-benefit decision criteria may be applied.

While the skeletal logic of the technique is simple, each task presents its own challenges.

Identifying Costs and Benefits

Many costs of a program are not obvious; many others are ignored by decision makers trying to minimize the internal cost to their agency. The criteria maximizing net social benefits, however, imply a comprehensive view of resource requirements and policy impacts. An initial challenge facing analysts is building a list of cost categories and program impacts (both positive and negative). Two categories of relevant (but nonobvious) impacts of a policy are particularly important in cost-benefit analysis—externalities and intangibles.

EXTERNALITIES

Actions taken for one purpose often have other, unintended consequences. A transaction in which a developer buys an apartment complex to construct a shopping center, for instance, will produce (unintended) costs for the tenants of the building. The costs or benefits of effects that go beyond primary purposes of the action are called externalities.

In the social perspective of cost-benefit logic, analysts must account for externalities. Indeed, "if you are an analyst for a public agency, you have an ethical and in most cases legal obligation to examine costs of alternative projects to be borne by others" (Welch and Comer, 1983:242). Externalities may be positive (producing benefits) as well as negative (producing costs). A successful drug-treatment program, for instance, might produce the positive externality of a reduced violent crime rate (Sylvia, Meier, and Gunn, 1985:54). Externalities, then, enter into both columns of the cost-benefit equation.

INTANGIBLES

The transaction between the developer and the apartment owner mentioned above produced relocation costs for displaced residents. These costs can be divided into tangible and intangible components. The dollar costs of searching for new housing, moving belongings, higher rent, increased transportation costs, and so forth, would be classified as tangible. These costs have relatively obvious monetary implications.

The real estate transaction, however, may have additional impacts on the displaced residents. Being uprooted from a stable community and friends may have psychological costs—depression, loss of identity, or reduced happiness. These are intangible costs. The distinction between tangible and intangible is that "tangible effects are relatively easy to value in dollar terms whereas intangible effects are not susceptible to being valued in dollar terms" (Anderson and Settle, 1977:22–23).

As with externalities, intangible effects may be positive or negative. The socio-psychological effects of relocation for the apartment dwellers would be negative. However, analysts of vocational rehabilitation programs have listed the future security that the program provides for citizens who may become disabled as a positive intangible. Analysts of criminal justice programs have similarly listed feelings of safety or security as positive program effects. While intangible effects are nebulous, they are relevant to citizen preferences and have a place in the logic of cost-benefit analysis.

SCOPE OF ANALYSIS

External and intangible policy effects underscore one of the inherent difficulties in doing satisfactory cost-benefit analyses. Simply put, analysts are faced with difficult decisions about the level of detail in conducting a cost-benefit analysis. Externalities and intangibles are frequently omitted from the list of effects because of limited resources (e.g., time or ability) or because policymakers are interested only in the direct and tangible effects for which they are most obviously accountable.

These incomplete cost-benefit analyses yield useful information for determining whether a policy makes a specific interest better off or worse off. However, analyses limited to direct and tangible effects do not yield information relevant to determining whether society as a whole is better off if the policy is implemented.

Establishing Dollar Values

Cost-benefit analysis offers the promise of representing complex choice situations with a single criterion—economic value. This promise is based upon the assumption that the dollar value of resources and impacts of a policy can be established, and that this value will relate to social value, not the preferences of a single individual. This assumption leads to some of the most difficult problems in implementing cost-benefit analyses, including the determination of market and shadow prices.

MARKET PRICES

In the absence of agreed-upon methods for measuring individual benefits from public actions, cost-benefit analysts assume that the standard for valuing benefits is best expressed in voluntary market transactions. If consumer A buys a product from producer B for $100, the value of that product to the consumer is at least $100. If it were not, the consumer would not voluntarily make the transaction. For those familiar with basic economics, this function of voluntary markets establishes the value of goods at varying levels of supply (as represented in demand curves).

For cost-benefit analysts, the concept of voluntary transactions underlies the acceptance of willingness to pay as a measure of value for project benefits. The value of a benefit is what consumers would be willing to pay for the benefit in a voluntary transaction. The preferred method for pricing benefits, then, is to identify a market price for the goods or services produced by a program. When the effect of the program on supply of the goods or services is relatively small, the sum of the units of the benefit provided by the program multiplied by the market price of each unit can be calculated as the social benefit of the program.

Regulation of the automobile industry provides an example of a program that is amenable to market pricing.

> The National Transportation Safety Board requires that all automobile bumpers be able to withstand a five-mile-an-hour collision, with no resulting damage to the vehicle. One benefit of this regulation is that fewer vehicles are damaged in low-speed accidents. The market price value of such an accident being avoided is the cost of repairing the vehicle. The total benefit is therefore the product of the number of accidents without damage and the cost of repairs had the accidents occurred. (Sylvia, Meier, and Gunn, 1985:56–57)

SHADOW PRICES

Many benefits of public programs, however, do not have easily identifiable market prices. Public goods are goods consumed by many persons at the same time; national defense, clean air and water, wilderness areas, police protection, and highways are examples. These goods are not typically provided through free markets; rather they are usually provided or protected by government. For these types of benefits, analysts attempt to establish shadow prices that estimate the market value of these goods.

Identifying the value of a human life graphically demonstrates pitfalls awaiting analysts attempting to establish shadow prices. Individuals generally perceive life to be a commodity of infinite value, but human activities frequently increase or decrease the probabilities of death, injury, or ill health. "In a world of scarce resources, it is often the case that hard choices have to be made concerning allocating resources to reducing the probability of illness, injury, or death as opposed to using them elsewhere in the economy" (Anderson and Settle, 1977:65).

In developing cost-benefit analyses of proposed regulatory activity, federal agencies sometimes make the appropriate value of life a subject of "macabre debate" (*New York Times*, 10/26/84). In proposing regulations to protect construction workers who handle concrete, OSHA estimated the value of a worker's life at $3.5 million. The Office of Management and Budget challenged this figure as "too high for a construction worker; a budget office economist says something like $1 million would be more reasonable" (*New York Times,* October 26, 1984). The Environmental Protection Agency has estimated the value of life in the range of $400,000 to $7 million.

The broad range in estimates reflects differing assumptions and differing approaches to calculating a shadow price for a human life. A simple approach to placing dollar value on human life is to estimate the amount of money individuals would have earned if they had reached full life expectancy. One rationale behind this approach is that the market value of individuals' potential earnings is an indication of the social value of their productivity.

This approach has the appeal of simplicity, but it demonstrates the hazards of shadow pricing. The foregone earnings approach has the disadvantage of devaluing the lives of those who generally have less earning potential—women, the elderly, minorities. Neither does the procedure account for the value of essential services not provided through the labor market, most notably homemaking. More sophisticated approaches to valuing lost productivity use methods for estimating true social value more fully, but the advantage of simplicity is lost.

Attempts to estimate the value of life present difficult challenges to cost-benefit analysts. Indeed, Thompson (1980) identifies a dozen distinct approaches to valuing life, each reflecting different assumptions. While the value of life is an extreme case, shadow pricing techniques are frequently necessary to conduct cost-benefit analyses. The value of citizen time, for instance, enters into many cost-benefit studies. Less expensive highway routing requiring greater driving time, for instance, may have to be weighed against more expensive routing that shortens driving time. The lower overhead achieved through centralized service provision may be weighed against the increased time required for citizens to use those services. Shadow prices also figure prominently in studies of environmental pollution or public recreation (Anderson and Settle, 1977:68–75).

Establishing the dollar value of nonmarket goods is one of the difficult tasks in cost-benefit analysis, one in which there is no objective solution. The dollar value of saving an endangered species, for instance, will vary widely between environmentalists and real estate and land-use developers. In many applications, cost-benefit analysis represents a clarification of the value that different groups place on policy outcomes rather than a detached calculation of net policy benefits to society.

Comparative Measures of Cost and Benefit

Once analysts have established and valued all costs relevant to a study, costs and benefits are compared. As a guide to making policy choices, the fundamental criterion underlying the technique is that the value of benefits to society will exceed the value of costs. Analysts have developed several criteria for making this comparison, each with its advantages and disadvantages.

BENEFIT-COST RATIO

A commonly applied criterion—indeed the one legally required to justify federal water projects—is the benefit-cost ratio. The measure is calculated in the following way:

$$\text{Benefit-Cost Ratio} = \frac{\text{Total Benefits}}{\text{Total Costs}}$$

The benefit-cost ratio provides a single numeric value that summarizes the relation between costs and benefits. A value of less than 1.0 indicates that project (or program) costs exceed benefits attributable to the project or program. The criterion would indicate a choice not to pursue the project because it would result in a net decrease in social value. A value greater than 1.0 indicates a net increase in social value; the higher the ratio the greater the social benefit given the cost. Thus, the benefit-cost ratio provides a means of comparing the relative social efficiency of alternative projects: a project with a benefit-cost ratio of 12 provides twice the dollar benefit for dollar expenditure as a project with a benefit-cost ratio of 6.

Since the criterion is a ratio, it standardizes results for projects of different absolute magnitude. While this characteristic of ratios is desirable for many applications, it has drawbacks in comparing alternative projects. The major difficulty is that the ratio focuses on the benefits per dollar of investment, not on the total net value of benefits. A small project to reduce flood damage in a riverfront town (e.g., raising a levy) may have a benefit-cost ratio of 5, but produce a net annual reduction in flood damage of only $30,000. A larger project may produce a ratio of 3, but result in a net annual reduction in damage of $800,000. A threatened community may well prefer the latter project despite its lower ratio.

In social programs, the efficiency focus of the benefit-cost ratio can be related to the practice of "creaming"—to goal displacement through concentrating services in those areas where results are easiest to achieve. An economic analysis of vocational rehabilitation programs in a major state found that the benefit-cost ratio for services to clients classified as "nonseverely disabled" was 11.30; for "severely disabled" clients the ratio was 3.92 (Collignon, Dodson, and Root, 1977:iii). If efficiency was the only criterion, limited program dollars would be applied to less severely disabled clients, undermining and distorting agency goals and public policy. The world of politics does not accept such unidimensional criteria without challenge. Indeed, federal legislation has increasingly channeled rehabilitation funds toward those most in need rather than to those who are the least expensive to rehabilitate.

NET PRESENT VALUE

A second widely used criterion for choosing between alternatives is "net present value" or the present value of total program benefits minus the total value of net present costs. The present value concept focuses on the fact that the value of a dollar is not constant over time. A simple household analogy makes the point.

> Let a household have a sum of, say, $1,000. If the household spends it all today, it can obviously spend $1,000. If it deposits the money in a bank ... offering a deposit rate of 5 percent each year, 1 year from now it will have $1050. The same $1000 is worth $1000 now and $1050 one year from now. (Gramlich, 1981:88)

A cost or benefit realized in the future is worth less in present dollars than its actual value at the time it will be realized. Net present value provides a comparison of future costs and benefits that are discounted to the value of current dollars.

Analysts use a variety of assumptions to determine just how much future costs and benefits should be discounted. The essential question is this: "How much is it worth spending now to achieve 'X' dollars in benefits or 'X' dollars of savings at a specific time in the future?" There is no consensus on exactly how to make this calculation, and most analysts will apply alternative assumptions to provide a range of estimates of present value. (For a full discussion of discounting, see Mishan, 1976.)

The net present value criterion can provide outcomes very different from the benefit-cost ratio. Rather than focusing on efficiency, it focuses on the absolute value of the net benefits provided for society. Therefore, it may favor relatively expensive projects that are effective in producing desired results over smaller projects that are more efficient.

Other criteria for comparing costs and benefits are available. The payback period may be calculated, e.g., how long does it take the value of project benefits to equal the value of project costs? Equity issues may be addressed by analyzing the relative distributions of who pays and who benefits. Indeed, one of the great dangers of cost-benefit analysis is that it can hide distributional consequences of public policies by applying the aggregate concept of net social benefit.

Using Cost-Benefit Analysis

Stakeholders using cost-benefit analysis information err if they assume the technique provides an objective and comprehensive guide to making policy choices. Cost-benefit analysis is largely a reflection of values—to identifying what should be considered as costs and benefits, and to assessing how much they should be valued.

Decision makers need to be aware of the various criteria for comparing costs and benefits, and apply the varying criteria according to the values they are attempting to maximize and the choice situations they confront. Decision makers deciding between alternative programs with a limited and determinant set of resources may lay greater weight on efficiency and benefit-cost ratios. When solving a pressing problem is the priority, effectiveness and sufficiency may be given more weight through comparing net present value. For decision makers concerned with equity, the distribution of costs and benefits across groups must be examined.

Policymakers also need to be aware of the sensitivity of cost-benefit results to the subjective decisions of analysts. Results are literally determined by factors included in the analysis and by dollar values assigned to them. Since costs and benefits are projected into the future, results are sensitive to the selection of a discount rate, particularly when there are significant long-term costs or benefits. Cost-benefit reports should include "sensitivity analyses" which analyze results with different levels for any value which cannot be established with great confidence (e.g., shadow prices, discount rates).

The realistic use of cost-benefit analysis must be grounded in an awareness of the tentative and value-laden nature of its results. The technique frequently does more to clarify the important components of a problem and to clarify differing interests and positions than it does in specifying optimum choices.

CONCLUDING COMMENTS

Costing approaches in policy research provide analysts with a variety of tools to address issues facing decision makers throughout policy processes. These tools provide means to (a) identify the costs of policies and programs, (b) compare the efficiency of alternative means for meeting policy objectives, and (c) compare the costs and benefits of policies or programs. The desirability of these types of information is undeniable. Providing this information, however, presents conceptual difficulties, particularly in political settings characterized by conflicting values and perspectives.

Establishing the costs of a public policy or program may appear a straightforward problem in record keeping and calculation. In fact, the subtleties of costing public programs frequently mean that costs are only partially identified or ignored altogether. Because democratic governments ideally represent all citizens rather than acting as self-interested individuals, the scope of relevant costs is greatly expanded. The total costs of a public program include more than an implementing agency's direct and indirect costs of providing services. To establish the true costs of public programs, analysts also consider costs borne by other levels of government, costs that may be created for other agencies, and contributed or imposed costs to private citizens and businesses. In many instances, the scope and value of these external program costs are not obvious. Policy analysts make an important contribution to determining what the real costs of particular programs and policies are, and to identifying who bears these costs.

Cost-effectiveness analyses are undertaken to identify alternatives that are most efficient in achieving specific public objectives—e.g., improved reading scores for school children. When measures of effectiveness in service delivery are available, average and marginal cost analyses provide bases for identifying alternatives that provide the greatest value. Cost-effectiveness analyses provide information relevant to a number of management decisions, including optimal program scale and incremental budget adjustments.

Cost-benefit analysis is sometimes reputed to be the best among economic techniques for policy analysis. Its promise is no less than providing a yardstick for measuring the degree of benefit that policies or programs will provide for society. Developing this measure requires that analysts identify and establish dollar values for total social benefits produced by a program as well as total costs. To do this, sophisticated approaches to identifying costs and benefits have been developed. Equally ingenious techniques for establishing dollar values for intangible and nonmarket goods and services have been developed and applied. As a result, analysts have produced measures of net benefit for a wide variety of environmental, public works, and social programs.

Such a yardstick, if it reflects agreed-upon standards and techniques, is a useful tool for policymakers facing choice decisions. However, the realities of cost-benefit analysis do not warrant unchallenged acceptance by stakeholders. "The number and complexity of the assumptions required to proceed on even a trivial cost-benefit problem . . . are truly impressive. It is easy to manipulate the assumptions" (Downs and Larkey, 1986:136).

Users of economic analyses appropriately question assumptions made by analysts conducting the studies. The monetary figures attached to saving an endangered species, to saving a life, to preserving a scenic coastline are expressions of human values as well as analysis. Decision makers also examine the criteria used to recommend policy choices in economic studies. A measure of net benefit says nothing about the distribution of costs and benefits. Decision makers concerned about equity, or concerned about effects on specific groups, need information about distributional effects.

A "major difficulty with analytic aproaches to improving government efficiency and effectiveness is that they greatly overestimate the orderliness possible in government decision making" (Downs and Larkey, 1986:136). Value diversity is a basic ingredient of American government, and analysis cannot impose a common mold. However, this does not invalidate the utility of economic analyses. As a tool of policy research, economic perspectives in policy analysis enhance and clarify public debate; they do not replace it.

REFERENCES

Anderson, Lee G., and Russell F. Settle. 1977. *Benefit-Cost Analysis: A Practical Guide.* Lexington, MA: D. C. Heath.

Bickner, Robert E. 1980. "Pitfalls in the Analysis of Costs," in G. Majone and E. S. Quade, eds., *Pitfalls of Analysis.* New York: John Wiley & Sons.

Browning, Edward K., and Jacquelene M. Browning. 1979. *Public Finance and the Price System.* New York: Macmillan.

Collignon, Frederick C., Richard B. Dodson, and Gloria Root. 1977. *Benefit-Cost Analysis of Vocational Rehabilitation Services Provided by the California Department of Rehabilitation.* Berkeley, CA: Berkeley Planning Associates.

Demone, H. W., Jr., and D. Harshbarger. 1973. *The Planning and Administration of Human Services.* New York: Behavioral Publications.

Downs, George W., and Patrick D. Larkey. 1986. *The Search for Government Efficiency: From Hubris to Helplessness.* New York: Random House.

Georgi, Hanspeter. 1973. *Cost-Benefit Analysis and Public Investment in Transport: A Survey.* London: Butterworths.

Gramlich, Edward M. 1981. *Benefit-Cost Analysis of Government Programs.* Englewood Cliffs, NJ: Prentice-Hall.

Levin, Henry M. 1975. "Cost-Effectiveness Analysis in Evaluation Research," in Marcia Guttentag and E. L. Struening, eds., *Handbook of Evaluation Research,* vol. 2. Beverly Hills, CA: Sage Publications.

Lindblom, Charles E. 1968. *The Policy-Making Process.* Englewood Cliffs, NJ: Prentice-Hall.

MacRae, Duncan, Jr., and James A. Wilde. 1979. *Policy Analysis for Public Decisions.* North Scituate, MA: Duxbury Press.

Mishan, E. J. 1976. *Cost-Benefit Analysis.* New York: Praeger.

Paris, David C., and James F. Reynolds. 1983. *The Logic of Policy Inquiry.* New York: Longman.

Patton, Carl V., and David S. Sawicki. 1986. *Basic Methods of Policy Analysis and Planning.* Englewood Cliffs, NJ: Prentice-Hall.

Posavac, Emil J., and Raymond G. Carey. 1984. *Program Evaluation: Methods and Case Studies,* 2d ed. Englewood Cliffs, NJ: Prentice-Hall.

Quade, Edward S. 1967. "Introduction and Overview," in T. A. Goldman, ed., *Cost-Effectiveness Analysis: New Approaches in Decision-Making.* New York: Praeger.

———. 1975. *Analysis for Public Decisions.* New York: Elsevier North-Holland.

Research and Education Association. 1982. *Handbook of Economic Analysis.* New York: Research and Education Association.

Robertson, David. 1984. "Program Implementation versus Program Design: Which Accounts for Policy 'Failure'?" *Policy Studies Review.* 3:391–405.

Rothenberg, Jerome. 1975. "Cost-Benefit Analysis: A Methodological Exposition," in M. Guttentag and E. L. Struening, eds., *Handbook of Evaluation Research,* vol. 2. Beverly Hills, CA: Sage Publications.

Schultze, Charles L . 1969. *The Politics and Economics of Public Spending.* Washington, DC: Brookings Institution.

Sinden, John A., and Albert C. Worrell. 1979. *Unpriced Values: Decisions Without Market Prices.* New York: John Wiley & Sons.

Springer, J. Fred. 1986. "Intents and Outcomes of Local Land Use Regulation: A Study in Policy Complexity." Presented to the Midwest Sociology Association, Des Moines, IA. Mimeo.

Springer, J. Fred, and Joel Phillips. 1982. "Implementation and Evaluation of Federal Policy: Lessons from the Career Criminal Program." Presented to the Midwestern Political Science Association, Chicago, IL.

Sylvia, Ronald D., Kenneth J. Meier, and Elizabeth M. Gunn. 1985. *Program Planning and Evaluation for the Public Manager.* Monterey, CA: Brooks/Cole Publishing.

Thompson, Mark S. 1980. *Benefit-Cost Analysis for Program Evaluation.* Beverly Hills, CA: Sage Publications.

Welch, Susan, and John C. Comer. 1983. *Quantitative Methods for Public Administration: Techniques and Applications.* Homewood, IL: Dorsey Press.

Weschler, Louis, and John Schunhoff. 1980. "Marginal Analysis for Public Systems," in M. J. Whyte et al., *Managing Public Systems.* North Scituate, MA: Duxbury Press.

Whyte, Michael J., Ross Clayton, Robert Myrtle, Gilbert Siegel, and Aaron Rose. 1980. *Managing Public Systems: Analytic Techniques for Public Administration.* North Scituate, MA: Duxbury Press.

13

Quick Analysis
Policy Research Under Pressure

As evidenced through increasing policy and programmatic initiatives, federal, state, and local governments are demonstrating significant concern about drug abuse in society. Community-based prevention represents one such program initiative. In contrast to traditional treatment and rehabilitation policies which attempt to ameliorate drug problems after they have occurred, prevention programs attempt to deter drug abuse before it occurs.

To provide programmatic guidance reflecting this community-based prevention policy, the director of a state's Department of Alcohol and Drug Programs (ADP) appointed the Director's Task Force on Drug Abuse Prevention to make recommendations on the funding and implementation of community drug prevention efforts. During its deliberations, the task force was aware of the importance of encouraging policy analysis on prevention programs—particularly in planning, implementing, and evaluating such efforts.

Recognizing the potential importance of policy research in guiding prevention efforts, one of the task force recommendations was that ADP should "encourage, support, and where appropriate, require prevention program evaluation." But the task force placed a qualification on its com-

mitment to encouraging policy research on prevention programs, recommending that "the level of evaluation should be reasonable and *within the
limits of funding* such that service delivery is not compromised" (Director's
Task Force on Drug Abuse Prevention, 1984:9; emphasis added).

This qualification accentuates a pervasive condition of doing policy
research. Research and analysis compete with other activities for scarce resources—time, money, and skill. Analysis is often accomplished within
short-term time frames imposed by stakeholders and by the immediacy of
problems. Analysts may not have the luxury of doing highly systematic research; instead, they may be faced with doing their best to produce quality
information quickly.

Recognizing the resource-sensitive nature of policy research, this chapter provides guidelines for doing policy research quickly. The objective is
to discuss approaches analysts employ in collecting information under conditions of limited time and effort.

The chapter is organized in several major sections. The first section
identifies sources of pressure on policy research. The second distinguishes
between "researched" analysis and "quick" analysis (Behn and Vaupel,
1982), and discusses the applicability of each. A third section presents principles and techniques of quick analysis, along with selected examples of
quick analysis in practice. The final section provides concluding comments.

SOURCES OF PRESSURE IN POLICY RESEARCH

Policy research encompasses a broad range of information needs. The need
for information is ongoing, and the means for providing it must be flexible
and capable of producing useful results under a variety of constraints and
pressures. The policy-making environment contains numerous sources of
pressure to produce quick results. These pressures are discussed below.

Time Lines

Time-sensitive pressures on producing information are often acute
when decision makers are elected officials. The comments of John Linner,
an analyst for Cleveland's Department of Community Development, illustrate the point. On first taking his job, Linner reports reading a quote
posted on the wall. The quote was from Tom Johnson, a former mayor of
Cleveland. It read, "A good executive always acts quickly, and is sometimes
right." At first the quote bothered Linner, who had just graduated from
planning school, but in time he learned to appreciate that politicians are
constantly pressured to take positions on issues on which they are to varying
degrees uninformed.

[Politicians] can't afford to deliberate for very long lest they be accused of being indecisive or wishy-washy. Therefore, when a Mayor asks ... for advice, ... [h]e wants a quick answer from someone whom he suspects knows a little bit more about the issue than he does. (Quoted in Patton and Sawicki, 1986:41)

Under the pressure of time lines, analysis must sometimes be quick (Behn and Vaupel, 1982). Results may be produced in days—or hours.

Staff Responsibilities

Staff members for decision makers carry numerous role responsibilities, only some of them involving policy research. The introduction to this chapter presented the ADP Director's Task Force recommendation that local prevention programs be encouraged or required to do evaluations without siphoning significant funds from program services. As a consequence, many of the evaluations will be self-evaluations conducted by program staff who have to fit these activities into their crowded schedules.

The necessity of meshing research activities with other responsibilities creates time pressures in generating accurate and useful evaluation information. Additionally, staff with multiple responsibilities are not likely to have advanced training in research methods; therefore, research methods they apply cannot be too intricate or complex. In these circumstances, policy research is quick and straightforward.

The Magnitude of the Problem

Decision makers develop positions on concerns that do not justify significant investments in research time or effort. Concerns emerge from a variety of sources—interest groups, staff, program recipients, legislators, political candidates, judicial rulings, prominent public figures, the media. Many of these concerns stand little chance of proceeding beyond the stimulation stage, but media interest and other factors may still require decision makers to take positions on the problem. Concerns of this magnitude do not justify elaborate policy research.

Similarly, "quick, basic analysis may be all that is justified for a one-time local problem where the cost of a large-scale study would exceed the benefit from the precise solution" (Patton and Sawicki, 1986:4). As with other public expenditures, costs of research must be weighed against reasonable expectations of benefit.

Budget Competition

In periods of cutback and tight budgets, resources for research and analysis are targets for reduction. During the budgetary retrenchment of recent years, for example, research and development funds (in nondefense areas) were a target for the budgetary scalpel. But the reduction of funds for analysis does not reduce the need for providing information useful in achieving accountability or improved efficiency. The result—a requirement for quick means of analysis.

In sum, a number of pressures produce needs for analysis yielding useful results quickly and with minimal resources. Time lines, staff responsibilities and capabilities, problem salience, and budget competition, all contribute to the demand for quick information.

The approaches suggested in this chapter do not replace techniques presented in previous chapters. Quick analysis often means modifying more complex techniques for quick application, thereby reducing technical quality and raising questions of accuracy and usefulness of study findings.

RESEARCHED ANALYSIS AND QUICK ANALYSIS

The pressures outlined above create an environment calling for a particular orientation to policy research. Behn and Vaupel (1982) define this orientation as "quick analysis" and contrast it with "researched" policy analysis. Patton and Sawicki (1986) make a similar distinction between "basic" analysis and full-blown "policy studies."

> Policy analysts are often required to give advice to policy makers in incredibly short periods of time, in contrast to university researchers and think tank consultants who are typically given comparatively large budgets and long periods of time to produce results, and they work with large sets of data. Consequently the methods they use are different than those used by staff who work for decision makers on a day-to-day basis. (Patton and Sawicki, 1986:3)

The following discussion contrasts "quick" and "researched" policy analysis. Major characteristics of each orientation to policy analysis are summarized in Table 13.1.

Researched Analysis

Researched analysis has the objective of examining policy problems and programs and developing a theoretical understanding that can guide future policy development. While researched policy analysis addresses issues useful to stakeholders, it is oriented to providing findings generally applicable within a policy community. Results are not focused on providing research responses to a narrow problem for a decision maker in a specific

TABLE 13.1   Characteristics of Quick Analysis and Researched Analysis

QUICK ANALYSIS	RESEARCHED ANALYSIS
• Decision-oriented • Context specific • Short/medium term • Recognizes resource limits/trade-offs • Less systematic	• Theory-oriented • Generalizable • Long term • Assumes resource adequacy • More systematic

context; rather the intent is to provide a foundation of understanding about an issue that has more general usage by the entire policy community.

From the researched perspective, time and resource constraints do not predominate as they do in quick analysis. Good theoretical knowledge takes time to build; sophisticated policy research requires significant expenditures of research dollars. Designing policy research primarily to produce broadly applicable knowledge may even require analysts to exercise significant control over the design of policy operations, such as in an experimental manipulation of study populations. Researched analysis is frequently conducted by experts specializing in research methods and techniques.

Quick Analysis

Quick analysis generates information immediately useful for developing positions on smaller-scale concerns facing policymakers. This type of analysis is intended to serve as a tool for making more routine decisions. Quick analysis takes place in a specific context and is intended to provide information for specific concerns within that context. Generalizability—the larger applicability of findings and recommendations—is not a primary concern.

Techniques of quick analysis are appropriate to the time and resource constraints of the problem context. Analysis efforts compete with other responsibilities and reflect a commensurate level of effort. Quick analysis presumes an interactive, supportive relation between research producer and user. Quick analysis is often conducted by staff who are not experts in research methods; thus the tools they use are based on less complex approaches.

The differences between researched analysis and quick analysis represent a continuum, and the distinction can be overdrawn. All research efforts, for example, take place within some limits on resources. Nevertheless, relative emphasis on one or the other approach is found at differing points in policy processes and in differing contextual settings.

The purposes and resource requirements of large-scale researched analysis mean that such information is primarily produced by large organizations, consulting firms, and academic institutions, and may be sponsored by the federal government or by state governments. Governmental research foundations such as the National Institute on Drug Abuse (NIDA) and the National Institute of Justice (NIJ) frequently fund researched analysis on policy issues. Major think tanks such as the RAND Corporation are primarily oriented toward this type of analysis. Researched analysis may also be funded by private foundations. In terms of the policy process, researched analysis will make its primary contribution to general questions that arise in policy stimulation, clarification, selection, or evaluation stages.

Quick analysis occurs anywhere stakeholders need to adopt quickly a position on an issue. However, quick analysis is particularly valuable to public officials who repeatedly respond to public demands and expectations. Quick analysis is also useful to program managers and staff responsible for policy implementation and to those confronting decisions arising in that process. The following section presents orienting principles for conducting quick analysis.

QUICK ANALYSIS: PROCESS AND TECHNIQUES

Conducting quick analysis does not involve a set of research methods distinct from more researched applications of policy research. Quick analysis is primarily a set of orientations leading analysts to focus on core dimensions of a problem and to gather rapidly information relevant to those core dimensions. An initial concern in quick analysis is to structure the problem so it can be rapidly and simply addressed. Problems must be structured so decision makers can focus on what is most important. They must be simplified, clarified, and specified. The following sections discuss methods of structuring problems in quick analysis.

More Thought—Less Data

Collecting new empirical data is the most time-consuming aspect of researched analysis; thus quick analysis proceeds with a reduced ability to collect original, primary data concerning the problem. Consequently, a key to successful quick analysis is to identify the right question(s)—the question(s) that (a) is relevant to users, and (b) that can be addressed, given the information and resources at hand. In quick analysis, the balance between thinking about the problem and collecting data tilts toward thinking.

Many issues facing decision makers are complex—correct responses to the problem depend on the perspectives and positions of stakeholders. The right question(s) in quick analysis incorporates preferences and responsibilities of stakeholders, of those impacted by such decisions.

Identifying the Range of Perspectives

Public policy issues are characterized by a diversity of values and viewpoints brought by different groups having a stake in the concern. Analysts and their clients "may want to consider the perspectives of some constituencies and not others, but it pays to think about all possible viewpoints as you start out and to narrow them down quickly, using a defensible rationale" (Patton and Sawicki, 1986:27). Quick analysis frequently begins with an attempt to identify the range of perspectives that will be brought to bear on an issue. This step avoids overlooking important points of view influencing the use of the results.

A useful beginning point for identifying the range of perspectives is to identify potential audiences in the policy community and what their interest in the issue might be. When possible, this exercise is undertaken in group brainstorming sessions involving decision makers, analysts, and other interested and knowledgeable people if feasible. The product should be a list of interested parties, their interests in the issue, and the concerns and suggestions they may have.

The Purpose/Audience Matrix

Hawkins and Nederhood (1986:39) provide guidance in identifying audiences for local managers undertaking self-evaluations of community-based drug abuse prevention programs. They emphasize the importance of identifying the right questions.

> When you choose a question for your evaluation study, you want a question that has stature—a question that will repay the effort you ... will invest in obtaining its answer. To assure yourself a question is worth answering, compare the top priority questions you're considering in light of these three:
> 1. What do we need to know about our program to solve a problem we have identified?
> 2. When we have the information, who will be interested in knowing it?
> 3. Why do we need to know this? What can we do differently with this new information?

To help reduce the number of potential study questions, self-evaluators may apply a "Purpose/Audience Matrix" to organize and prioritize the range of questions they could address.

The configuration of a purpose/audience matrix varies according to the particular issue being analyzed, but it demonstrates important principles useful in initial stages of quick analysis. The audience dimension of the matrix focuses attention on identifying the range of parties potentially interested in the issue. Thus, analysts and policymakers make decisions about which audiences require most attention and which audiences are less important for the purposes of the specific problem they face.

Second, the purpose dimension of the matrix focuses on the ways in which the answers to study questions might be used. In advocating quick analysis to achieve "rapid feed-back evaluation," Wholey (1983:119) argues that evaluators tend to "rush into the field without careful attention to the feasibility and likely usefulness of data collection." Analysts and their sponsors cannot afford this ineffective and inefficient use of scarce resources. As Hawkins and Nederhood (1986:39) caution, "If you don't know how you will use the information, don't bother to . . . answer the question."

The purposes arrayed in Figure 13.1 allow analysts to focus on information useful in securing funding if this were the major objective of program decision makers. The purposes included in the matrix again depend on the nature of the concern under study.

Other approaches to quick analysis accomplish essentially the same objective through structuring techniques different from the purpose/audience matrix. Moberg (1984:8), for instance, suggests another means of selecting the most relevant questions from a list of potential study questions. After identifying potential questions, he suggests that analysts have key users complete the following statement for each.

We need to know:

Because we need to (decide/demonstrate/account for):

Although this process consumes time, answers to this statement provide a basis for selecting useful questions.

The selection of specific questions for quick analysis reflects an approach to analysis sometimes called "backward problem solving" (Polya, 1957). The idea is to look ahead at the uses of information and at the feasibility of analysis, and to restate questions so they can be resolved within these criteria. No research adequately addresses all possible questions, and questions must be structured in a way amenable to the level of analysis possible.

Quick Analysis: A Specific Technique

Behn and Vaupel developed a more concentrated technique for structuring questions to be addressed through quick analysis. Their technique focuses directly on the decision situation confronting policymakers and

	Planning & Development	Management Control/ Operational Decisions	Secure Funding	Public Relations
Management				
Clients				
Funders				
Other Agencies				
Public or Community				
Evaluators Researchers				
???				

FIGURE 13.1 Hypothetical Purpose/Audience Matrix for Local Prevention Programs. (*Source:* Adapted from David J. Hawkins and Britt Nederhood, *Staff/Team Evaluation of Prevention Programs: STEPP Handbook* (Washington, DC: National Institute of Drug Abuse, 1986), p. 42.)

provides a means of structuring problems so that priorities can be set and alternatives can be quickly assessed.

The first step in Behn and Vaupel's approach to quick decision analysis is to provide a simple structuring of the concern. To accomplish this, analysts develop "decision saplings (simple decision trees with only a few branches to capture the essence of the decision dilemma)" (Behn and Vaupel, 1982:328). These decision saplings use the following symbols to structure the decision situation.

Decision Node (□): the basic point of decision between identified alternatives.

Uncertainty Node (○): the uncertainty (risk) about the consequences of an identified alternative.

Terminal Node (△): the potential end consequences of identified alternatives.

Figure 13.2 presents an example. The decision sapling structures a problem confronting the mayor of St. Louis, Missouri, the former home of the "football Cardinals"—a team in the National Foodball League. The team, locally nicknamed the "Big Red," had played its home games in Busch stadium in the heart of the city. The stadium, however, was one of the smallest in the NFL, seating only 55,000 fans. Claiming that 70,000 seats were the minimum required to keep the team financially healthy, team ownership made it known they wanted a new stadium and began listening to proposals to bring the Big Red to cities seeking an NFL franchise.

The mayor faced a dilemma. In addition to the economic and prestige losses that would accompany the team's departure, the potential electoral impacts of thousands of irate football fans would be felt. To attempt to avoid losing the team, the mayor had to make a quick decision about whether to use city funds and the influence of his office to push for the construction of a new sports complex. The basic decision, portrayed in Figure 13.2, was whether to construct a stadium or to do nothing.

Either decision, whether to support the stadium or to do nothing, carries uncertainty with respect to the desired outcome—keeping the Big Red in town. Thus, each branch of the sapling passes through an uncertainty node with two possible terminal outcomes: the team leaves or the team stays. In other words, building the stadium will not guarantee that the team will stay in town, but it will change the probabilities.

As part of structuring the problem, the decision sapling allows the mayor and his staff to set their priorities among the outcomes. The best possible outcome is that the team stays without the new stadium, thereby gaining the objective without expending scarce development dollars and

FIGURE 13.2 Should the Mayor Support a Stadium? An Example of a Decision Sapling

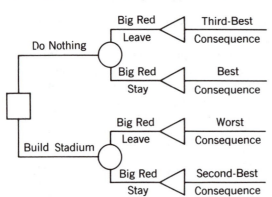

influence that can be used elsewhere. The worst outcome is to build the stadium and lose the team. Such an outcome is economically and politically damaging since the team's revenues are necessary to make the stadium economically feasible. Building the stadium and keeping the team is the second-best consequence, and not building the stadium and losing the team the third best.

In some cases, this simple structuring of a problem itself recommends a decision. If, for example, the first and second preferred consequences are on one branch of the decision node, the appropriate decision would be clear. If the new stadium was seen to have strong positive outcomes, regardless of whether the team left or not, the first and second preferences could both be on the support-the-stadium side. The mayor's choice, then, is obvious.

However, the decision sapling in Figure 13.2 portrays a different situation. The best consequence and the third-best consequence are on the do-nothing branch. The worst and second-best outcomes are on the support-the-stadium branch. The sapling portrays a decision dilemma in which the mayor's decision is not obvious. The mayor's alternatives are greatly clarified if the probabilities associated with each branch of the uncertainty nodes can be estimated.

Quick analysis draws on "subjective probabilities" (Behn and Vaupel, 1982:328)—estimates of the probability of different outcomes based on available knowledge. In this case, reports in the media, the mayor's conversations with the Cardinals' ownership, and other sources would form a basis for estimating the probabilities of the different consequences associated with each decision branch.

Figure 13.3 portrays one possible set of estimates. If the mayor and his staff are convinced Big Red owners are serious about their demand for

FIGURE 13.3 Should the Mayor Support a Stadium? Decision Sapling with Subjective Probabilities

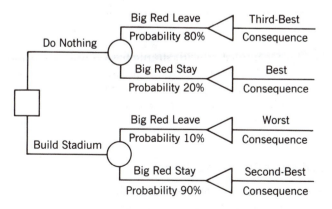

70,000 seats, they may estimate the chances of losing the team at 80 percent if there is no new stadium. Thus, the chances of the most desirable outcome are $100 - 80 = 20$ percent. On the other hand, they may have sufficient assurances from the ownership to produce an estimate that the chances of retaining the team are 90 percent if the new stadium is built. Thus, the chances of the team leaving if the new stadium is built would be $100 - 90 = 10$ percent. Under these conditions, the mayor may well opt for the 90 percent chance of achieving his second preferred consequence through supporting the stadium.

On the other hand, the mayor and his staff may not feel secure that the team will not move even if there is a new stadium. Their best information may support an estimate of a 50-50 chance that the team will leave, even with the new stadium. This estimate may produce different actions by the mayor. He may opt to do nothing, hoping for the possibility of his most preferred outcome. Alternatively, he may try to reduce the uncertainty associated with building the stadium. One option, for example, would be to seek a guaranteed lease with the football team, were the stadium to be built.

Back-of-the-Envelope Calculations

Behn and Vaupel (1982:7) report the experiences of Richard Zeckhauser (an accomplished policy analyst) on his first day as an analyst in the Defense Department. On arriving at the job, Zeckhauser had a conversation with his new boss in which he discussed the nuances of his highly quantitative college thesis. Following the conversation, his new supervisor commented:

> That was good fun. Let's talk about your work here in the Defense Department.
> Do you know how to add, subtract, multiply, and divide?
> Yes.
> Do you understand what marginal analysis is?
> Yes.
> Good, that and common sense is what you will need. (Quoted in Behn and Vaupel, 1982:7.)

Useful analysis can be accomplished with simple back-of-the-envelope calculations (Patton and Sawicki, 1986:110). Many basic facts can be reasonably estimated by using existing information as a base and by performing simple logical and mathematical operations. An example demonstrates the potential value of obtaining useful data with simple arithmetic computations.

Estimating Reductions in Prison Populations

Prison overcrowding is a nationwide criminal justice issue. Get-tough sentencing laws and an increased willingness for judges to send offenders to prison have combined to fill prisons in many states beyond their capacity (Austin, 1986). Under pressure from courts and interest groups, officials in one state were forced to explore various means of reducing overcrowding in corrections facilities (EMT Associates, 1987).

Confronted with a prison population at 150 percent of capacity, the director of the Department of Corrections in a large state was asked by the governor to come up with recommendations to alleviate the problem as quickly as possible. The director consulted with staff and determined that instituting a program of "administrative good time" might be the most feasible and effective means of reducing prison populations. "Good time" programs credit inmates with time off their sentences as long as they are on good behavior in prison. However, the director wanted some specifics to give the governor when they met the following morning. Just how many prison beds would a good time policy save in its first year?

The director asked a staff member to come up with a defensible estimate, which means a conservative estimate using conservative assumptions. There was no time for a full-blown estimation study, so the staff member turned to back-of-the-envelope calculations. The first step was to set boundaries on the estimate—to identify a numerical foundation which could be used to develop the estimate. Where to start? The staff member reasoned that the good time policy would simply accelerate the release of inmates who were close to release anyhow. Therefore, if she could determine how many inmates would be released in the first year, she would have a place to start.

A spokesperson at the statistics division of the Department of Corrections told her that just over 32,000 inmates were released in the previous year and that the number of annual releases had increased only slightly over the last half decade. Thus, an estimate of 32,000 releases in the next year would be safe and conservative.

The next question posed by the staff member was, How much will the release of these inmates be accelerated by the new policy? The answer would depend on how much time off would be credited for good behavior. To establish a reasonable number, the staff member called corrections agencies in several other states that had good time policies. These states credited from 5 to 15 days for each month of good behavior. A conservative policy would credit 5 days for each 30 days of good behavior. The analyst chose this figure as a basis for her calculations.

One further figure was needed to set some boundaries for the estimate. Since the good time credit was dependent on good behavior, not all 32,000 annual releases would receive the credit. Another call to the statistics section revealed that approximately 80 percent of the state's inmates were classified as minimum risk—a reasonable basis for estimating the number of inmates who would be eligible for good time credit. Now, the staff member was ready to come up with some numbers.

Some quick calculations told the analyst that approximately 25,600 inmates would be eligible for good time credit in the first year (80 percent of total releases). She also determined that the policy, when fully implemented, would reduce the demand for bed space by 16.7 percent (5 days' credit per month would reduce sentences by that amount). However, the director needed an estimate of the savings in the first year. The governor had made it clear he would not accept a retroactive policy, and the program would not achieve its full effect immediately.

Yet another call to the statistics section revealed that releases were fairly stable through the year; they did not fluctuate significantly from month to month. She determined that 25,600/12 = 2,133 inmates would be released each month in the next year. Thus, the first month of the policy 2,133 inmates × 5 days credit = 10,665 days saved. The second month would produce 2,133 × 10 days = 21,330 days saved, and so on. Figure 13.4 displays the work sheet for developing an estimate of bed savings in the first year of the proposed policy.

The calculations are straightforward, arrived at through multiplying the number of expected eligible releases each month by the number of days of credit they would have accumulated since the policy was implemented (5 days for each month since implementation). The calculations included potential releases for the next 14 months because the accelerated release rates would mean that inmates scheduled for release in the first two months of year 2 would be released toward the end of year 1. Multiplication and

FIGURE 13.4 Administrative Good Time First-Year Savings

Releases per month for year 1

$$25,600 \div 12 = 2,133$$

Monthly savings

Month 1	2,133 × 5 days =	10,665 days saved
Month 2	2,133 × 10 days =	21,330 days saved
Month 3	2,133 × 15 days =	31,995 days saved
Month 4	2,133 × 20 days =	42,660 days saved
Month 5	2,133 × 25 days =	53,325 days saved
Month 6	2,133 × 30 days =	63,990 days saved
Month 7	2,133 × 35 days =	74,655 days saved
Month 8	2,133 × 40 days =	85,320 days saved
Month 9	2,133 × 45 days =	95,985 days saved
Month 10	2,133 × 50 days =	106,650 days saved
Month 11	2,133 × 55 days =	117,315 days saved
Month 12	2,133 × 60 days =	127,980 days saved
Month 13	2,133 × 65 days =	138,645 days saved
Month 14	2,133 × 70 days =	149,310 days saved
		1,119,825 days saved

1,119,825 ÷ 365 = 3,068 bed years saved.

3,068 ÷ 118,000 total inmates = 2.6 percent savings in first year.

addition produced a reduction of 1,119,825 days of incarceration in the first year of the policy. A few simple divisions reveal that 3,068 bed years would be saved in the first year of implementation, a reduction of 2.6 percent in the total demand for bed space in the correction system.

Thus, with a few select telephone inquiries and simple hand calculations, the staff member produced an estimate of the effect of a good time policy on the state's prison population in the first year, and when fully implemented. With little additional effort, the effects of altering the policy (e.g., crediting 10 days per month of good behavior) could be calculated. The use of spread-sheet programs available for microcomputers allows even quicker calculations of assumptions underlying preceding estimates. The example demonstrates general procedures for conducting back-of-the-envelope calculations. These include:

- Use available information to develop a starting point for performing the necessary calculations.
- Calculate boundaries for estimates: what are reasonable maximums and minimums?
- Refine estimates using logic, additional available information, and arithmetic.
- Test the sensitivity of the calculations by altering assumptions and assessing the effects on results.

As with most quick analysis, back-of-the-envelope calculations rely heavily on the common sense of analysts. Although common sense may result in inaccurate assumptions and flawed information, back-of-the-envelope calculations may yield valuable returns to stakeholders.

Using Available Information

Quick analysis relies on easily retrievable information; collecting new empirical data is time consuming and expensive. The analyst is involved in putting together a puzzle based on information produced by others for other purposes.

> Quick analysis largely consists of putting the pieces together. Locating the pieces and finding the way they match is the primary job of the analyst.... It is better to analyze roughly appropriate existing data exhaustively than to conduct a superficial analysis of hastily collected new data. (Patton and Sawicki, 1986:43)

Skills at quickly identifying and assessing the quality of relevant existing data are important to quick analysis. This section briefly discusses approaches to finding and assembling pieces of relevant information. A more complete treatment is presented in the chapter on documentary research.

RECORDS AND REPORTS

Public and private organizations produce volumes of data on many topics. Governmental units provide numerous regular reports on social and economic conditions; agencies collect and store management records that contain a variety of information on agency activities, clients, and finances; interest groups and business associations collect and maintain data on issues of interest to them. All are sources of information for quick analysis.

Statistical reports produced by the Bureau of the Census are an example of useful existing information. The census provides demographic, economic, and social data for governmental units and geographic subdivisions within those units. Census data provide a basis for quick estimates of potential need or potential clientele for public programs. When a city's Office for the Disabled was asked to estimate the need for its services in the city, it used information produced by new questions on physical and mental handicaps in the 1980 census.

When analysts use information collected by others, data quality becomes a concern. Analysts take care to assess the relevance and quality of the data they are reviewing using criteria discussed in Chapter 7. While records and reports are essential to quick analysis, they are first assessed for technical worth and for their relevancy to the immediate issue.

EXPERT SURVEYS

Individuals knowledgeable about the issue being studied are a second source of information for quick analysis. When asked to develop an estimate of the effects of administrative good time, the analyst in the example got on the phone to the statistics section and to knowledgeable officials in states that had experience with the policy. In many instances, data can be located most quickly by contacting individuals in the policy community. Quick, expert surveys are often conducted by telephone and use open-ended interview techniques such as those discussed in Chapter 6.

Use Multiple Sources

The value of triangulation has been stressed throughout this text. Nowhere is it more important than in conducting quick analysis. Quick analysis attempts to produce reasonably accurate and useful answers to core questions; precise and detailed empirical results lie beyond its scope. Quick analysis is not as systematic as is researched analysis. The use of triangulated approaches is well suited to producing more accurate and useful and quick analysis.

Typically, no single data source provides complete responses to questions facing analysts and users. Operational definitions, target populations, time periods, or other details of the data source commonly differ from those that would ideally address research questions. When faced by such a problem, Patton and Sawicki (1986:111) suggest analysts "employ triangulation; estimate the unknown quantity using several completely separate approaches and data sources, and compare the results for reasonableness."

Similarly, when there is a need to develop subjective probabilities concerning policy outcomes, or when the feasibility of a given policy option is being assessed, analysts apply principles of triangulation to ensure that a variety of perspectives are considered. The opinions of representatives from opposing or divergent interests are solicited and combined to produce a more complete and balanced portrait of the issue. Analysts relying on a single data source or a single point of view are making their analysis partial and vulnerable to charges of biased and incomplete information.

CONCLUDING COMMENTS

Policy research is an action-oriented set of skills. As such, its techniques are adaptable to a variety of problems and decision situations faced by users. Much policy research takes place under pressure. Time lines, multiple demands on staff, budget competition, and the magnitude of many problems combine to limit time and other resources available for analysis.

When under pressure to produce information with limited time and resources, analysts adopt the orientations of quick analysis. As contrasted with researched analysis, quick analysis provides information used by specific decision makers to develop positions on particular concerns.

Choices between quick analysis and researched analysis approaches depend on the policy context: the resources available, the consequences of error, the opportunities for reconsideration, and so forth. Often, research efforts include a mix of quick analysis and more researched approaches, particularly in triangulated studies.

Quick analysis requires analysts to focus more on thinking the problem through and less on collecting primary data. In the structuring stages of quick analysis, attention is devoted to identifying the range of perspectives or questions that may be attached to the issue at hand. Understanding the range of perspectives is important for clarifying the dimensions and boundaries of a concern. Analysts continue to structure the issue, working with stakeholders to specify the major aspects of the problem from their point of view. Techniques such as Behn and Vaupel's (1982) decision saplings help simplify and focus questions addressed in quick analysis.

Quick analysis involves approximations and adaptations of data gathered elsewhere for other purposes. It is not as systematic and thorough as is more researched analysis. Analysts using quick analysis methodology clearly communicate limitations of analysis, identifying the implications of the limitations for the accuracy and usefulness of resulting information.

In conducting quick analysis, analysts keep it simple. They refer to existing sources of information to find data relevant to the concern, and manipulate data through straightforward calculations. While quick analysis seems less glamorous than researched policy studies, its importance should not be underestimated. Quick analysis plays a fundamental role in contributing to the resolution of concerns cumulatively shaping public policies and programs.

REFERENCES

Austin, James. 1986. *The Use of Early Release and Sentencing Guidelines to Ease Prison Crowding: The Shifting Sands of Reform.* San Francisco, CA: National Council on Crime and Delinquency.

Behn, Robert D., and James W. Vaupel. 1982. *Quick Analysis for Busy Decision Makers.* New York: Basic Books.

Director's Task Force on Drug Abuse Prevention. 1984. *Final Report.* Sacramento, CA: California Department of Alcohol and Drug Programs.

EMT Associates. 1987. *Alternative to Incarceration Programs: A Review of Evaluation Literature.* Sacramento, CA: California Department of Corrections.

Hawkins, J. David, and Britt Nederhood. 1986. *Staff/Team Evaluation of Prevention Programs: STEPP Handbook.* Washington, DC: National Institute of Drug Abuse.

Kummer, James A. 1986. "Part-Time Bus Operators at the Bi-State Development Agency: A Cost-Saving Analysis." St. Louis, MO: Final Report to the Bi-State Development Agency.

Moberg, Paul D. 1984. *Evaluation of Prevention Programs: A Basic Guide for Practitioners.* Madison, WI: Wisconsin Clearinghouse.

Patton, Carl V., and David S. Sawicki. 1986. *Basic Methods of Policy Analysis and Planning.* Englewood Cliffs, NJ: Prentice-Hall.

Polya, George. 1957. *How to Solve It.* New York: Doubleday.

Stokey, Edith, and Richard Zeckhauser. 1978. *A Primer for Policy Analysis.* New York: W. W. Norton.

Wholey, Joseph. 1983. *Evaluation and Effective Public Management.* Boston: Little, Brown.

14

Planning and Managing Policy Research

Consider the examples of policy studies used throughout prior chapters. Many of these studies were complex, multifaceted, requiring combined efforts. Some studies involved teams of analysts; others involved multiple organizations—public agencies, legislative committees, universities, and consulting firms. All of the studies required analysts skilled in planning and managing research activities to meet the information needs of stakeholders.

Research activities must be designed so they achieve study objectives within resource constraints; communications and coordination must be maintained within the research team and with users; teams of principal analysts and research assistants must be supervised. Policy research is an activity requiring skills in planning and management.

This chapter discusses planning and management skills used by policy analysts. An introduction to project planning and management is an essential complement to the skills of structuring research questions, collecting information, and interpreting study results. Planning and management skills provide the means through which analysts put together the pieces of policy research projects.

The chapter first discusses the functions of planning and management for projects of differing size and character. Second, it identifies techniques for planning research tasks, staffing requirements, and resource needs. Third, it examines problems and approaches to supervising and to facilitating the work of members of the research team. Finally, it discusses approaches to managing the communication and use of study results.

POLICY RESEARCH: PLANNING AND MANAGEMENT REQUIREMENTS

Policy research projects vary in magnitude. At one extreme are massive research efforts such as the development of a "star wars" missile defense system in space, or efforts at managing major public health threats such as AIDS. Efforts of this magnitude require major commitments of resources, calling for research programs that commission and coordinate numerous specific research efforts in meeting information needs.

At the other extreme is quick analysis requiring only a few minutes, hours, or days. This type of policy research is often carried out by single individuals who rely on their personal skills in understanding problems and quickly finding relevant information.

The majority of research projects that policy analysts implement fall between these extremes. These projects vary in scope, duration, and complexity, but do share common characteristics (Burman, 1972:3).

- Policy research projects are *finite.* Unlike research programs which serve a general ongoing goal such as controlling crime, research projects have specific information needs such as testing whether a particular intervention reduces neighborhood burglaries. The research objectives of a project are accomplished within specified limits of time, dollars, and other resources. They have a definite end point at which they can be said to be complete and their objectives met.
- Policy research projects are *nonrepetitive.* They address specific problems within a particular context. Even though they may be designed to contribute to the cumulation of general knowledge through a research program, they are one-time efforts for the particular analyst(s) involved. This means that policy research projects are creative, designed to meet unique requirements of the situation.
- Policy research projects are *complex.* While projects may be limited, requiring only limited participation of staff and limited time, they are complex in the sense that their results are not obvious. They require problem structuring, identification of appropriate information needs, and skillful interpretation of results. They frequently require consideration of the multiple perspectives and multiple stakeholders in the policy process.

There are also differences in the way research projects are accomplished. A major difference is between projects that are carried out by in-house staff of an organization responsible for implementing study results—*inside research*—and projects that are carried out by an external analytic team—*outside research* (Mayer and Greenwood, 1983:265).

Inside and Outside Research Projects

Policy research is undertaken in a number of ways. In many instances, organizations undertake self-analyses in which they research topics relevant to their organizational concerns. Staff of community-based drug abuse prevention programs may, for instance, conduct an evaluation of their services to seek ways of improving them. Inside research occurs when agencies use their own staff to produce information about their own program activities and outcomes.

Outside research is policy analysis conducted by an organization that "does not carry out any of the activities under investigation" (Mayer and Greenwood, 1983:256). Outside research can be either requested or imposed. An example of imposed research is an evaluation of programs in a state department of human resources carried out by staff in a legislative research unit. This type of outside research is often mandated by legislatures or funding agencies in order to assess the performance of specific programs.

In other instances, agencies or programs may request outside research. In this case, the research will serve the purposes of the agency responsible for the activity being studied, but is conducted by another organization. Governmental agencies rely on a number of sources for outside research. Research services may be provided by private consulting firms, colleges and universities, or research staffs in other governmental agencies such as councils of government or other planning bodies. For larger projects, outside analysts are usually selected through a competitive process in which the agencies evaluate research proposals from several bidders.

In some instances, policy research projects involve a combination of inside and outside organizations. Organizations often have the basic capability and resources to carry out systematic policy research, but require assistance on designing the analysis or other areas requiring special skills. In these cases, outside consultants may be used to provide assistance in the design phases, in training staff in particular research skills, or in assisting the internal staff with tasks such as sampling, statistical analysis, and computer modeling.

USING OUTSIDE CONSULTANTS OR INSIDE STAFF

Often, the decision about whether a policy research project is to be done by inside or outside analysts is dictated by circumstances. In many cases, funds may not be available for securing outside assistance. If analysis is needed, there is no choice but to have in-house staff do the work. In other cases, a lack of in-house capability or a prior commitment of staff time leaves little choice but to contract for outside research consultants, assuming funding is available. When there is discretion in choosing between inside or outside research work, or in choosing a creative mix of both, several considerations are relevant.

An initial consideration is that contracting with outside researchers carries distinct benefits. For example, consulting firms, universities, and governmental research units employ personnel specializing in policy research tasks. They bring training, experience, and technical competence to research projects. Since these specialized organizations have policy research as their primary activity, they produce more technically sophisticated research than do internal staff.

Second, outside research often has greater credibility and impartiality than does inside research. Staff in the organization responsible for the activities under study may have an interest in finding favorable program results, for example. When the purposes of policy research are to hold a program accountable (is it effectively and efficiently accomplishing its publicly mandated objectives?), these considerations may point to outside research assistance. Similarly, if an agency or program wants to provide credible evidence of effective performance (say for representing themselves to a funding agency), outside research may counteract perceptions that study results are self-serving, lacking detachment.

On the other hand, contracting with outside researchers to conduct policy research presents drawbacks.

- Costs and time requirements may exceed those of an in-house analysis. Part of the reason is that outside analysts are not familiar with the program under study and consume time learning about it.
- Outside analysts may not acquire an adequate understanding of a dynamic complex policy issue, leading to less relevant findings and recommendations. A result may be that "implementing outside findings may not be as palatable to those inside who have to live with the consequences of recommendations which were 'invented' elsewhere. Thus, although outside studies may be of higher technical quality, they may represent problems when the time comes to implement their recommendations" (Hatry, Winnie, and Fisk, 1976:23).
- Outside analysts may be perceived as more threatening than an internal team and may meet more resistance in obtaining information and in eliciting assistance from staff.

Strengths and weaknesses of outside research also vary with the type of organization conducting the study. Consulting firms often specialize in certain policy areas or analytic techniques. Some specialize in community services; others in management audits, work load studies, or analyses of personnel systems. When decision makers desire information of these specialized types, firms with developed techniques and experience offer advantages.

In other instances, using the research services of colleges and universities offers advantages. University researchers are helpful in exploring less well-defined information needs which cannot be easily met with a standardized approach. Contracting with academics, however, also brings drawbacks.

> Users should be [alerted], however, that some academics prefer to work on federal level problems, may be inclined toward ivory tower solutions, or may emphasize work that is publishable from a disciplinary perspective rather than practical for the government. (Hatry, Winnie, and Fisk, 1976:21)

In brief, policy research projects come in a variety of sizes and organizational settings. In deciding whether to undertake or to commission a research project, policymakers consider what is necessary to meet information objectives. Regardless of the choices made, once it is decided to undertake a policy research effort, projects require the planning of activities and the management of resources. Subsequent sections present basic skills in planning and managing projects.

PLANNING RESEARCH PROJECTS

Project planning is carried out with different degrees of formality and precision. For a small in-house project relying on quick analysis techniques, planning may be accomplished in a brief period of time. The responsibilities for planning and managing research tasks will probably be left to staff member(s) assigned to complete the project. Larger projects require detailed written plans that guide the course of the research program.

In any project, a well-designed plan provides benefits for producers and users of policy research (Davis and Cosenza, 1985:64–65). Users who request the project can

- assess the plan to see if the proposed research and its information products are likely to yield useful information at an efficient and affordable cost;
- assess the relative value of the planned research in relation to other organizational priorities;
- use the plan as a basis for monitoring and controlling research activities, helping to ensure the study produces what was promised.

Analysts also benefit. A well-designed plan:

- Assists analysts in thinking through the research problem. Explicitly identifying tasks helps assure the project produces the necessary information.
- Assists analysts in designing projects that are realistic. Explicitly planning the allocation of resources in the project helps identify tasks that can or cannot be accomplished with available resources.
- Provides analysts with a specific plan of action that focuses their activities once the project is under way.

Project planning refers to developing a game plan for a policy research endeavor. Planning tasks are usually drafted by those performing and supervising research activities, although it is often a good idea to include a range of stakeholders in the process.

Since policy research projects are nonrepetitive, the substance of each plan is uniquely tailored to information needs. Nevertheless, some standard procedures aid analysts through important steps of the planning process. While all projects do not need or warrant such detailed planning, the major components presented are relevant to any policy research project. First discussed is scheduling tasks.

Scheduling Research Tasks

The scheduling component categorizes specific tasks and orders them in a sequence of planned activities. The planned schedules of tasks, frequently displayed graphically, provide management with a basis to monitor planned performance of project activities. Major approaches to scheduling tasks include the use of Gantt charts and network analysis techniques.

GANTT CHARTS

The best-known type of display for showing the flow of tasks and activities in a research project is the Gantt chart developed by Henry L. Gantt, who first used the procedure in the early 1900s (Burman, 1972:8). Gantt charts are most commonly employed in presenting project progress and in clarifying work activities required to accomplish information objectives. They include such items as listings of events, event durations, schedule dates, and progress to date. Figure 14.1 provides a sample Gantt chart adapted from the Lake Tahoe transportation study. Each bar in the figure represents a single category of activity.

Gantt charts are advantageous because they are easy to understand

Research Activity

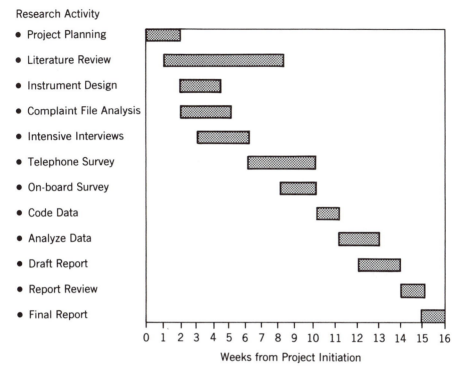

- Project Planning
- Literature Review
- Instrument Design
- Complaint File Analysis
- Intensive Interviews
- Telephone Survey
- On-board Survey
- Code Data
- Analyze Data
- Draft Report
- Report Review
- Final Report

0 1 2 3 4 5 6 7 8 9 10 11 12 13 14 15 16

Weeks from Project Initiation

FIGURE 14.1 Illustration of a Gantt Chart Displaying Major Research Activities and Time Lines

and easy to change in projects the magnitude of the Lake Tahoe transportation study. They are the least complex means of portraying progress and are frequently employed in projects of low or moderate complexity.

Simple scheduling tools such as Gantt charts have drawbacks, particularly in complex one-time projects. Burman (1972:13–14) observes that Gantt charts and similar techniques

> use time as the basis against which the plan is drawn. They are, therefore, only truly applicable where time estimates can be made with reasonable accuracy, and adhered to during the project. This is generally . . . not [true] in a 'one time' project, where times are often only educated guesses at the best. Any major error in time estimation requires a complete re-drawing of the plan, and the simpler techniques are thus not sufficiently dynamic in a large project.

Large projects may be composed of hundreds of interrelated activities. A Gantt chart attempting to detail these tasks quickly becomes unmanageable and unreadable. Further, no simple scheduling technique is capable of showing the interdependencies of research tasks and activities. When using simple scheduling techniques like Gantt charts in larger projects, management loses control over the course of the study, not knowing where to concentrate efforts necessary for the project to finish in the minimum time and at least costs.

NETWORK ANALYSIS

In larger projects, network-based scheduling techniques enable "the project manager to plan diverse undertakings on an integrated basis, as well as to coordinate project tasks and to control work accomplishment" (Digman and Green, 1981:10). Network analysis is an approach to planning, scheduling, and coordinating project tasks by recording their interrelationships in diagrammatic form. Networks model the flow of work necessary in completing a project. "They visually portray the events and activities that are planned for the project and show their sequential relationships and interdependencies" (White et al., 1980:87).

Network models are constructed through a network diagram in which each project task is represented by a circle and an arrow on the graphic. How circles and arrows are linked indicates the dependencies of research events and activities on one another. Figure 14.2 displays a simple arrow representation of sequence. The direction of the arrows specifies that the activity "draw survey sample" precedes the activity "conduct survey," which in turn comes before "code and analyze data." The diagram also indicates that designing and pretesting the survey instrument will occur while the

FIGURE 14.2 Arrow Representation of Sequence

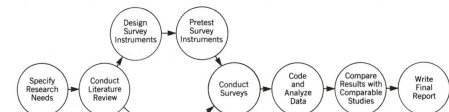

sample is being drawn. All of these activities must be finished before the final report can be written.

While many separate techniques exist, perhaps the best-known and most-used network approach is PERT (Program Evaluation and Review Technique). PERT is an approach developed in the late 1950s, in part by the Special Projects Office of the U.S. Navy:

> The Special Projects Office of the Navy, concerned with performance trends on large military development programs, introduced PERT on its Polaris Weapon System in 1958, after the technique had been developed with the aid of the management consulting firm of Booze, Allen and Hamilton (Kerzner, 1979:335).

The introduction of PERT in scheduling and coordinating activities succeeded in "reducing the development time for the Polaris missile by over two years, a reduction of some 45%" (Burman, 1972:15). Since that time, PERT has found wide acceptance in planning larger projects.

Similar to other network approaches, PERT requires that analysts first identify individual tasks comprising a project. These tasks (activities and events) are sequentially organized into a network diagram to reflect the order required for project completion. Time estimates are made for each task in the network. Cost estimates may also be included. After network calculations have been performed, the resulting information is used by project directors to "reallocate resources between activities as required or desired, resulting in a schedule of activities and events which efficiently utilizes resources and meets schedule constraints (to the extent possible)" (Digman and Green, 1981:13).

PERT and other network-based techniques are advantageous in larger policy projects for good reason:

- Network techniques display interrelations between activities, allowing analysts to see not only the flow of work, but also the ways in which their own activities depend upon or are influenced by those of others.
- The detail required in constructing network diagrams helps minimize, if not avoid, unrealistic or superficial planning errors.
- Network techniques allow a large amount of relevant data to be presented in a well-organized, decision-relevant format.
- Network techniques help managers identify potential problems. Management attention and resources can be focused on these potential problems.

Although valuable in planning larger projects, network analysis is tedious and exacting, particularly if attempted manually. Standard computer programs are available in sequencing tasks and in developing time and cost data, making it technically an easier task. For large, complex, and costly projects, the investment in detailed scheduling techniques is well rewarded.

Developing a Plan

The scope of a project and the complexity of its research and administrative tasks determine personnel requirements. Analysts specify the way they will meet these tasks through a staffing plan that accomplishes three objectives: (1) it defines the responsibilities of project personnel, (2) it identifies the administrative organization of the project, and (3) it identifies staff time required for project tasks.

Staff responsibilities are specified by identifying skills necessary to carry out project tasks and then incorporating them into job descriptions. The following job descriptions are adapted from the Lake Tahoe transportation study:

1. *Project Director.* Responsible for the overall direction and supervision of the project. Maintains close coordination with the sponsoring agencies. Monitors project progress. Coordinates tasks and resources. Disseminates research findings.
2. *Research Coordinator.* Responsible for the technical management of the project. Designs research components of the study, e.g., questionnaire construction, data analysis specifications; coordinates and supervises collection of data. Writes research reports.
3. *Resource Consultants.* Provides technical assistance where needed, e.g., designing research, data processing, data analysis, report writing.
4. *Research Assistants.* Responsible for collecting and coding data, and providing assistance in data analysis.
5. *Project Secretary.* Maintains project files and accounting and financial data. Prepares vouchers and payrolls. Orders supplies and services. Types and duplicates project-related material (questionnaires, correspondence, codebooks and coding instructions, training materials, and so forth).

The set of job duties for the transportation study provided the basis for developing an organization chart for the project (Figure 14.3). An organization chart is useful in clarifying the organizational setting of the project, the type and number of personnel constituting the study, and the "chain of responsibility that links them" (Mayer and Greenwood, 1983:267).

Finally, the staff plan specifies the allocation of staff time necessary for each task identified in the work plan. This "task loading" function is an important component of project planning because it links the project's ma-

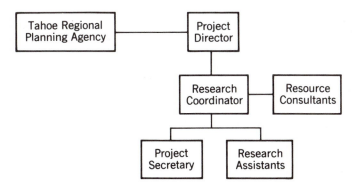

FIGURE 14.3 Organization Chart for Lake Tahoe Transportation Study

jor resource—staff time—directly to the work being proposed. Table 14.1 presents a portion of a task loading chart for the Tahoe study.

A complete chart specifies staff time for each task identified in the project Gantt chart (Figure 14.1). The task loading chart is a major indicator of whether a proposed project can be completed with proposed resources. It forces project planners to consider time requirements of proposed activities in detail, e.g., how long will it take to produce a completed telephone interview? Task loading warrants significant attention in the planning process.

Producing a Budget Plan

The budget of the proposed project documents the amount and type of resources needed to execute research plans. Its development includes estimating the costs of personnel and nonpersonnel resources necessary for completing the project. Where total estimated costs exceed funding reali-

TABLE 14.1 Task Loading Chart for Tahoe Study (partial; staff time in hours)

	DESIGN DATA COLLECTION INSTRUMENTS	CONDUCT TELEPHONE SURVEYS	WRITE FINAL REPORT
Project Director	10	20	40
Research Coordinator	24	20	40
Resource Consultants	10	—	—
Research Assistants	8	250	20
Project Secretary	4	—	50
TOTAL	(56)	(290)	(150)

ties, research proposals require modification to conform to resource limitations. Table 14.2 provides a budget adapted from the Tahoe project.

PERSONNEL COSTS

Research projects are labor intensive; the primary components of most research budgets are wages, salaries, and benefits. The sample budget in Table 14.2 is not unusual—87 percent of the total is personnel costs. Errors in estimating staff time requirements translate directly into errors in proposed budget.

The Tahoe budget demonstrates a straightforward approach to estimating personnel costs. The detailed estimates of staff hours from the task loading chart provide estimates of total hours for each staff position. Multiplying projected hours by hourly rate for each position yields estimated personnel costs.

A second method in estimating personnel costs is to determine "the per unit cost of completing discrete tasks, such as conducting or coding interviews . . . [for personnel] employed on an hourly basis for those tasks" (Mayer and Greenwood, 1983:275). To arrive at total costs, the per unit cost is multiplied by the times the activity will be performed. For repetitive, standardized tasks such as conducting structured interviews and coding and key punching, wages can be reasonably estimated using the per unit costs of completing activities. Whatever the specific method for estimating person-

TABLE 14.2 Sample Research Budget
(adapted from the Lake Tahoe transportation study)

BUDGET ITEM	RATE PER HOUR	HOURS FOR PROJECT	COSTS
Personnel			
Project Manager	$38	152	$5776.00
Research Coordinator	36	136	4896.00
Resource Consultants	30	40	1200.00
Project Secretary	12	152	1824.00
Research Assistants	10	377	3770.00
			Subtotal: $17466.00
Equipment, Supplies, and Related Services			
Long distance telephone			$ 606.00
Key punching			228.00
Computer analysis			100.00
Reproduction (including final report)			600.00
Travel			1000.00
			Subtotal: $2534.00

nel costs, their importance for accurate project budgeting cannot be overestimated.

NONPERSONNEL COSTS

The sample budget in Table 14.2 includes three types of nonpersonnel costs commonly incurred by research projects: (1) equipment and supplies, (2) services, and (3) travel and living expenses. Organizations may include equipment and service requirements in an indirect overhead rate which is calculated as a percentage of specified direct costs (see Chapter 12 for a discussion of indirect costs).

Equipment and supplies may include vehicles, office equipment, telephones and other communication devices, printing and reproduction costs, paper, and so on. These items may be estimated "on the basis of the average monthly expenditures for such items ... for an office with a comparable number of full-time equivalent professional and clerical staff" (Mayer and Greenwood, 1983:280). Average monthly expenditures are multiplied by the expected length of the project in estimating costs of equipment and supplies. Additional items needed specifically to accomplish study activities are then determined and added to office costs, yielding an overall estimate of equipment and supplies.

Services include vehicle operation and maintenance, coding and computer services, and publication costs (editing, typing, printing). Service costs are frequently estimated, using standard rates established by the sponsoring organization or by private companies, and through determining the costs of conducting similar projects. Services in the sample research budget include keypunching and computer time (Table 14.2).

Travel and living expenses in the Lake Tahoe transportation study were budgeted at $1,000. This included travel costs and maintenance of project personnel who were supervising and conducting interviews and surveys in the resort area. Estimates of living expenses are usually based on standard per diem rates paid by governmental agencies.

When research funding is competitively sought from sources outside an existing agency, the need for a well-developed budget is obvious. Less obvious is the need for a budget when research projects are funded through existing agency resources.

> Yet the fact that no new monies are to be spent does not mean that no cost is incurred in carrying out the research. The cost of a given research project is expressed in terms of the loss of alternate activities that could have been conducted with the same resources. Good management practice encourages the budgeting of any activity, even though monies for it already exist, so that efficient choices can be made between alternative ways of spending that money. (Mayer and Greenwood, 1983:273)

Research budgets are required components of project planning, whether or not funded through agency resources.

But budgets are estimates of projected research needs. They are plans, and few planned efforts escape problems in application. Common causes of budget problems in research projects include:

- poor estimation techniques and/or cost standards resulting in unrealistic budgets;
- inadequate planning resulting in unnoticed or often uncontrolled increase in the scope of effort required by project members; and
- unforeseen technical problems, e.g., developing adequate data sources (Kerzner and Thamhain, 1984:188–89).

Critically assessing the feasibility and accuracy of planning decisions is crucial to minimizing error. The consequences of planning errors are long uncompensated hours, strained relations among members of the research team, and incomplete or inadequate project results. No analyst who has ever arrived at the report writing phase and found the money gone will doubt the importance of financial skills in budgeting policy research.

Approval of Project Plans

Approval of project plans helps build commitment by decision makers. Approvals are sought from sponsors of the project and from "the people who can cause the project to fail, by any means, fair or foul" (Miller, 1978:25). Such people may include staff, clients, advocacy groups, agency management, advisory groups, elected officials, and others in the policy community.

Seeking approval from diverse individuals and groups inevitably highlights objections to the proposed research. Depending on what the objections are, project staff may choose the following options (Miller, 1978:26):

- modify the format and presentation, making the plan more understandable and useful for consumers;
- apply more, less, or different resources to activities in order to change completion dates of key research tasks;
- reduce the scope of the project in order to accelerate results and to conserve resources; or
- take a position that the plan as presented is necessary for the successful completion of information objectives.

When approvals for larger projects have been secured, the proposal should be published with its revisions. Published plans have a positive, reinforcing effect on persons approving them, an effect strengthening user obligations and commitments to project objectives and outcomes. Published plans are equally beneficial for analysts, providing focus and direction to research endeavors.

MANAGING RESEARCH PROJECTS

Implementing the plan is what a research project is all about. Effectively managing the plan's implementation promotes the subsequent use of information products. In project environments, effective management means skillfully fulfilling leadership tasks arising throughout the course of the study. Major leadership tasks of project directors include:

1. Developing project teams
2. Managing team conflict
3. Monitoring resource expenditures
4. Maintaining ties with stakeholders
5. Reporting research
6. Bringing projects to completion

Developing Project Teams

Selecting proper key staff in inside research is critical to successful project outcomes. In larger policy studies, staffing is typically conducted in two phases. First, sponsors—e.g., agency management, elected officials—select the project manager (and sometimes other major project members). Second, personnel directly reporting to the project managers are recruited and assigned to the study, typically by the director. Also during this time, support personnel, task specialists, and individual contributors are identified, selected, and assigned to the project.

Projects fail or succeed based on the skills project managers bring to their duties. Project directors require a high level of skill in integrating specialists from diverse disciplinary and professional perspectives into effective working teams. They cope with constant change in an evolving work environment affecting the course of the research. They understand the subtle interplay of organizational and behavioral dynamics to maximize subsequent acceptance and usage of project results. They possess a high degree of leadership in guiding research activities in relatively unstructured project environments.

Since policy research is labor-intensive, the quality of project outcomes depends on the selection of project personnel. Research is a complex activity involving varied operations ranging from creative and open-ended activities such as problem structuring and information interpretation, to repetitive and detailed work such as coding information from agency records. It is crucial to match the skills, expectations, and motivations of staff to the particular requirements of the tasks they will perform. A person who expects to exercise discretion and creativity should not be hired in a position that will involve only routine duties.

In some projects, team members are selected by senior management or department managers; the project director may have little or no say in who is selected. When this occurs, project managers may be given available personnel rather than those most motivated and qualified for project tasks. The result can be uninterested, unskilled personnel. Generally, "the more power the project leader has over the selection of his team members, . . . the more likely team building efforts will be fruitful" (Kerzner and Thamhain, 1984:306).

A primary responsibility of project managers is developing a work climate conducive to effective team functioning. A first step to create such a climate is to establish a team of sufficient size to realistically do the necessary work. Understaffed projects inevitably suffer from tension and frustration. It is also important to establish a flexible team organization that encourages communications and participation in management decisions (Baker, Fisher, and Murphy, 1983:697).

Further, it is important to ensure that basic research tasks are stated in clear, succinct terms and that information products of projects are specified with as much accuracy as possible. Successful project managers establish definite objectives for the project and seek understanding among project participants regarding the significance of the objectives and the potential usefulness of research products. Again, participative decision-making styles are generally more successful in creating and maintaining commitment than are other styles (Wilemon and Baker, 1983:639). Establishing a communicative, supportive team climate at the outset of a project reaps dividends in those periods when the project requires redirection, when deadlines approach, and when team members must cooperate in producing final research products.

Managing Team Conflict

Effectively managing conflict is a responsibility challenging project directors throughout the life cycle of a study. Conflict is an inescapable, pervasive feature of organizational landscapes, and "any organization in which it doesn't occur, or occurs only rarely, is one in which people either don't feel free to think for themselves or don't feel free to express their thoughts and ideas" (Labovitz, 1984:600).

Free expression and discussion of different opinions and conclusions is particularly important to policy research. The open-ended nature of research problems requires active discussion and debate to improve decisions. In this context, conflict is desirable. It represents attempts to change established thought and action. It is beneficial when it produces new information and improved project outcomes. It serves as a creative force in adapting to changing circumstances characteristic of project environments.

But when conflict is detrimental, it cripples project functioning. "It often results in poor program decision making, lengthy delays over operational issues, and a disruption of the team's efforts—all negative influences on program performance" (Kerzner and Thamhain, 1984:273). Considering the multiple roles of conflict—beneficial and detrimental—project directors do not attempt to muzzle or avoid dissension, but to recognize and harness its constructive potential to study objectives.

Conflict has many sources in research projects. Thamhain and Wilemon (1975) identified seven potential sources of conflict in projects:

1. *Scheduling:* disagreement over the timing and sequencing of research tasks
2. *Project Priorities:* differing views over the issues and outcomes most important to complete projects successfully, possibly requiring a reallocation of resources
3. *Human Resources:* conflict over the staffing of projects, particularly between departments supporting the effort
4. *Technical Concerns:* disagreement over performance specifications, technical trade-offs, and technical means to achieve performance objectives
5. *Administrative Procedures:* dissension over operational issues, e.g., definition of responsibilities, plan of execution, procedures for administrative support, reporting relationships
6. *Cost:* conflict over resources allocated for project activities
7. *Personality Conflict:* interpersonal differences among project participants

While any of these sources of conflict emerge in project life cycles, project directors report the most intense conflict surrounds scheduling, project priorities, and manpower decisions (Thamhain and Wilemon, 1975:31–50).

Recognizing potential sources of conflict helps directors anticipate and prepare for positive conflict resolution. Project directors handle conflict in several ways (Burke, 1969:48–55):

- *Withdrawal:* ignoring or retreating from conflicts
- *Smoothing:* suppressing or deemphasizing disagreements
- *Forcing:* imposing solutions to resolve issues
- *Compromising:* negotiating and searching for solutions bringing some degree of satisfaction to participants involved in disputes; and
- *Confronting or Problem Solving:* resolving differences through an integra-

tive problem-solving process, attempting to find ways to mesh conflicting parties' goals and needs

To determine actual conflict approaches used by project managers,
research was conducted by Thamhain and Wilemon (1975) in conjunction
with their work on conflict in project life cycles. While project managers
reported using a combination of approaches, they showed a clear preference for the problem-solving approach. Seventy percent of a sample of project directors reported they used that method most frequently.

There are good reasons project managers use problem-solving approaches to conflict resolution. In the labor-intensive and frequently stress-
ful project work environment, decisions about scheduling, research approaches, and so forth, create or modify tasks that are carried out by other
members of the research team. In this environment, a forcing approach
to conflict resolution leads to resentment and resistance. In comparison, a
problem-solving approach incorporates a "win-win" approach to conflict
resolution.

> Win-win strategies are typically the result of participative management tech-
> niques in which all parties to a conflict collaborate in establishing common
> or superordinate goals, and also engage in joint problem-solving efforts to
> determine how those goals can best be met. (Labovitz, 1984:604)

Naturally, conflict resolution approaches are tailored to the content
of the conflict, the persons involved, the implications for project objectives,
and other contextual features. Project directors employ the full range of
conflict-resolution approaches in their capacity as team leaders and facilita-
tors.

Monitoring Resource Expenditures

Another responsibility of project managers is to monitor and guide
the allocation of funds during the study. The basis of the resource allocation
process is the budget, illustrated in Table 14.2. The budget states the total
amount of funds expected to be available, along with information on how
the funds will be distributed.

Sometimes budgets are prepared and promptly forgotten, a regretta-
ble error. The consequences of the error become increasingly evident in
later phases of projects (we're out of money), resulting in frayed tempers
amid charges and countercharges. It takes only one such experience to convince project managers of the efficacy of using the budget as a guide against
which performance is measured—as a financial plan of action for achieving
research aims.

In larger research projects, a desirable practice is establishing written
policies and procedures for authorizing expenditures. When policies are

stated and understood, rules of the game have been established, resulting in fewer misunderstandings and unnecessary conflict. Project managers fulfill an important responsibility in monitoring research expenditures as they oversee and manage the course of the project. Increasingly, their performance is evaluated not only on information products of the research, but also on their sophistication in making financial decisions relative to facilitating successful project outcomes.

> These [financial] controls need not be unduly restrictive. Properly designed, they can be a real help to the manager in using his resources well. When they are sensible, applied with discretion, and explained to the professional staff, there need be little resentment or opposition by the staff. If, on the other hand, they are used to control rather than assist, they will be resented and flouted. (Blake, 1978:223)

Maintaining Ties with Stakeholders

A common theme in prior chapters is the necessity of involving users in research projects. Project directors assume the prime responsibility of maintaining collaborative efforts and coordinating activities with stakeholders in programs under study. The quality of relationships of the project team with concerned groups may spell the difference between successful or unsuccessful project outcomes (Baker, Fisher, and Murphy, 1983:685).

Although linkages with decision makers are most keenly needed in formulating and planning policy research, project managers continue the ties in carrying out research. Potential users are afforded opportunities to express ideas and concerns. Project directors remain accessible to policymakers and relevant others. Periodic progress reports on project status are transmitted through written and oral communication channels. Insights and suggestions are sought by project managers as alternatives, conclusions, recommendations, and action plans are developed. Stakeholders are asked to review drafts to identify and correct factual errors, omissions, misinterpretations, misleading statements, unworkable alternatives and recommendations. Through maintaining linkages with users, project directors reap dividends in keeping interested parties committed to the project, thereby enhancing subsequent usage.

Much policy research requires data collection from staff or records in the programs being studied. To accomplish this work, members of the research team work with staff in the agency. In conducting the evaluation of career criminal programs (introduced in Chapter 2), for instance, data were coded from prosecutors' case files. Coding required several weeks of work in each of seven prosecutors' offices. It required finding work space and sampling and retrieving the files. The project director was careful to establish and maintain friendly and cooperative working relations with the records supervisor in each site. Project staff did as much of the retrieval themselves as possible and minimized their intrusion into office activities. Successful project management requires maintaining ties with nonproject staff as well as with stakeholders.

Reporting Research

Reporting research information to stakeholders is an ongoing responsibility of project leaders. How well they report information influences user perceptions of the merit and relevancy of project results. Two primary communication tasks of project managers and analysts are the writing of a final report of the study and making oral presentations to users.

WRITING FINAL REPORTS

During project life cycles, research proposals, progress reports, and final reports constitute major written communication linkages between analysts and users. Final research reports include full documentation and detail. They typically survive original data files and working papers, and become sole or major source documents. Decision makers, analysts, and others reference them because they provide the most complete coverage of what was done, how it was done, and what the results were. Final reports are the information products of research projects. Following discussions emphasize two key concerns in final reports: report format and report writing.

REPORT FORMAT

Well-organized final reports provide road maps for readers, guiding them through a maze of concepts. An effective format lets them know in logical, understandable fashion the content of the report and how the content will be presented.

Outlines of final reports vary. In some organizations, a preferred outline for report formats may be established in writing or through convention. Project writers often reference related technical reports in creating working outlines for communicating research information. Although each final report has its individual characteristics of organization and format, most contain the following components:

1. *The Title Page.* The title page includes four items: the title of the report, the date of submission, for whom the report was prepared, and by whom it was prepared.
2. *The Executive Summary.* This is the report in miniature. It provides a statement of the issue, how the study was conducted, and a summary

of conclusions and recommendations emerging from the analysis. It may be the only section of a long report read by users.

3. *Tables of Contents, Charts, and Illustrations.* Listing major headings and subheadings in a contents section is useful because it aids readers in going directly to relevant sections in final reports, and because it provides order and flow to topics. Tables, charts, and other exhibits are listed after the table of contents, perhaps in a separate table of illustrations.

4. *Introduction to the Study.* This section discusses the purpose, information objectives, and background of the research. It describes the issue under analysis and the scope of the study. It presents technical methods and procedures used to collect and analyze data, and it informs readers of the limitations of procedures used in fulfilling research objectives. Limitations of the study may also be placed in the section on conclusions and recommendations. In larger studies, a separate chapter (or chapters) is included detailing technical methods and procedures.

5. *Findings of the Study.* Frequently, the longest section of a final report, the discussion of findings may extend over several chapters and include tables and graphics. It should be an organized presentation of findings giving readers a clear sense of direction—not a jungle of facts, figures, and prose defying order, purpose, and clarity.

6. *Conclusions and Recommendations.* Like executive summaries, conclusions contain no new material. Findings provide the basis for conclusions, and conclusions provide the basis for alternatives and recommendations.

7. *Appendices.* Appendices include detailed tables and statistical analyses, data collection instruments, coding instructions and forms, fieldwork procedures, supporting documents, and other information necessary for a complete research report. Any material disrupting the flow of the report is best placed in an appendix and referenced in the body of the report.

Whatever format is created, effective organization presents material in "manageable chunks that are carefully grouped, logically ordered, clearly marked, and labeled as to their importance. The reader can quickly grasp the main points and know where the report is heading...." (Murphy, 1980:178).

REPORT WRITING

Bad writing ... does not get read.... [T]he writer who wants to keep his audience bears always in mind that at any moment it can get up and leave. (McCloskey, 1985:189)

Good report writing makes for easy reading. It does not force readers constantly to stop and reread passages, trying to determine what is being said or what the connections are to earlier points. Guidelines in improving report writing include:

- *Write to an audience of human beings.*
  A research report is a vehicle for communicating information to users. Determine who those stakeholders are and tailor writing to them. Consider their questions, concerns, needs, and backgrounds. Orient report contents to agency problems, constantly linking discussions to key issues and decisions confronting users. Consider individual and organizational dynamics in reporting findings and recommendations. "Try not to offend, threaten, or put off potential users" (Rothman, 1980:175).
- *Use direct, nontechnical language.*
  Except when writing for a specialized audience, keep writing plain, to the point, understandable to the nonexpert. Avoid jargon, particularly in writing for diverse individuals and groups. Keep reports as brief as possible.
- *Strive for clarity of expression.*
  "The rule of clearness is not to write so that the reader can understand, but so that he cannot possibly misunderstand" (Morley, cited in McCloskey, 1985:191). Clarity is enhanced through good organization of ideas, using words precisely and providing examples. Have others review the report to improve clarity.
- *Make writing coherent.*
  Link sentences and paragraphs to previous ones. Readers understand ideas that are interconnected, related to one another. If readers have to make the connections themselves, some will give up, leaving report writers talking to themselves.
- *Ensure that tables and graphics are readable.*
  Use simple visual displays to communicate major findings. Most visuals are best when they are brief, confined to a single idea. Use descriptive titles that concretely reflect the contents of the visual.
- *Keep writing interesting.*
  A final report need not be lifeless. Create sentences that are on target, accurate and vivid in their description. Use verbs, active ones. Mix short sentences with long ones; include quotations and examples. Vary paragraph length. A good final report "is not a novel, but it need not be a stuffy tome lulling your readers to sleep" (Murphy, 1980:179).

ORAL PRESENTATIONS

Stakeholders expect oral and written reports from project managers. Oral presentations are useful in clarifying and exploring the implications of research information. In-person presentations better ensure that findings, conclusions, alternatives, and recommendations are accurately interpreted and operationally shaped for implementation purposes.

In large measure, principles of effective writing apply to verbal presentations. Use language specifically adapted to the audience. Be direct, to the point, brief. Suggest concrete action steps implied by findings. Point out changes in policy, practice, and organizational structure required to implement results. Show how agency resources are influenced by recommended actions.

Organize the presentation, ensuring that relevant research information is conveyed in the time available. Punctuate the presentation with reference to visual aids. Visual aids maintain audience interest, improve understanding of complex material, and direct the flow of discussion in presentations. Make them a part of the report story.

Keep an even temper, even when faced with unfair opposition.

> When you present your results in person, you can expect questions, comments, and criticisms. Make a strong effort to be receptive to these and to respond tolerantly and openly. This may be difficult if the person or group reviewing your work is inattentive, focused on details, or biased against you or your findings. Under these circumstances your responsiveness is even more important. (Patton and Sawicki, 1986:97)

An idea is to brief stakeholders informally before the meeting. The briefing does not require decision-maker approval or agreement to the contents of final reports, but an advanced understanding may prevent defensive reactions or outright rejections of project recommendations. "This kind of preview is especially important if the recommendations involve major changes in organization structure, budget allocations, or strategic focus for any of the executives who will be present at the formal presentation" (Ware, 1984:129).

Bringing Projects to Completion

As important as the oral presentation to users is, it does not signal the completion of the project or the end of the project manager's responsibilities. Unless recommendations for change are simple and noncontroversial, for example, stakeholders will not be able to understand, assess the implications of the recommendations, and act on them in a single meeting. Subsequent working sessions between stakeholders and project directors are likely to be necessary.

Further responsibilities of project directors in closing out a project include (Kerzner and Thamhain, 1984:326–30):

- Establishing manpower phaseout schedules
- Preparing personnel evaluations of project members

- Analyzing overall project performance with regard to financial data, schedules, and technical efforts
- Completing and securing project files
- Transferring or selling nonpersonnel resources, e.g., equipment originally allocated to the project

Closing out the project merits as much planning and management as do other phases in policy research. Project managers establish closeout procedures by identifying major steps and responsibilities. They handle the closeout phase like any other project task with agreed-upon activities and responsibilities, schedules, budgets, and end products. They continue to promote a work climate conducive to teamwork in bringing the project to completion.

CONCLUDING COMMENTS

This chapter reviewed planning and management skills used in formulating and implementing research projects. Successful project outcomes hinge on how well these tasks are performed by project participants. The objective of project planning is to develop operational, realistic guidelines for implementing research. Planning documents specify the research to be done, how it will be done, by whom and by when, in meeting project aims. Components of project plans include scheduling research tasks, staffing, budgeting, and securing approval of planning documents.

The scheduling components of project proposals include information on the sequencing and timing of research tasks. A planned schedule of tasks provides management with a basis to compare and monitor planned to actual performance of activities. Major approaches to scheduling range from simple techniques such as Gantt charts to sophisticated network analysis approaches such as PERT.

The staffing plan describes the responsibilities of each staff position, identifies the organization of the research team, and indicates the amount of time each team member will devote to specific project tasks.

Budgeting components of research planning document the amount and type of resources needed to achieve performance objectives. Critically evaluating the accuracy of assumptions on which cost estimates are based is a major approach to avoiding painful budgetary problems.

Combined with the technical aspects of research proposals, planning components provide a detailed picture of what information users can expect from the study, and at what costs. A concluding activity in planning research projects is to seek final approval of project proposals. Approvals are sought from those associated with and affected by potential study results. With approvals secured, plans are published with agreed-upon changes in larger projects.

In managing research projects, a key initial responsibility of project directors is creating a work climate conducive to productive teamwork. Their skill in performing this task relates to the quality of research products produced through team efforts. Through effectively communicating with project participants, a sense of mission and unity is fostered.

Conflict management is a responsibility challenging research managers throughout project life cycles. Conflict is beneficial when it serves as a stimulus in responding to changing circumstances characteristic of project environments. When detrimental, it cripples project performance. Conflict-resolution approaches are necessarily tailored to the content of the dispute, the parties involved, the implications for project performance, and other features of the research environment, although a participative approach is a favored conflict-resolution method of project directors.

Project managers further assume responsibility for maintaining communication linkages with stakeholders. The quality of relations—formal and informal—between research producers and consumers is critical to planned project outcomes. Maintaining ties with relevant individuals and groups promotes commitment to the project, increasing the chances of usable research products.

Like conflict management, reporting research information is a continuing responsibility of project leaders. Reports may be written or oral; how well they are communicated influences user perceptions of their worth and utility.

Written and oral presentations do not complete the responsibilities of project managers. Dealing with personnel issues, working with other groups in implementing recommendations, and evaluating overall project performance are frequent closeout activities for project directors.

Policy research is a complex activity placing challenging demands on producers and stakeholders responsible for its planning and management and for its end products. Policy skills are necessary to understand effectively the issues addressed in policy research and to produce usable study results. Skills in structuring research problems, collecting information, and analyzing and interpreting results are necessary for conducting technically sound studies. Planning and management skills allow analysts to integrate the various pieces of policy research.

As these skills become more widespread in governmental agencies and related organizations, policy research will increasingly permeate public decision making. In the 1990s and beyond, the public will continue to demand "government programs and agencies that are demonstrably efficient, demonstrably effective, and demonstrably responsive to public needs" (Wholey, 1983:205). Policy research will remain an essential information source for citizens, public policymakers, and other stakeholders as all strive to meet the challenges of an evolving community.

REFERENCES

Baker, Bruce N., Delmar Fisher, and David C. Murphy. 1983. "Factors Affecting Project Success," pp. 669–85, in David I. Cleland and William R. King, eds., *Project Management Handbook*. New York: Van Nostrand Reinhold Company.

———. 1983. "Project Management in the Public Sector: Success and Failure Patterns Compared to Private Sector Projects," pp. 686–99, in David I. Cleland and William R. King, eds., *Project Management Handbook*. New York: Van Nostrand Reinhold Company.

Blake, Stewart P. 1978. *Managing for Responsive Research and Development*. San Francisco: W. H. Freeman.

Burke, Ronald J. 1969. "Methods of Resolving Interpersonal Conflict," *Personnel Administration* (July-August).

Burman, Peter J. 1972. *Precedence Networks for Project Planning and Control*. London: McGraw-Hill.

Davis, Duane, and Robert M. Cosenza. 1985. *Business Research for Decision Making*. Belmont, CA: Kent Publishing.

Digman, L. A., and Gary I. Green. 1981. "A Framework for Evaluating Network Planning and Control Techniques," *Research Management* 24 (January):10–17.

Hatry, Harry P., Richard E. Winnie, and Donald M. Fisk. 1976. *Practical Program Evaluation for State and Local Governments*. Washington, DC: Urban Institute.

Kerzner, Harold. 1979. *Project Management: A Systems Approach to Planning, Scheduling and Controlling*. New York: Van Nostrand Reinhold Company.

Kerzner, Harold, and Hans J. Thamhain. 1984. *Project Management for Small and Medium Size Businesses*. New York: Van Nostrand Reinhold Company.

Labovitz, George H. 1984. "Managing Conflicts in Matrix Organizations," pp. 600–7, in David I. Cleland, ed., *Matrix Management Systems*. New York: Van Nostrand Reinhold Company.

McCloskey, Donald. 1985. "Economical Writing," *Economic Inquiry* 24:187–222.

Mayer, Robert R., and Ernest Greenwood. 1983. *The Design of Social Policy Research*. Englewood Cliffs, NJ: Prentice-Hall.

Miller, William B. 1978. "Fundamentals of Project Management," *Journal of Systems Management* 29 (November):22–29.

Murphy, Jerome T. 1980. *Getting the Facts: A Fieldwork Guide for Evaluators and Policy Analysts*. Santa Monica, CA: Goodyear Publishing.

Patton, Carl V., and David S. Sawicki. 1986. *Basic Methods of Policy Analysis and Planning*. Englewood Cliffs, NJ: Prentice-Hall.

Rothman, Jack. 1980. *Using Research in Organizations: A Guide to Successful Application*. Beverly Hills, CA: Sage.

Thamhain, Hans J., and David L. Wilemon. 1975. "Conflict Management in Project Life Cycles," *Sloan Management Review* (Summer).

Ware, James P. 1984. "Making the Matrix Come Alive: Managing a Task Force," pp. 112–31, in David I. Cleland, ed., *Matrix Management Systems*. New York: Van Nostrand Reinhold Company.

Wholey, Joseph S. 1983. *Evaluation and Effective Public Management*. Boston: Little, Brown.

White, Michael J., Ross Clayton, Robert Myrtle, Gilbert Siegel, and Aaron Rose. 1980. *Managing Public Systems: Analytic Techniques for Public Administration.* North Scituate, MA: Duxbury Press.

Wilemon, David L. and Bruce N. Baker. 1983. "Some Major Research Findings Regarding the Human Element in Project Management," pp. 623–41, in David I. Cleland and William R. King, eds., *Project Management Handbook.* New York: Van Nostrand Reinhold Company.

Acknowledgments continued from page ii.

Jerome T. Murphy, *Getting the Facts: A Fieldwork Guide for Evaluators and Policy Analysts.* Santa Monica, Calif.: Goodyear, 1980.

Carl V. Patton and David S. Sawicki, *Basic Methods of Policy Analysis and Planning.* Englewood Cliffs, N.J.: Prentice Hall, 1986.

Harold Sigal and Nancy Ostrove, "Beautiful But Dangerous: Effects of Offender Attractiveness and Nature of the Crime on Juridic Judgement," *The Journal of Personality and Social Psychology* (1975), 31: 410–414. Copyright 1987 by the American Psychological Association. Reprinted by permission.

Susan Welch and John C. Comer, *Quantitative Methods for Public Administration: Techniques and Applications.* Homewood, Ill.: Dorsey Press, 1983.

Carol H. Weiss, *Evaluation Research: Methods for Assessing Program Effectiveness.* Englewood Cliffs, N.J.: Prentice Hall, 1972.

Index